DUBLIN

MARY-ANN GALLAGHER

About the author

Mary-Ann Gallagher has written, and contributed to, more than a dozen Cadogan guides, including *Flying Visits Ireland*. Her travels have taken her everywhere from Japanese hill villages to glossy European capitals. She still loves Dublin, but recently exchanged its changeable skies for the bluer ones of Barcelona.

Acknowledgements

Mary-Ann would like to extend heartfelt thanks to Susannah, Ed, Brendan, Alex, Declan, Paul, Barney, Rob, and Mary Gibbons (of Mary Gibbons tours). Big thanks, too, to everyone at Cadogan, particularly Matthew Teller for his Buddha-like patience.

Cadogan Guides
Network House, 1 Ariel Way, London, W12 7SL
info@cadoganguides.co.uk
www.cadoganguides.com

The Globe Pequot Press
246 Goose Lane, PO Box 480, Guilford, Connecticut 06437–0480

Copyright © Mary-Ann Gallagher 2004

Series book design: Andrew Barker
Series cover design: Sheridan Wall
Art direction: Sarah Rianhard-Gardner
Photography: © Susannah Sayler
Maps © Cadogan Guides, drawn by Map Creation
Additional cartography: Angie Watts
Mapping based on Ordnance Survey Ireland permit No. 7964
© Ordnance Survey Ireland and Government of Ireland.

Managing Editor: Natalie Pomier
Editorial Assistant: Nicola Jessop
Editor: Matthew Teller
Proofreading: Catherine Bradley
Indexing: Isobel McLean
Production: Navigator Guides
Printed in Italy by Legoprint
A catalogue record for this book is available from the British Library
ISBN 1-86011-136-x

The author and the publishers have made every effort to ensure the accuracy of the information in this book at the time of going to press. However they cannot accept any responsibility for any loss, injury or inconvenience resulting from the use of information contained in this guide.

Please help us to keep this guide up to date. We have done our best to ensure that the information in this guide is correct at the time of going to press. But places and facilities are constantly changing, and standards and prices in hotels and restaurants fluctuate. We would be delighted to receive any comments concerning existing entries or omissions. Authors of the best letters will receive a copy of the Cadogan Guide of their choice.

All rights reserved. No part of this publication may be reproduced, stored in a retrieval system, or transmitted, in any form or by any means, electronic or mechanical, including photocopying and recording, or by any information storage and retrieval system except as may be expressly permitted in the UK 1988 Copyright Design & Patents Act and the USA 1976 Copyright Act or in writing from the publisher. Requests for permission should be addressed to Cadogan Guides, Network House, 1 Ariel Way, London W12 7SL, in the UK, or The Globe Pequot Press, 246 Goose Lane, PO Box 480, Guilford, Connecticut 06437–0480, in the USA.

Contents

Introducing
- Introduction 1
- The Neighbourhoods 2
- Days Out in Dublin 9
- Roots of the City 19
- Art and Architecture 31

The Guide

01
Travel 37
- Getting There 38
- Specialist Tour Operators 40
- Entry Formalities 41
- Arrival 42
- Getting Around 43

02
Practical A–Z 47
- Climate and When To Go 48
- Crime and the Police 48
- Disabled Travellers 49
- Electricity, Weights and Measures 49
- Embassies and Consulates 50
- Etiquette 50
- Genealogy 50
- Health and Insurance 51
- Internet 51
- Lost Property 52
- Media 52
- Money, Banks and Taxes 52
- Opening Hours and Public Holidays 53
- Packing 53
- Phones 53
- Post 54
- Religious Services 54
- Smoking 54
- Students 54
- Time 55
- Tipping 55
- Toilets 55
- Tourist Offices 55
- Women Travellers 56
- Working and Long Stays 56

03
Southeast Dublin: The Georgian Heart 57
- Trinity College and the Book of Kells 60
- Around College Green 64
- Grafton Street 65
- National Museum of Ireland 68
- St Stephen's Green 72
- Newman House 73
- Irish Jewish Museum 74
- Merrion Square 76
- National Gallery of Ireland 76
- Further Southeast 80

04
Southwest Dublin: Temple Bar and Old Dublin 81
- Temple Bar 84
- Dublin Castle 85
- Christchurch Cathedral 89
- Dublinia 90
- St Patrick's Cathedral 91
- The Liberties 94
- Guinness Storehouse 95
- Kilmainham Gaol 96
- Irish Museum of Modern Art (IMMA) 97

05
Northeast Dublin: Around O'Connell Street 99
- O'Connell Street 102
- Abbey Theatre 103
- St Mary's Pro Cathedral 104
- Parnell Square 105
- Gate Theatre 105
- Hugh Lane Gallery and Francis Bacon's Studio 106
- Dublin Writers Museum 107
- James Joyce Centre 108
- Mountjoy Square 110
- The Quays North of the Liffey 111
- International Financial Services Centre (IFSC) 111
- Custom House 111
- Ha'Penny Bridge 112
- Millennium Bridge 112
- Grattan Bridge 112

06
Northwest Dublin: The Four Courts to Phoenix Park 113
- Four Courts 116
- St Mary's Abbey 116
- St Michan's Church 117
- King's Inns 118
- Smithfield 118
- Old Jameson Distillery 119
- Dublin Brewing Company 120
- Stoneybatter 120
- Collins Barracks 120
- Croppies Acre 121
- Phoenix Park 121
- Áras an Uachtaráin (President's House) 123
- Dublin Zoo 123

07
Outside the Centre 125

South of the Centre 126
Pearse Museum 126
Rathfarnham Castle 128
Drimnagh Castle 128
Dillon Garden 129
North of the Centre 129
Glasnevin Cemetery 129
National Botanic Gardens 130
Croke Park: the GAA Museum 131
Casino at Marino 131
The Coast Around Dublin Bay 132
Bull Island Nature Reserve 132
Malahide 132
Howth 134
Dún Laoghaire and Sandycove 135
Dalkey and Killiney Bay 136
Bray 138

08
Walks 139

A Literary Walk 141
Viking and Medieval Dublin 143
The Docks and the Grand Canal 149

10
Day Trips 153

The Coast North of Dublin 155
Swords 155
Donabate 155
Skerries 156
The Valley of the Boyne 157
Drogheda 157
Slane 159
Brú na Boinne: Newgrange, Knowth and Dowth 160
Hill of Tara 162
Trim 163
Kells 164
Southwest to Kildare 165
Celbridge 165
Kildare Town 166
The Wicklow Mountains 167
Glendalough 167
Powerscourt Estate 169
Blessington Lakes 171

Listings

Where to Stay 172
Eating Out 185
Nightlife 202
Entertainment 210
Shopping 214
Sports 219
Children's and Teenagers' Dublin 222
Gay and Lesbian Dublin 225
Festivals and Events 227

Reference

Language 229
Index 232

Maps

Unmissable Dublin *inside front cover*
The Neighbourhoods 2–3
Southeast Dublin: The Georgian Heart 58–9
Trinity College and St Stephen's Green 64
Southwest Dublin: Temple Bar and Old Dublin 82–3
Temple Bar 85
Northeast Dublin: Around O'Connell Street 100–1
Northwest Dublin: The Four Courts to Phoenix Park 114–5
Outside the Centre 126
A Literary Walk 140
Viking and Medieval Dublin Walk 144–5
The Docks and the Grand Canal Walk 148–9
Day Trips 154
Dublin Southside Hotels 174–5
Dublin Northside Hotels 180–1
Dublin Southside Cafés and Restaurants 188–9
Temple Bar Cafés and Restaurants 194
Dublin Northside Cafés and Restaurants 196–7
Colour Street Maps *end of guide*
Off the Beaten Track *inside back cover*

Introduction

'...it's a dreary little dump most of the time...'

Roddy Doyle, author

Whatever Dubliners – always their own harshest critics – may say, Dublin at the dawn of the 21st century is on the up. Rock stars, film-makers and celebrities love the place; the fashion pack have taken over its shiny new bars and clubs; arts and culture are booming; and the skyline has been transformed with startling new architecture. And yet beneath this glossy veneer, the city's traditional charms remain (for the most part) intact: you'll still find serene ranks of Georgian mansions, dreamy parks and glorious gardens, and time-raddled pubs replete with burnished wood and polished mirrors.

This phenomenal transformation hasn't been easy: when Ireland joined the EEC (now the EU) in 1973, it was considered a 'disadvantaged region'. By the end of the 1980s, the country was reaping the rewards of the EU cash injection and the resulting flood of new investment. By the 1990s, the 'Celtic Tiger' economy was booming and Dubliners were brimming with new-found confidence and optimism. Glitzy new bars, restaurants and nightclubs sprang up, whole neighbourhoods were transformed and endless amounts of money seemed to be sloshing around. But, by the dawning of the new millennium, the decade-long party was over. Dublin, having thrust itself forward as a major European capital, now finds itself confronted by the same social and administrative problems that confound other big cities – from racism, corruption and drug addiction to traffic congestion and a severe shortage of affordable housing. And while Ireland continues to boast one of the healthiest economies in Europe, the free-spending days of the 1990s are definitely over.

But the sheen which the city has acquired hasn't undermined the old Dublin: its links with the past remain tangible in the soaring spires of the medieval cathedrals, the graceful Georgian mansions and the bullet-pocked façades which recall the terrible struggles for independence. Would-be writers still flock here, seeking inspiration from a city which has produced an extraordinary number of literary giants – Goldsmith, Swift, Beckett and Joyce among them. The yellowing, ancient pubs may now rub shoulders with neon-lit super-bars, but they still thrive – despite grim warnings of their demise after the introduction of an EU-imposed smoking ban. And the Dubliners themselves, at the core of the city's appeal, remain their famously genial, talkative, fascinating selves.

The Neighbourhoods

9 Phoenix Park, p.121

Northwest Dublin: The Four Courts to Phoenix Park

8 Kilmainham Gaol, p.96

Southwest Dublin: Temple Bar and Old Dublin

In this guide, the city is divided into the four neighbourhoods outlined on the map above, each with its own sightseeing chapter. This map also shows our suggestions for the Top Ten activities and places to visit in Dublin. The following colour pages introduce the neighbourhoods in more detail, explaining the distinctive character and highlights of each.

3 Guinness Storehouse, p.95

The Neighbourhoods 3

6 Glasnevin Cemetery, p.129

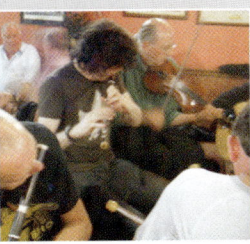
10 Traditional Music, p.211

4 Chester Beatty Library, p.87

Northeast Dublin: Around O'Connell Street

1 Book of Kells, p.61

Southeast Dublin: The Georgian Heart

5 Iveagh Gardens, p.74

2 Bronze Age gold in the National Museum, p.68

7 National Gallery, p.76

Southeast Dublin: The Georgian Heart

In the late 18th century, fashionable Dublin ventured across the River Liffey and began an extravagant building spree, creating the serene Georgian townhouses, spanking new avenues and manicured gardens which still characterize this elegant and affluent southeastern neighbourhood. Even ancient institutions like Trinity College underwent a Georgian facelift, and the university still contains a sumptuous 18th-century library as well as the dazzling Book of Kells. Many of the most venerable public museums, including the National Museum of Archeology and History and the National Gallery, are clustered here, along with many of the finest hotels, most stylish restaurants, smartest boutiques and hottest clubs.

From top: Bank of Ireland, Grafton Street, Trinity College, architectural detail and National Gallery.

Southeast: The Georgian Heart
Southeast Dublin chapter p.57
Hotels p.173 Restaurants p.186 Bars p.203

Clockwise from top left: St Patrick's, Dublin Castle, Gogarty's Restaurant, Queen of Tarts and the Guinness Brewery.

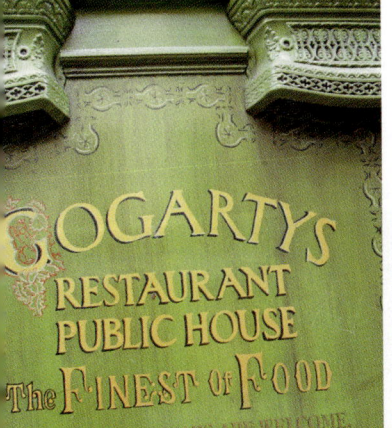

Southwest Dublin: Temple Bar and Old Dublin

Southwest Dublin is a curious hotchpotch of the old and new: meandering medieval lanes dominated by the glorious cathedrals of Christchurch and St Patrick's are nudged up against the city's most popular entertainment district, Temple Bar, which is packed with shops, galleries, bars, restaurants – and hordes of tourists. Dublin Castle still dominates the city from its hill, and behind it sits the Chester Beatty Library, one of the most singular and fascinating museums in Europe. Spreading west is the earthy neighbourhood of The Liberties, famously home to the Guinness Brewery, which is still brewing 'the black stuff' after more than two hundred years.

> Southwest Dublin:
> Temple Bar and Old Dublin »
> Southwest Dublin: Temple Bar and Old Dublin chapter p.81
> Hotels p.178 Restaurants p.193 Bars p.205

From top: General Post Office, Dublin Writers Museum and the Millennium Spire.

Northeast Dublin: Around O'Connell Street – Writers And War Heroes

O'Connell Street, once a Georgian beauty and now blighted with thoughtless modern development, is characteristic of this once grand and now faded neighbourhood. But renovation is finally underway, with spectacular (if controversial) new developments like the Millennium Spire and the belated restoration of early Georgian mansions. Dublin's literary giants, notably James Joyce, are commemorated in a pair of fine museums, and the legendary Abbey Theatre and the General Post Office (scene of the Easter Rising of 1916) are reminders of two very different approaches to Irish nationalism. Down by the river, the Ha'Penny Bridge is still Dublin's prettiest symbol, now flanked by a sleek 21st-century companion and boardwalk.

Northeast Dublin: Around O'Connell Street
Northeast Dublin: Around O'Connell Street chapter p.99
Hotels p.179 Restaurants p.195 Bars p.207

Northwest Dublin: The Four Courts to Phoenix Park

From the pomp and grandeur of the Four Courts to the glorious, green expanse of Phoenix Park, passing by the huddled workers' cottages of Stoneybatter and the slick new developments of Smithfield, northwest Dublin encompasses several centuries of history. Mummified corpses in ancient churches are still touched for luck, while only a few blocks away Dublin's yuppies are buying up loft-style apartments around the newly revamped Smithfield Plaza. One of the few vestiges of the industrial past of this neighbourhood is the Jameson's whiskey distillery, which has now wholeheartedly embraced the tourist trade. But not everything is changing: these sidestreets contain some of Dublin's most genuine and untouched pubs.

Clockwise from top: Jameson distillery, graffiti at Smithfield, Smithfield Horse Fair, Phoenix Park.

Northwest Dublin:
The Four Courts to Phoenix Park
Northwest Dublin: The Four Courts to Phoenix Park chapter p.113
Hotels p.182 Restaurants p.199 Bars p.207

Outside the Centre: Castles, Gardens and Dublin Bay

Dublin's suburbs contain some of the city's most fascinating sights, including the elegant Botanic Gardens, the atmospheric cemetery at Glasnevin (where many of Ireland's legendary heroes are buried), the magical Casino at Marino and the GAA museum at Croke Park, dedicated to Irish sports. A pair of picture-book castles are still redolent of Dublin's early history. And while it's easy to forget that Dublin sits on the coast, a string of pretty seaside towns lines the lovely arc of Dublin Bay and beyond, easily accessible for a breath of fresh air from the city.

Clockwise from top: National Botanic Gardens, view of Dublin Bay, and the Glasnevin Cemetery.

Outside the Centre
Outside the Centre chapter p.125
Hotels p.182 Restaurants p.199 Bars p.208

Days Out in Dublin

Georgian Dublin p.10

Indoor Dublin p.12

Dubliner's Dublin p.14

Green Dublin p.16

21st-Century Dublin p.18

GEORGIAN DUBLIN

Dublin at the end of the 18th century was the second city of the British Empire: business was booming, and its heady social calendar rivalled that of any European capital. The entire city was transformed as landowners began to build sumptuous mansions and broad boulevards. The first of these building projects were north of the River Liffey, but the fashionable Dubliners soon turned their attention south, where the legacy of the Georgians is still most keenly felt.

One

Start: Start with a filling breakfast crêpe at **Lemon**.
Morning: Discover how the other half lived in the opulent **Newman House**, Dublin's finest Georgian mansion.
Lunch: The **Hodges Figgis** bookshop has been going since the 18th century: its café is new, but a good spot for lunch.
Afternoon: Stroll around **Merrion Square**, still lined with a virtually unbroken line of superb Georgian town houses, most with blue plaques denoting their famous residents of years gone by.
Dinner: The stylish **Browne's Brasserie** is housed in a graceful 18th-century town house, and the food is superb.
Evening: Hang out with the new aristocrats at the exclusive nightclub **Lillie's Bordello**.

Days Out in Dublin 11

Two

Start: **Chompys Deli** is an institution for brunch and it's set in the gorgeous Powerscourt Townhouse.

Morning: A magnificently converted Georgian mansion, the **Powerscourt Townhouse** is now an excellent shopping centre. Make sure you visit the Irish Design Centre.

Lunch: On an elegant Georgian street, with high 18th-century ceilings, the **Cobalt Café** and Gallery is a great place for a relaxed lunch.

Afternoon: Take in the **James Joyce Centre** and the nearby **Dublin Writers Museum**, both occupying beautifully preserved Georgian mansions.

Dinner: **Chapter One**, one of the city's best restaurants, is tucked away in the Dublin Writers Museum.

Evening: Finish the evening at the bar in the **Gresham**, a popular watering-hole in one of the oldest hotels in Dublin.

Food and Drinks
Browne's Brasserie, p.186
Chapter One, p.195
Chompys Deli, p.191
Cobalt Café, p.198
Hodges Figgis, p.192
Lemon, p.192

Sights and Activities
Dublin Writers Museum, p.107
James Joyce Centre, p.108
Merrion Square, p.76
Newman House, p.73
Powerscourt Townhouse, p.218

Nightlife
Lillie's Bordello, p.209
Gresham, p.179

INDOOR DUBLIN

It isn't true that it rains all the time in Dublin – but you should bring your brolly anyway. Luckily, the city is stuffed full of indoor attractions (and not just pubs) to keep you entertained and out of the wet and cold. Excellent museums, a thriving cultural scene, great restaurants and a buzzing nightlife scene mean that you'll rarely have to brave the elements.

Three

Start: Set yourself up for the day with a tasty breakfast at the **Queen of Tarts**.
Morning: Gaze at the dazzling **Book of Kells** and the sumptuous 18th-century library in **Trinity College.**
Lunch: Have a delicious light lunch at the **Avoca** café and shop.
Afternoon: Stroll around the **National Gallery** collection of Irish art, and then take afternoon tea at the **Shelbourne Hotel**.
Dinner: Try **Bruno's** for excellent modern Irish fare.
Evening: Take in a play – the **Abbey Theatre** for classic Irish drama, or the **Project Arts Centre** for cutting-edge performances.

Days Out in Dublin 13

Four

Start: Begin with some delicious coffee and croissants at the delightful **La Maison des Gourmets**.
Morning: Visit the enthralling **Chester Beatty Library**, for its fabulous collection of Oriental art and manuscripts.
Lunch: Follow Dublin's smart crowd to ultra-chic **Halo** at the Morrison Hotel, which serves a good-value lunch menu.
Afternoon: Pamper yourself with some beauty treatments at **Thérapie**, or catch an arty film at the excellent **Irish Film Centre**.

Dinner: Try the oysters washed down with Guinness at **Davy Byrne's** pub, which famously featured in James Joyce's *Ulysses*.
Evening: Catch a gig at Dublin's best known live-music spot, **Whelan's.**

Food and Drinks
Avoca, p.190
Bruno's, p.187
Davy Byrne's, p.203
Halo, p.195
La Maison des Gourmets, p.192
Queen of Tarts, p.195
Shelbourne Hotel, p.173

Sights and Activities
Abbey Theatre, p.103
Book of Kells, p.61
Chester Beatty Library, p.87
Irish Film Centre, p.213
National Gallery, p.76
Project Arts Centre, p.212
Thérapie, p.217
Trinity College, p.60

Nightlife
Whelan's, p.209

DUBLINER'S DUBLIN

The tourist path in Dublin is well worn, and Temple Bar in particular is always crammed with map-toting foreigners (although the locals love the organic market held here on Saturdays). For a taste of traditional Dublin, don't miss the chance to see a Gaelic football or hurling match, and catch some genuine Irish music if you can. To see the changes which have been wrought in the last affluent decades, check out the new ultra-chic bars and restaurants.

Five

Start: Try out a few words of Gaelic at the Irish-speaking **Caife Trí-D**.
Morning: Explore the little-visited **Liberties** district: stroll among the antique shops of **Francis Street**, and muse on the names carved into the gateway of the long-demolished maternity hospital.
Lunch: Squeeze onto one of the tiny tables at the **Gallic Kitchen**.
Afternoon: Visit the atmospheric **Glasnevin Cemetery** and follow it up with a pint at **Kavanagh's** pub – better known as 'The Gravediggers' – which has barely changed in centuries.
Dinner: Settle in with the well-heeled crowd at **Dobbins Wine Bistro** for dinner.
Evening: If you're in the mood to party, head for **PoD**. If not, savour Dublin's finest pint of Guinness at **Mulligan's**.

Days Out in Dublin 15

Six (Saturdays only)

Start: Begin with a coffee at arty **Gruel**, on the edge of Temple Bar.

Morning: Potter around the organic market in **Cow's Lane** (Sat 10–6) and select from the fabulous range of local produce.

Lunch: If the weather's good, pick up a picnic at the market; if not, head for the excellent **Silk Road Café** in the Chester Beatty Library.

Afternoon: See a Gaelic football or hurling game – at the legendary **Croke Park** stadium if possible (or the tourist office can give you details of local matches).

Dinner: Dine on the best modern Irish cuisine at the eminently fashionable **Dish**.

Evening: Head to the **Cobblestone** (no longer smoky but still atmospheric) for live Irish music.

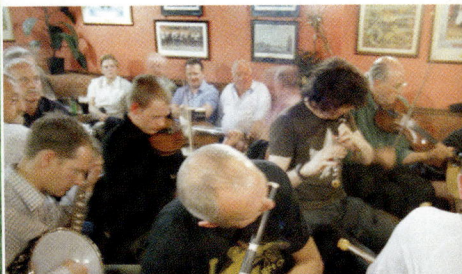

Food and Drinks
Café Tri-D, p.192
Dish, p.199
Dobbins Wine Bistro, p.187
Gallic Kitchen, p.195
Gruel, p.194
Kavanagh's, p.208
Mulligan's, p.204
Silk Road Café, p.87

Sights and Activities
Cow's Lane market, p.218
Croke Park, p.131
Francis Street antiques shops, p.215
Gaelic football and hurling, p.220
Glasnevin Cemetery, p.129
The Liberties, p.94

Nightlife
Cobblestone, p.207
PoD, p.209

GREEN DUBLIN

Dublin is crammed with parks and gardens, at their finest in spring, when the grass is impossibly green and fresh and the flower beds are dazzling in their multicoloured profusion. There are secret hideaways like the Iveagh Gardens, right in the heart of the city, and immaculate manicured lawns, like those in St Stephen's Green, but the best place to wander is the vast, verdant expanse of Phoenix Park.

Seven

Start: Breakfast at **Cornucopia**, one of the longest-established vegetarian cafés in Dublin.

Morning: Feed the ducks in **St Stephen's Green**, Dublin's best-loved central public park, with lawns, flower beds and a host of statues dedicated to famous Dubliners.

Lunch: Take a picnic to the magical **Iveagh Gardens**, tucked away behind huge stone walls.

Afternoon: Hop on the bus to Glasnevin, for a visit to the elegant **Botanic Gardens**, with their exquisite wrought-iron greenhouses.

Dinner: Dine amongst a profusion of palms in the lavishly decorated **Café en Seine**.

Evening: Have a perfectly mixed cocktail at the **Shelbourne Hotel's Horseshoe Bar**, just a short step from St Stephen's Green.

Days Out in Dublin

Eight

Start: Take your time over a freshly squeezed juice or smoothie at **Nude**.

Morning: Visit the **Irish Museum of Modern Art**, where the 18th-century formal gardens have been exquisitely restored.

Lunch: The **Grass Roots Café** has wonderful views of the museum gardens.

Afternoon: While away the afternoon in **Phoenix Park**, one of the largest and loveliest public parks in Europe. Catch a polo match if you can.

Dinner: Sit out on the terrace at **Tá Sá Mahogani Gaspipes**, where you can enjoy the gardens while dining on unusual international cuisine.

Evening: **Solas** used to be known as the Modern Green Bar, and still has its funky green décor.

Food and Drinks
Cornucopia, p.191
Café en Seine, p.203
Grass Roots Café, p.195
Nude, p.193
Tá Sá Mahogani Gaspipes, p.199

Sights and Activities
National Botanic Gardens, p.130
Irish Museum of Modern Art, p.97
Iveagh Gardens, p.74
Phoenix Park, p.121
St Stephen's Green, p.72

Nightlife
Horseshoe Bar, p.204
Solas, p.205

21ST-CENTURY DUBLIN

A swathe of new projects to celebrate the millennium have transformed the city centre: some, like the Millennium Spire, have been roundly criticized, but others, like the new boardwalk along the River Liffey, are enormously popular. The once-neglected docklands are now glittering with glassy new apartments and the city is packed with hip new boutiques, cafés, bars and restaurants.

Nine

Start: Head for the **Epicurean Food Hall** for breakfast – you'll find everything from bagels to samosas.
Morning: Take a stroll on **O'Connell Street**, undergoing major redevelopment which will bring a tree-lined pedestrian avenue to the once traffic-choked street. In the centre is the controversial **Millennium Spire**.
Lunch: Try and get a table at tiny **Panem**, one of the best bakeries in Dublin.
Afternoon: Saunter along the new boardwalk and cross the river via the sleek **Millennium Bridge**, and browse through Dublin's chic boutiques around **South William Street**.
Dinner: The huge windows of the glassy **Ocean** bar and restaurant is a good place to see the new development around the docklands.
Evening: Dance the night away at **Spirit**, one of the new generation of ultra-hip clubs.

Food and Drinks
Epicurean Food Hall, p.198
Panem, p.198
Ocean, p.199

Sights and Activities
O'Connell Street, p.102
Millennium Spire, p.102
Millennium Bridge, p.112
South William Street, p.67

Nightlife
Spirit, p.209

Roots of the City

STONES, BONES AND SAINTS 20
THE VIKINGS 20
MEDIEVAL DUBLIN 21
THE REFORMATION AND
THE ARRIVAL OF CROMWELL 22
RESTORATION AND GEORGIAN DUBLIN 23
THE STRUGGLE FOR HOME RULE 25
THE GREAT FAMINE 25
TOWARDS INDEPENDENCE 26
BIRTH OF THE REPUBLIC 29
THE IRISH 'TROUBLES' 29
CONTEMPORARY DUBLIN 30

Stones, Bones and Saints

The Dublin area has probably been settled since around 8000 BC, and traces of human habitation dating back to 5000 BC have been found on **Dalkey Island**, off the southern shore of Dublin Bay. At that time Ireland was thickly covered with dense forest; the early hunter-gatherers lived in lake dwellings called *crannógs*, and travelled primarily by boats known as *curraghs*, similar to those still used today by fisherfolk in the west of Ireland. By 4000 BC, Neolithic farmers were building stone walls, domesticating animals and clearing woodland to cultivate crops. They buried their dead in gallery graves and burial cists such as the ones still being excavated in Phoenix Park, which pre-date the passage tombs at Newgrange, Knowth and Dowth. Dublin's first **dolmen**, which dates from 3000 BC, survives on the Hill of Howth.

The Bronze Age reached Ireland around 2050 BC with the arrival of the **Beaker People**, who became known in Irish myth as the *Tuatha Dé Danaan*, and who got their name from the delicate pottery vessels they created. The Beaker People were skilled metalworkers, and established trading routes with Brittany, the Baltic and the Iberian peninsula. Between 2050 BC and 700 BC there were major advances in metalworking: some extraordinary gold jewellery was produced, including the **Gleninsheen Collar**, on view at the National Museum.

No one knows when the first wave of **Celtic** invaders arrived – perhaps as early as 900 BC, but certainly by 700 BC. The Celts (also known as **Gaels**) had spread from southern Germany, France and Spain and quickly established themselves as the dominant culture, easily defeating the Beaker People. The Celts brought with them a highly organized social structure which divided Ireland into different clans with three classes: the Free, made up of warriors and landowners with cattle; the Professionals, who were lawmakers, Druids, storytellers and poets; and the Slaves. Each clan had a petty king who was subject to the High King or *Ard Rí* who held court on the Hill of Tara. The second wave of Celtic settlers in c. 250 BC brought with them a style of pottery known as La Tène, characterised by its spiral motif or whorl. The legacy of the Celts survives in epic tales of heroic and superhuman deeds.

Finally, Dublin enters the history books. During the Celtic period, a settlement developed on the banks of the Liffey called **Áth Cliath**, meaning Hurdle Ford. (*Baile Atha Cliath* is the modern Gaelic name for Dublin.) It was the only crossing over the river, and stood at the junction of four major roads. **Dubh Linn**, meaning 'Black Pool', was a later settlement which got its name from a tidal pool close to the junction of the Rivers Liffey and Poddle; its location is marked by the Dubh Linn gardens behind Dublin Castle.

Christianity arrived in Ireland with St Patrick in AD 452; according to legend, he baptised early converts on a well which stood on the site of St Patrick's Cathedral. The Celts embraced Christianity peacefully (there are no early Christian martyrs in Ireland) and monasteries, churches, holy wells and hermit cells began to appear, including several in the Dublin area. These monastic settlements, which functioned as small, virtually self-sufficient communities supporting large numbers of people, were important centres of learning. Ireland became renowned for its scholarship and skilful artistry, which reached its greatest heights in the early 9th-century **Book of Kells**, an exquisitely illustrated copy of the Four Gospels. However, when the legendary wealth of the monasteries reached the ears of the Vikings they started raiding the coastal monasteries.

The Vikings

Lambay Island, off Dublin Bay, suffered the first **Viking** raid, in 795. Initially, the Vikings carried out hit-and-run style raids on unprotected monasteries, returning to their bases in Scandinavia with the spoils. In 837, a Viking force with more than 60 longships landed at the mouth of the River Liffey and remained there for the winter. In 841, they set up a permanent trading base called a *longphort* by contemporary annalists. It may have been located near Islandbridge and Kilmainham, where a Viking cemetery was discovered in the 19th century.

The Vikings were harried by local Irish tribes, who eventually got rid of them in 902. But they returned in 917 under the leadership of **Ivar the Boneless**, and built a new fortified settlement on the banks of the Liffey in the area now known as Wood Quay. The remnants of this town, considered by many to be the best preserved Viking remains outside Scandinavia, were uncovered by accident in the 1960s and controversially built over, but the excavations provided historians with a wealth of new information. The Vikings were skilled at a range of crafts including metalwork, woodcarving, leatherwork, weaving and shipbuilding – but they continued to supplement their income from trade with raids on monasteries and native settlements. The round towers that still survive, such as at **Glendalough**, were watchtowers and repositories for valuables.

Under **King Sitric 'Silkbeard'**, Viking Dublin prospered: the first coins were minted in 997 and several important buildings, including Christchurch Cathedral and the Thingmote (an assembly place and parliament of sorts), were constructed. But in 1014 **Brian Ború**, who had usurped the High Kingship of Ireland, decisively defeated the Vikings at the Battle of Clontarf. He was murdered in his tent after the battle, and his death left a power vacuum which the O'Briens, the O'Loughlins and the O'Connors each sought to fill. The conflict came to a head when the king of Leinster, **Dermot MacMurragh**, angered the head of the O'Rourke clan by stealing his wife, Devorgilla. In the war that followed, MacMurragh offered his allegiance to the English king, Henry II, in return for military aid. The first Anglo-Norman force, sent by Richard de Clare, better known as Strongbow, landed in Wexford in 1169.

Medieval Dublin

The Anglo-Normans were ambitious and Henry II promised that they would be given any lands they managed to wrest from the Irish. Before setting sail for Ireland, Strongbow had already negotiated an agreement with MacMurragh to marry the king's daughter Aoife, and succeed to the throne of Leinster on the king's death. After laying waste to Waterford, Strongbow and Aoife were married, and the army immediately marched on Dublin. The Vikings, who had killed MacMurragh's father and insultingly buried him with a dog, sought the help of the High King **Rory O'Connor**, who gathered an army which far outnumbered the Normans. Nonetheless, the city fell on 21 September 1170, marking the beginning of an occupation that would last 750 years.

In 1171 MacMurragh died, and Strongbow declared himself king of Leinster. Other barons had grabbed huge swathes of land. Henry II became alarmed at the success of his barons in Ireland, and sent a large force to check their ambition. The barons and chieftains were required to swear their allegiance to the Crown, and, although Strongbow was confirmed as king of Leinster, Henry II appointed **William de Burgo** as viceroy. He issued a charter – on view at Dublin's City Hall – giving Dublin to 'my men of Bristol', which ensured that Strongbow could never gain control of the city and also opened up important trade links with England.

The Normans fortified and reorganized Dublin. In 1213 Henry II ordered the building of **Dublin Castle**, which served as the centre for British rule until 1922. Christchurch Cathedral was rebuilt in stone in 1173, and was soon joined by St Patrick's Cathedral. The Anglo-Normans extended their territory outside the city walls into an area which became known as **The Pale**. It ran in an arc from Dalkey in the south to Drogheda in the north. Despite its defences, the Pale was under constant attack from Gaelic lords.

In 1314, the Irish **Chieftains** enlisted the help of Robert the Bruce against the English in Ireland. Bruce saw this as an opportunity to fulfil his dream of a unified Celtic kingdom with himself as King of Scotland and his brother, Edward, on the throne of Ireland. Edward waged a bloody campaign throughout Ireland. In 1317 Robert the Bruce arrived to aid his brother's campaign and laid siege to Dublin. Fearing a merciless attack, the mayor gave the order to set fire to the city's suburbs, but the fire rapidly grew out of control. The Scottish army were apparently so impressed by this determination that they gave up the siege and marched on to Limerick, which proved impregnable; the Scots eventually returned home. It was not only war that plagued medieval Dublin, but also **disease**: the Black Death arrived in 1348 and wiped out a third of the Irish population.

Ireland was largely ignored by the English kings until the accession of Henry VII. The Anglo-Irish families had become embroiled in the English Wars of the Roses, with the Geraldines traditionally supporting the House of York and the Butlers siding with the House of Lancaster. The Earl of Kildare, a Geraldine and Yorkist, was Lord Deputy of Ireland with control over state offices, which caused widespread resentment. Henry VII summoned the earl to London to answer charges of insubordination, but somehow news reached Dublin that he had been executed. This was untrue, but the earl's headstrong son, Silken Thomas, furiously renounced his allegiance to Henry at the Chapter House of St Mary's Abbey in 1534 and took control of the Pale with the support of the Irish chieftains. The rebellion was quickly crushed, and Silken Thomas was hanged at Tyburn in London in 1537.

The Reformation and the Arrival of Cromwell

In 1532 **Henry VIII** split with the Pope and declared himself Supreme Head of the Church in England. This caused consternation among the nobles in Ireland, particularly when all holders of public office were required to take an Oath of Supremacy or face a charge of treason. In 1537, the monasteries were dissolved and stripped of their lands, which were redistributed to nobles loyal to the king. Many of their greatest treasures went up in flames the following year, when all relics and other evidence of 'popish superstition' were ordered to be burned.

In 1541 Henry was declared **King of Ireland** at a huge parliament, to which many Irish chieftains were invited. When his daughter Mary acceded to the throne, Catholics hoped that their church would be restored, but she retained the title 'Queen of Ireland' and refused to return the confiscated lands to the monasteries. She was succeeded by Elizabeth I, who zealously spread the Reformation by reviving the Act of Supremacy and ordering the widespread use of the Book of Common Prayer. The confiscation of monastic lands opened up vast areas of Dublin to redevelopment, providing the blueprint for the present-day city.

In 1592 Elizabeth founded the College of the Most Holy Trinity on former monastic land, in order to provide education within the Protestant tradition. She tried to bring the Gaelic lords to heel by forcing them to surrender their lands to the Crown and then immediately re-granting them, but, while Dublin and the area within the Pale was relatively peaceful, wars between the Irish lords still divided the rest of the country. Stability was threatened by the Nine Years' War, when two Ulster chieftains Hugh O'Neill and Red Hugh O'Donnell rose up against the English. The rebellion was crushed, and O'Neill was forced to sign the Treaty of Mellifont on 23 March 1603 – only to discover that Elizabeth had died the day before. He was forbidden to practise Catholicism and stripped of his lands. His power was broken and he eventually abandoned the Irish people and sailed with his followers to Europe. This 'Flight of the Earls' marked the final nail in the coffin of the hopes of the Irish lords: the English conquest of Ireland was complete.

The Irish Catholics continued to be persecuted under the staunchly Protestant King

James I. Families who refused to renounce their Catholicism were dispossessed, and their lands given to Protestant families from Scotland, particularly in the Catholic-dominated northern province of Ulster. This practice of '**plantation**' was bitterly resented. With the accession of Charles I, the Catholics began to hope for leniency. In 1625 the Irish gentry offered to pay £120,000 to the king in return for concessions, assuring the security of their estates and the protection of Catholics against discrimination. The king received the money, but reneged on his promise to grant concessions. When the roundly despised **Thomas Wentworth** (known as 'Black Tom') was appointed Lord Deputy in 1633, he tried to wring as much money as he could from the local nobles. Irish families, Catholic and Protestant, native-Irish and old-English, were tricked into giving £20,000 to the king to secure the very concessions that they had previously been promised. Wentworth sucked another £240,000 from the gentry at an assembly of the government at Dublin Castle in return for more empty promises. Wentworth alienated every element of Irish society, and eventually his enemies forced Charles to recall him in 1640. The following year he was impeached by the House of Commons and beheaded.

The **Civil War** that engulfed England inevitably spread to Ireland, and the disgruntled Irish adopted the maxim 'England's difficulty is Ireland's opportunity'. By 1642, rebels had taken most of Ireland, and established a provisional government at Kilkenny. Charles I entered into negotiations with this government, hoping to gain their support against the Puritans. In Dublin, the government awaited reinforcements from **Cromwell**, alienating the old English families who were assumed to be Royalist sympathizers. It was a time for action, but the Irish rebels were once again confounded by their own internal power struggles and dithered in their support for the king. By the time they finally promised their allegiance, he had been executed. Cromwell and his armies arrived in Ireland and embarked on a campaign so brutal that his name still evokes hatred in many parts of the country. He intended to crush the Gaelic lords once and for all, and avenge the slaughter of Protestants in Ulster in 1641. At the infamous **Siege of Drogheda**, many thousands were massacred. By 1652, Ireland had been subdued; many Irish lords were forced into exile, their lands redistributed to former Roundhead soldiers in lieu of unpaid salaries.

Restoration and Georgian Dublin

The succession of the Catholic **James II** in 1685 brought renewed hope for the Irish. New acts of religious toleration were passed and the king attempted to re-establish the Catholic Church in Ireland. The Catholic Earl of Tyrconnell became commander of the army and later, the Chief Governor. Catholics were appointed to powerful positions in the army, administration, judiciary and town corporations. The supremacy of the Protestant landowners, many of whom lived in England, was under threat and in 1688 James's son-in-law, **William of Orange**, was invited by the English Protestants to take the throne of England and Ireland. James retreated to Ireland, where he counted on the support of the Irish Catholics. By March 1689 only Enniskillen and Londonderry were under Protestant control. Londonderry, tucked behind its walls, held out for 15 weeks before finally being relieved. It was a disaster for James and his exhausted army. In 1690 William met James's army at the legendary **Battle of the Boyne**. William's highly trained army of English, Scots, Dutch, Germans and French Huguenots was 36,000 strong; James commanded just 25,000 worn-out and ill-fed troops. The Catholic king was roundly defeated and fled to France.

After William's victory, he strengthened his grip on Ireland by passing the first **Penal Laws** in 1695. Catholics were banned from purchasing freehold property; any son of a Catholic who converted to Protestantism had the right to turn his parents off their estate;

the property of Catholic families was divided equally among all their children (so large estates quickly became uneconomic); all Catholics had to pay a tithe to maintain the Anglican Church; all priests were banished; no Catholic schools were allowed; and no Catholic could hold a commission in the army, enter one of the professions or own a horse worth more than £5. Spies were employed to report on the 'hedge schools' where banished priests would teach and celebrate Mass. These laws prevented Catholics from gaining political power in Ireland, and simultaneously appeased the Protestant landowners who in return acted as a garrison to keep the peace. The Irish were not just persecuted through their religion: the English also imposed heavy taxes on all Irish produce including cloth, wool, glass and cattle, which ensured that the Irish economy was unable to compete.

Although the Catholics were suffering, Dublin, as the seat of English rule, was booming. Protestant landowners commissioned the beautiful **Georgian** buildings which still define the cityscape, including the Four Courts, Leinster House and Custom House. A National Parliament was founded at College Green and passed the **Wide Streets Act** in 1751, making Dublin the first city in the world to enjoy planned development. The elegant squares and boulevards of Henrietta Street, Merrion Street, Merrion Square and O'Connell Street were laid out and lined with opulent mansions, designed and decorated by the foremost artists of the age. In 1731 the Royal Dublin Society was founded to promote the arts, science and agriculture; in 1742 the city saw the première of Handel's *Messiah*; and the city produced writers such as Jonathan Swift and Edmund Burke. Canals were built, and Arthur Guinness opened his brewery on the banks of the River Liffey.

When the American War of Independence broke out, Dublin found itself in a precarious position. The English were preoccupied with their former colony across the Atlantic, and the city felt vulnerable to attack from Spain or France. A volunteer force was raised, mainly from the Protestant landowning classes, which began to turn its attention towards the question of **home rule** as fears of invasion gradually receded. In 1782, Henry Grattan convinced the British Government to acknowledge that Ireland should be bound only by laws that were made by the king or by the Irish parliament. The Declaration of Rights was passed, which repealed the most vicious of the Penal Laws, made Trinity College accessible to people of all religions and established a Catholic seminary. Much had been achieved, and yet the parliament never fully embraced the emancipation of Catholics. As it became apparent that there would be no more reforms, resentment bubbled among the disenfranchised Catholics and middle classes, who were heartily sick of a government which represented only a minority of society.

The French Revolution of 1789 made change seem possible. The United Irishmen, led by **Wolfe Tone** and inspired by Tom Paine's *The Rights of Man*, declared their belief that government should be open to all. A rebellion in 1796 was quickly stamped out. Two years later, another country-wide rebellion was planned, but Wolfe Tone and the other leaders were betrayed by spies before they could take Dublin Castle. In 1798 the government imposed martial law. The United Irishmen, bereft of their leaders, drifted to the city once it was known that the rebellion had failed. Their short haircuts copied from the French gave them the nickname '**Croppies**', but made them easily identifiable and most were executed. Their bodies were thrown into a pit near Collins Barracks, now known as Croppies Acre.

As late as May 1797 Grattan was still trying to gain concessions on Catholic Emancipation from the Irish parliament, but he was voted down by the government side and finally resigned in disgust. This inability to forge links with the Catholic population was the downfall of the Irish parliament: in 1800, they found themselves in the ignominious position of having to vote themselves out of existence, and the **Act of Union** was passed in 1801, uniting Ireland with Great Britain.

The Struggle for Home Rule

The striving for Catholic emancipation continued, and found a charismatic leader in **Daniel O'Connell**. Catholics were still not allowed to sit in government, or hold important state office, judicial or civil service posts. O'Connell, a barrister, and Richard Lalor Shiel set up the Catholic Association to provide free legal aid to Catholics who had fallen foul of the law, and finance political campaigns fought by the Association. Several pro-emancipation candidates were elected, including O'Connell himself.

Support for O'Connell was considerable and eventually the Westminster government was forced to allow him to take his seat, passing the **Catholic Emancipation Act** in 1829. O'Connell began to focus on the abolition of the Act of Union, and founded the Repeal Association in 1840. In 1841 he was elected **Lord Mayor of Dublin**, becoming the first Catholic mayor for 150 years. He held huge rallies campaigning for home rule at sites which recalled the heroes of Irish history, including a massive meeting on the Hill of Tara, mythical home of the High Kings of Ireland, which attracted more than a million people. He announced another meeting at Clontarf, where Brian Ború had defeated the Vikings in 1014, but the British authorities, unnerved by his popularity, declared the meeting an unlawful assembly. Faced with the possibility of a violent clash, O'Connell, who believed that 'no political change is worth the shedding of a single drop of human blood', cancelled the meeting. He was arrested for conspiracy and found guilty by a stacked jury, although he was exonerated by the House of Lords on appeal.

By now, the **Great Famine** was devastating Ireland, and O'Connell's pleas for help in the British parliament fell on deaf ears. His political power and his health were waning, and in 1847 he set out for Rome. He never arrived, dying in Genoa on 15 May 1849. His heart was given to Rome, as he had instructed (it has subsequently been lost), and the rest of his body was returned to Ireland, where his funeral was attended by enormous crowds. His remains lie in Glasnevin Cemetery. The newly acquired freedoms for Catholics led to a shift in Dublin society, as the middle classes grew more prosperous and the city began to expand to the leafy southern suburbs.

The Great Famine

The daily diet of the average Irishman in the 19th century was six pounds of **potatoes** and a pint of milk. The potato could feed a large family on a small plot of land and in the west of Ireland it was the only crop that could be grown effectively. In 1845 the whole crop was devastated by a fungus; for the next three years Ireland suffered its worst **famine**. In 1846, three-quarters of the country's potato crop lay blackened and inedible in the ground. There were half-hearted attempts on the part of the British government to stave off famine, but the supplies of corn ordered from America were kept in government depots for five months. Two million people died of starvation and related diseases, and almost as many **emigrated**. The emigrants, packed into overcrowded, disease-ridden ships, were the lucky ones: thousands simply dropped dead of starvation on the quays. 'I pray to god that you Nor one of yers may [neither] know Nor ever Suffer what we are Suffering At the present,' wrote one stricken mother to her more fortunate son, who had sailed for the USA. The rural Irish were the first to suffer, and poured in their thousands to Dublin in search of work and food. By 1846, the numbers flooding into the city were so great that guards were posted to turn away as many people as possible. The government finally passed the **Soup Kitchen Act**, which established soup kitchens to feed each adult a bowl of soup and a loaf of bread a day. The most famous of these kitchens was a huge tent erected on Croppies Acre which could feed a hundred people at a sitting.

By 1847, three million were receiving relief, but the authorities grew resentful of the drain upon their coffers and ordered that all government relief under the Soup Kitchen Act cease by October 1847. The blight that hit the potato harvest in 1848 was as bad as ever, and thousands more died of starvation and cholera. Meanwhile, the wealthy middle and upper classes remained untouched, continuing their social whirl of balls and dinners.

In 1849, **Queen Victoria** made her first visit to Dublin, where she was greeted by cheering crowds; Nelson's Pillar on O'Connell Street was specially lit by newly introduced electricity in her honour. Incredibly, her letters home make no mention of the famine at all. In 1853, she returned to the city to open the Great Dublin Industrial Exhibition, which only underlined the wealth divide. The creation of the railways and the canal network and the success of the brewing and distilling industries all contributed to the wealth of the middle classes, who moved out to the elegant Victorian suburbs being created to the south of the city. They abandoned great swathes of the city centre and their former mansions were chopped up into tenements, into which scores of families were crammed in unspeakable squalor by profiteering landlords.

Resentment at British indifference to the plight of the Irish during and after the famine was reaching a head. The **Irish Republican Brotherhood**, also known as the **Fenian Brotherhood**, was formally established in Dublin on St Patrick's Day 1858 by James Stephens and James O'Mahony. The Fenians orchestrated another uprising in 1865, but were betrayed by an informer (this was becoming a predictable pattern for thwarted Irish rebellions), and their leaders were arrested or forced to flee. Nonetheless, they continued to harass the authorities, attacking police barracks and stealing weapons throughout the 1860s.

The Irish economy was substantially weakened by the famine, and in the 1870s starving tenant farmers were evicted from their lands as agricultural prices plummeted. Famine threatened again after a particularly wet winter, and, with the memory of British indifference still strong, the issue of **home rule** became the burning topic of the day. In 1875, **Charles Stewart Parnell** won a seat in the British parliament for the Home Rule Party, and in 1879 the Land League was formed to gain ownership of the land for tenants. The British Prime Minister, **William Gladstone**, was broadly sympathetic to their cause and between 1870 and 1903 a series of Land Acts were passed, under which the majority of Irish landlords were bought out and their lands transferred to tenant farmers.

However, the Irish Land League's tactics were becoming increasingly aggressive, and there were several clashes with the authorities. Eventually, Parnell was arrested and taken to Kilmainham Gaol in 1881, charged with conspiracy. The following year, the Phoenix Park murders, in which two British officials were stabbed to death, set back the cause for home rule dramatically. The murder was the work of a Fenian splinter group called The Invincibles, but Parnell, who was horrified by the event, offered to resign in order to avoid suspicion falling on his party. Gladstone urged him to remain in office, but public opinion in Britain had swung firmly against the Irish, and the Home Rule Bill of 1886 was defeated. In 1889, Parnell was cited as co-respondent in a divorce case brought by Captain Willie O'Shea against his wife, Kitty, with whom Parnell had conducted a long-standing affair. The revelation divided the Home Rule Party, Parnell was deposed, and he died in Kitty's arms in 1891.

Towards Independence

The growing support for the **nationalist** cause in Ireland was harnessed to a burgeoning pride in all things Irish. In 1884, the Gaelic Athletic Association (GAA) was formed to promote the ancient Gaelic sports of hurling and football. In 1889, the Gaelic

League was established to revive the Gaelic language and all aspects of the Irish arts, and was a major influence on the Celtic revival spearheaded by W.B Yeats and Lady Gregory around the turn of the century. At this time English was taught in schools and Gaelic was a dying language, spoken by only 14 per cent of the population. The president of the GAA, Douglas Hyde, campaigned successfully for the reinstatement of Gaelic lessons and for universities to accept Gaelic as an entry qualification. The Athletic Association acted as a link between the Catholic Church and the Irish Nationalists, and became a source of recruitment for the nationalist cause.

In 1902, Arthur Griffith established the nationalist newspaper **Sinn Féin**, out of which a political party emerged in 1905. The name means 'Ourselves Alone' and the party's central creed was home rule for Ireland. By 1910, the passing of the Home Rule Bill seemed inevitable, despite protests from the north of the country. In 1913, as the Bill was going through parliament, 500,000 people in Belfast signed their names to a covenant pledging resistance to home rule.

In Dublin tensions rose between the native Irish workers and the factory owners. By 1913, Dublin's largely unskilled labour force were living in some of the most notorious slums in Europe, and the wealth of the professional classes stood in stark contrast to the poverty of the workers. Almost 90,000 people in Dublin lived in squalid, cramped tenements, with most families occupying just one room. Tensions reached boiling point in 1913 when William Martin Murphy, who ran the Tramway Company, locked out all workers who had joined the Irish Transport General Workers Union. Soon labourers across the city found themselves locked out, and by the end of the week 25,000 people were out of a job. The lockout strike lasted for eight months, and there were serious clashes: a particularly vicious attack took place during a speech by Jim Larkin, when the crowd was charged by baton-wielding government forces who injured several hundred people.

Meanwhile, in response to the impending passing of the Home Rule Bill, the **Ulster Volunteer Force**, or UVF, was established to protect the Protestant north. James Connolly, a trade unionist and workers' leader during the 1913 lockout, responded by creating the Irish Citizens Army. The Irish Volunteers, a precursor of the Irish Republican Brotherhood (IRB), was also founded in the same year. When news broke that arms had been imported to Larne to supply the UVF, revolution seemed inevitable.

With the outbreak of the **First World War** in 1914, the question of home rule was put on hold. Many thousands of Irishmen volunteered to join the British Army, hoping to win concessions that would lead to home rule. But not all Nationalists felt the same way: some believed that the British entanglements in Europe meant that the time was ripe for a rising. A secret plan for an uprising on Easter Sunday 1916 was hatched by some members of the Irish Volunteers, led by **Patrick Pearse**, but it was kept from the leaders of the organization. The conspirators hoped to use military manoeuvres planned for Easter Sunday as a cover for the uprising, but Eoin MacNeil, the official leader of the Irish Volunteers, discovered the plot and cancelled the manoeuvres.

Foiled in this first attempt, the uprising was moved forward a day, and on **Easter Monday 1916** 2,000 troops, led by Patrick Pearse, took control of the General Post Office and other strategic locations across Dublin. A Proclamation declaring 'the right of the people of Ireland to the ownership of Ireland and to the unfettered control of Irish destinies' was papered across the city at dawn, and Pearse read it out on the steps of the GPO. The Nationalists had hoped for support from the Germans, which failed to materialize, but they managed to hold out for almost a week against 20,000 government troops. The city suffered enormous damage, and hundreds died. Finally, on 29 April, Pearse and his men surrendered and were taken to Kilmainham Gaol. Patrick Pearse, James Connolly, Thomas Clarke and 11 other leaders of the rebellion were court-martialled and summarily executed. The brutality with which they were treated outraged the Irish; public opinion – which had initially been against the uprising – swung firmly behind the rebels. They were fêted as martyrs, and their burial ground in Arbour Hill Cemetery remains a focus for political and republican leaders.

In the wake of the Easter 1916 rising, republican support swelled enormously. The Sinn Féin party under the influence of American-born **Eamon De Valera** sought to mobilize public support through propaganda and electioneering. In 1918, the British government passed a law extending conscription to Ireland, but support for the war against Germany was at an all-time low and the news caused uproar in Ireland. Many of the Sinn Féin leaders, including De Valera, were arrested by the British, who feared another uprising, and imprisoned in English gaols.

In the 1918 general election, Sinn Féin won three-quarters of the Irish seats (partly, it must be said, thanks to impersonation and election rigging), although more than half of their elected members were in prison. Those who were not in prison refused to take their seats in Westminster, and convened an Irish Assembly, the Dáil Éireaan, at which the **Irish Republic** was declared. De Valera escaped from Lincoln Prison in 1919, and was appointed president of the new – still unrecognized – Irish state. **Michael Collins** was appointed Minister of Finance, but his main responsibility was to train the military arm of the Irish Volunteers, which would later be known as the **Irish Republican Army**, or IRA. He led a bitter guerrilla campaign which targeted policemen and informers, including the infamous 'G-Men' who were the information-gatherers of the Dublin Metropolitan Police's G-Division. But the Royal Irish Constabulary fought back with ruthless brutality, their ranks supplemented with huge numbers of English recruits. There were not enough uniforms to go around, and these recruits were dressed in khaki with black hats, which gave rise to their nickname: the **Black and Tans**. On 21 November 1920, Collins ordered the assassination of 14 undercover British officers who had infiltrated the IRB in Dublin, but the following day the Black and Tans machine-gunned crowds at a Gaelic football match in Croke Park. Twelve men and women were killed and dozens were injured in what became known as the **Bloody Sunday Massacre**. In 1921, the IRA attacked the Customs House at the instigation of De Valera, and the British government finally called a truce. Negotiations began to find a compromise.

An Irish delegation headed by Michael Collins went to London to meet with Lloyd George. A treaty was signed on 6 December 1921 which approved the establishment of an **Irish Free State** with dominion status similar to that of Canada. Ireland was to be divided into a 26-county Irish Free State with Dublin as the capital, while six counties in Ulster would remain under British rule. Collins was also forced to agree that legislators should swear an oath of allegiance to the Crown and that the British Navy would have access to certain ports. As he signed the treaty, he is rumoured to have remarked, 'I have signed my death warrant'.

The terms of the treaty, particularly the partition and the oath of allegiance, horrified some members of the Dáil, who refused to accept it, but Collins viewed it as a stepping stone to greater freedom. De Valera rejected it, and, when the Dáil debate was narrowly won by the pro-treaty side, he resigned as president. In January 1922, Dublin Castle was officially handed over to the Irish Free State.

A general election held in June showed overwhelming support for the treaty, but the Dáil Eireann and the Irish Republican Army were irrevocably split. Anti-treaty forces, known now as the 'Irregulars', took over the Four Courts as their headquarters, and Collins was warned by the British government that if he refused to attack the Four Courts they would consider the treaty abrogated and bring in British forces. He gave the order to shell the building on 28 June: the **Irish Civil War** had begun. The pro-treaty section of the IRA became known as the Irish

Free Army, and they found themselves pitted against men with whom they had recently fought side by side. De Valera's forces in the Four Courts were finally forced out, but not before they had mined the adjoining Public Records Office, destroying irreplaceable records dating back to the Middle Ages. The Civil War dragged on for a terrible year, which left thousands dead and tens of thousands imprisoned. Michael Collins himself was ambushed and killed in Cork. His body was returned to Dublin and interred in the largest public funeral since Parnell's. Finally, on 24 May 1923, the Republican leadership gave the order to cease fire, although they still refused to accept the legitimacy of the Free State.

Birth of the Republic

In 1926 Eamon De Valera founded a new political party to represent the anti-treaty side called **Fianna Fáil**, or Warriors of Ireland. They did well at the 1927 elections, but were refused admittance to the Dáil because they wouldn't take the oath of allegiance to the British king. De Valera stood outside the parliament and denounced the 'false oath' to the gathered crowd, and promised to hold a referendum to abolish it. His party was more successful in the 1932 elections, although there were widespread rumours of election-rigging. Nonetheless, Fianna Fáil took power with the support of the Labour Party in 1932. The oath of allegiance was dropped, and many IRA prisoners were released. But De Valera became increasingly disillusioned with the IRA, which he finally declared an illegal organization in 1936. After the IRA stole a huge amount of ammunition in 1939, the authorities began cracking down: many leaders were arrested or executed. In the 1937 constitution, the country's official name was changed to **Eire**, and Roman Catholicism was established as the primary religion. Work began on restoring the devastation inflicted during the early years of the 20th century; slums were cleared, and construction began on local authority housing schemes on the outskirts of the city.

The country was neutral during the **Second World War**, but it still suffered from German bombs which caused more than 30 deaths and 80 casualties. There were food shortages, and rationing was introduced in 1942. In 1948, Fianna Fáil were ousted by a coalition between Fine Gael (Tribes of Gaels) and Clann na Poblachta (Republican Party), and in 1949 Ireland was finally declared a **republic**.

The Irish 'Troubles'

During the 1950s, the government concentrated on introducing better health care and other social issues. It clashed regularly with the Church authorities, particularly the authoritarian **Archbishop McQuaid**. Dublin was expanding rapidly, as people from rural communities arrived to find work. The city's Georgian heritage was still linked in the public imagination with British imperialism; much of the 18th-century architecture was destroyed and replaced by anonymous concrete buildings. In 1957, Fianna Fáil were back in power under Eamon De Valera, who became President of Ireland two years later and was replaced as Taoiseach by **Séan Lemass**. Under Lemass, Ireland finally began to open up to international influences and its economy improved. The fiftieth anniversary of the Easter Rising in 1966 was celebrated with the construction of the Garden of Remembrance by the government, and the bombing of Nelson's Pillar on O'Connell Street by the IRA.

The '**Troubles**' in Northern Ireland began to escalate in the 1960s, although they had little effect on the Republic until 1968, when members of the Irish Cabinet were accused of providing the North with weapons. They were dismissed from office, but the subsequent trial found them all not guilty. In the North, things went from bad to worse: in 1971, internment without trial was introduced, and the following year, on what came to be known as **Bloody Sunday**, British paratroopers opened fire on a civil rights march in Londonderry, killing 13 people. There was a demonstration in Dublin, and the British

Embassy on Merrion Square was firebombed. In the face of increasing IRA activity, the Irish government proposed an Offences against the State Bill, which gave the police wide-ranging powers against the IRA. It was initially opposed by Fine Gael and the Labour Party, but when two bombs exploded in Dublin, killing two people and injuring more than a hundred others, they offered their support and the bill was passed. There were more bombings in 1974 and 1976 and the decade was marked by political and economic instability. Things improved somewhat once the Republic joined **the EEC** in 1973, but the country continued to struggle with rising unemployment.

Contemporary Dublin

During the 1980s, Dublin's preferential tax regimes began to attract foreign investment, and the enormous International Financial Services Centre on Custom House Quay was constructed as a symbol of the new financial optimism. As employment grew, social issues came to the fore, particularly the political hot potatoes of **abortion** and **divorce**. The Church, which had exerted its considerable powers to enforce their prohibition for so long, found itself embroiled in a series of scandals relating to sexual abuse and paedophilia which dramatically undermined its authority. Divorce was finally approved in 1995, but abortion remains a delicate political issue unresolved by the results of several referenda. In 1990, Ireland's first female president, **Mary Robinson**, was elected, and was succeeded by Mary McAleese in 1997. The influx of investment, the dot-com boom and the transformation of some inner city slums (in particular, Temple Bar) which contributed to the rapid rejuvenation of Ireland's fortunes, led to the country's new nickname of the '**Celtic Tiger**'.

But underneath the shiny exterior of the new Dublin with its fancy fashion boutiques and stylish bars, some long-standing problems, notably drug addiction, remain. This issue was highlighted terribly in 1996, when journalist **Veronica Guerin** was killed by the drug barons she was investigating.

By 1999, a worldwide recession was taking its toll on Ireland. This downturn in Dublin's fortunes was reflected in the botched celebrations for the millennium; they included a glowing clock which was supposed to be submerged in the Liffey for the countdown on New Year's Eve – but the river was so murky that the clockface couldn't be deciphered, and Dublin wags quickly nicknamed the project 'the Chime in the Slime'. Construction was also stalled on the controversial Millennium Spire, which was only finally erected in 2003. And successive governments have found themselves caught up in financial scandals: former Taoiseach Charles Haughey took millions of pounds in bribes from businessmen in the 1980s, and members of Bertie Ahern's government were implicated in another corruption scandal which even Ahern, nicknamed the 'Tefal Taoiseach' for his ability to dodge trouble, may have difficulty surviving unscathed.

One of Dublin's biggest future challenges is set to be coping with its burgeoning **multicultural population**. The city's new-found wealth has reversed the centuries-old trend for emigration, and now there are more immigrants than emigrants. Learning to accommodate and appreciate different cultures is only part of the challenge: another effect of the huge influx of people is simply a question of numbers. Gentrification and development have meant that house prices have risen to such dizzying heights that most people are priced out of the market, and the shortage of accommodation means that rent prices are also incredibly high. The city is crammed with traffic and public transport is overstretched. The new Luas tram system is finally taking some of the strain, and the DART suburban railway is next up for a major overhaul, in an attempt to ease the city's transport overcrowding.

Art and Architecture

PREHISTORY 32
THE EARLY CHRISTIAN ERA 32
VIKING DUBLIN 32
MEDIEVAL DUBLIN 33
NEOCLASSICAL AND GEORGIAN DUBLIN 33
NINETEENTH-CENTURY DUBLIN 35
TWENTIETH-CENTURY DUBLIN 35
INTO THE 21ST CENTURY 36

Prehistory

Evidence of the first settlers in Dublin survives in the **burial cists** discovered in **Phoenix Park**, and in an ancient dolmen which still stands on the **Head of Howth**. The most spectacular prehistoric ruins are clustered in the **Boyne Valley** north of Dublin, where the passage tombs at **Newgrange**, **Knowth** and **Dowth** illustrate the engineering skills and artistic craftsmanship of the early Irish settlers and have been declared a UNESCO World Heritage Site. A Stone Age tomb was discovered on the **Hill of Tara**, seat of the High Kings of Ireland, where grassy undulations still delineate the ancient ring-fort. The National Museum on Kildare Street contains a dazzling collection of **Bronze Age gold**.

The Early Christian Era

According to legend, Christianity was introduced to Ireland by St Patrick in AD 452. The **early Christians** often lived in remote caves, which gradually developed into hermitages and monasteries; remnants of early churches have survived on **Dalkey Island** and **Ireland's Eye**. The monastic complex at **Glendalough**, established by St Kevin, is one of the most beautiful and haunting sites in Ireland, although much of the surviving architecture dates back only to the 10th and 11th centuries: earlier constructions were usually made of wood and have long since rotted.

High crosses, such as at Monasterboice, Glendalough and Trim, appeared in the 7th century. They usually feature a Celtic ring and were carved with biblical events, a pictorial sermon for the largely illiterate population.

> ### Prehistory
> **Phoenix Park**, for its ancient burial cists, p.123
> **Newgrange, Knowth and Dowth**, for their superb passage tombs, p.160
> **Hill of Tara**, where you'll find a Neolithic tomb, p.162
> The **National Museum of Ireland** has an unparalleled collection of Bronze Age gold, p.69

> ### The Early Christian Era
> **Glendalough**, an early monastic complex, is one of Dublin's most compelling historical sites, p.167
> **Book of Kells**, on view at Trinity College, p.60
> The **National Museum of Ireland** is crammed with superb examples of early medieval craftsmanship, p.70

As the rest of Europe was submerged in the Dark Ages, the Irish monasteries were becoming renowned for scholarship and artistry which reached new heights in the exquisitely illuminated **Book of Kells**. The collection of early medieval treasures on display at the **National Museum of Ireland** – jewel-encrusted shrines, chalices and elaborately carved crosses – attest to the outstanding craftsmanship of the period.

As Viking raids became more common, the Irish began to build **round towers**, of which about a hundred still survive across the country. These acted as watchtowers and repositories for valuables; the finest extant example can be found at **Glendalough**.

During the Celtic period there were two small settlements on the banks of the Liffey, which survive only in the names of the modern city in Gaelic (*Áth Cliath*) and English (*Dubh Linn*). By the end of the 8th century there were a large number of monasteries and churches around Dublin, the most important being those at **Tallaght**, **Clondalkin** and **Finglas**; the riches they contained were a major enticement for the Vikings, who first raided Ireland in 795.

Viking Dublin

The **Vikings** founded the first major settlement in Dublin when they established a *longphort* on the riverbank in 841. Their first berthing was marked by a stone marker or *Steyne* which stood intact until the 17th century. Excavations in Kilmainham and Islandbridge turned up a **Viking cemetery** which may date back to this first settlement, but otherwise almost nothing is known about it.

Viking Dublin

The **National Museum of Ireland** displays a collection of Viking pieces saved from the Wood Quay development, p.69

Dublinia also has a fine collection of Viking artefacts, p.90

A second, more permanent, Viking settlement was established in 917, and rapidly grew into a prosperous community. This was the origin of modern Dublin, and the remnants were discovered by accident when construction began on the new Corporation buildings on **Wood Quay**. The foundation remains of about 200 buildings from the 10th and 11th centuries were discovered, mostly rectangular in design, which would have had post-and-wattle walls and thatched roofs. It was the best preserved Viking site discovered outside Scandinavia, and the decision to continue construction on top of the excavations met with outraged protest from locals – but went ahead anyway. The **National Museum of Ireland** displays many of the artefacts discovered on the site, and others are on show at **Dublinia**.

Other Viking remains, including pathways and wattle-screens, were unearthed in the 1960s beneath Dublin Castle.

Medieval Dublin

The Anglo-Normans, who conquered Viking Dublin in the late 12th century, introduced new building techniques and European architectural styles. They constructed stone walls, a fortified castle and the magnificent cathedrals of **Christchurch** and **St Patrick**.

Medieval Dublin

Christchurch Cathedral, although restored later, is a fine example of medieval church architecture, p.89

St Patrick's Cathedral is another beautiful example, p.91

City walls – just a short stretch of the walls still exists, p.146

Tower houses survive, just like those at Malahide and Drimnagh, p.128

However, just a short stretch of the original **city walls** survives (near St Audoen's Church), and the castle was later destroyed by fire; very little of the fortification survives. The two cathedrals were patched up through the centuries and renovated so thoroughly that only fragments – notably the crypt at Christchurch – remain intact.

Tower houses, such as the ones that form the core of Malahide Castle and Drimnagh Castle, began to be built, and included defensive features such as 'murder holes' (concealed openings above the entrance from which boiling water or lime would be poured onto the heads of intruders) and 'trip stairs'. The dissolution of the monasteries in 1537 meant that great tracts of land suddenly became available for new development. This led to, among other major works, the establishment of Trinity College.

Neoclassical and Georgian Dublin

By the late 17th century, Dublin's newfound prosperity was being reflected in the construction of major public buildings such as the **Royal Hospital Kilmainham** in 1680, the first classical revival edifice in Dublin. It was designed by Sir William Robinson, who was also responsible for Marsh's Library (1701) and the remodelling of Dublin Castle in the early 1700s. Sir Edward Lovett Pearce introduced neoclassical Palladianism to Ireland; this became the dominant style of the early 18th century and heralded a construction boom which would utterly transform the cityscape. Over the next century, Dublin would develop from an enclosed medieval city into one of the most significant modern cities in 18th-century Europe. Pearce's masterpiece was the magnificent **Parliament House** (now the Bank of Ireland) on College Green, but he also established the model for the majority of the Georgian townhouses built over the next century: four-storey edifices with tall, symmetrical windows, and a flight of granite steps leading to a door surmounted with a fanlight window.

In the early part of the 18th century, the most fashionable Dublin neighbourhoods were on the north side of the river: **Henrietta Street**, laid out by the wealthy landowner Luke Gardiner in the 1720s, was one of the earliest Georgian streets. More splendid mansions lined **Parnell Square**, including Charlemont House which now houses the **Hugh Lane Gallery**. By the latter half of the century, fashionable Dublin had moved south of the river, and the northside and its Georgian heritage began the steady decline which has only recently been reversed.

Pearce's protegé and collaborator on the Bank of Ireland was the Anglo-German architect Richard Cassels (also known as Richard Castle), who settled in Ireland around 1728 and became the leading country house architect of his day. In Dublin, his major works include **Leinster House**, which became the model for the White House in Washington DC and is now the seat of the Irish parliament, and **Clanwilliam House** on St Stephen's Green, which has been immaculately restored and opened to the public as part of Newman House.

The often austerely simple façades of the Georgian townhouses belie the richness of the decoration within: most featured elaborate, creamy stucco ceilings, delicate marquetry floors, gleaming marble chimney pieces and huge crystal chandeliers. The Swiss stucco craftsmen Paulo and Fillipo LaFranchini were responsible for much of the finest plasterwork of the age, including the Apollo Room in **Newman House**, but their work was regularly matched in skill and beauty by Irish stucco craftsmen such as Michael Stapleton and Robert West.

One of the most remarkable architects of the later 18th century was Sir William Chambers. He never set foot in Ireland, but his designs were used in some of the finest Georgian architectural monuments, including the magnificent **Casino** at Marino. The other great architect of the period was James Gandon, best known for the imposing **Custom House** and **Four Courts**. James Cooley beat his better-known rival, Gandon, to win the commission for Dublin's **City Hall**, another showy neoclassical building which reflected the city's optimism. The last great architect of the era was Francis Johnston, who built the **General Post Office**.

The National Museum in **Collins Barracks** displays a wonderful collection of 18th-century Irish furniture, glass, jewellery and silverwork from the period. Dublin was the second city of the British Empire during this period, and Irish painters and sculptors looked to England for their livelihoods. This is reflected in their output, which generally conformed to the prevailing English taste for landscapes and portraiture, the best of which is on view at the **National Gallery of Ireland**, and includes George Barret's luminous landscapes and Hugh Douglas Hamilton's portraits.

> ## Neoclassical and Georgian Dublin
>
> **Royal Hospital Kilmainham**, Dublin's first neoclassical building, p.97
>
> **Parliament House** has some fine stucco ceilings, p.65
>
> **Henrietta Street** is one of the earliest Georgian streets in Dublin, p.118
>
> **Parnell Square** was once a fashionable address, p.105
>
> **Leinster House** is one of the finest surviving Georgian mansions, p.71
>
> **Newman House** has been exquisitely restored, p.73
>
> **Collins Barracks** contains beautiful examples of Georgian decorative arts, p.120
>
> **Casino at Marino** is a magical 18th-century pavilion, p.131
>
> **Custom House** magnificently dominates the riverside, p.111
>
> **Four Courts** is another of Gandon's masterpieces, p.116
>
> **City Hall** has been lavishly restored, p.88
>
> **General Post Office** makes buying a stamp a glamorous transaction, p.103
>
> **National Gallery of Ireland** contains the best Irish art of the Georgian period, p.76

Nineteenth-Century Dublin

When Ireland was united with Great Britain by the Act of Union in 1801, it lost its parliament and most of its power. The great building boom of the Georgian era was over. However, ecclesiastical architecture flourished – scores of churches were built and many more underwent restoration. One of the grandest new projects was **St Mary's Pro-Cathedral**, built in 1814. This was followed by the **Black Church** and the church of **St Francis Xavier**, both built immediately after the Emancipation Act of 1829 which relaxed laws governing the construction of Catholic churches. Dublin's much-loved **Church of St Stephen** was erected in 1825 and topped with a cupola which has given it the nickname 'the Peppercanister Church'.

In the latter half of the 19th century, many of Dublin's major churches underwent renovations by architects influenced by the Gothic revival. The renovation of **St Patrick's Cathedral** was relatively sensitive and mostly adhered to the original designs, but other works, including George Edmund Street's restoration of **Christchurch Cathedral** in the 1870s, involved parts of the original structures being arrogantly destroyed.

The Great Famine of the 1840s brought a flood of desperate immigrants to the city from the countryside. Meanwhile Dublin's middle classes were becoming wealthy, largely on the profits from brewing and distilling. They moved south to the elegant new suburbs, abandoning their Georgian mansions to unscrupulous landlords who stripped them of their opulent interior decoration and turned them into tenements.

A host of new buildings were constructed during the late 19th century to house national Irish cultural institutions, including the **National Museum** and the **National Library**, which are fine examples of Victorian Palladianism. The most innovative of the Gothic revival architects was Benjamin Woodward, who designed the Museum buildings in **Trinity College**.

The Romantic movement had a profound impact on early 19th-century art, evident in the work of landscape artists such as Francis Danby and James Arthur O'Connor (which you can see at the **National Gallery**). Later 19th-century artists like Daniel Maclise, Richard Moynam, Henry Jones Thadeus and Frederick Wiliam Burton excelled at the genre painting popular in Britain at the time.

Twentieth-Century Dublin

During the early 20th century, the 'Celtic revival' had a profound effect across the arts, and decorative arts in particular flourished under the patronage of the Arts and Crafts Council. The Harry Clark and An Túr Gloine studios were established, and produced exquisitely crafted **stained glass windows** for ecclesiastical and secular buildings. You can see some Harry Clark windows at the former **Bewley's Oriental Café** on Grafton Street, itself a fine example of the Art Deco tradition. The Arts and Crafts movement produced some exceptional buildings, including the graceful **Iveagh Trust Buildings and Baths**.

The greatest painter of the early 20th century was Jack B. Yeats, brother of William, and son of the portraitist Jack Butler Yeats. There is a comprehensive collection of his works at the **National Gallery** and more at the **Hugh Lane Gallery**. They show the evolution of his paintings from the early Celtic revival-influenced pieces, which

---

Nineteenth-Century Dublin

St Mary's Pro-Cathedral is the grandest Catholic church in the city, p.104

Black Church was built of black calp stone, p.111

St Francis Xavier, a Parisian-style Catholic church, p.110

Trinity College boasts the fanciful 19th-century museum buildings, p.63

National Gallery displays 19th-century landscapes and genre painting, p.74

Twentieth-Century Dublin

Bewley's Oriental Café is a colourful Art Deco gem, p.66

Iveagh Trust, now battered but still graceful, p.93

Dún Laoghaire, to see Andrew O'Connor's *Christ the King*, p.135

Sandycove, where Michael Scott's home is found, p.135

Abbey Theatre, an unloved 1960s replacement for the original, p.104

Corporation Buildings, among the most controversial architecture in Dublin, p.89

Temple Bar, the most famous of Dublin's regeneration schemes, p.84

romanticize the rural landscapes of people of the west of Ireland, to the experimental Expressionist works at the end of his career.

Other Irish artists were being influenced by the modernist movement, including Roderic O'Conor, Walter Osborne, Paul Henry and Mary Swanzy. One of the most innovative Irish sculptors of the early 20th century was Andrew O'Connor, whose intriguing *Christ the King* (1929) was deemed unsuitable by Church authorities and only finally erected in Dún Laoghaire in a secret ceremony in 1979.

Dublin's first truly modern building was the starkly modernist **Busáras** (main bus station), designed by Michael Scott and built in 1947. The sleek, glassy home which he designed for himself and his family in the 1930s is visible next to the James Joyce Tower in **Sandycove**, and he was also responsible for the new **Abbey Theatre**, built in 1966 after the original theatre burned down.

Dublin was expanding rapidly, as people arrived to find work. The city's Georgian heritage was still linked in the public imagination with British imperialism: much of it was erased by concrete in the 1960s and '70s. The establishment of the Irish Georgian Society in 1958 ensured that some buildings survived, but terrible planning decisions included destroying many Georgian townhouses along **Fitzwilliam Street** to make way for a brutally ugly office building. **Liberty Hall**, the city's first – and last – skyscraper, was erected in 1964, to general antipathy. Sam Stephenson's designs for the **Corporation Buildings**, which were controversially erected over a Viking settlement in the 1980s, also met with criticism. Only the first of his two buildings was erected; a second glass tower on the site was added later and, unlike its predecessor, met with public approval.

The rundown inner city neighbourhood of **Temple Bar** was completely transformed in the 1980s and 1990s, when the 17th- and 18th-century warehouses and townhouses were restored, and a slew of sharply modern new buildings were erected, including **The Ark** children's theatre, the **DESIGNyard** arts centre and the **Temple Bar Music Centre**.

Into the 21st Century

Major redevelopment took off during the 1990s as the 'Celtic Tiger' economy boomed. The once-grimy quays are now filling up with swanky new apartment buildings, and the **Waterways Visitor Centre**, one of the most imaginative contemporary buildings in the city, opened in 1995. In **Smithfield**, a former distillery has been converted into a still-unfinished leisure complex, set around a restored cobbled market-square. Several historic buildings have been converted for use as showcase museums, including **Collins Barracks**, now an outpost of the National Museum of Ireland, and Kilmainham Hospital, now the **Irish Museum of Modern Art**. IMMA is the best place to see modern and contemporary Irish artists, including Jack B. Yeats, Louis Le Brocquy, Ciarán Lennon, Sean Scully, Caroline McCarthy and Richard Deacon. In 2001, the Hugh Lane Gallery opened a permanent exhibition which contains the perfectly preserved studio of **Francis Bacon**, who was born in Dublin.

Into the 21st Century

Waterways Visitor Centre, an elegant, glassy, architectural gem, p.80

Smithfield is still a work-in-progress, p.118

Irish Museum of Modern Art shows the finest young Irish contemporary artists, p.97

Travel

GETTING THERE 38
By air 38
By train 39
By coach 39
By ferry 40
By car 40

SPECIALIST TOUR OPERATORS 40

ENTRY FORMALITIES 41

ARRIVAL 42

GETTING AROUND 43
By bus 43
By train 43
By tram 44
By taxi 44
By bicycle 44
Hiring a car 45
Guided tours 45

GETTING THERE
By Air
From the UK

Dublin is just an hour's flight away from most UK cities, and it's a massively popular weekend destination. There are plenty of cheap deals to be found, particularly on the web, but you will need to book well in advance if you are looking for weekend flights at any time of year. Midweek travel can be substantially cheaper. Count on paying around £80–100 for a weekend flight during the peak season, and as little as £30 return for a midweek flight in low season. Competition on these busy routes is intense and there are regular special offers which are usually featured on airline websites, or in the travel supplements of the big newspapers. Flight prices rise during peak periods – summer holidays, Easter and around Christmas – and you will need to book flights and accommodation months in advance when there are big festivals or sporting events happening in Dublin (St Patrick's Day or the Six Nations rugby championship, for example).

Aer Arann: *t 0800 587 2324, www.aerarann.ie*. From Belfast.

British Airways: *t 0870 850 9850, www.ba.com*. From Bristol and Gatwick.

Bmibaby: *t 0870 254 2229, www.bmibaby.com*. From Nottingham.

Aer Lingus: *t 0845 084 4444, www.aerlingus.com*. From Birmingham, Bristol, Edinburgh, Gatwick, Glasgow, Heathrow, London City and Manchester.

FlyBE: *t 0870 567 6676, www.flybe.com*. From Exeter and Southampton.

Ryanair: *t 0871 246 0000, www.ryanair.com*. From Aberdeen, Birmingham, Blackpool, Bournemouth, Bristol, Cardiff, Durham Tees Valley, Edinburgh, Gatwick, Leeds-Bradford, Liverpool, Luton, Manchester, Newcastle, Prestwick and Stansted.

Flights on the Internet

The best place to start looking for flights is the web – just about everyone has a site where you can compare prices, and booking online usually confers a 10–20% discount.

In the UK and Ireland
www.airtickets.co.uk
www.cheapflights.com
www.lastminute.com
www.skydeals.co.uk
www.sky-tours.co.uk
www.thomascook.co.uk
www.trailfinders.com
www.travelselect.com
www.kelcoo.co.uk
www.opodo.co.uk

In the USA
www.air-fare.com
www.airhitch.org
www.expedia.com
www.flights.com
www.orbitz.com
www.priceline.com
www.travellersweb.ws
www.travelocity.com
www.smarterliving.com

In Canada
www.destina.ca
www.lastminuteclub.com
www.newfrontiers.com

Student and Youth Travel Specialists

Several agencies offer special flights and deals for students. You may have to show a student ID card to get the discounts.

CTS Travel: *t (020) 7290 0630, www.ctstravel.co.uk*

STA Travel: *t 0870 160 6070, www.sta-travel.com*

USIT Campus: *t 0870 240 1010, www.usitcampus.co.uk*

Trailfinders: *t (020) 7937 1234, www.trailfinders.co.uk*

From the USA and Canada

The Irish national carrier Aer Lingus operates direct flights to Dublin from several major US cities. There are direct flights from New York to Dublin with Continental and Delta, which also flies directly from Atlanta. Fares to Dublin are surprisingly high, and it may be worth picking up a cheap deal to London and getting a connection from there (see above). There are currently no direct flights from Canada to Dublin: the cheapest option is usually to get a flight to London and pick up a connection there. Average season prices for a return ticket from the US are around US$1000 in high season, or about US$450 in low season. Special deals are few and far between, but it's always worth checking out airline websites and the travel supplements of the major Sunday newspapers.

Airlines

Aer Lingus: *t 800 474 7424, www.aerlingus.com*. Baltimore, Boston, Chicago, Los Angeles, New York and Newark direct to Dublin.

American Airlines: *t 800 433 7300, www.aa.com*. Code-shares with Aer Lingus: you can book flights from most major US cities.

British Airways: *t 800 247 9297, www.ba.com*. Flights via London.

Continental: *t 800 231 0856, www.continental.com*. Newark to Dublin direct.

Delta: *t 800 241 4141, www.delta.com*. Atlanta direct to Shannon and Dublin; New York direct to Dublin.

Lufthansa: *t 800 645 3880, www.lufthansa.com*. Flights via Frankfurt.

Northwest/KLM: *t 800 777 5553, www.klm.com*. Flights via Amsterdam.

TAP Air Portugal: *t 800 221 7370, www.tap-airportugal.us*. Flights via Lisbon.

United Airlines: *t 800 538 2929, www.united.com*. Flights to Dublin via London Heathrow.

Virgin Atlantic: *t 800 862 8621, www.virginatlantic.com*. Flights from major US cities via London Heathrow or Brussels.

Student and Youth Travel Specialists

Council Travel: USA *t 888 COUNCIL, www.counciltravel.com*

CTS Travel: USA *t 877 287 6665, www.ctstravelusa.com*

STA Travel: USA *t 800 777 0112, www.sta-travel.com*

Travel Cuts: Canada *t 800 667 2887, www.travelcuts.com*

By Train

Most ferry services making the crossing between Britain and Ireland connect with rail services from London and other UK destinations. Rail-sea tickets are available from stations across the UK, but cannot be bought online. Prices and journey times vary, but a standard journey from London Euston to Dún Laoghaire takes just under 7 hours if you cross with the high-speed Stena boat, or just under 11 hours if you cross with Irish Ferries. A return fare costs up to £88; for the cheapest £29 fare, book at least 14 days in advance. You can get reliable, entertaining information on all kinds of train journeys from the Man In Seat 61, *www.seat61.com*.

For information and train times, contact the Iarnrod Éireann (Irish Rail) in Dublin, or National Rail Enquiries in the UK.

Iarnród Éireann (Irish Rail): *35 Lower Abbey St, Dublin, t (01) 836 6222, www.irishrail.ie*

National Rail enquiries (UK): *t 0845 748 4950, www.nationalrail.co.uk*

By Coach

Eurolines offers direct coach services to Dublin from Bristol, Leeds, London, Manchester and Glasgow. The journey time is about 10–12 hours, and they often run overnight. With cheap air fares so easy to find, the long and tedious coach journey is only worth considering if you are on a very tight budget or have a student or pensioner pass (which offer big discounts). Prices can be as low as £33 for a return trip from London to Dublin, rising to £80 in the high season.

There are several smaller companies also offering coach connections between the UK and Ireland: check newspapers for details.

Eurolines (UK): *52 Grosvenor Gardens, London SW1,* **t** *0870 514 3219, www.eurolines.co.uk*

Bus Eireann (Dublin): **t** *(01) 836 6111, www.buseireann.ie*

By Ferry

Dublin Harbour and nearby Dún Laoghaire (pronounced "dunleary") are served by ferries from Holyhead in north Wales, Liverpool and the Isle of Man (summer only). Other Irish ports include Rosslare (for crossings from Fishguard and Pembroke in Wales, and Cherbourg and Roscoff in France); Belfast and nearby Larne (for crossings from Cairnryan and Stranraer in Scotland); and Cork (for crossings from Swansea in Wales and Roscoff in France).

Prices depend on time of year and length of crossing, the length of your stay (five-day deals are often the cheapest) and whether you are taking your car. Book as early as possible for the best deals, and look out for special offers online. Note that at peak times (such as Christmas and Easter) passenger numbers are strictly controlled. During these periods, foot passengers will need to obtain a 'sailing control ticket' (available when the booking is made or from ferry offices).

Irish Ferries: *UK* **t** *0870 517 1717, Republic of Ireland* **t** *1890 313131, www.irishferries.com.* Car and foot passenger ferry services at least five times daily between Holyhead and Dublin Port.

Stena Line: *UK* **t** *0870 570 7070, Republic of Ireland* **t** *(01) 280 7777, www.stenaline.com.* Car and foot-passenger ferry services between Dún Laoghaire and Holyhead, and car ferry services between Holyhead and Dublin Port. Also operates a high-speed catamaran service Holyhead–Dún Laoghaire which crosses the Irish Sea in 1hr 40min.

Isle of Man Steam Packet Company: *UK* **t** *0870 552 3523, Republic of Ireland* **t** *1800 805055, www.steam-packet.com.* Twice-daily Seacat ferry services from Liverpool to Dublin Port and a seasonal (summer-only) ferry service to Dublin from the Isle of Man.

By Car

If you are driving to Dublin, be prepared for traffic jams around the city and total gridlock in the centre: traffic congestion is one of the city's biggest headaches. Once you get there, park the car and do not bother using it until it is time to leave. The main access roads for the city are the N11 dual carriageway from the port in Dún Laoghaire, the N1 and the M1 motorway from Belfast, the N6 and N4 from Galway and the N8 and N7 from Cork. Traffic circulates on the left, and signposts are usually bilingual. When driving in Ireland, a valid national driving licence is required and a Green Card and Motor Insurance certificate are recommended. A country identification sticker is compulsory, as are seat belts in the front and, where fitted, in the rear. The official alcohol-to-blood ratio for drivers is 0.08% (the same as in the UK and most of the USA): this is regularly blithely disregarded by locals, but there are stiff fines for those who get caught over the limit. You can get more information from:

Irish Visiting Motorists Bureau: *Insurance House, 39 Molesworth St, Dublin,* **t** *(01) 676 9944*

Automobile Association of Ireland: **t** *(01) 617 9999, www.aaireland.ie*

Emergency breakdown services are provided by Automobile Association Rescue **t** 1800 667788 and the RAC **t** 1800 535005.

SPECIALIST TOUR OPERATORS
In the UK

Abercrombie & Kent: *Sloane Square House, Holbein Place, London SW1W 8NS,* **t** *0845 070 0610,* **f** *(020) 7730 9376, www.abercrombiekent.co.uk.* Quality city breaks.

Kirker Travel: *3 New Concordia Wharf, Mill Street, London SE1 2BB,* **t** *(020) 7231 3333,* **f** *7231 4771, www.kirkerholidays.com.* City breaks.

Martin Randall Travel: *10 Barley Mow Passage, Chiswick, London W4 4PH,* **t** *(020) 8742 3355,* **f** *8742 7766, www.martinrandall.com.* Cultural tours accompanied by a lecturer.

Prospect Music and Art Tours: *36 Manchester St, London W1U 7LH,* **t** *(020) 7486 5705,* **f** *7486 5868, www.prospecttours.com.* Tours of the big museums.

Saga Holidays: *Enbrook Park, Sandgate High St, Folkestone CT20 3SE,* **t** *0800 300 500,* **f** *(01303) 771 010, www.saga.co.uk.* Holidays for the over-50s.

In Ireland

Irish Cycling Safaris: *Belfield House, UCD, Dublin 4,* **t** *(01) 260 0749,* **f** *706 1168, www.cyclingsafaris.com.* Cycling tours around Ireland.

Golf and Leisure Ireland: *8 Portersgate Close, Clonsilla, Dublin 15,* **t** *(01) 822 0396,* **f** *820 3053.* Golfing holidays.

Moloney & Kelly Travel: *18 Fitzwilliam Place, Dublin 2,* **t** *(01) 676 5511, www.maloneykelly.com.* City breaks.

Paddywagon Tours Ltd: *17 Westmoreland Street, Dublin 2,* **t** *(01) 672 6007, UK freefone 0800 783 4191, www.paddywagontours.com.* 1-, 2-, and 6-day backpacking tours around Ireland.

In the USA

Abercrombie and Kent: *1520 Kensington Rd, Oak Brook, IL 60523,* **t** *800 323 7208, www.abercrombiekent.com.* Quality city breaks.

Abreu Tours: *350 Fifth Ave #2414, New York, NY 10118-2414,* **t** *800 223 1580, www.abreu-tours.com.* Independent and escorted tours including fly-drives.

Central Holidays: *120 Sylvan Ave, 2nd Floor, Englewood Cliffs, NJ 07632,* **t** *800 935 5000, www.centralholidays.com.* Offers fly-drives and cruise tours.

Quantum Tours: *4165 Silverton Rd NE, Salem, OR 97305,* **t** *800 995 2666.* Small, accompanied tours of Ireland, including garden tours.

ENTRY FORMALITIES

Passports and Visas

There are no formal entry requirements for EU passport holders travelling to Ireland, regardless of the purpose or duration of the visit. Holders of US, Canadian, Australian and New Zealand passports do not require visas for stays of up to three months. For the most up-to-date information, check with the Irish embassy or consulate in your home country, or visit the Irish government website *www.irlgov.ie/iveagh/services/visas*.

Customs

Since 1999, duty-free goods have been unavailable on journeys within the EU, but this does not necessarily mean that prices have gone up, as shops at ports and airports do not always choose to pass on the cost of the duty. It does mean that there is no limit on how much you can buy, as long as it is for your own use. Guidelines are issued (e.g. 10 litres of spirits, 800 cigarettes, 90 litres of wine, 110 litres of beer) and, if they are exceeded, you may be asked to prove that it is all for your own use.

Non-EU citizens flying from an EU country to a non-EU country (e.g. flying home from Dublin) can still buy duty-free. Americans can take home 1 litre of alcohol, 200 cigarettes and 100 cigars. Canadians can take home 200 cigarettes and 1.5 litres of wine or 1.14 litres of spirits or 8.5 litres of beer.

ARRIVAL
Dublin Airport

Dublin Airport is located 7 miles (12km) north of the city centre. There is currently just one terminal (which was massively expanded in 2001), and it has plenty of facilities including a tourist office in the arrivals hall, bureaux de change, a branch of the Bank of Ireland and currency exchange machines, a post office, left luggage facilities, shops, cafés and several car hire companies.

Dublin Airport: *t (01) 814 1111, www.dublin-airport.com*

Getting to and from Dublin Airport
By Bus

All bus services depart from outside the arrivals hall.

The Airlink Express is a fast coach service which operates two routes. Bus 747 runs between the airport and O'Connell St (every 30min, Mon–Sat 5.45am–11.30pm, Sun 7.15am–11.30pm). Bus 748 links the airport with the central bus station (Busáras) on Store St and the two main railway stations, Connolly and Heuston (every 25–30min, Mon–Sat 6.50am–9.30pm, Sun 7am–10.05pm). Journey time for both services is around 25 minutes to the city centre, depending on traffic, and cost €5 for adults, €2 for children.

The cheap but achingly slow option is to take the regular public bus. From the airport, buses 16, 16A/B, 41, 41a/b/c and 46A run to the city centre (O'Connell Street) every 10–20 minutes (8am–11.30pm), and take around 45 minutes – or longer if there is lots of traffic, which you can usually count on in Dublin. Tickets (€1.45) are available from the travel information desk near the arrivals exit, from machines by the bus stop, or on board if you have the exact change.

The other option is the privately run Aircoach (every 15min. daily 6.30am–11.30pm), which has stops in O'Connell St, near the main tourist information centre close to Grafton St, and outside several of the larger hotels throughout the city including those in Ballsbridge. It costs €6, and takes around 25 minutes.

Dublin Bus (for Airlink Express and the public buses): *t (01) 873 4222, www.dublinbus.ie*

Aircoach: *t (01) 844 7118, www.aircoach.ie*

By Train

There are no direct train services from Dublin Airport, but the Aerdart bus service from outside the arrivals hall (every 15min, Mon–Fri 5.45am–11.20pm, Sat–Sun 6.30am–8.10pm) runs from the airport to the DART station at Howth Junction in 20 minutes. This alone costs €4.30, or ask for the special €6 all-in DART/Aerdart ticket from the airport to any DART station.

Aerdart: *t (01) 814 1062, www.aerdart.ie*

By taxi

A taxi from the airport into Dublin costs around €18–23. Supplements apply for baggage, and for journeys between 8pm and 8am.

Dublin Port

Dublin Port is about 2 miles (3km) east of the city centre. Local buses, run by Dublin Bus (see above), serve the terminal – a ride into the city costs €2.50 (children €1.25). Taxis are also available outside the terminal building, charging around €8–12 to the city centre. Local transport websites (see above) have sections dedicated to ferry connections.

Dún Laoghaire

The ferry terminal at Dún Laoghaire, about 9 miles (15km) southeast of Dublin, is connected by escalator to the adjacent DART station, where DART trains run every 10–20 minutes into Dublin city centre, as do regular local buses on several route lines (including 7, 7A/B/D and the Express 46X service). Taxis from outside the terminal charge around €20–25 to Dublin city centre. Local transport websites (see above) have sections dedicated to ferry connections.

GETTING AROUND
By Bus

Dublin Bus run the local buses, which are still the most common way of getting around the city. Their crowded, chaotic information office is at 59 Upper O'Connell St. You can pick up timetables here, but there is currently no bus map on offer, although they will hand out a blurred, photocopied version which is better than nothing. Negotiating the city's bus services is tricky, although bus stops are plentiful, and are all marked with the bus route numbers and (usually) timetables. Having said that, don't rely on timetables: Dublin buses seem to operate according to the whim of the driver, and you should resign yourself to a wait of 10–20 minutes in the city centre and considerably longer in the suburbs.

Buses are usually double-deckers, and passengers board at the front and leave at the back. You must have the exact fare when you are boarding the bus, but as fares vary depending on the distance covered, it is often hard to work out in advance how much you will need to pay. If you don't have the correct fare, you will be given a refund ticket and will have to reclaim your change from the Dublin Bus offices on O'Connell Street.

To avoid clanking around the city with pockets full of small change, consider buying one of the **bus passes** on offer. There are several available, all of which must be validated in the machines at the front of the bus. **Rambler** passes offer unlimited travel on city buses (including the Airlink bus, so it is worth buying it at the CIE travel information desk at the airport when you arrive) and cost €5 for one day, €10 for three days, €15 for five days and €18 for seven days. A one-day **Family Rambler** pass for two adults and up to four children costs €7.50. You can also buy a special 'handy pack' of five adult one-day Rambler passes for €16. The **Travel 90 Handy Pack** contains 10 individual bus tickets, each valid for unlimited travel within 90 minutes.

Some tickets are valid for buses and trains, including the DART: the **3-Day Short Hop** costs €15 and offers unlimited travel on all Dublin Bus, DART and suburban rail services (excluding Airlink and Nitelink).

Dublin Bus: *59 Upper O'Connell St,* **t** *(01) 873 4222, www.dublinbus.ie*

By Train

Notoriously expensive, often grubby and not particularly reliable, Irish trains are still poor, despite investment in recent years. The big exception to this is the sleek Enterprise service to Belfast, which is fast and efficient. The DART rail service around Dublin is also good, and reasonably priced. Dublin has two main stations for national train services: Connolly, on Amiens Street **t** (01) 703 2358, and Heuston, by the Quays **t** (01) 703 2131. Both have bureaux de change, lockers, left luggage facilities and a few shops, bars and cafés. As a rough guide, Connolly station serves Belfast, Rosslare and Sligo, while Heuston station serves Galway, Tralee, Westport, Kildare, Cork, Kerry, Kilkenny, Waterford, Clonmel and Limerick.

There are a number of special **visitor passes** available, which cover national rail and/or bus travel – but these are only worth considering if you are going to be making several long journeys around the country.

By DART and Suburban Rail

The Dublin Area Rapid Transit system (or DART) hugs the coastline from Greystones in the south to Howth and Malahide in the north (the line divides at Howth Junction, so make sure you are getting on the right train for your destination). Of the two central Dublin stations with DART services, Connolly is more convenient if you are based north of the Liffey; Pearse Street is more convenient if you are south of the Liffey. Trains are reasonably clean and efficient and a number of special integrated passes are available for visitors (see above). DART services run roughly every 15–20 minutes Monday to Saturday, less frequently on Sundays and public holidays. Note that major improvements to DART stations and services are planned for 2005: this will mean some service disruption (particularly at weekends), so check your route in advance.

Ticket prices depend on how far you are travelling, but as a general guide, a single ticket from central Dublin to Greystones in the south (takes 50min) costs €3.35 for adults and €1.45 for children; central Dublin to Malahide (takes 15min) or Howth (takes 25min) costs €1.80 for adults, €0.90 for children.

Suburban Rail services link the city centre with nearby towns. They run less frequently than DART services, but cover a larger geographical area. Many visitor passes (see p.43) include Suburban Rail services.

DART: www.irishrail.ie/dart

By Tram (Luas)

A new tram network, called the Luas, is under construction as an attempt to solve Dublin's chronic traffic problems. It will eventually be integrated into a new metro system, but the whole project is not expected to be completed until 2016. The first sections of the tram lines opened in 2004 and, until the network is complete, it seems that half of the major streets in central Dublin are being dug up to lay the tram lines – making traffic jams, at least in the short term, even more of an issue than they were before.

There are currently two Luas lines: the Red Line, which links Tallaght to Connolly station (total journey time 43 minutes), and the Green Line, which links Sandyford with St Stephen's Green (total journey time 22 minutes). Fares vary depending on how many zones you travel through; a single ticket within the central zone (for example, from Connolly to Heuston stations) currently costs €1.30. There are several other tickets available, including a 7-day Luas-only pass for €10 (Zone 1 only) and a 7-day Combi-Pass which offers unlimited travel on buses and trams for €23. Check the website for details of other tickets, including 1-day, 7-day and 30-day passes. Tickets are available from machines at the tram stops and should be date-stamped when you enter the tram.

Luas: *t* 1800 300 604, www.luas.ie

By Taxi

Dublin taxis come in a variety of shapes and sizes. They can be hailed on the street, but it is usually easiest to pick one up at one of the central taxi ranks: on the northside at the corner of Abbey Street and North O'Connell Street, and on the southside at Aston Quay, College Green and St Stephen's Green (at the top of Grafton St). Although the taxi industry was deregulated some years ago and several hundred new permits were issued, it is still almost impossible to get a taxi after pubs and clubs close, particularly at weekends. At peak times, you could easily wait an hour or more at a taxi rank – although your driver is almost certain to give you a hard luck story about how tough it is to scrape a living now that there are so many taxis competing for business. Fares are high (roughly equivalent to London fares), and there are supplements for luggage, animals, extra passengers and night journeys between 8pm and 8am. Of the firms below, City Cabs also offers wheelchair accessible cabs, but call well in advance to book one.

Access Metro Cabs: *t* (01) 668 3333.
A to B Taxicabs: *t* (01) 677 2222.
City Cabs: *t* (01) 872 7272.
Pony Cabs: *t* (01) 661 2233.

By Bicycle

Cycling in central Dublin is only for the brave. The fleets of students casually negotiating the traffic jams on their boneshakers make it look easy, but in fact the lack of bike lanes, the potholes, the oblivious attitude of Dublin drivers and the sheer amount of road traffic make it a tough proposition for all but the most experienced cyclists. The big exception to this is the leafy expanse of Phoenix Park, which is perfect for exploring on two wheels. Bike theft is very common, which has resulted in massive hikes in the cost of insurance, which in turn has meant that very few places now rent out bikes. A refundable €100 deposit is usually required. If you bring your own bike to Ireland, make sure you find somewhere safe to store it (your hotel or hostel should be able to help, but enquire in advance). Bikes are usually accepted on DART trains for a small fee, although there are restrictions on rush hour services.

Belfield Bike Shop: *Belfield House, UCD, Dublin 4,* **t** *(01) 706 1697.* Bikes to rent from €18 per day.

Macdonalds: *38–39 Wexford St,* **t** *(01) 475 2586.* Bikes to rent from €25 per day.

Hiring a Car

Car rental is expensive in Dublin. The best deals are usually available online and you should check whether your airline offers any special deals or discounts. Book well in advance to get the best deals, and to ensure that there are cars available if you are travelling in summer or at other peak periods. Most car hire offices can be found at the airport, but several have branches in the city centre. To rent a car, you will need to be at least 23 (sometimes 21), and to have held a valid driving licence for at least 12 months. Find out if a supplement is payable if you intend to take the car across the border into Northern Ireland.

Access Car Rentals: *airport* **t** *(01) 844 4848.*
Avis: *airport* **t** *(01) 605 7500, www.avis.ie.*
Atlas Eurodrive: *airport* **t** *(01) 844 4859.*
Belgard: **t** *1800 451 452 or (01) 404 9999.*
Budget: *airport* **t** *(01) 844 5150, city centre (01) 837 9802, www.budgetcarrental.ie.*
Dan Dooley/Kenning: **t** *(01) 677 2723, www.dan-dooley.ie.*
Hertz: *airport* **t** *(01) 844 1200, city centre* **t** *(01) 660 2255, www.hertz.com.*
Murrays Europcar: *airport* **t** *(01) 812 0410, city centre* **t** *(01) 614 2800, www.europcar.ie.*
Thrifty: **t** *1800 515 800 or (01) 840 0800, www.thrifty.ie.*

Guided Tours

Bus and Coach Tours

Dublin Bus City Tours: *59 Upper O'Connell St, Dublin 1,* **t** *(01) 873 4222,* **f** *(01) 703 3031, www.dublinbus.ie.* The official 'hop-on hop-off' sightseeing tours on double-decker buses. There are 19 stops which take in Dublin's major attractions, and tickets are valid for 24 hours. Bus runs roughly every 10 minutes 9.20am–6.30pm (every 30min 5–6.30pm). Adults pay €12.50, children under 14 €6, students and seniors €11. The ticket includes discounts at some sights. Dublin Bus also run half-day and full-day tours outside the city, including the South Coast Tour, which takes in coastal towns from Dún Laoghaire to Greystones, and a city tour combined with a trip to the village which has become famous as the setting for the popular TV show *Ballykissangel*. Another coastal tour heads north of Dublin and includes a visit to Malahide Castle. Prices range from €20 to €35. All tours begin at Dublin Bus offices on O'Connell St.

Mary Gibbons Tours: **t** *(01) 283 9973.* Mary Gibbons is a very experienced tour guide with an incredible amount of fascinating historical and archaeological information at her fingertips. Her tours are easily the most informative and illuminating, but she wears her knowledge lightly, and her excellent in-depth commentary is peppered with gossipy asides on politicians and celebrities. She runs two tours: one to the Hill of Tara, Newgrange and the Boyne Valley, and another to Glendalough and Powerscourt. Prices are €28 for each tour. Highly recommended.

Over the Top Tours: **t** *(01) 838 6128 or 1800 424252 (for reservations only), www.overthetoptours.com.* A very friendly, accommodating and reliable company with enthusiastic driver-guides. The one-day tours include the Celtic Experience, which covers the Boyne Valley and Hill of Tara, Mellifont Abbey and the Hill of Slane, and costs €25 (students €23). The Wicklow-Glendalough tour crosses the Wicklow mountains to Glendalough, taking in some beautiful scenery along the way, and costs €24 (students €21). Highly recommended.

Wild Coach Tours: *t (01) 280 1899, www.wildcoachtours.com*. Minibus tours with irreverent and amusing driver-guides which promise to take you 'off the beaten track'. The Wild Wicklow tour takes a full day and includes a visit to Glendalough. It costs €28 (child/student €25). They also offer two half-day tours: Wild Powerscourt and the Wild Castle Tour (to Howth and Malahide) which cost €20.

Rail Tours

Railtours Ireland: *58 Lower Gardiner St, Dublin 1,* **t** *(01) 856 0045, www.railtoursireland.com*. One-day (or longer) rail tours to some of the best-known sights around Ireland, including Ballykissangel, Glendalough and the Wicklow Mountains, Waterford, Cork, Connemara and Galway Bay, Ring of Kerry, Cliffs of Moher, Giants Causeway and the Aran Islands. Prices vary according to the tour.

Walking Tours

The city tourist office has designed several self-guided walking trails around the main sights, with signposts to guide you: there's the Georgian Trail, the Cultural Trail, the Old City Trail and the Rock 'n' Stroll Trail. There are dozens of guided walking tours on offer, particularly in summer, which range from high-brow historical affairs to increasingly drunken pub crawls around the city's famous literary haunts. Most tours cost around €10 per person, with reductions for children and students. Advance booking is often required and always recommended.

1916 Rebellion Walking Tour: *t (01) 676 2493, www.1916rising.com*. A chilling and fascinating tour around the sites associated with the 1916 Rebellion. Departs from the International Bar, Mon–Sat 11.30am and 2.30pm, Sun 1pm. No 2.30pm tours during March and October.

Dublin Literary Pub Crawl: *37 Exchequer St,* **t** *(01) 670 5602,* **f** *670 5603/454 5680, www.dublinpubcrawl.com*. Meets at the Duke pub on Duke Street. Tickets are sold on a first-come-first-served basis. April–Nov nightly at 7.30pm; Dec–March Thurs–Sat 7.30pm; Sun all year at noon and 7.30pm.

Dublin Rock & Roll Tour: *t (01) 241 1500, tours@hotpress.ie*. Dublin's musical haunts, from the site of U2's first gig to the bar where Sinead O'Connor used to waitress.

Historical Walking Tours of Dublin: *t (01) 878 0227, www.historicalinsights.ie*. Assemble at the front gate of Trinity College. Besides the excellent historical tour, they also runs a series of themed tours in summer which focus on a particular aspect of Irish history, from sex to architecture. Tours run April–Sept daily 11am, noon and 3pm; Oct–March, Fri, Sat and Sun at noon.

Musical Pub Crawl: *t (01) 478 0193, www.musicalpubcrawl.com*. Two knowledgeable musicians lead you through several traditional music pubs. Tours leave from upstairs at the Oliver St John Goggarty Pub in Temple Bar. May–Oct nightly 7.30pm; Nov, Feb, March and April Thurs–Sat only 7.30pm. Private tours only in Dec and Jan.

Old Dublin: *t (01) 679 4291*. Assemble at Bewley's on Grafton Street, or Dublin Writer's Museum at 18 Parnell Square; call for times.

Revolutionary Dublin 1916–23: *t (01) 662 9976*. These tours are conducted by Trinity College graduate students. Daily tours, call for times.

Zozimus Experience: *t (01) 661 8646, www.zozimus.com*. A creepy but fun tour with a mysterious hooded guide, with ghost stories and a chilling surprise at the end. Departs from the gates of Dublin Castle. May–Oct 9pm, Nov–April 7pm.

Practical A–Z

Climate and When to Go 48
Crime and the Police 48
Disabled Travellers 49
Electricity, Weights and Measures 49
Embassies and Consulates 50
Etiquette 50
Genealogy 50
Health and Insurance 51
Internet 51
Lost Property 52
Media 52
Money, Banks and Taxes 52
Opening Hours and Public Holidays 53
Packing 53
Phones 53
Post 54
Religious Services 54
Smoking 54
Students 54
Time 55
Tipping 55
Toilets 55
Tourist Offices 55
Women Travellers 56
Working and Long Stays 56

Climate and When to Go

The last thing you might expect to see in Dublin is a palm tree, but the city is full of them: steady rainfall and year-round mild temperatures are perfect growing conditions. The vegetation may like the climate, but Dubliners don't: complaints about the weather are almost as common as complaints about the traffic. With an average of 200 days of **rain** a year, chances are you will get a soaking, so pack an umbrella and a waterproof coat whenever you visit.

The summer of 2003 was freakishly hot, with temperatures of 45°C recorded in some Dublin back gardens, but July and August usually peak at a mellow 18–20°C. Oddly, these are both the sunniest and wettest months: to get the sunshine without the rain, consider coming in June or September – which also have the advantage of being outside the tourist season. Winters are mild, with temperatures rarely dropping below freezing, although there are sharp winds.

Dublin is a popular year-round destination, but it gets particularly crowded in **July** and **August**. It also gets packed during the city's big festivals, especially around **St Patrick's Day** (17 March) and to a lesser extent on **Bloomsday** (16 June). Flight prices will be high and accommodation scarce during these times, so be sure to book well in advance. The city is regularly flooded at weekends all year round, often with rowdy stag and hen parties, which means that flights and accommodation are often more expensive from Thursday to Saturday.

When you decide to visit is largely dependent on what your interests are. If you want to join in with the party crowd, visit on a summer weekend. If you prefer to avoid the throngs, visit in spring or autumn and avoid Temple Bar at weekends. To see the formal gardens in full bloom, visit in May and June (and try to catch the **Wicklow Gardens festival**). In the dark winter months, the days are short, some tourist facilities may be closed and smaller museums may have restricted hours, but at least you can warm up around a roaring fire in a traditional pub and you won't have to fight the crowds.

Average daily minimum and maximum temperatures		
Jan	1–8°C	(34–47°F)
April	4–13°C	(40–56°F)
July	11–20°C	(52–68°F)
Oct	6–14°C	(43–58°F)

There are a number of festivals and events which take place all year round: see the chapter on Festivals (p.227), and check out the Dublin tourist office's excellent website, *www.visitdublin.com*.

Crime and the Police

Dublin's crime rate has risen dramatically over the last decade or so. Petty crime, particularly bag-snatching and pickpocketing, has long been a problem on the city streets, and fights between drunken youths are also pretty commonplace at weekends, but visitors are unlikely to get caught up in anything more serious. Simple precautions – the kind that anyone should take in any big city – should mean that you'll avoid trouble. Make a photocopy of your **passport** and other important documents and keep them separately. Make use of the **hotel safe** and don't carry large amounts of cash or valuables with you unless you have to: if you do, keep them in a **money belt** which goes under your clothing. Use **ATMs** (cash machines) inside bank premises wherever possible; if you use one on the street, make sure it hasn't been tampered with before you insert your card, hide your PIN while entering it, and don't stand around counting the money. **Backpacks** are easy to steal from: wear a bag that straps across you with the opening facing inwards. Be particularly careful on crowded buses and trains. Don't leave bags or jackets containing valuables on the back of your chair in pubs or restaurants, and don't leave wallets on the table. If you bring your **car**, don't leave any valuables inside and leave the glove compartment open so that thieves know there is nothing worth stealing. Most of Dublin's rougher areas are well off the tourist trail, but be careful late at night in some of the shabbier neighbourhoods north of the Liffey near the bus station and in parts of the Liberties area near Christchurch Cathedral.

If you are robbed or encounter any other problems, head for the nearest **police station**: the Irish police are called **Garda Siochana** (or Garda for short) and police stations have a blue lantern outside. There is a special **Tourist Victim Support Service** at Harcourt St, Harcourt Square, *t (01) 478 5295*, with a 24-hour freephone helpline, *t 1800 661 771*. To make an insurance claim, you will need to get a copy of the police report.

In emergencies, dial 999 or 112.

Disabled Travellers

Dublin is not well geared towards **travellers with disabilities**, but things are improving. Many of the major sights and museums offer at least partial wheelchair access. These include: Chester Beatty Library; Christchurch Cathedral; City Hall; Dublinia; Guinness Storehouse; National Gallery; National History Museum (ground floor only); National Museum (ground floor only); Royal Hospital Kilmainham; and St Patrick's Cathedral. Facilities vary widely and it is always advisable to call in advance to check out exactly what is on offer. Many **hotels** are now wheelchair accessible (these are listed in the Where to Stay section), particularly in the moderate to expensive price ranges. **Public transport** is much better than it used to be: about 40 per cent of city buses are now fully wheelchair accessible. The Dublin Bus information office has a list of bus routes featuring accessible buses; these include the 747 and 748 airport bus link and several of their bus tours. Work is underway to make DART trains and stations wheelchair accessible, and to introduce hearing loops and Braille tiles. The mainline and suburban trains run by Iarnród Éireann are less well equipped, but they do offer certain services for travellers with disabilities (a traveller's meeting service, special ramps, etc) with at least 24 hours notice. The Luas tram system is fully wheelchair accessible. The airport is also now fully accessible.

Organizations and Helplines

In Dublin

National Disability Resource Centre: *44 North Great George's St, t (01) 874 7503.*

Irish Wheelchair Association: *Blackheath Drive, Clontarf, Dublin 3, t (01) 833 8241, www.iwa.ie.* Publishes guides with advice for holidaymakers with disabilities.

Catholic Institute for the Deaf: *Lower Drumcondra Rd, Dublin 9, t (01) 830 0522.*

Cerebral Palsy Ireland: *Sandmount Ave, Dublin 4, t (01) 269 5355.*

Cystic Fibrosis Association of Ireland: *24 Lower Rathmines Rd, Dublin 6, t (01) 496 2433.*

In the UK

Holiday Care Information Unit: *2nd floor, Imperial Building, Victoria Rd, Horley RH6 7PZ, t (01293) 774 535, www.holidaycare.org.uk.* Information on accommodation, transportation, services, tour operators and contacts.

RADAR (Royal Association for Disability and Rehabilitation): *12 City Forum, 250 City Rd, London EC1V 8AF, t (020) 7259 3222, www.radar.org.uk.*

In the USA

SATH (Society for Accessible Travel and Hospitality): *347 Fifth Ave #610, New York, NY 10016, t (212) 447 7284, www.sath.org.* Advice on all aspects of travel for the disabled.

Electricity, Weights and Measures

The electric current is 225AC or 220V, the same as in most of Europe. North American appliances will need transformers. Wall sockets take the standard British-style three-pin (flat) fused plugs.

Ireland, like the UK, is officially metric, but occasionally reverts to the imperial system, most importantly in the pubs (where a pint is still a pint). Road distances are usually marked in kilometres, but speed limits are still displayed in miles per hour.

Embassies and Consulates

In Dublin

Most of these are open Monday to Friday (closed at lunchtimes). It is best to ring first.

Australia: *2nd Floor, Fitzwilton House, Wilton Terrace, Dublin 2,* **t** *(01) 664 5300*.

Canada: *4th Floor, 65–68 St Stephen's Green, Dublin 2,* **t** *(01) 417 4100*.

UK: *31 Merrion Rd, Dublin 4,* **t** *(01) 205 3700*.

USA: *43 Elgin Rd, Dublin 5,* **t** *(01) 668 8777*.

Irish Embassies Abroad

Details are at **www.foreignaffairs.gov.ie**.

Australia: *20 Arkana St, Yarralumla, Canberra ACT 2600,* **t** *(02) 6273 3022, irishemb@cyberone.com.au*. Also consulate in Sydney.

Canada: *130 Albert St, Ottawa, ON, K1P 5G4,* **t** *(613) 233 6281, embassyofireland@ rogers.com*. Also consulate in Vancouver.

UK: *17 Grosvenor Place, London SW1X 7HR,* **t** *(020) 7235 2171*. Also consulates in Edinburgh and Cardiff.

USA: *2234 Massachusetts Ave NW, Washington DC 20008,* **t** *(202) 462 3939, www.irelandemb.org*. Also consulates in Boston, Chicago, Houston, New York, Reno, St Louis and San Francisco.

Etiquette

Dubliners are generally easygoing, and most enjoy nothing more than a good debate, preferably over a drop of the black stuff (that is, Guinness). Religion, sex and related issues like contraception used to be conversational taboos, but this has changed nowadays, particularly among young Dubliners. Abortion remains a hot potato, however. Dubliners tend to dress casually most of the time, although many people make an effort to get dressed up when going out at the weekend. Some churches request modest dress (no shorts or strappy tops). Dining times are similar to those in the UK and the US, with lunch usually around 1pm and dinner around 7pm.

Genealogy

Anyone with any Irish blood seems to be drawn to genealogy. Tracing your ancestors is a tricky and time-consuming business, but can be incredibly rewarding. A good first port of call is the Genealogy Advisory Service at the National Library.

Genealogy Advisory Service: *At the National Library, Kildare Street, Dublin 2,* **t** *(01) 603 0200, www.nli.ie*. Contact them in advance to arrange an appointment, and give them details of any information and papers which you might already have. Their hours are Mon–Fri 10–4.45, Sat 10–12.30. Friendly staff will help you begin your search, and they also have lists of genealogists who provide tracing services for a fee. Get hold of their leaflet *Getting Started* which contains a list of useful organizations. The National Library has microfilm copies of the registers of most Catholic parishes, including those in Northern Ireland, up to 1880.

General Register Office (Births, Marriages and Deaths): *Joyce House, 8–11 Lombard St East, Dublin 2,* **t** *(01) 671 1000*. Marriages of non-Catholics were recorded from 1845, and those of Catholics from 1864. You can obtain birth, marriage and death certificates for a small fee.

Metric conversions

All figures are approximate.

1 centimetre = 0.4 inches; 1 inch = 2.5cm; 1 foot = 30cm.
1 metre (100cm) = 1.1 yards or 39 inches; 1 yard = 0.9m.
1 kilometre (1000m) = 0.6 miles; 1 mile = 1.6km; 8km = 5 miles.
1 kilogram or kilo (1000g) = 2.2lb; 1lb = 45g/0.45kg; 1oz = 28g.
1 litre = 1.8 UK pints or 0.25 UK gallons; 1 UK pint = 0.6 litres.
1 litre = 2.1 US pints or 0.3 US gallons; 1 US pint = 0.5 litres.

Registry of Deeds: *Henrietta St, Dublin 2,* **t** *(01) 670 7500, www.irlgov.ie/landreg*. This houses records of land purchases and other related matters from 1708 onwards. They also charge a small fee to researchers.

National Archives: *Bishop St, Dublin 8,* **t** *(01) 407 2300, www.nationalarchives.ie*. Dublin's Public Record Office was burnt in 1922, but the National Archives house a copy of Griffith's *Primary Valuation of Ireland 1848–63*. This records the names of those owning or occupying land and property, rebellion reports and records relating to 1798, and other records pertaining to transportees to Australia. You will need to bring ID to obtain a Reader's Ticket.

Irish Genealogical Research Society: *c/o The Irish Club, 82 Eaton Sq, London SW1W 9AJ, www.igrsoc.org*. A charity which promotes research and has a valuable library containing manuscripts of family histories, memoirs and pedigrees, useful for those whose research is pre-1864. There is a fee for admission to the library (open at the above address on Saturdays only).

Health and Insurance

In a medical emergency, call an ambulance on 999 or 112, or go to the Accident and Emergency (A&E) department of the nearest **hospital**. The most central are St James' Hospital, James St, Kilmainham, **t** *(01) 410 3000, www.stjames.ie*, and Beaumont Hospital, Beaumont Road, **t** *(01) 809 2714*. Note that all A&E patients must pay a fee of around €35 to be treated.

For non-emergency medical care, there is a standard agreement for EU citizens which will entitle you to a certain amount of free treatment. You must obtain a **form E111** before you leave (available from post offices in the UK), but if you need treatment you will have to pay costs upfront and then reclaim them on your return. You should always also take out travel insurance: take it from your travel agent or airline at the time of booking, or shop around for a better deal. Non-EU travellers should check with their policies at home to see if they're covered in Ireland; travel insurance is always advisable. If treated, be sure to save all doctors' receipts, pharmacy receipts and police documents.

Chemists (pharmacies) have remedies for minor ailments like colds and flu, but prescription medicines are expensive. O'Connells Late Night Pharmacy, 55 O'Connell St, **t** *(01) 873 0427*, and Dame Street Pharmacy, 16 Dame St, **t** *(01) 670 4523*, are open daily until 10pm.

Internet

There are dozens of Internet cafés in Dublin and finding one is never difficult. Count on paying around €2–3 per hour. Most of the more expensive hotels have Internet access in rooms. You can find a list of Wi-Fi service providers in Dublin at *www.intel.jiwire.com*.

Internet cafés

Central Café: *6 Grafton St, Dublin 2,* **t** *(01) 677 8298, info@centralcafe.ie*.

Global Café: *8 Lower O'Connell St, Dublin 1,* **t** *(01) 878 0295, info@globalcafe.ie*.

Cyberia: *Temple Lane South, Temple Bar, Dublin 2,* **t** *(01) 679 7607*.

Does Not Compute: *Unit 2, Pudding Row, Essex St West, Temple Bar,* **t** *(01) 670 4464*.

Internet Exchange: *3 Cecilia St, Dublin 2,* **t** *(01) 670 3000, www.internet-exchange.co.uk*.

Useful websites

www.visitdublin.com. Official tourist website. Accommodation and car rental services and online shop.

www.softguides.com/dublin. Information on hotels, pubs and sightseeing and a hotel-booking service.

www.dublinpubscene.com. Lots of information on Dublin's pubs.

www.ireland.com. Online version of the Irish Times newspaper, with a special section dedicated to Dublin.

www.temple-bar.ie. A good source of information on what's happening in Temple Bar.

www.dublinbus.ie. Local bus information.

www.eventguide.ie. Online version of the free listings guide.

Lost Property

Make sure you report lost property to the police if you want to make a claim on your insurance: the insurance company will require a copy of the police report. Visit the helpful **Tourist Victim Support Service** at Harcourt St, Harcourt Square, **t** *(01) 478 5295*; it has a 24-hour freephone helpline **t** *1800 661 771*. To track down items lost on public transport, call the following numbers:

Dublin Bus: t *(01) 703 2489*.
Connolly station: t *(01) 703 2363*.
Dublin Airport: t *(01) 814 4480*.
Heuston station: t *(01) 703 2102*.
Taxis: t *(01) 666 9854*.

Media

Newspapers and magazines

There are three main broadsheet **newspapers** in Ireland, of which two are based in Dublin. *The Irish Times*, at www.ireland.com, is the longest-established and enjoys an excellent reputation, with a good mix of objective reporting, scholarly meanderings and thoughtful comment. *The Irish Independent*, at www.independent.ie, is a little less highbrow but still a good read. The third national broadsheet is the *Irish Examiner*, www.examiner.ie, based in Cork. Of the tabloids, the *Evening Herald* has the best small ads and *The Star* emulates the UK's 'red-tops'.

The most useful **listings guide** is *InDublin* (€2.50), a glossy magazine which appears fortnightly and is available from newsagents. There are a couple of good freebies, including the excellent *Event Guide*, at www.eventguide.ie, and the sketchier *t.t. (What to Do in Dublin)*, both available from most bars and cafés in the city centre.

Magazines include the upmarket women's glossy *Image* and the *Dubliner*, which has good restaurant reviews and plenty of spicy gossip. The *Phoenix* offers a satirical spin on Irish politics, and *Magill* is a fine monthly news magazine. The best new writing and criticism is in the quarterly *Dublin Review*.

TV and Radio

The government-sponsored national **TV** station Radio Telefís Éireann (RTÉ) has three channels: RTÉ 1, with a staid schedule of chat shows and soap operas; Network 2, which is more youthful and inventive; and the Gaelic-language Telefís na Gaelige (TG4). The independent station TV3 imports American and British soaps and sitcoms. The five British terrestrial channels – BBC1, BBC2, ITV1, Channel 4 and Five – can be picked up in most places. Cable or satellite TV is common, and can be found in most hotels and B&Bs.

RTÉ runs four national **radio** stations: RTÉ Radio 1, with a general mixture of music, sports and talk shows; the more upbeat RTÉ 2FM; the Irish-language Raidio Na Gaeltachta; and RTÉ Radio Lyric FM, for classical music and arts. Other Dublin-based stations include Today FM (100–102 FM) and chart-based stations at 98 and 104 FM.

Money, Banks and Taxes

The euro (€) – made up of 100 cents – is the currency of Ireland, along with most other EU countries. The bills come in denominations of €5, €10, €20, €50, €100, €200 and €500. Coins come as 1, 2, 5, 10 and 50 cents, €1 and €2. All euro coins and notes are legal tender in all eurozone countries. At the time of writing, €1 is worth about UK£0.69, US$1.28 and C$1.53.

For shop purchases over €90, it is possible to get the tax refunded. Ask for a Global Refund Form in the shop where you made your purchase. You must have your passport with you to prove your citizenship. At the airport when you leave, bring the receipt to the VAT office (near the duty-free shops), where a refund will be made. You can get more information at www.globalrefund.com.

Banks and changing money

Banks are open Mon–Fri 10–5, and most offer money exhange services. The main post offices also have exchange offices, which, along with the banks, usually offer better rates than the various bureaux de change scattered around the city centre (particularly around Grafton Street). Many hotels will change money and traveller's cheques, but the rates are always worse than those of the banks. ATMs are widely available: all major credit and debit cards with the Cirrus or Plus symbol are usually accepted (but note that the British 'Switch' system is not used in Ireland). Traveller's cheques are widely accepted, but are usually exchanged at a poor rate, so bring them in euros if possible. The two best-known issuers of traveller's cheques have adjacent offices: Thomas Cook, *118 Grafton St*, **t** *01 677 1307*, and American Express, *116 Grafton St*, **t** *01 677 2874*.

Lost or stolen cards

Report lost or stolen credit cards immediately, either at any bank or by calling the following freephone numbers:
American Express: t *1800 626 000*
Diners Club: t *1800 409 204*
Visa: t *1800 558 002*
Mastercard: t *1800 557 378*

Opening Hours and Public Holidays

For bank and post office opening hours, see Money, Banks and Taxes' and 'Post'.

Shops are usually open Mon–Sat from 9 or 9.30am to 5.30 or 6pm, with slightly shorter hours outside the city centre. Craft and gift shops will usually open on Sundays, especially during the summer.

Most **museums** are open 10–5, closing early or perhaps altogether on Sundays. Most close or run to Sunday schedules on bank holidays. A few are closed on Mondays.

Tourist information offices, except the main office on Suffolk St, are usually closed on Sundays, and most operate reduced hours during the winter months.

Pubs are usually open from 11.30am Monday to Saturday, and from 4pm on Sundays.

On **public holidays**, banks, offices, shops and many restaurants close, while most museums and public transport run to Sunday schedules.

Public Holidays (Bank Holidays)

1 January: *New Year's Day*
17 March: *St Patrick's Day*
Easter: *Good Friday* (this is not an official public holiday, but is widely treated as one) and *Easter Monday*
First Monday in May: *May Day*
First Monday in June: *June Holiday*
First Monday in August: *August Holiday*
Last Monday in October: *October Holiday*
25 December: *Christmas Day*
26 December: *Boxing Day*

Packing

An umbrella, comfortable shoes and a waterproof jacket are essential whatever time of year you are visiting. Most things are more expensive in Dublin than at home, including toiletries, clothes and prescription medicines, so be sure to stock up before you arrive. Travellers from the US or continental Europe will need adaptors and/or transformers for electrical goods, but these are readily available in Dublin. You will need your own sleeping bag at the official youth hostel, but requirements vary in the many independently owned hostels.

Phones

Most of the phone boxes are run by Eircom. Most will only accept **phonecards**, available from newsagents, post offices and supermarkets, although some still accept coins and a few take credit cards. Calls within Ireland and to the UK are cheaper between 6pm and 8am and all day on Saturday and Sunday, but off-peak calling times vary for other countries. Calls from hotel rooms are very expensive. Most UK and European **mobile phones** will work in Ireland, although you should check before you leave home that you have a roaming agreement with your service provider. US mobiles are usually incompatible: again, check in advance.

If you're calling within Dublin, you don't need the 01 code: just dial the 7-digit number. From outside, use the 01 prefix.

To call Dublin from abroad, dial your country's international access number (00 in the UK, 011 in the US), then 353 (the country code for Ireland), then 1 for Dublin (the zero is dropped), then the 7-digit number.

To call abroad from Dublin, dial 00 plus the country code (44 for the UK, 1 for the US or Canada), then the area code (omitting the zero if there is one), then the number.

Post

The Irish **postal system** is efficient and reliable. Letterboxes are green and usually have two slots: one for delivery within Dublin and one for everywhere else. The main post office is the GPO on O'Connell St, which is open Mon–Fri 8am–8pm, Sat 8am–1pm. Most post offices are open shorter hours (Mon–Fri 9–5.30, Sat 8–1), and many smaller branches close for lunch and often on one afternoon each week (usually Wednesday or Thursday). Standard-value stamps are available from newsagents around the city. Letters or postcards to the UK cost the same as those sent within Ireland. Airmail letters (including those to the UK) should carry a blue Priority 'Aerphost' sticker.

Religious Services

An overwhelming majority of Irish citizens are Roman Catholic, although the Catholic Church's influence has waned over the last decades. Dublin also has a sizeable minority of Protestants and small communities of other religions.

Catholic: *St Teresa's, Clarendon Street, t (01) 671 8466. St Mary's Pro-Cathedral, Marlborough Street, t (01) 874 5441.*

Church of Ireland: *Christchurch Cathedral, Christchurch Place, t (01) 677 8099. St Patrick's Cathedral, St Patrick's Close, t (01) 475 4817.*

Jewish: *Terenure Synagogue, Rathfarnham Road, Terenure, t (01) 492 3751.*

Muslim: *Islamic Cultural Centre, Roebuck Road, Clonskeagh, t (01) 260 3740.*

Sikh: *Gurdwarea Guru Nanak Durbar, 78 Serpentine Avenue, Ballsbridge, t (01) 667 1558.*

Smoking

Historically, Dubliners have had a relaxed attitude to smoking. But a recent EU directive making it illegal to smoke in the workplace got the entire capital in a frenzy. In a much-publicized move, from early 2004 all of Dublin's pubs were declared no-smoking zones. Despite the torrent of objections from irate pub landlords, who imagined their profits going up in smoke (or the absence of it), the ban has been widely enforced. Pubs aside, efforts are also being made to accommodate non-smokers elsewhere: many hotels offer no-smoking rooms (some establishments are even completely smoke-free) and restaurants will usually have a separate no-smoking section.

Students

Dublin has a huge student population, with several big universities and colleges, a vast number of language schools (in summer it sometimes seems that Spanish is the lingua franca of Grafton Street) and a wealth of summer courses. The tourist office leaflet *Live and Learn* lists summer schools throughout Ireland. Citizens of EU member states do not require visas to study in Ireland but all long-term visitors must register with the Immigration Department at the Garda National Immigration Bureau, Harcourt Square, *t (01) 475 5555*.

Universities and Colleges

Trinity College: *College Green, t (01) 677 6545.*
City University: *Glasnevin, t (01) 700 5165.*
University College: *Belfield, t (01) 269 3244.*

Summer Schools

James Joyce Summer School: *UCD International Summer School Office, Newman House, 86 St Stephen's Green, t (01) 706 8480.*

Irish Georgian Society: *74 Merrion Sq, t (01) 676 7053.*

Language Schools

Alliance Francaise: *1 Kildare St, t (01) 679 1732, www.alliance-francaise.ie.*

Istituto Cervantes: *58 Northumberland Rd, t (01) 668 2024*.
Casa Italia: *45 Kildare St, t (01) 494 1389*.
Goethe-Institut: *62 Fitzwilliam Sq, t (01) 661 8508*.
Language Centre of Ireland: *45 Kildare St, t (01) 671 6266, www.lci.ie*. Long-established school offering English as a foreign language.
Dublin School of English: *11 Westmoreland St, Temple Bar, t (01) 677 3322, www.dse.ie*. English as a foreign language (TEFL) courses.

Student Travel

For details of student travel organisations in the UK and North America, *see* p.39. USIT Now, *19–21 Aston Quay, t (01) 602 1600, www.usitnow.ie*, is the biggest Irish student and youth travel organization, with branches across the country. It also has noticeboards for information on accommodation, courses, jobs etc. Note that you will need an internationally recognized student card like the ISIC to qualify for student reductions.

Time

Ireland is in the same **time zone** as the UK, following GMT in winter and GMT+1 in summer. Clocks go forward one hour for Summer Time on the last Sunday in March, and back one hour on the last Sunday in October. If you're travelling around these times, it's worth checking the exact date of the changeover, and confirming precise travelling times. For all but a week or two around the changeovers, Dublin remains five hours ahead of US Eastern Time.

Tipping

It is usual to tip 10–15% in restaurants, and many eating places now include an optional service charge on the bill. Ask if the staff get the tip before you sign for it on your credit card – if not, you might prefer to leave the tip in cash.

Tip taxi drivers 5–10% if they have been helpful. It is not customary to tip staff in pubs, but it is fairly common to buy them a drink if they have been particularly genial.

In hotels, €1 or €2 per bag is acceptable for porters. Some people choose to leave a few euros (€1 or €2 per day) for the chambermaids at the smartest hotels, but this is not common or expected.

Toilets

Public loos (*leithreas*) are few and far between in Dublin and they are usually shockingly grim. If you get caught short, duck into a department store, one of the big museums (the National Gallery is always handy) or find a bar.

It's polite to ask in pubs if you can use the loos, but usually, nobody minds. They are often labelled in Irish: Fir (men) and Mná (women).

Tourist Offices

Abroad

UK: *All Ireland Desk, British Visitors Centre, Regent St, London SW1Y 4 XT, t 0800 039 7000 or (020) 7519 0800, www.tourismireland.com*.
USA: *345 Park Ave, New York, NY 10017, t (212) 418 0800, www.shamrock.org*.
Canada: (no personal callers) *160 Bloor St E, Suite 1150, Toronto, ON, M4W 1B9, t (416) 929 2777*.

In Dublin

The excellent **Dublin Tourism Centre** is set in the former church of St Andrew on Suffolk St. It's a very slick affair, with every service imaginable on offer, from accommodation booking (with a special counter for backpackers) to transport details and information and booking services for dozens of trips and tours. There is a wealth of leaflets, a TicketMaster counter for tickets to all Dublin's major venues, a bureau de change, and even a book and gift shop. You have to take a ticket and wait for your number to flash up on the screen, which means you'll have a chance to try out the **café**, too. There are several branches around the city, but none is contactable directly by phone. Call the following numbers to access tourist information and various booking services (for accommodation, transport, theatres etc): from within Ireland **t** 1850 230 330; from the UK **t** 0800 039 7000; from elsewhere worldwide **t** +353 66 979 2083.

There's also a vast amount of information online at *www.visitdublin.com*.

Dublin Tourism Centre: *St Andrew's Church, Suffolk St. Open July–Aug Mon–Sat 9–7, Sun 10.30–3; Sept–June Mon–Sat 9–5.30, Sun (Sept only) 10.30–3, bank holidays 10.30–3.*

O'Connell Street Tourism Centre: *14 Upper O'Connell St. Open Mon–Sat 9–5, closed bank holidays.*

Baggot Street Bridge: *Baggot St. Open Mon–Fri 9.30–noon and 12.30–5, closed bank holidays.*

Dublin Airport: *Arrivals Hall. Open daily 8am–10pm, including bank holidays.*

Dún Laoghaire Harbour: *Ferry Terminal. Open Mon–Sat 10–1 and 2–6, including bank holidays.*

The Square Towncentre: *Tallaght, Dublin 24. Open Mon–Sat 9.30–noon and 12.30–5, closed bank holidays.*

Women Travellers

Women are treated much the same in Dublin as in most European cities, and, although women may get some unwanted attention in the pubs, a polite but firm refusal is usually all that's needed. In rural areas outside Dublin, some astonishingly old-fashioned ideas linger on, but the formerly patriarchal Irish society has had a few sharp shocks recently, notably with the presidency of Mary Robinson and the legalization of divorce (finally) in 1995. As a result, women's issues now enjoy a much higher profile, but change is slow.

Working and Long Stays

Most international visitors can stay in Ireland up to three months without any special visa. For longer stays, it is necessary to obtain a **resident card**, available from the Immigration Department at the Garda National Immigration Bureau, Harcourt Square, **t** (01) 475 5555. You will not need a **work permit** if you, your spouse or child are an Irish or other EEA national (the EEA comprises EU member states plus Norway, Iceland and Liechtenstein). Postgraduate students who need to do research in Dublin, and postgraduate doctors and dentists with temporary registration, are also exempt from the requirement for work permits. If your company transfers you to Dublin (for a maximum of four years), you will not need a work permit so long as the company has operations in more than one country. Contact the Irish government's Foreign Affairs department for up-to-date information, *www.foreignaffairs.gov.ie*.

For those trying to find short-term and freelance work, **teaching English** is a popular choice, particularly during the summer. Be warned that it is not highly paid, there is stiff competition for positions and many institutions require either an ESL or a TEFL certificate. Some people find it simpler to look for private students.

There is lots of **casual work** to be had in bars and restaurants, particularly in the summer.

Southeast Dublin: The Georgian Heart

TRINITY COLLEGE & THE BOOK OF KELLS 60

AROUND COLLEGE GREEN 64
Bank of Ireland (House of Lords) 64

GRAFTON STREET AND AROUND 65
South William Street and around 67
Dublin Civic Museum 67
St Teresa's Carmelite Church and Friary 67

KILDARE STREET AND AROUND 68
National Museum of Ireland 68
National Library of Ireland 70
Leinster House 71

ST STEPHEN'S GREEN AND AROUND 72
Newman House 73

OUT TO PORTOBELLO 74
Irish Jewish Museum 74
Shaw's Birthplace 75

MERRION SQUARE AND AROUND 76
National Gallery of Ireland 76
Number Twenty-Nine 79
Oscar Wilde House 79

FURTHER SOUTHEAST 80
National Print Museum 80

1 Lunch

Bleu Bistro Moderne, *Joshua House, Dawson St*, **t** *(01) 676 7015*. **Open** daily noon–11. Stylish, reasonably priced brasserie.

2 Tea and cakes

Brown's Bar, *88–95 Grafton St*, **t** *(01) 679 5666*. **Open** Mon–Sat 9am–6pm (Thurs until 8pm), Sun noon–6pm. Smart café.

3 Drinks

James Toner's, *139 Lower Baggot St*. Linger over your pint at this old-fashioned pub.

Highlights

Georgian Dublin: Visit the fabulous Newman House, p.73

Indoor Dublin: Admire the exquisite Book of Kells, p.62

Dubliner's Dublin: Shopping at the Powerscourt Townhouse Shopping Centre, p.67

Green Dublin: Stroll through the magical Iveagh gardens, p.74

21st-century Dublin: A cocktail on the terrace at Bailey's, p.203

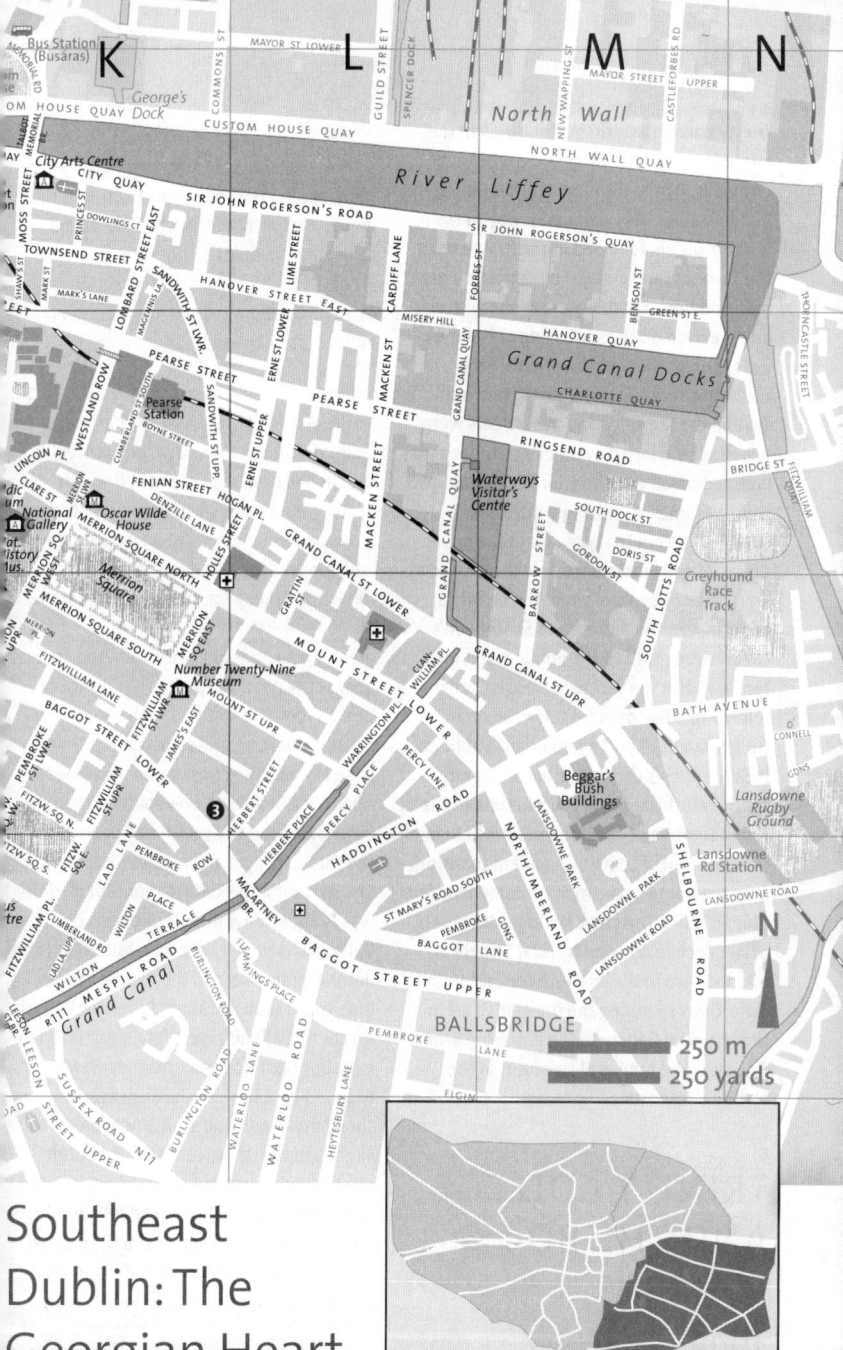

Southeast Dublin: The Georgian Heart

The heart of Georgian Dublin, this is still the city's most elegant and affluent neighbourhood. It contains the finest of its Georgian squares, the prettiest of its public parks, the cream of the national museums and Ireland's most prestigious university – which happens to house one of the most celebrated illuminated manuscripts in the world, the legendary Book of Kells. When

Trinity College was first established in the late 16th century, it stood well outside the city walls. By the 18th century, the Georgian building spree was well under way as fashionable Dublin followed in the footsteps of the Duke of Leinster who built the first great mansion here. Suddenly, everyone who was anyone lived on the south side of the river – a state of affairs that lasted until very recently. Graceful townhouses were built around garden-filled squares, streets were widened into broad avenues and money was lavished on opulent interior decoration. Two centuries later, surprisingly little has changed, except that nowadays the public are admitted where once only the aristocrats would have been welcome. The beautiful parks in Merrion Square and St Stephen's Green were given to the public in the 19th century, with the secluded Iveagh Gardens following a few decades later. Newman House, overlooking the luxuriant public park in St Stephen's Green, has been magnificently refurbished and contains one of the finest surviving Georgian interiors in Ireland. Even the Earl of Leinster's opulent mansion, now the home of the Irish Parliament, offers guided tours. The great National Museums of Art, Archeology and Natural Science opened here in the late 19th century, with collections spanning the finest Irish art in the National Gallery to the glittering Bronze Age gold and medieval treasures in the National Museum.

TRINITY COLLEGE AND THE BOOK OF KELLS
Trinity College J7

*College Street, Dublin 2, **t** (01) 608 2320, **f** (01) 608 2690, www.tcd.ie/library; all cross-city buses. Grounds **open** daily 8am–10pm, **adm** free. No public admission to Chapel, Dining Hall or Examination Hall, although visits of the Chapel can be arranged with prior notice.*

> ### Trinity College walking tours
> Trinity students lead interesting walking tours around the college during the summer, which start at a booth just inside the gates at the main entrance. There are usually around nine tours a day. The ticket price of €10 includes admission to the Old Library and the Book of Kells.

In 1592, the 'College of the Most Holy and Undivided Trinity' received its charter from Queen Elizabeth I. The idea for a university in Dublin had first been raised in the 14th century, but it took the Reformation to make it happen: Ireland needed an institution which would provide it with Protestant ministers to keep Catholicism firmly at bay. Students who travelled to be educated at the great universities of France, Italy and Spain had, as the queen wrote to the Council of Ireland, 'become infected with popery and other ill qualities, and so become evil subjects'. The site chosen was the ruined Abbey of All Hallows, on what was then the outskirts of the city, which had been given to the Dublin people as a reward for their loyalty during the Reformation. But if Trinity was founded on anti-Catholic principles, the Catholics viewed it with equal suspicion and antipathy and warned the Pope that 'the Irish youth shall be taught heresy by English teachers'. Catholics were finally admitted in 1793, but right up until 1970 they were required to obtain special dispensation from the Archbishop to do so. Women fared slightly better: they were admitted from 1904, some years before Oxford and Cambridge universities would follow suit. As late as 1927, a synod declared that there were three other colleges in Ireland, including the University College of Dublin, which were 'sufficiently safe as regards faith and morals' and that there was therefore no reason for Catholics to attend Trinity.

The West Front

Today, nothing remains of the original Elizabethan construction. Trinity was swept up in the grandiose Georgian architectural

Trinity College and the Book of Kells

schemes of the 18th century, which transformed the face of Dublin almost beyond recognition, and the earliest surviving building is the Rubics, dating from 1700 (see below). The university complex currently covers around 40 acres of what has become prime real estate right at the very heart of the city. The main entrance faces College Green, no longer a green at all, but a noisy, chaotic intersection of major roads which is always crammed with buses, bicycles and crowds (Trinity Gates remains one of the main meeting points in central Dublin).

The graceful **West Front** which overlooks this bedlam is one of the finest Georgian façades in the city, but it's almost impossible to appreciate it in all the chaos. Attributed to Theodore Jackson, it was built in 1752, a harmonious ensemble of sober granite and Portland stone with a generous portico flanked with columns. Statues of two of the College's most famous alumni stand at the entrance gate: the political philosopher Edmund Burke (1729–97) and the playwright Oliver Goldsmith (1728–74). These are just two on the heady list of writers, politicians, philosophers and scientists that the College has produced; it also includes Oscar Wilde, Samuel Beckett and, most recently, Irish presidents Mary Robinson and Mary McAleese.

Parliament Square

Once through the main gate, the hubbub of the street quickly fades as you enter **Parliament Square**, the first of the elegant squares around which the university buildings are arranged. The pretty mid-19th century **Campanile** in the centre is often used as a symbol of the university, and is said to mark the location of the former abbey on which the college was built. Behind it is a voluptuous sculpture by Henry Moore, *Reclining Connected Forms* (1969), and to the left is its antithesis: a statue of the dour Provost Salmon. Salmon's oath that women would attend the university 'over my dead body' was fulfilled when he died in 1903 (women were admitted the following year).

On the left of the square is the **Chapel**, built in 1798 and boasting an impressive columned portico elegantly echoed by that of the **Examination Hall** (1791) opposite. Both were designed by Sir William Chambers (who never actually set foot in Ireland) and both feature superb plasterwork by the foremost Irish stucco artist of the era, Michael Stapleton. The windows in the Chapel would originally have been clear, making it lighter than it has been, since painted, rather than stained, glass windows were added in the 19th century. Since 1970, it has become the only chapel in Ireland to be shared by all denominations.

Next to the Chapel is the university **Dining Hall**, rebuilt in 1761 after the previous version collapsed – twice. Its run of bad luck continued until 1984 when it was gutted by fire (a student with a grudge was suspected of an arson attack), but the award-winning restoration has returned it to its former glory.

Library Square

Behind the Campanile spreads the grassy expanse of **Library Square**, overlooked by the mellow red-brick **Rubrics** (1700), used for accommodating students and faculty. This is the College's oldest surviving building, although it was meddled with in the 1890s and again in the 1970s. Next to it, along the southern end of the square, is the famous Old Library (see below). The northern side is enclosed by the **Graduates' Memorial Building** (1892), and behind it are the tennis courts and accommodation area known as **Botany Bay**, which supposedly got its name because the students who lived here were wicked enough to deserve transportation; Oscar Wilde was one of those with rooms here while a student.

The Book of Kells and the Old Library J7

*Entrance on Fellow's Square, to the right off Parliament Square. Exhibition, Book of Kells and Old Library all **open** Mon–Sat 9.30–5; also open Sun: June–Sept 9.30–4.30, Oct–May noon–4.30. Closed 10 days over Christmas and New Year. **Adm** €7.50, students/seniors €6.50,* *family ticket €15, under 12s free. Large book- and gift-shop.*

The exhibition area containing the highly prized illuminated manuscript of the **Book of Kells** is a slick, high-tech operation. This is Dublin's – and possibly Ireland's – most popular visitor attraction, and the crowds, particularly in summer, are staggering. Visit as early as possible, and try to avoid weekends if you don't want to jostle for space.

The Book of Kells is kept in a tiny, low-lit gallery, where just two pages are displayed at a time (although they are turned periodically). Alongside it are selections from some of the library's other illuminated treasures, the Books of Armagh, Durrow, Dimma and Mulling. To reach this small chamber, visitors pass through a large contemporary exhibition space, which offers a fascinating and handsomely presented introduction to the history of writing in Ireland, from the earliest Ogham stones inscribed with an ancient script (which looks like a series of notches) to the arrival of the first Christians, and the brilliantly illuminated manuscripts of the early medieval period. Huge coloured screens with plenty of pictures and diagrams describe the lives of the early monks and the methods by which they created their miniature marvels; they also give an interesting and lively overview of the historical and cultural context in which these beautiful books were produced. It is worth lingering here over the vast reproductions of some of the highlights of the Book of Kells itself.

Stairs lead up to the magnificent **Old Library**, signalling a complete change of pace: if the downstairs exhibition area is a slick display of 21st-century media savvy, the imposing Long Room at the heart of the Old Library exudes Enlightenment principles and 19th-century rigour. Hushed, solemn and majestic, its bust-lined length extends for 213ft (almost 65m), and is neatly edged with elegant book bays and tall, narrow windows. The original flat ceiling was replaced with a lofty, barrel-vaulted version in 1860, in order to expand the amount of available shelf space. Since the 1801 Copyright Act, Trinity

The Book of Kells: 'Chief Glory of the Western World'

The Book of Kells is the most famous, the most lavish and the most beautiful of Ireland's illuminated manuscripts, described by Giraldus Cambrensis, the first Norman historian of Ireland, in the 12th century as 'the chief glory of the western world'. It is an exquisitely decorated copy of the four gospels in Latin, and probably dates back to the early 9th century, although its origins remain unclear. It is thought to have been produced on the island of Iona off the west coast of Scotland, where St Colum Cille founded a monastery in about 561, and it is possible that it was created to commemorate the bicentenary of the saint's death. The monks abandoned their monastery after a Viking attack in 806, and set up a new community in Kells, County Meath (about 70km northwest of Dublin), bringing their treasured book with them. The existence of the Book of Kells was first documented in the Annals of Ulster, which recorded in 1007 that 'the great gospel book of Colum Cille was stolen from the stone church at Kells'. It was discovered a few months later, tossed in a bog, and minus its valuable covers. In 1654, it was brought to Dublin for safekeeping, and was presented to Trinity College by the Bishop of Meath a few years later. The book contains 340 decorated folios (so, 680 pages) – although about 30 have been lost – and each page is painstakingly illuminated in vivid colours, the dyes made by crushing pearls or beetles' wings. The most famous and lavishly embellished page is the Chi Rho page, which is crammed with breathtakingly detailed Christian imagery from fish to peacocks, the latter a symbol of the incorruptible body of Christ from an ancient belief that peacock's flesh didn't putrefy. If this isn't one of the pages currently on view, you can see a blown-up copy of it in the exhibition which precedes the gallery.

has received a copy of every book published in Great Britain and Ireland, and currently owns around 3 million printed books and manuscripts, of which just the earliest are kept here. The busts, mainly 19th-century, are of famous writers from antiquity onwards. Among the other treasures kept here is an original print of the Proclamation of 1916 which sparked the Easter Rising (*see* p.27), one of only a dozen or so survivors of a print run of 2,500. There's also a battered harp, one of the oldest in the country, popularly attributed to Brian Ború, even though he was long dead by the time it was made in the early 15th century.

The Dublin Experience
Entrance in the Arts and Social Sciences building, opposite the Old Library, or from Nassau St. **Open** *late May–early Oct daily 10–5;* **adm** *€4.50, seniors, students and under 18s €4.*

The shamelessly touristy **Dublin Experience** gives a speed-of-light overview of the city's history – a thousand years is covered in 45 minutes. It's tacky, but not a bad way to get a sense of how the city has developed over the last millennium, and there are lots of crowd-pleasing special effects and audio-visuals. It's located in the modern Arts and Sciences building, which also has a couple of coffee shops, where you can queue up with the students for drinks and snacks.

Douglas Hyde Gallery
Entrance in the Arts and Social Sciences Building, opposite the Old Library, or from Nassau St, **t** *(01) 608 1116, www.douglashydegallery.com.* **Open** *Mon–Fri 11–6, Thurs until 7, Sat 11–4.45;* **adm** *free.*

A wing of the streamlined modern Arts and Social Sciences building houses the Douglas Hyde Gallery, one of Ireland's most prestigious contemporary art spaces. Established and emerging artists from Ireland and abroad are featured in wide-ranging temporary exhibitions held in two galleries, which cover everything from painting and sculpture to film and installations.

New Berkeley Library
No public access.

The main student library closes off Fellow's Square at its eastern end, an unmemorable modern box from 1967. It is named for the philosopher and former student **George Berkeley**, who founded the University of Philadelphia and for whom the famous university in California is named. Next to it is Arnaldo Pomodoro's 1962 sculpture *Sphere Within Sphere* – better known to students as 'the half-eaten Malteser'.

Provost's House
No public access.

Tucked into an elegant corner of the university complex is the **Provost's House**, the oldest continuously inhabited Georgian building in the city. It was built in 1761 and modelled on a London mansion designed by Lord Burlington from drawings by Palladio. The gorgeous interior features celebrated paintings, a fine coffered ceiling and some elaborate plasterwork, but, as it functions as a private home, ordinary mortals won't get past the front door without an invitation.

Old Museum
No public access.

Beyond the Old Library is the 19th-century former **Museum**, a handsome Victorian building full of whimsical, medieval-style stone carvings. It delighted Ruskin, but the fabulous menagerie appalled the university authorities, who ordered that the stonemasons be dismissed when they saw what had been done. The building is now a university department, but the skeletons of two giant deer (extinct since about 9000 BC) still guard the entrance.

Samuel Beckett Theatre
For information on performances and tickets, see p.212.

Across the playing fields is the wooden pavilion that houses the **Samuel Beckett Theatre** – a setting Beckett himself might have appreciated given his passion for cricket. Although it is largely used for student productions, it's regularly hired by professional companies and presents a broad range of performance arts.

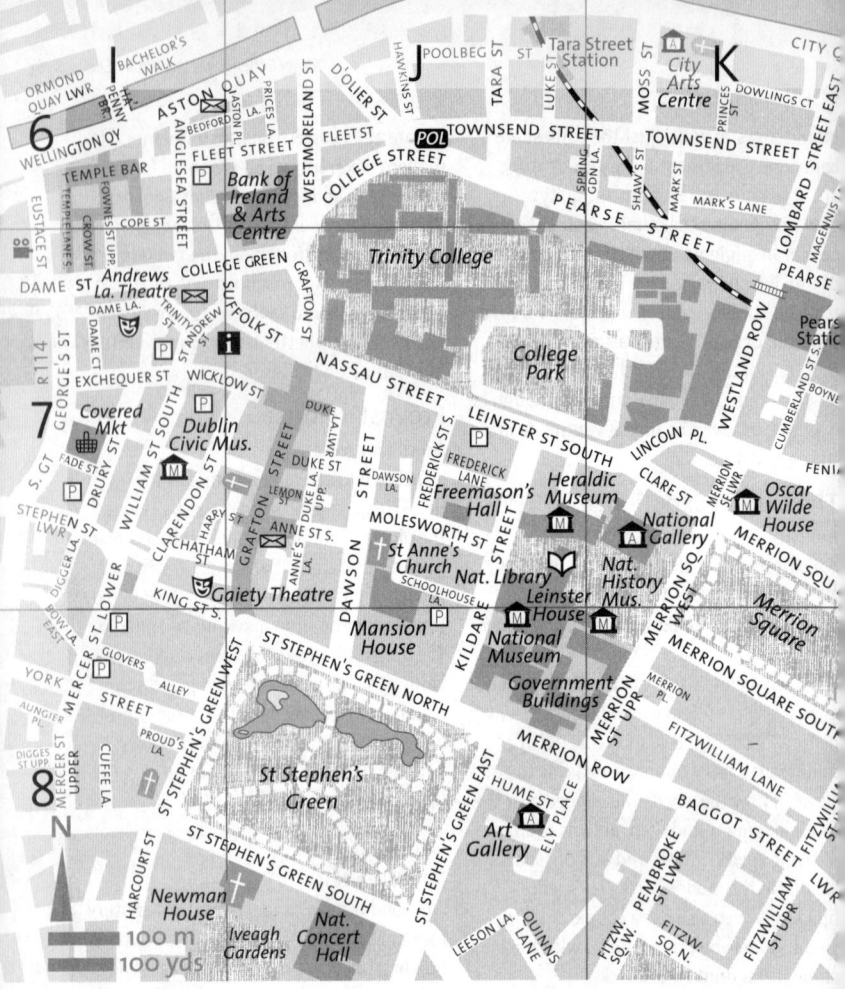

Close by, the graceful little building which looks like a miniature classical temple is the **Printing House** (1734) by Richard Cassels, architect of Leinster House (*see* p.71).

AROUND COLLEGE GREEN

Bank of Ireland (House of Lords) J6

College Green, **t** *(01) 671 2261,* **f** *(01) 670 7556; all cross-city buses.* **Open** *Mon–Fri 10–4, Thurs until 5;* **adm** *free. Free guided tours of the House of Lords Tues 10.30, 11.30 and 1.45.*

'*An independent country was thus degraded into a province, Ireland as a nation, was EXTINGUISHED.*'

Sir Jonah Barrington, *The Rise and Fall of the Irish Nation* (1833)

The vast columned building which curves majestically around College Green was originally built to house the **Irish Parliament**. It was designed in 1727 by Edward Pearce, who was inspired by the great Palladian mansions of Italy, and quickly became one of the most spectacular landmarks of a city already swept up in a great building frenzy. The Irish parliament sat here for 70 years, and it was in these chambers that the independence of the Irish nation was declared in 1782 by the formidable orator Henry Grattan. But the members of parliament were from the Protestant ascendancy class, unable and unwilling to reach any compromise with the

Public Art Around College Green

There are lots of statues scattered around the Bank of Ireland and College Green, including John Foley's statue of the formidable 18th-century politician **Henry Grattan** near the entrance. Two more statues are stranded on traffic islands, almost lost in the frenzied traffic: the first is a statue of the composer **Thomas Moore** (1779–1852), which stands on top of some disused public toilets – the best place, according to James Joyce in *Ulysses*, for the author of *The Meeting of the Waters*. The second is the **Steyne Monument** (1986) by Cliodna Cussen, which marks the spot where the original Viking *steyne* (a monolith commonly used to mark the location of the first berthing) stood for almost nine centuries.

Catholic majority, and therefore heavily reliant on the protection provided by the British. As a result, only 18 years later they were in the ignominious position of voting themselves out of existence when the Act of Union was passed in 1801, uniting Ireland with Great Britain. The Irish parliament was dissolved, and the building was promptly sold to the **Bank of Ireland**, which still owns it. The Bank continues to run it as an ordinary high street bank, albeit an unusually grand one.

Inside, the House of Commons has gone, and the only reminder of its former opulence is the vast rotunda which rises loftily over the bank's main cash hall. The **House of Lords** survives, a surprisingly small panelled room with a beautiful vaulted ceiling, embellished with delicate stucco decoration and gilded medallions. From the centre hangs a lavish 18th-century crystal chandelier, apparently a mere bauble in comparison with the original, and two vast tapestries depicting the 1689 Defence of Derry and the 1690 Battle of the Boyne adorn the walls. In the old days, the Lord Lieutenant would sit in the small recess under a scarlet canopy 'surrounded by more splendour than His Majesty on the throne of England'.

Bank of Ireland Arts Centre J6

Foster Place, t (01) 671 1488; all cross-city buses. Museum of Banking open Tues–Fri 10–4; adm €1.50, seniors/students €1. Arts Centre box office open Tues–Fri 11–4.

The **Bank of Ireland Arts Centre** is tucked around the back of the main building, on quiet, cobbled Foster Place. It is set in the former armoury (which still has carved cannons on the roof) and offers regular lunchtime concerts and recitals, along with poetry readings and other cultural events. The Centre also contains the **Museum of Banking**, an enjoyable meander through the history of both the Bank of Ireland and the historic premises which it occupies. Among the exhibits is the mace used in the House of Commons before it was dissolved, which was recovered in the 1930s.

GRAFTON STREET AND AROUND

Grafton Street has long been Dublin's favourite shopping street. For a while it was almost too popular: when the endless stream of honking traffic got too much, in 1982, the city pedestrianized it. As rents have shot up, many of the smaller traditional establishments have been forced to move elsewhere, leaving the street to the major chain stores with deeper pockets, but there are some sturdy survivors: one of the city's best department stores (Brown Thomas), a couple of great cafés (Brown's Bar, Butler's Chocolate Café) and some of the most celebrated pubs and literary haunts scattered around the side streets.

Molly Malone Statue J7

Corner of Grafton St and Suffolk St. All cross-city buses.

The introduction to Dublin's snootiest shopping street is surprisingly brash: a shiny bronze statue by Jeanne Rynhart, from 1988, of Molly Malone – heroine of the 19th-century music-hall song ('In Dublin's fair city/ Where the girls are so pretty/ I first set my eyes on sweet Molly Malone...'). Dubliners have given cheeky nicknames to most of their public statues, and this rather curvaceous depiction of Molly is no exception: she is known as 'the tart with the cart'. She pushes her barrow of cockles and mussels ('...alive, alive o!' as the song goes) with a jaunty air, but Dubliners despise her, probably because the tourists love her: she's regularly surrounded by bus parties.

Brown Thomas Department Store J7

88–95 Grafton St, t (01) 605 6666; all cross-city buses. Open Mon–Sat 9–6, Thurs until 8, Sun noon–6.

Brown Thomas was one of Dublin's first and fanciest department stores, first established across the street where the Marks and Spencer's store is now located. No longer quite as upmarket as it used to be, it's still a favourite with the 'ladies who lunch' who gather in the smart café to gossip over their purchases.

Bewley's Oriental Café J7

78 Grafton St; all cross-city buses.

Bewley's Oriental Café closed down at the end of 2004. It was a Dublin institution, and had been since it was begun in the mid-19th century by a teetotal Quaker family, who hoped to encourage temperance by giving Dubliners another option besides the pub to meet socially. They had only patchy success in encouraging locals to give up the demon drink, but the cafés still took off. There were several branches, but this one was the first and most spectacular, revamped in the 1920s at the height of 'Tutmania' – when all things Egyptian were fashionable in the wake of the discovery of Tutankhamun's tomb. The façade is encrusted with dazzling mosaics of Egyptian symbols, and boasts delicate stained-glass windows by Henry Clarke. At the time of writing, it is not yet known what will become of the venue, but if you walk down busy Grafton street, make sure you stop at number 78 to admire the façade. Bewley's is still trading as a tea and coffee merchant both in Ireland and internationally, and it has kept an outlet in Dublin, but to the disappointment of many Dubliners, it was decided to close the much loved cafés (there also used to be a branch in Westmoreland street).

Davy Byrne's J7

21 Duke St, t (01) 677 5217, f (01) 671 7619, www.davybyrnespub.com; all cross-city buses. Open daily 11am–12.30am.

Davy Byrne's pub has been going since 1798, but is best known for its association with James Joyce who mentioned it in *Ulysses* ('He entered Davy Byrnes once a year. Moral pub. Doesn't chat, stands a drink now and then. But in a leap year once in four. Cashed a cheque for me once.') Each year on Bloomsday (16 June), the pub prepares the traditional Leopold Bloom lunch of a glass of burgundy and a gorgonzola sandwich, and Joyce himself stares out of a 1940s mural by Harry Kernoff from the pub walls. This isn't one of Dublin's unchanged Victorian pubs, and it keeps up with the times with periodic renovations. But it's bright and comfortable and it serves decent pub food all day (the seafood is particularly good). Best of all, it's conveniently close to Grafton Street, so you can take the weight off your feet after a hard day's shopping.

McDaid's I7

3 Harry St, t (01) 679 4395, f (01) 679 4852; all cross-city buses. Open Mon–Wed 10.30am–11.30pm, Thurs–Sat 10.30am–12.30am.

Another 18th-century pub just off Grafton Street with literary associations, McDaid's was a favourite with the likes of Patrick

Kavanagh (1904–67) and Brendan Behan (1923–64). Behan – a self-confessed 'brawling, boozing exhibitionist' – would bring his typewriter in here and work. Once, apparently, he chucked it through the window in a fit of temper. (You can see this very typewriter at the Dublin Writers Museum, see p.107.)

South William Street and around I7

Bus 10, 11, 13, 122, 19, 16, 16A.

South William Street runs parallel to Grafton Street. It's another chic shopping street with fashionable boutiques, hip cafés and restaurants, and the elegant Powerscourt Townhouse shopping centre (see below). Off it is the Drury Arcade, a trendy shopping arcade set in a Victorian covered market, packed with unusual shops and stalls selling everything from the latest fashions to fine foods (the olive stall is a favourite with locals). Pedestrianized Castle Street has more bars, restaurants and great cafés, including the heavenly Maison des Gourmets for French pastries.

Powerscourt Townhouse Shopping Centre I7

59 South William St, t (01) 679 4144; bus 10, 11, 13, 122, 19, 16, 16A.

The elegant 18th-century Powerscourt Townhouse was built for Viscount Powerscourt, owner of the magnificent estate near Enniskerry (see p.170). It has been beautifully restored to house a fashionable shopping centre, set around a glassed-over courtyard. Many of the original details have been preserved, including some delicate plasterwork ceilings by Michael Stapleton.

There are stacks of bars, cafés and restaurants, and plenty of shops to blow your holiday budget, including the Irish Design Centre (see p.217) for fabulous homegrown fashion.

Dublin Civic Museum I7

South William St, t (01) 679 4260, www.dublincitycouncil.ie; bus 10, 11, 13, 122, 19, 16, 16A. Open Tues–Sat 10–6, Sun 11–2; adm free.

This is a likeable, shabby little museum which rarely sees visitors. It's set in another formal Georgian mansion, which once served as the City Assembly House. There's an eccentric and eclectic collection, which spans all kinds of oddities from Viking artefacts to historic shop signs for everything from abattoirs to workhouses. There's also a very battered 18th-century bench from the former House of Commons (now the Bank of Ireland, see p.64), one of the few pieces of furniture which has survived. The enormous pair of leather shoes belonged to the Irish giant Patrick Cotter O'Brae (c.1761–1806), who stood about eight feet six inches tall. An absorbing collection of postcards display old views of the city (O'Connell Street, surprisingly, used to be even busier than it is now), including some curious ones printed on peat: 'I was a piece of turf/ But now am paper brown/ And used for wrapping parcels up/ For every house in town'. Also here is part of the head of Nelson, blown off its pedestal after the IRA dynamited Nelson's Pillar in 1966 to mark the fiftieth anniversary of the Easter Rising.

St Teresa's Carmelite Church and Friary I8

56 Aungier St, t (01) 475 8821, f (01) 475 8825 www.carmelites.ie; bus 16, 16A 19, 19A. Open Mon–Fri 7.45–6, Tues until 9.15pm, Sat 7.45–7, Sun 7.45–7.30, bank holidays 9.30–1; adm free.

This large, light church (dating from 1793, but remodelled since) is one of the earliest post-Reformation Catholic churches in Dublin, and probably the most popular with Dubliners. Unlike the grand, hushed cathedrals with their fleets of tour groups, this is filled with local worshippers, who come to light candles at the numerous shrines and pray to the patron saint of their cause: St Valentine for lovers, St Jude for lost causes or Our Lady of Lourdes for health problems. The waters of the Well of St Albert of Sicily, near the main entrance on Aungier Street, are popularly regarded as curative. The complex has a genuine community ambience, with a small section devoted to the history of the church and the Carmelite order in Dublin, a coffee shop and secondhand bookshop. The original Carmelite church was dispossessed during the Reformation when its sacred treasures, like those of all the city's Catholic churches, were tossed into the great bonfire outside Christchurch Cathedral. Only one holy statue survived the inferno: an early 16th-century image carved in Irish oak of Our Lady of Dublin, much-venerated protector of the city, which a priest found in a junk shop in 1824 and which has found a more suitable home here.

KILDARE STREET AND AROUND
National Museum of Ireland J8

Kildare St, t (01) 677 7444, f (01) 677 7450, www.museum.ie; bus 7, 7A, 8, 10, 11, 13. Open Tues–Sat 10–5, Sun 2–5; adm free. Daily guided tours of different sections, times vary; €1.50. Free lunchtime lectures on Wednesdays. Partially wheelchair accessible (ground floor only). Giftshop, café-restaurant.

The **National Museum of Ireland** opened to great fanfare in 1890. It's a fine example of Victorian Palladianism, with a lofty, domed rotunda in the entrance hall. The collection is now divided into four locations: this one contains the archaeology and history collection; Collins Barracks on the northside (*see* p.120) has the decorative arts and furniture; there are ranks of stuffed animals in the Museum of Natural History (*see* p.78); and there's a National Museum of Country Life in Castlebar, County Mayo. The Kildare Street building contains a vast array of ancient treasures, including dazzling Bronze Age gold and beautiful examples of Celtic and medieval art. It is divided into seven sections, some of which have excellent short film presentations (regular showings) which put the exhibits in context.

Pick up a plan of the museum at the information desk under the rotunda, where you can also find out what time the museum's guided tours depart.

Prehistoric Ireland

The exhibition begins with flint heads and stone chisels which date back to around 7000 BC, when the earliest Irish settlers were living in woodland, making weapons and beginning to domesticate animals. The Lurgan Logboat, a vast boat made from a hollowed-out log, was discovered in 1902, and is thought to have been made around 2500 BC. Reconstructions of early habitations and passage tombs show how these early settlers might have lived. The curious image carved from yew, known as the Ralaghan Figure (*c.*1100–1000 BC), was probably a fertility idol. The earliest metalworkers were farmers, who are credited with importing two things that the Irish would come to excel at: metalworking and making beer. The earliest metal objects were cold-hammered from copper and gold, and the Lissan Rapier (c. 1400–1000 BC), the longest rapier known from Bronze Age Europe, attests to the skill of the Irish craftsmen. Metalworking techniques became increasingly sophisticated, and the Dowris Hoard (discovered in 1820) displays a magnificent collection of 8th–6th century BC shields, cauldrons, bells and knives. Plans and reconstructions outline the importance of the Hill of Tara (see p.162), one of the most important prehistoric burial sites, imbued with a legendary significance which endured until the early Christian period. Among the most gruesome exhibits is the Bog Man, still dressed in his deerskin cape; he had been throttled with a length of willow and tossed into the bog along with two pointed stakes – probably the victim of a ritual murder, a relatively common occurrence around 400–200 BC. His remarkably well preserved body was discovered in County Galway in 1821.

Ór – Ireland's Gold

The central area of the elegant wrought-iron main hall at the heart of the museum is devoted to its most spectacular treasures: a dazzling display of Bronze Age **gold** jewellery which ranks among the finest collections of prehistoric gold artefacts in Europe. Curiously, though, despite the wealth of gold jewellery and decorative objects which have come to light in Ireland, no one knows for sure where all the gold came from in the first place.

The highlight is the stunning **Glenisheen Collar** (*c*.700 BC), a thick gold collar with intricate decoration. It is one of the latest pieces in the collection and admirably illustrates the apotheosis of this strand of Irish craftsmanship. The earliest pieces date back to around 2200 BC, simple disks or crescent shapes called *lunulae* made of thin sheets of beaten gold and decorated with simple incisions or raised patterns. Around 1200 BC, the jewellery became more elaborate, with incredibly intricate torcs, bracelets, armlets, rings and ear-spools (disks around which the ear lobe was stretched). By around 800–700 BC, a wider variety of objects was produced using new techniques, including the use of gold wire and gold foil (the latter was used to cover small objects made of base metal used as amulets). One of the most spectacular collections is the **Mooghaun Hoard**, discovered by navvies digging the West Clare railway in the 1850s. Of around 150 pieces, only 29 have survived (the rest probably found their way to jewellers' shops to be melted down), but the museum displays facsimiles of the originals.

The Treasury

Most of the museum's finest treasures are contained in these galleries, which concentrate mainly on ecclesiastical art of the pre- and early medieval period. The **Ardagh Hoard** is a small collection of silver cups and brooches, of which the most outstanding piece is also the earliest, the famous **Ardagh Chalice**, thought to have been produced in the early 8th century. This dazzling two-handed cup is widely considered to be the finest example of Celtic art, and is intricately decorated with gold filigree, enamel and glass studs, and elaborate patterned bands. There are also several richly ornamented croziers, including the 11th-century **Clonmacnoise crozier**, and several bell-shrines, of which the most famous is the 12th-century **Shrine of St Patrick's Bell**, said to have belonged to Ireland's patron saint. Other highlights include the **Cross of Cong** (1123), an oak cross sumptuously decorated with interlacing patterns in silver and gilt bronze. Along with a gorgeous collection of ecclesiastical chalices, patens and crucifixes, it forms the Derrynaflan Hoard. The **Tullylough Cross** is another outstanding piece of early medieval Irish craftsmanship, with panels displaying interlaced patterns and tiny scenes (including what seems to be St Patrick chasing out the snakes from Ireland). The early brooches, which remain a typical feature of Celtic jewellery, are simple, but very beautiful; the most exquisite is the famous **Tara Brooch**, a delicate 8th-century ornament of the palest bronze, studded with amber and decorated with intricate patterns including some fierce-looking creatures traced in gold. It is thought to have belonged to a high-ranking member of the court of the Irish kings at Tara, before falling into the hands of the Vikings.

Viking Age Ireland

Make your way upstairs for the next part of the visit, which begins with the galleries dedicated to the **Vikings**, who first arrived in Dublin in AD 795 on a raiding mission, and then built a settlement about 50 years later. Many of the artefacts on display come from the excavations in Wood Quay (*see* p.89), on which the city controversially erected their civic offices despite a public outcry. The Vikings were not Christianized until the late 10th century, and were buried according to ancient pagan custom. The wealthiest were buried with their possessions; warriors, like the skeleton of a tall Viking warrior shown here, were buried with their weapons. Reconstructions show what Viking homes would have looked like and jewellery, tools, leather shoes and domestic implements collected from the Wood Quay excavations serve to fill in the picture of daily life. There are some gruesome reminders of how tough life was for some members of their society – a human skull scored with axe blows was found alongside an iron chain; probably evidence of how an unfortunate slave met his end. There are also some early coins, first minted in Dublin by the Vikings in 997.

Medieval Ireland 1150–1550

These galleries are divided into themes, each bringing a different aspect of medieval society into focus using illustrations, information panels and artefacts from the period. The first theme is **prayer**, and outlines the history of the medieval church which was already a powerful and highly developed organization by the 8th century. The churches were the main centres of learning; many had acquired huge estates, and some became the residences of provincial kings. The cult of relics is enjoyably illustrated by the curious relic-shrines of the period, including a peculiar shoe-shaped one made to house St Brigid's shoe. There are examples of ecclesiastical architecture, including a plaster cast of the Romanesque doorway from Cormac's chapel in County Tipperary, and some unusual inscribed headstones – one is made from a recycled millstone. The second theme is **power**, focusing on the Irish kings and lords. The last High King of Ireland was Ruaidhrí Ó Couchbhair, who died in 1183, and for the rest of the medieval period Irish rulers were mainly provincial kings and lords. Art Mac Murchadha Caomhámanach, King of Leinster (c.1357–1416), famously cultured and learned, won his place as a hero of Irish history by challenging the authority of the English in Ireland. The Kavanagh Charter Horn, a beautiful ceremonial drinking horn, is the only piece of Irish regalia to have survived the Middle Ages. Margaret Butler (c.1480–1542), a 'rare woman and able for wisdom to rule a realm' is also singled out. Weaponry, jewellery, seals, rings and even medieval board games give a flavour of medieval courtly life. The final section is devoted to **people**, and deals with everyday life during the period, with exhibits of cooking implements, coins and pottery. Among the most curious exhibits are the strange wooden jugs of 'bog butter': jugs of milk which were preserved in bogs hundreds of years ago and then forgotten still regularly turn up in the Irish countryside.

Ancient Egypt

A small section of the museum's upper level is devoted to a collection of ancient Egyptian artefacts, with jewellery, ceramics, tools, funerary amulets and mummies – including a mummified cat.

The Road to Independence

This small and rather patchy collection is found on the ground floor, in a gallery off the main exhibition area. It covers the period from 1798, when the rebellion of the United Irishmen was summarily quashed by the British, to the declaration of the Irish Free State in 1922. Flags, uniforms, guns belonging to the early IRA, photographs and posters illustrate the period's history.

From here, it's just a short step to the excellent museum café.

National Library of Ireland J7

Kildare St, t (01) 603 0200, f (01) 676 6690, www.nli.ie; bus 7, 7A, 8, 10, 11, 13. **Open** *Mon–Wed 10–9, Thurs–Fri 10–5, Sat 10–1;* **adm** *free. Wheelchair access can be arranged with advance notice.*

Opposite the National Museum stands the equally grand **National Library**, which also opened in 1890. The core of its holdings came from the library of the Royal Dublin Society, founded in 1731, but its collections have been massively expanded since then. It now contains an unrivalled array of Irish documentary material, including manuscripts, letters and first editions of the works of Yeats, Joyce, Swift and other eminent Irish authors, a beautifully illuminated 13th-century manuscript *Topographia Hibernica* by Giraldus Cambrensis and a Gaelic manuscript collection.

From the circular entrance hall, a staircase lined with splendid stained glass windows leads up to the main reading hall, under a vast pale dome which echoes the rotunda in the museum opposite.

The National Library also contains the Genealogical Advice Centre, a good first port-of-call for anyone seeking to find out more about their Irish ancestry (*see* p.50).

Heraldic Museum J7

*2–3 Kildare St, **t** (01) 603 0311, **f** (01) 662 1061, www.nli.ie; **bus** 7, 7A, 8, 10, 11, 13. **Open** Mon–Wed 10–9, Thurs–Fri 10–5, Sat 10–1; **adm** free. Wheelchair access can be arranged with advance notice.*

The Heraldic Museum, also part of the National Library, is really only for committed fans of heraldry. It's an old-fashioned little museum with ranks of battered cabinets containing seals, crests, insignias and stamps. Irish citizens, or those with a strong connection to the country, can apply here to be granted their own coat-of-arms.

Leinster House J7

*Kildare St, **t** (01) 618 3066, **f** (01) 618 4118, www.oireachtas.ie; **bus** 7, 7A, 8, 10, 11, 13. **Open** only when parliament is not in session: call in advance to find out tour times.*

Leinster House, grandly set back from the hubbub of Kildare Street, was commissioned in 1745 by James Fitzgerald, Earl of Kildare. When questioned about the location of his new residence, so remote from the then-fashionable hub on the north side of the city, he is said to have replied: 'They will follow me wherever I go'. He was the first of the great magnates to build south of the river, and, as prophesied, the rest of fashionable Dublin was not slow to follow. The house, designed by the leading Palladian architect Richard Cassels, was the grandest of the period, surrounded by elegant lawns and gardens (where the crowds were dazzled in 1785 by the ascent of a hot-air balloon) and said to have been the inspiration for the White House in Washington DC. It was renamed in 1766 when the earl was elevated to become the Duke of Leinster. His son Lord Edward Fitzgerald was one of the leaders of the Irish Rebellion, who was forced to flee from the house in March 1798, only to be captured eleven weeks later (*see* p.93). He died in Newgate Prison of a bullet wound received during his arrest. The house was sold to the Royal Dublin Society in 1815 by the third Duke of Leinster, and acquired by the government after the establishment of the Irish Free State in 1922.

Today Leinster House is the seat of the two Houses of the Oireachtas (National Parliament), comprising **Dáil Éireann** (the House of Representatives) and **Seanad Éireann** (the Senate). Despite substantial remodelling, many of the original decorative elements have been retained, and you can admire these on the guided tours offered when parliament is not in session.

Freemason's Hall J7

*17 Molesworth St, **t** (01) 679 5465; **bus** 10, 25X, 32, 51X, 66X, 67X, 84X. **Open** June–Aug Mon–Fri 11.30–2; **adm** €1.50.*

Just off Kildare Street, the **Freemason's Hall** was built as a Grand Lodge in 1866, and its extravagant High Victorian façade incorporates masonic symbols. The interior is a dizzying mixture of clashing Victorian styles, from neo-Gothic to neoclassical, with a dollop of Orientalism for good measure. The halls and meeting rooms contain exhibits outlining the history of the notoriously secretive masonic society in Ireland, from its establishment in 1725 to the present day. Unsettling or fascinating depending on your point of view, it's easily one of Dublin's most eccentric museums.

St Anne's Church J7

*Dawson St, **t** (01) 676 7727; **bus** 10, 25X, 32, 51X, 66X, 67X, 84X. **Open** Mon–Fri 10–4, Sun for services; **adm** free.*

The cartoonish 19th-century neo-Romanesque façade of the **church of St Anne** was never finished because of lack of funds. Fortunately, the delightful, light-filled Georgian interior was left untouched, and retains its elegant wooden galleries and box pews. Bram Stoker, author of *Dracula*, was married here (his wife was taken with Oscar Wilde, but changed her mind), and Mrs Felician Hemans, the sentimental English poet who penned *The Boy Stood On the Burning Deck*, is buried in the southern aisle. The 18th-century Bread Shelf is usually stacked with loaves of bread for the poor, a charitable tradition which has been going for 300 years. A more up-to-date charitable tradition is the over-55s cybercafé hosted here (Mon–Fri noon–3pm).

Mansion House J8

*Dawson St; **bus** 7, 7A, 8, 10, 11, 13. No public access.*

The grandest mansion on Dawson Street is home to Dublin's Lord Mayor. The original Queen Anne townhouse was built in 1710 for Joshua Dawson (who gave the street its name), but a pompous façade was tacked on in the late 19th century. This is where the first meeting of the Dáil adopted the Declaration of Irish Independence in 1919.

ST STEPHEN'S GREEN AND AROUND

St Stephen's Green, with its leafy park and elegant ranks of Georgian mansions, has long been one of the most fashionable squares in Dublin. Taking afternoon tea at the historic Shelbourne Hotel (*see* p.173), with its bay windows overlooking the gardens, remains an institution, but the square hasn't been untouched by time. Several of the opulent mansions created here in the 18th century were bulldozed in the 1960s and 1970s, and the western end is a noisy, grubby construction site, where tracks are being laid for Dublin's new tram stystem, the Luas. Traffic clogs the roads, but the formal gardens at the centre are still a popular retreat from the hectic city.

St Stephen's Green J8

*t (01) 475 7816; all cross-city buses. **Open** Mon–Sat 8am–dusk, Sun 10am–dusk; **adm** free.*

> 'But the trees in Stephen's Green were fragrant of rain and the rainsodden earth gave forth its mortal odour, a faint incense rising upward through the mould from many hearts.'
>
> James Joyce, *Portrait of the Artist as a Young Man* (1916)

St Stephen's Green is Dublin's most popular public park. Shady paths lined with tall trees crisscross the park, past rose gardens, a broad ornamental lake with bobbing ducks, undulating lawns, rockeries and glades. But it wasn't always such a tranquil retreat: the site was first used to build a hospital for lepers, destroyed during the Reformation. The land became a public common, the site of hangings, markets and fairs, until the 17th century when gardens were first created. By the 18th century, it was a fashionable promenade, particularly the northern side which was nicknamed 'Beau Walk' for the young men who came to strut. By the early 19th century, the park had been fenced and an admission fee of one guinea was charged, putting it out of reach of all but the richest. In 1880, the philanthropist Lord Arthur Guinness pushed through an Act of Parliament which gave the park back to the public, and then paid for its redesign. It remains a favourite with Dubliners, who picnic on sunny days or come to hear the summer concerts at the bandstand.

St Stephen's Green Monuments

There is a dizzying collection of busts and statues of Dublin's most famous characters scattered all over St Stephen's Green. Of the revolutionaries, **Wolfe Tone** (1763–98), leader of the United Irishmen, stands at the northeast corner, and there's a bust of the colourful **Countess Markievicz** (1868–1927), heroine of the Easter Rising, on the western side. There are plenty of writers, too, including a statue of **James Joyce** (1882–1941) opposite his former college Newman House on the southern flank. An abstract memorial to **W.B. Yeats** by Henry Moore, *Knife Edge*, overlooks the flowerbeds at the western end.

Newman House 18

*85–86 St Stephen's Green South, **t** (01) 716 7422, **f** (01) 716 7211; all cross-city buses. **Open** June–Aug for guided tours only: Tues–Fri noon, 2pm, 3pm & 4pm; **adm** €4.50, seniors/students €3.*

Newman House comprises two exceptionally fine Georgian mansions on the south side of St Stephen's Green, which have been opened to the public after a magnificent and sensitive restoration. Clanwilliam House (1736–8) at no. 86 and the adjoining mansion at no. 85 were acquired in the mid-19th century by the fledgling Catholic University, and later renamed Newman House for Cardinal John Henry Newman, first rector of the university. Among the many writers who taught or were educated here are Gerald Manley Hopkins, who described Dublin as 'a joyless place', and James Joyce, who wasn't much happier. Hopkins' bedroom is preserved as it was during his time here, as is the **Physics Theatre**, where the 'tundish' episode took place in Joyce's autobiographical *Portrait of the Artist as a Young Man*. (This passage, in which the dean doesn't understand the Irish word 'tundish' and the young Stephen Dedalus realizes that, for him, English will always be an 'acquired speech', was described by the poet Seamus Heaney as being 'to Irish literature as the 1916 Easter Rising is to Irish nationalism'.)

Clanwilliam House was designed by Richard Cassels, the Palladianist who was responsible for some of Ireland's grandest country houses as well as Leinster House (*see* p.71). It was commissioned by Captain Hugh Montgomery, who wanted a pleasure palace to entertain in while in Dublin for 'the Season', rather than an ordinary residence. The stone façade (the first in Dublin) is sombre, but the interior is breathtakingly light and opulent. The house contains some of the finest stucco decoration in Ireland, the work of the celebrated Swiss stucco artists Paolo and Fillipo Lafranchini. The dazzling **Apollo Room**, with its sumptuously decorated panels of Apollo and the Muses, is considered one of the finest interiors of 18th-century Dublin. The Lafranchini brothers also produced the elaborate allegorical relief of good government and prudent economy in the main **Saloon**, which stretches for almost the whole length of the first floor. The Catholic University decided the figures were too risqué and chastely covered some of the more lascivious-looking gods and goddesses, but many of their 'improvements' have been undone in restoration and only Juno still coyly wears her 19th-century bathing-costume. The marble fireplace was recreated from designs of the long-lost original.

A hidden stairway leads to no. 86 next door, a much larger mansion built in 1765 for the notorious priest-baiter Richard Chapel Whaley, who fully deserved his nickname 'Burn-Chapel'. The swirling rococo stucco in the main Saloon is the work of the Irish artist Richard West.

Newman University Church 18

*87A St Stephen's Green South, **t** (01) 478 0616; all cross-city buses. **Open** Mon–Sat 8.45–6, Sun for services; **adm** free.*

Next to Newman House stands the University Church, now a favourite for weddings between chic Dubliners, but once derided for its eccentricity. It was designed in 1855 by the Catholic University's Fine Art professor John Pollen, with help from Cardinal Newman; the man bucked the trend for fashionable Gothic revivalism and classicism with their dazzling neo-Byzantine creation, full of intricate marble and gold leaf decoration. Newman's bust still gazes over the cheerful wedding parties.

Royal College of Surgeons J8

St Stephen's Green West; all cross-city buses. No public access.

Few Georgian buildings have survived on the western side of the Green, but the **Royal College of Surgeons**, built in 1806, is a fine exception. During the Easter Rising of 1916, it was used as the headquarters of the rebel army, led by the redoubtable Countess de Markievicz (1868–1927) in a uniform tailored specially for the event, and bullet holes still pock the columns. During the firing, some bullets went wildly astray and hit the ducks in the pond on St Stephen's Green: there were six duck casualties altogether.

St Stephen's Green Centre J8

South King St; all cross-city buses.

This glassy, pavilion-style **shopping mall** sits at the top of Grafton Street and overlooks St Stephen's Green. It's filled with largely unremarkable small shops and chain stores, but there's a good café (the Dome, *see* p.191) at the very top.

National Concert Hall J8

Earlsfort Terrace, t (01) 475 1666, f (01) 478 3797, www.nch.ie; all cross-city buses. Open Mon–Sat 10–7 and for concerts (see p.212 for details). Restaurant.

Earlsfort Terrace leads off St Stephen's Green to this imposing building, designed in the classical style as a pavilion for the Great Exhibition in 1865 and altered to house University College Dublin in the early 20th century. It was remodelled and reopened as the National Concert Hall, Ireland's premier classical music venue, in 1981. Almost hidden in the wall in the car park behind the hall is one of the entrances to the Iveagh Gardens.

Iveagh Gardens J8

Entrances on Earlsfort Terrace and Clonmel St, t (01) 475 7816; all cross-city buses. Open Mon–Sat 8am–dusk, Sun 10am–dusk.

These beautiful, rarely visited gardens are tucked behind high stone walls without an obvious entrance, making them feel deliciously secret. The gardens belonged variously to nearby Clonmel House, Iveagh House and now to University College Dublin. They were substantially redesigned by Ninian Niven for the 1865 Great Exhibition, and are filled with shady, tree-lined paths and ponds, cascades, fountains, a rose garden and even an archery field (once flooded in winter for skating and in summer for sailing). It is a tranquil retreat from the crowds, and a perfect summer picnic spot.

OUT TO PORTOBELLO

Irish Jewish Museum I10

3–4 Walworth Rd, off Victoria Rd, t (01) 453 1797; bus 16, 19, 22. Open May–Sept Tues, Thurs & Sun 11–3.30; Oct–April, Sun 10.30–2.30; adm free, but donations gratefully received.

The Portobello area of Dublin was once known as 'Little Jerusalem', and this delightful, welcoming museum is housed in two adjoining terrace houses which were used as the local synagogue until the mid-1970s. The ground floor exhibits relate the community's history: the first documentary evidence of Jews in Ireland dates back to 1079, when the Annals of Innisfallen recorded the visit of 'five Jews from across the sea' who came bearing gifts and were then sent home. It wasn't until the late 19th and early 20th centuries that Ireland gained a Jewish population of any size, and even at its height in the 1940s it only numbered 5,500 people. Daniel O'Connell, who fought for Catholic Emancipation, was also a stalwart supporter of the Jews, and told the Jewish community: 'Ireland has claims on your ancient race, it is the only country that I know of unsullied by any one act of persecution of the Jews'. This record was spoiled in 1902 when Fr Creagh of Limerick preached a sermon attacking the Jews, suggesting that they would 'kill and slay Christian children'. More than two-thirds of Limerick's tiny Jewish population fled as a result.

Today there are only about 1,800 Jews in the whole of Ireland; this tiny synagogue shut its doors in the mid-1970s after falling into disuse. It reopened as a museum in 1985, with the Irish-born former president of Israel Dr Chaim Herzog officiating at the ceremony. Next to the historical exhibits is an old-fashioned kitchen, with a special Sabbath meal laid out on the table (the kitchen belonged to the museum's caretaker), and photographs and other mementoes lining the corridors offer a fascinating glimpse into Jewish life in Dublin over the past century. Upstairs is the handsome original synagogue, still kitted out with all its ritual paraphernalia, and at the back are exhibition cases displaying Jewish religious objects.

Shaw's Birthplace I9

33 Synge St, t (01) 475 0854, shawhouse@dublintourism.ie; bus 16, 19, 122. Open May–Sept Mon–Sat 10–5, Sun 2–6; closed for lunch daily 1–2; adm €6, seniors/students €5, children €3.50, family ticket €16.50; includes audio-guide. Bookshop. Guided tours with prior notice.

George Bernard Shaw was born in this modest little house on a leafy suburban street on 26 July 1856, and lived here until he was ten. He remembered it as a 'loveless'

George Bernard Shaw

The playwright and critic **George Bernard Shaw** was born in 1856 in the modest Dublin suburb of Portobello. Shaw and his two sisters lived in fear of their drunken father – his mother was confronted with her new husband's drinking problem on honeymoon, when she discovered a wardrobe full of bottles. She escaped into music and began an affair with Vandeleur Lee, a charismatic singing teacher, holding many musical soirées in her drawing room. (Shaw would later write that 'Hell is full of amateur musicians'.) When she left Dublin for London with her lover, Shaw followed, and set about educating himself in the British Library. He began writing novels, and became a familiar figure at Speaker's Corner and at socialist rallies, overcoming his stammer to gain a reputation as a passionate orator. He was one of the founders of the Fabian Society, later instrumental in the establishment of the Labour Party and the London School of Economics.

Shaw wrote his first play – heavily influenced by Ibsen – in 1891, but it wasn't until 1904 that he began to gain any recognition. In the meantime, he made ends meet by working as a music and theatre critic, and finally moved out of his mother's house in 1898 to marry Charlotte Payne-Townsend, a wealthy Irish woman.

When war broke out in 1914, Shaw expressed his horror at the tragic waste of young lives under the guise of patriotism in a series of newspaper articles which were very badly received – some outraged readers even talked of having him tried for treason. That year he also wrote *Pygmalion*, which would become his best-known work after it was later adapted into the musical *My Fair Lady*. *Heartbreak House*, the only major play he produced during the First World War, reveals his bitterness and disillusion with British politics. His post-war plays – particularly *Saint Joan* (1923) – re-established his reputation, and he was awarded the Nobel Prize in 1925.

Shaw lived an abstemious life (he was a teetotal vegetarian who never smoked), and died at the age of 94 after falling off a ladder at his country home.

> ### Discount Tickets
>
> The Shaw Birthplace offers a special combined ticket with the Dublin Writers Museum (see p.107), James Joyce Museum (see p.136), Malahide Castle and Fry Model Railway Museum (see p.133) – you can choose any two of these attractions for €10 (students/seniors €8, children €5.50, family ticket €28.50).

house, and followed his mother to England in 1876 when she finally left Shaw's feckless father for good. It has been recreated to look much as it would have done when he lived here as a child, and an audio guide gives an entertaining, anecdotal account of his early life. The kitchen, which Shaw described as 'an awful little kennel with primitive sanitary arrangements', has a flagged stone floor and a huge range, but it's dark and gloomy. The pretty walled garden is remembered as having 'high dark walls, much too high to climb', evoking his childish desire to escape the threatening atmosphere inside the house. The grander upstairs apartments, where Mrs Shaw held her musical soirées and conducted her not-very-discreet affair with a flamboyant music teacher, are full of Victorian clutter. A plaque above the bed where Shaw was born feet-first states simply 'Bernard Shaw, author of many plays', an inscription he chose himself (he hated the name George and never used it).

MERRION SQUARE AND AROUND
Merrion Square K7

All cross-city buses.

When fashionable Dublin migrated south of the river in the 18th century, the Earl of Kildare and Lord Fitzwilliam of Merrion became the largest private landlords of the era. Lord Fitzwilliam laid out the grand expanse of Merrion Street and followed it up 30 years later with **Merrion Square**, flanked with the splendid townhouses of Dublin's social élite. The back of Leinster House, the National Gallery of Ireland and the Museum of Natural History give an imposing flourish to its western end, and the other three sides are still lined with impeccable Georgian residences. Most are now owned by businesses and private clubs, but almost all bear a plaque attesting to their famous residents, including Oscar Wilde at no. 1 (*see p.79*), W.B. Yeats at no. 82 and Daniel O'Connell at no. 58. The formal gardens at the centre of the square are particularly lovely, with an elegant maze of paths leading apparently at random to a clear grassy expanse at the centre.

National Gallery of Ireland K7

*Entrances on Merrion Square West and Clare St, **t** (01) 661 5133, **f** (01) 661 5372, www.nationalgallery.ie; **bus** 5, 7, 7A, 10, 44, 48A. **Open** Mon–Sat 9.30–5, Thurs until 8.30, Sun noon–5.30; **adm** free. Free guided tours Sat 3pm, Sun 2pm, 3pm, and 4pm. Free public lectures Sun 3pm, Tues 10.30am. Partial wheelchair access; tactile picture sets available from the information desk. Guided tours for visually and hearing impaired visitors may be booked by writing at least three weeks in advance. Café, restaurant, gift shop.*

The **National Gallery of Ireland** opened in 1864, in a spectacular building which featured ultra-modern top-lit galleries illuminated by over 2,000 gas burners. The original building, known as the Dargan Wing, was extended in 1903 to include the Milltown Wing), again in 1968 to take in the Beit Wing and most recently in 2002 into the Millennium Wing. Negotiating the museum's labyrinthine galleries is not easy, so arm yourself with a plan from the information desks, located at both the Merrion Square and Clare Street entrances.

As a general guide, Level 1 contains most of the Irish paintings, including the Yeats Museum, which is divided between the Milltown and Millennium Wings. This level also contains the British art collection in the

Beit Wing. On Level 2, you'll find the Spanish, Italian, German, Dutch, Flemish and French painting spread across the Milltown, Beit and Dargan Wings. On Level 2 in the Millennium Wing are galleries for temporary exhibitions. The café is on Level 1 of the Millennium Wing, with the restaurant and shop below it at entrance level.

Level 1

The **Irish art** collection spans three centuries, from the landscapes and portraiture of the 18th century to Jack B. Yeats' Expressionistic works of the mid-20th century. Rooms 14–19 contain some fine 18th-century portraiture and landscapes, including George Barret's *Powerscourt Waterfall* (c.1760) – in which the spectacular waterfall (*see* p.170) emerges from a dusky landscape drenched in golden light – and the superb double portrait *Bishop of Derry with His Granddaughter Lady Caroline Crichton* (c.1790). Probably the most famous piece here is Nathaniel Hone the Elder's *The Conjuror* (1775), a portrait of a grey-bearded magician conjuring up a painting from prints of Old Masters – clearly a pointed attack on Sir Joshua Reynolds, president of the Royal Academy in London, where the picture was first exhibited.

The emotionally charged influence of the Romantics is evident in Francis Danby's intense *The Opening of the Sixth Seal* (1828), which was a big hit with the public. Later Impressionistic and post-Impressionistic works include Roderick O'Conor's vivid *Farm at Lezaven* (1894) and Walter Osborne's dreamy *Apple Gathering, Quimperlé* (1895), both painted in Brittany, a popular retreat for Irish artists of the period.

Modern Irish art is held in Rooms 1–5 of the Millennium Wing, and begins with Paul Henry's haunting portraits and landscapes of the west of Ireland, which recall the works of the Catalan artist Isidre Nonell. William Orpen's vast canvas *The Holy Well* (1916) reveals his contempt for the popular romantic view of the bucolic west.

Back in the Dargan Wing, the **Yeats Museum** (Room 21) is devoted to the works of the remarkable family of poets, painters and artists. John Butler Yeats, father of William (the poet) and Jack (the painter), was a skilful portraitist himself, who unfortunately couldn't bring himself to charge his society friends for their portraits, putting his family in severe financial straits. Eventually, he went on holiday to New York and refused to return. His daughters founded the Irish Arts and Crafts movement, whose work is also displayed here, but the galleries are dominated by an extensive collection of paintings by Jack B. Yeats, who is considered one of the finest Irish painters of the 20th century. Notebooks, sketchbooks and other memorabilia are scattered though the rooms, which display works spanning his entire career. One of the earliest and best-loved is *The Liffey Swim* (1923), but it's the anguished later Expressionist works such as *Grief* (1951) that really stand out.

Next to the Yeats Museum is the **Shaw Room** (Room 22), named in honour of George Bernard Shaw who bequeathed one-third of his posthumous royalties to the National Gallery, which he called 'that cherished asylum of my childhood'. A life-sized bronze statue (1927) by Troubetzkoy of the author, arms folded, with a secret smile on his lips, stands guard over the room. There is a fine series of 17th- and 18th-century portraits of simpering aristocrats, and Daniel Maclise's vast *Marriage of Strongbow and Aoife* (1854) dominates an entire wall.

The highlights of the **British and American painting** collection (in the Beit Wing, Rooms 7–10) are 18th-century portraits by Hogarth, Gainsborough and Reynolds, among them Reynolds' sly depiction of *Charles Coote, 1st Earl of Bellamont* (1773–4). Standing jauntily in his glossy pink robes and velvet slippers, it's easy to see why he was known as a 'man ruled by vanity'.

Level 2

The first room of Level 2 (Room 25, Beit Wing) is devoted to **Art in Rome in the 18th Century**, highlighting the importance of Rome on the all-important Grand Tour which was the crowning glory in the education of any well-to-do young man of the period. Joshua Reynolds, later lampooned by Nathanial Hone (*see* p.77), does some satirizing of his own in the *Parody of the School of Athens* (1751), which pokes fun at the pretensions of the artists and travellers in Rome at the time. Look out, too, for Antonio **Canova's** delicate, pale marble sculpture, *Amorino* (1789).

In the succeeding galleries of the Beit Wing (Rooms 26–33) there are several sentimental pieces by the prolific Luca Giordano (nicknamed 'Luca fa presto' because he was such a fast worker) and some powerful Bolognese paintings, such as Ludovico Mazzolino's *The Coming of the Red Sea* (1521). Room 28 contains **Titian's** haunting *Supper at Emmaus* and **Tintoretto's** vivid *Portrait of a Venetian Senator* (1575–80). There are some beautiful Renaissance paintings in Room 29, among them **Filippo Lippi's** delicate *Portrait of a Musician* (late 1480s) and Perugina's sombre *Lamentation over the Dead Christ* (1495). The adjoining gallery contains one of the Gallery's earliest purchases and finest pieces, **Fra Angelico's** *Saints Cosmas and Damien their Brothers Surviving the Stake* (c.1440–42).

Room 31 is devoted to naturalistic and meticulous early paintings from **Germany and the Netherlands**, including Gerard David's *Christ Bidding Farewell to his Mother* (c.1510) and some sumptuous portraits of merchants dressed in their best finery. The **Spanish** collection in Room 32 boasts a couple of portraits by Goya and a languid, lazy allegory *El Sueño* (c.1800). Velázquez's remarkable *Kitchen Maid with Supper at Emmaus* is one of his very earliest known paintings, soft, intimate and revealing. El Greco's *St Francis Receiving Stigmata* is characteristically vivid and swirling.

Moving into the Milltown Wing, there are some fine Greek and Roman icons in Room 36. Among the **Flemish** paintings in Room 37 are Breughel the Younger's bawdy *At A Peasant Wedding* (1620), in which a drunk tries unsuccessfully to grope a fed-up guest, Van Dyck's sharp-faced *Boy Standing on a Terrace* (c.1623–4) and Rubens' *Christ in the House of Martha and Mary* (1628). One small gallery is devoted entirely to the fluffy Spanish Mannerist **Murillo**, and another to the striking Italian Tenebrist with a murky past, **Caravaggio**. Vermeer's exquisite *Woman Writing a Letter* and Rembrandt's *Rest on the Flight to Egypt* (1647) are among the later **Dutch** works in Room 40.

Rooms 45–48 in the Dargan Wing contain **French** art (with the earliest pieces in Room 48), including Nicolas Poussin's dark and moving *Lamentation over the Dead Christ* (c.1657–60). Later works include an earthy *Still Life* (1731) by Chardin and Gérard's masterful portrait of *Julie Bonaparte with her Two Daughters* (1808–9), painted during her brief reign as Queen of Spain. Among the Impressionist and post-Impressionist works are **Monet's** shimmering *River Scene* (1874), Signac's startling *Lady on the Terrace* (1898) and **Picasso's** dynamic *Still Life with a Mandolin*.

Natural History Museum K7

Merrion St, **t** *(01) 677 7444,* **f** *(01) 677 7450, www.museum.ie;* **bus** *7, 7A, 8.* **Open** *Tues–Sat 10–5, Sun 2–5;* **adm** *free. Free guided tours available, times vary. Gift shop.*

This is an endearingly old-fashioned museum, where virtually nothing has changed since Dr David Livingstone delivered the inaugural lecture in 1857. The Victorian devotion to stuffing and labelling reaches a climax in this lofty hall, where row upon row of wooden cabinets are crammed with all kinds of creatures which silently snarl and scamper in an alarmingly natural manner. At the entrance stands the skeleton of a gigantic Irish deer, extinct for 11,000 years, and a basking shark and the skeleton of an enormous whale float high above the main gallery. The cabinets are stuffed with all kinds of curiosities, from long-extinct creatures to iridescent butterflies and beetles, and from strange marine creatures such as the bulbous sunfish found off County Donegal to gruesome furry spiders.

Number Twenty-Nine K8

29 Fitzwilliam St Lower, t (01) 702 6165, f (01) 702 7796, www.esb.ie/education; all cross city buses. Open Tues–Sat 10–5, Sun 2–5; adm €3.50, students/seniors €1.50. Café, gift shop.

Fitzwilliam Street, which links Merrion Square with Fitzwilliam Square, contained the longest unbroken stretch of Georgian townhouses in the world until the 1960s. Then the Irish Electricity Board pulled down 26 of them and erected a brutally ugly office block in their place. Perhaps in an effort to make amends, they have restored a Georgian mansion at no. 29, and amiable retired EIB workers (like friendly Charlie) run regular tours of the house.

Unlike the aristocratic splendours of Newman House on St Stephen's Green, **Number Twenty-Nine**' recreates the life of an upper-middle-class merchant family around 1800. The tour begins with a short video, ostensibly narrated by the mistress of the house, which puts the exhibition in context. The basement contains the kitchen with its sturdy range and pre-electric version of the hostess trolley, a pantry where rocks of salt were kept and pulverized each day for table use and the housekeeper's spartan quarters. The ground floor is much grander, with fine stucco decoration on the ceilings and Waterford crystal chandeliers. These public apartments were designed to impress visitors, but the most opulent room in the house is the Salon on the first floor, with a Carrara marble fireplace, crystal chandeliers and delicate stucco. Behind it is the pretty boudoir, where the ladies would sit on what seems impossibly delicate furniture and sew or write letters. Next door is the bedroom, with a handsome four-poster bed in which the couple would sleep sitting up in the custom of the day, and an early mobile exercise gym which simulated riding on a horse. The adjoining dressing room contains ranks of identical shoes, which curiously were not formed for left and right feet. Upstairs is the children's bedroom, with antique toys including an extravagant doll's house and an early walking frame for babies. The governess lived in the adjoining room, where girls were taught while boys were sent away to school. It has a pretty stencilled floor and contains framed extracts from typical lessons of the period.

Fitzwilliam Square K8

All cross-city buses.

Fitzwilliam Square is a delightful little corner of Georgian Dublin, where the elegant houses are still largely residential – unlike the grander versions on St Stephen's Green and Merrion Square. Unfortunately, visitors can't linger to enjoy its quiet charm, as the gardens are for the square's residents only.

Oscar Wilde House K7

American College Dublin, 1 Merrion Sq, t (01) 662 0281; all cross-city buses. Open for guided tours only: Mon, Wed, Thurs 10.15am and 11.15am; obligatory donation €2.50.

1 Merrion Square was the childhood home of **Oscar Wilde** (1854–1900), the legendary writer and wit. His father was the surgeon and architect Sir William Wilde, and his mother a nationalist poet who wrote under the pen name Speranza and repeatedly attacked the British for their inaction during the Irish Famine. Her literary *salons* were the most famous and best attended in the city.

After major renovation by the American College Dublin, the house is now open for guided tours, which will take you around Dr Wilde's study and surgery and Speranza's drawing room and dining room.

Opposite the house, a statue of Oscar Wilde, looking disconcertingly like a leprechaun in a bright green jacket, sits on a boulder inscribed with some of his most famous quips – including the classic 'Only dull people sparkle at breakfast'.

FURTHER SOUTHEAST

St Stephen's Church L8

*Mount Street Crescent, off Upper Mount St, **t** (01) 288 0663; **bus** 5, 7, 8, 45. **Open** for services and concerts.*

This delightful little church, built in 1825, is nicknamed 'the peppercanister' for its whimsical cupola. Its situation, though, is less than delightful: it is continually circled by dense traffic and is a well-known cruising spot for prostitutes after dark. Inside, it is rather dull and overblown Victorian, but it does have a fine 18th-century organ. It's best viewed from Merrion Square, where it forms the perfect punctuation mark to the harmonious Georgian lines of Upper Mount Street. As a result of this picture-postcard aspect, the church is a seasoned movie performer, regularly showing up in historical dramas such as *Michael Collins*. It often hosts concerts as well (*see p.212*).

National Print Museum M8

*Garrison Chapel, Beggar's Bush Barracks, Haddington Rd, **t** (01) 660 3770; **bus** 5, 7, 8, 45; **DART** to Lansdowne Road. **Open** Mon–Fri 10–12.30 and 2–5; **adm** €3.50, students/seniors €1.50, family ticket €6.50. Café.*

Beggar's Bush was once one of the roughest neighbourhoods in Dublin, and these barracks were built by the British in the 1860 to try to keep the locals under control. The revolutionary Erskine Childers, who gained notoriety for smuggling guns to Ireland in 1914, was shot here in 1922, one of the very last executions before the barracks were handed over to the new Irish Free State in the same year. They have now been immaculately restored to house the engaging **National Print Museum**. The tour begins with an interesting video outlining some of the old skills and shows many of the museum's machines in operation. The exhibits illustrate the history of printing from Johann Gutenberg's invention of moveable type in 1455 to the present day; exhibits include some extravagantly ornate 19th-century presses and early computers. The upper gallery contains newspaper pages commemorating headline events in a range of typefaces and styles. There's also a unique ruling machine, which made lines on children's copy books and ledgers, and was usually operated by women who would sit and knit while it clanked away. There's a pleasant café for lunch, too.

Waterways Visitors Centre L7

*Grand Canal Quay, **t** (01) 677 7510, www.waterwaysireland.org; **bus** 2, 3; **DART** to Grand Canal Dock. **Open** June–Sept daily 9.30–5.30; Oct–May Wed–Sun 12.30–5; **adm** €2.50, seniors €1.90, children/students €1.20, family ticket €6.35. Wheelchair access to ground floor only.*

This elegant glass and concrete box seems to float above the canal, and is a tangible reminder of how much this once-seedy neighbourhood has been transformed by recent development. It contains an audio-visual display on the history of Dublin's waterways, including the network of canals which were developed in the 1700s and were widely used for trade and public transport until the railways took away most of the passenger business in the late 19th century. But the canals were still used for freight – particularly delicate cargoes such as bottles (the Guinness barges were once a common sight) – right up until 1960 when they were finally closed to commercial traffic.

The two main canals, the Grand to the south and the Royal to the north, were built in the 1760s; traditionally, it is said that true Dubliners are born somewhere between the two.

Southwest Dublin: Temple Bar and Old Dublin

TEMPLE BAR 84

DUBLIN CASTLE AND AROUND 85
Chester Beatty Library 87
City Hall 88
Wood Quay and Corporation Buildings 89

THE CATHEDRALS AND AROUND 89
Christchurch Cathedral 89
'Dublinia' 90
St Audoen's Church 90
St Werburgh's Church 91
St Patrick's Cathedral 91
Marsh's Library 94

THE LIBERTIES AND KILMAINHAM 94
Thomas Street 95
Guinness Storehouse/St James's Gate Brewery 95
Kilmainham Gaol 96
Irish Museum of Modern Art (IMMA) 97
War Memorial Gardens 97

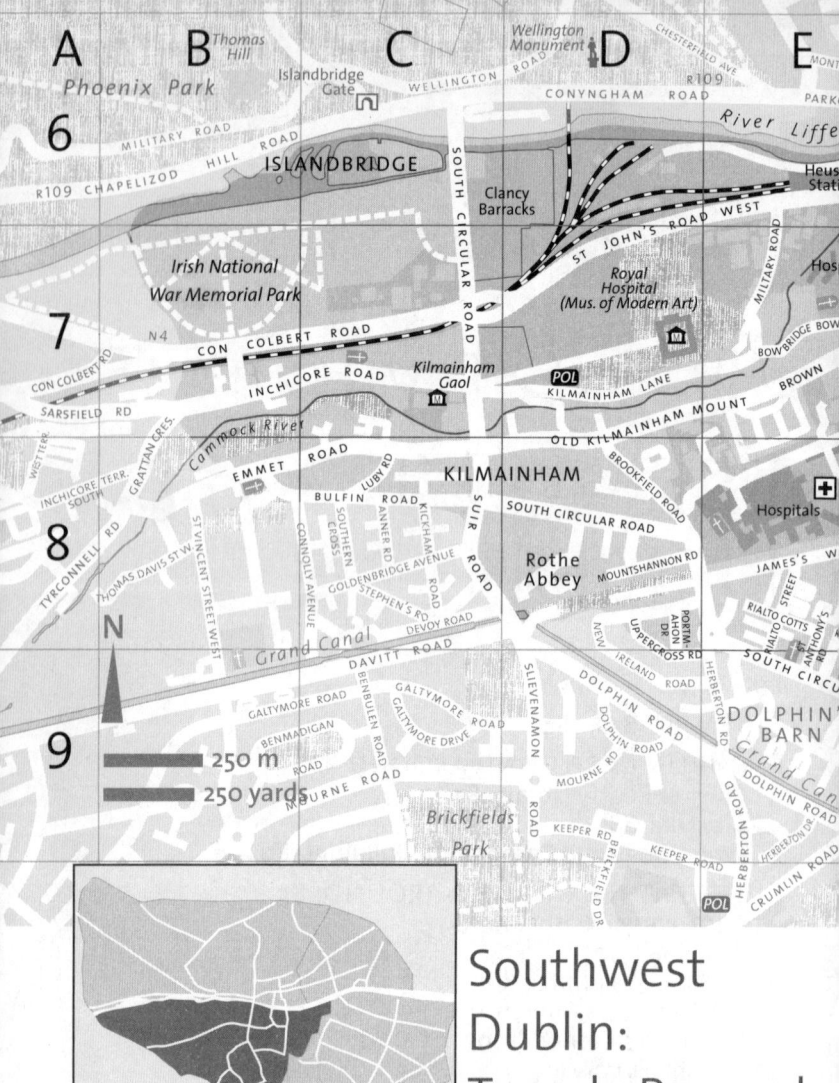

Southwest Dublin: Temple Bar and Old Dublin

Highlights

Georgian Dublin: See the beautifully restored City Hall, p.88

Indoor Dublin: Linger in old-fashioned pubs such as the Long Hall, p.206

Dubliner's Dublin: Tour Kilmainham Gaol, redolent of the struggles for Irish independence, p.96

Green Dublin: Explore the elegant, formal War Memorial Gardens, p.97

21st-Century Dublin: Take in a performance at the Project Arts Theatre, p.212

This is where Dublin began, with a small Viking settlement on the banks of the River Liffey. A crooked warren of narrow, medieval streets meanders around the dramatic cathedrals of Christchurch and St Patrick's, and up to the former fortress of Dublin Castle. The fortress became a palatial Georgian abode in the 18th century, and the magnificent Royal Exchange (now the City Hall) is a testament to the city's wealth and affluence at that time. Ships were unloaded

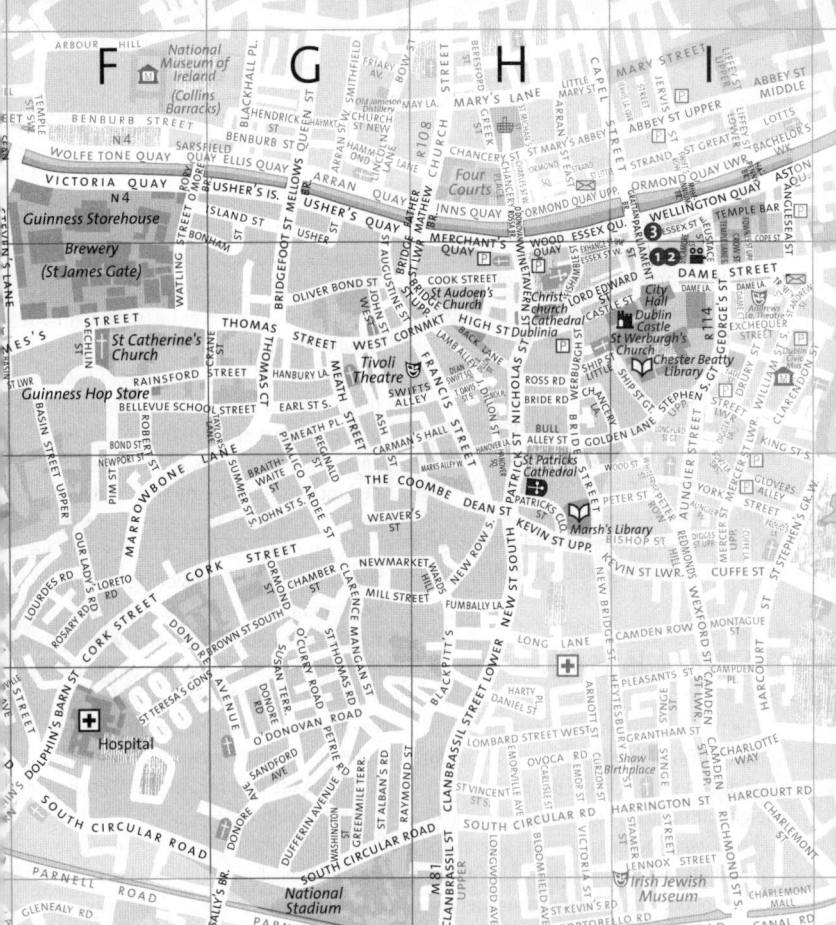

at the docks in nearby Temple Bar, a district which filled up with warehouses and taverns only to decline when the shipping trade was moved upriver. The area languished for years before being dramatically revamped in the 1990s. Now Temple Bar is Dublin's most popular entertainment district (at least with tourists), packed with bars, shops, restaurants and clubs. For Dubs, it has been too much of a good thing, and most look down their noses at this ersatz chunk of 'Oirland': few locals can be found among the vast Saturday night crowds.

The area west of the great cathedrals, known from the Middle Ages as 'The Liberties' because of its special privileges, belonged first to great landowners and was then settled by Huguenot weavers fleeing persecution from France. But when trade slumped, the area slumped with it, and

1 Lunch

Gruel, *68a Dame St,* **t** *(01) 670 7119.* **Open** *daily 8am–9.30pm.* A laid-back, arty little café on the fringes of Temple Bar with good daily specials and friendly staff.

2 Tea and cakes

Queen of Tarts, *Dame St,* **t** *(01) 670 7499, and also in City Hall.* **Open** *Mon–Fri 7.30–6, Sat 9–6, Sun 10–6.* Freshly baked tarts, quiches and cakes to go with delicious, freshly brewed coffee.

3 Drinks

Octagon Bar, *in Clarence Hotel, 6–8 Wellington Quay, Temple Bar,* **t** *(01) 670 9000.* **Open** *Mon–Sat 11–11, Sun 12.30–10.30.* Located in the luxurious celebrity haunt of the Clarence Hotel, this is one of the most glamorous – and expensive – bars in Dublin.

became a poverty-ridden slum. The tenements have been cleared, but the neighbourhood is still one of the poorest in the inner city despite recent efforts to entice new businesses here. One business, now more than three hundred years old, continues to do well: the famous St James's Gate brewery, home of Guinness, which contains a slick museum with a panoramic bar. Further west, another excellent museum, this one devoted to modern art, has opened in the elegant neoclassical Royal Kilmainham Hospital. Close by, Kilmainham Gaol, where the leaders of the Easter Rising in 1916 were shot, offers a stark glimpse into Ireland's turbulent political history.

TEMPLE BAR

The transformation of the **Temple Bar** district is Dublin's biggest success story. Just two decades ago, it was a dank and grimy neighbourhood of mouldering 17th- and 18th-century warehouses, where rats scampered in the ill-lit cobbled alleys. It had been slated for demolition since the 1960s in order to make way for a bus station. Now it has become a buzzing micro-village of galleries, arts centres, shops and bars, and its cobbled streets are continually humming with crowds of revellers.

When the Vikings arrived in Dublin, the area now known as Temple Bar didn't exist. As the river shrank, silted up with rubbish, the land was reclaimed and gradually became the centre of the city's trade. Temple Bar's luxurious Clarence Hotel (famously owned by the rock band U2) now stands on the site of Dublin's medieval Custom House, where all goods shipped into the city were weighed, measured and taxed. While trade flourished, warehouses, taverns, brothels and theatres sprang up.

However, when the new Custom House was built in 1791 on the North Quays (*see* p.111), Temple Bar's economic importance quickly vanished as the shipping trades were

Beyond the Bars

Temple Bar may be famous for boozing and debauchery, but there's plenty to do beyond the bars. You could catch some music at The Temple Bar Music Centre (see p.211), one of the best live music venues in the city, or a film at the Irish Film Centre (see p.213), both of which have good cafés. Try and catch a performance at the cutting-edge Project (see p.212) or the Olympia Theatre (see p.212), one of the oldest theatres in Dublin. Kids will enjoy the events at the The Ark (see p.224), a dedicated cultural centre and theatre for children. There are also some good festivals and cultural events to look out for, including the summer-long Diversions festival of performing arts (see p.228), and the Temple Bar Outside Visual Arts project, which exhibits new film and video work outdoors in Market Square (more information at *www.templebar.ie*). If you want to pick up some contemporary Irish art, check out ArtSelect, the Graphic Studio Gallery and the DESIGNyard (p.216).

moved downstream. The area became an inner-city slum, and stayed that way well into the 20th century.

The artists, musicians and film-makers who moved into Temple Bar in the 1970s and 1980s, attracted by the cheap rents, were the impetus behind the area's transformation. However, their relaxed bohemian style is now struggling amidst the new, commercialized Temple Bar.

And for Dubliners, the area has become a victim of its own success: few join the hordes of tourists who trawl the theme bars, overpriced restaurants and tacky souvenir shops at weekends. Matters improved slightly when stag and hen parties were banned, but Temple Bar is still the first, predictable stop for cheerful boozers from out of town in search of fun. Still, there is plenty to interest visitors looking for something besides a hangover, with a slew of galleries, unusual design shops and arts centres, and a great organic market held on Meeting House

Square and Cow's Lane on Saturday mornings (see p.218).

Temple Bar Gallery and Studios 16

5–9 Temple Bar, **t** *(01) 671 0073,* **f** *(01) 677 7527, www.templegallery.com;* **bus** *51B, 68, 69X, 79, 78A, 90, 150.* **Open** *Tues–Sat 11–6, Thurs until 7;* **adm** *free. Wheelchair accessible.*

This is a glittering, ultra-modern gallery which exhibits work by Irish and international artists – particularly emerging artists who aren't attached to commercial galleries. The complex also contains 30 artists' studios, and it's possible to see them at work if you make arrangements in advance.

National Photographic Archive 17

Meeting House Square, **t** *(01) 603 0200,* **f** *(01) 603 0371, www.nli.ie;* **bus** *51B, 68, 69X, 79, 78A, 90, 150.* **Open** *Mon–Fri 10–5, Sat 10–2;* **adm** *free. Bookshop.*

The National Library's huge collection of almost 300,000 photographs was moved to this gleaming new archive building in 1999. You need a library card to enter the reading rooms, but a small gallery area displays some of the collection in a series of temporary exhibitions (forthcoming events are listed on the website). The family portraits, landscapes and street scenes offer a fascinating glimpse of Ireland a century or more ago.

DUBLIN CASTLE AND AROUND

Dublin Castle 17

Dame St, **t** *(01) 677 7129,* **f** *(01) 679 7831, www.dublincastle.ie;* **bus** *77, 77A, 56A, 49, 123. State apartments* **open** *Mon–Sat 10–5, Sun and bank hols 2–5, closed during state visits,* *admission on guided tours only; **adm** €4.50, seniors/students €3.50, children under 12 €1.50. Café, craft shop.*

Gazing around the serene courtyards enclosed by harmonious Georgian apartments, it's hard to imagine the Anglo-Norman keep which once stood here. For seven centuries, **Dublin Castle** was home to English-appointed governors and viceroys, a symbol of foreign oppression until it was formally handed over to the Irish Free State in 1922.

In 1204, with the Irish battering at the city gates, King John commanded the construction of a 'strong fortress' which was erected on the area now covered by the Upper Yard. Part-prison, part-garrison and part-palace, it held a miniature town behind its impregnable walls, which were studded with the heads of traitors as a bloody warning to would-be rebels.

The fortress was unsuccessfully besieged time and time again, most famously holding out against the armies of 'Silken Thomas' Fitzgerald in 1534. Fitzgerald furiously renounced his oath of loyalty to Henry VIII of England, whom he believed – mistakenly – had executed his father, but his unsuccessful rebellion was to lead him only to the scaffold at Tyburn.

Over the years, a hotchpotch of buildings were tacked on to the original fort, but the castle remained fundamentally unchanged until the late 17th century, when it was ravaged by fire. Now virtually nothing remains of the original construction, apart from some sturdy walls at the base of the Record Tower and subterranean ruins under the Gun Powder Tower (visited as part of the tour) discovered recently in the Lower Yard. The castle complex was expanded and rebuilt in the early 18th century by the Surveyor General, Sir William Robinson, to designs which echo his Royal Hospital at Kilmainham, and it grew progressively grander and more splendid under the 18th- and 19th-century viceroys.

State Apartments

The Georgian **state apartments** were built mostly over the period 1700–1750, and contain some opulent decoration, including lavish stucco ceilings and Waterford crystal chandeliers. But the magnificence is muted by a strong whiff of the institutional, and the apartments' giddy days as the social centre of the Dublin Season are long gone, the grey uniforms of bureaucrats replacing the swish of silk and lace.

The tour begins at Battleaxe Landing, named for the axe-wielding guards who guarded the Throne Room, and hung with some fine Gobelins tapestries. The viceroy's former apartments have been divided up into smaller chambers and contain some uninspiring art (with the exception of a portrait by Van Dyck and Thomas Ryan's *Flight of the Earls*), but offer wonderful views of the manicured formal gardens.

The **Room of the Arts and Sciences** is named for the remarkable stucco ceiling, brought here from a drawing room in Tracton House on Merrion Square. The room contains a rather garish wooden table elaborately carved with figures – a prisoner made it as a gift for Queen Victoria in the hope that she would commute his sentence, but the tiny demons and short-skirted dancing girls offended rather than charmed her.

The **Queen's Bedroom** has lodged several famous visitors, from Nelson Mandela to Margaret Thatcher.

The **Drawing Room** was almost completely destroyed by fire in the 1940s and few furnishings are original: an important exception is the valuable Apollo Mirror, which a sheep-farmer in County Wexford had picked up for £5, painted black and used as a headboard for his bed.

The **Throne Room** still contains symbols of British rule – the lions and unicorns of England – as well as an extravagant chandelier made to commemorate the 1801 Act of Union; it manages to meld the rose of England with the thistle of Scotland and the

Irish shamrock. The exquisite 18th-century panels are by the Italian artist Gaetano Gandolfi.

Next comes the **Banquet Hall**, still used for grand state occasions. In the past, the viceroy would sit in the centre and secretly survey his guests with the specially constructed convex mirrors. There are endless dull portraits of the viceroys, many wearing the insignia of the Order of St Patrick, a knightly order established by George III.

St Patrick's Hall is the grandest chamber of these apartments, once the ballroom, and now used to inaugurate Irish presidents. What was once a musicians' balcony is now the press gallery.

The tour then heads outside to the **Lower Yard**, overlooked by the Record Tower, parts of which are 800 years old. Its sister tower was the Powder Tower, where the gunpowder was stored, of which only some stony ruins remain. They were discovered, along with the fragments of a wall from the ancient Viking settlement, in 1986. The **moat** which surrounded the original fortress was actually the diverted River Poddle, a tributary of the Liffey and now little more than a muddy, rather smelly, puddle.

Chester Beatty Library 17

Dublin Castle, t (01) 407 0750, f (01) 407 0760, www.cbl.ie; bus 54A, 50, 50A, 56A, 77, 77A, 77B. Open Mon–Fri 10–5, Sat 11–5, Sun 1–5; Oct–April closed Mon; adm free. Free public tours Wed 1pm, Sun 3pm & 4pm. Wheelchair accessible. Restaurant, gift shop, roof garden.

The **Chester Beatty Library**, at the back of Dublin Castle, contains a mesmerizing collection bequeathed to the state by the Irish-American mining magnate Sir Alfred Chester Beatty. Beatty, who was Ireland's first honorary citizen and lived in Dublin from 1950 until his death in 1968, spent over six decades gathering one of the finest private collections of Western and Oriental illuminated manuscripts and rare books in the world, as well as a breathtaking array of related objects including paintings, sculpture and engravings. They are now beautifully displayed in purpose-built galleries attached to the 18th-century Clock Tower building, deliberately low-lit to reduce damage to the precious objects they contain. The library won the European Museum of the Year award in 2002.

The first floor is devoted to Artistic Traditions, but the visit is best begun with the section on Spiritual Traditions on the second floor. Owing to the extent of the collection, only a tiny part is on view at any one time: the exhibits which illustrate each theme are rotated every six months or so, although the themes remain the same.

The rooftop garden, a quiet, contemplative, Japanese-style space, is the perfect place to ponder on all the treasures, and the Silk Road café downstairs (*see* p.143) is one of the best lunch spots in Dublin.

Second Floor: Spiritual Traditions

These exhibits explore the traditions of many of the world's religions, with a priceless collection of ancient texts and ritual objects. Short films and illuminating fact panels offer fascinating insights into aspects of many of the major religions. There are Buddhist *sutras* delicately written on palm leaves, exquisitely illuminated descriptions of the Hindu gods and a beautifully detailed cosmological painting depicting the Hindu concept of the universe. The ritual objects from Tibet include Buddhist prayer bells and a stupa representing the Buddha's final nirvana. From Japan come delicate scroll paintings with floating calligraphy, frightening statues of the protective deities and a serene bronze of Kannon, Bodhisattva of compassion. There is a magnificent collection of the central religious text of Islam, the Qur'an, including some exquisite early manuscripts dating back to the 13th century. The Qur'an does not explicitly prohibit the depiction of images, but a Hadith (a saying of the Prophet) condemns those who attempt to usurp God by creating images. As a result, these Qur'ans – and Islamic art in general – feature superbly intricate geometric and vegetal patterns, but never a human figure. Some of the oldest and most precious books in the collection are fragments of early copies of the Christian gospels, from around AD 250.

First Floor: Artistic Traditions

One of the most extraordinary exhibits on this floor is a 16th-century encyclopedia from China, produced when the emperor asked his experts for a book which would cover all the subjects under the sun. Their response ran to 11,000 volumes. Also from China is a rare and extensive collection of jade books, mostly from the late 18th century; ornate snuff bottles (Western traders imported the habit of taking snuff); rhino horn cups, which were said to make liquids bubble up if they contained poison; the gorgeous silk 'Dragon Robe', which was decorated with the Imperial symbol of a five-clawed dragon and worn by the Emperor; and a dazzling array of seals, scrolls and paintings. Among the Japanese collection is a handscroll which tells the story of a Chinese emperor whose obsessive love for a concubine caused him to neglect his lands, which then fell into civil war. There are vicious-looking samurai swords and armour and some elaborate picture books hand-painted by monks in the ancient capital of Nara. From Burma and Thailand are more illustrated folding books, including a quirky 19th-century one from Thailand which describes the characteristics of mythical and real elephants. There are books of spells and incantations from Sumatra used by priests and sorcerors, and Persian poetry books which shimmer with gold.

The European art collection includes a spectacular collection of engravings, with works by Goya, Rembrandt, Van Dyck, Piranesi and Delacroix, but the most important are Albrecht Dürer's woodcuts from the late 15th century, produced soon after the introduction of the printing press to Europe. Among the illustrated books are volumes illustrated by Turner and Blake, and a striking book of poetry presented to Beatty by its illustrator, Matisse.

City Hall 17

Cork Hill, Dame St, t (01) 672 2204, f (01) 672 2620, www.dublincity.ie/cityhall; bus 50, 50A, 54A, 56A, 77, 77A, 77B. Open Mon–Sat 10–5.15, Sun 2–5; adm to city hall free; adm to exhibition 'The Story of the Capital' €4, concessions €2, children €1.50. Wheelchair accessible. Audio-guides, café.

Dublin's **City Hall** began life as the Royal Exchange, built in 1769. It was designed by Thomas Cooley, who beat his better known rival James Gandon to win the commission. This was one of the first neoclassical buildings in Ireland, with a stately, column-lined portico and a magnificent gilded rotunda supported by 12 carved columns in the main hall. Its opulent interior reflects the unprecedented prosperity that Dublin was enjoying at the time – and delighting in displaying to the world. The rotunda, under which the merchants would transact their business, soars splendidly, glittering with golden mosaics and inset with stained glass. The stone-carving and stucco decoration are among the finest in the city. When hard times hit after the Act of Union in 1801 and Dublin became a political and financial backwater, the building fell into disuse. It was bought by the Corporation to be converted into the City Hall in the mid-19th century, when its magnificent space was divided up into boxy offices. A massive restoration project in 2000 returned it to its former glory, removing the fussy 19th-century additions and making the original gilt and marble sparkle anew. The ambulatory around the rotunda contains 18th- and 19th-century sculptures of some of Dublin's well known heroes, including 'The Great Liberator' Daniel O'Connell, who was also the first Catholic to hold the office of Lord Mayor.

The basement contains 'The Story of the

'Capital', a well-designed exhibition which gives a good potted history of the city. Cabinets contain a sparse collection of ancient documents and other treasures, put into context by plenty of interactive information points and short videos. Among the earliest documents is the charter granted by Henry II in 1171, in which English settlers in Dublin were give the same liberties and freedoms as the people of the city of Bristol. There's a curious 16th-century (or perhaps earlier) six-sided cabinet made to contain the City Seal, which could only be opened when all six key-holders were present, and you'll also see the ostentatious 17th-century Great Mace of Dublin which is still carried before the Lord Mayor on ceremonial occasions.

Wood Quay and Corporation Buildings H6

Wood Quay; **bus** *50, 78A.*

The first Viking settlement in Dublin was a trading-cum-pirate base established in AD 841, but almost nothing from this first *longphort* has been discovered. A larger, more permanent settlement which developed into a sizeable town was established in the early 10th century on what is now Wood Quay.

In the 1970s, work had begun on a new riverside HQ for the Dublin Corporation when the remains of this Viking town were unearthed. It was one of the biggest Viking-age discoveries in Europe and caused great local and international excitement. Dubliners wanted the remains to be preserved intact, but the Corporation decided to press ahead with their building scheme. Outraged citizens marched and lobbied, brought the Corporation to the courts and kept press interest at fever pitch with a series of high-profile marches and site invasions.

But to no avail: the excavations disappeared beneath the monolithic new corporation headquarters, better known as 'the Bunkers', and the valuable artefacts were transferred to the National Museum of Ireland.

THE CATHEDRALS AND AROUND
Christchurch Cathedral H7

Christchurch Place, **t** *(01) 677 8099,* **f** *(01) 679 8991, www.cccdub.ie;* **bus** *49, 50, 51B, 54A, 56A, 65, 77, 77A, 78A, 123.* **Open** *Mon–Fri 9.45–5, Sat–Sun 10–5;* **adm** *free. Guided tours available. Wheelchair accessible. Gift shop.*

The earliest church on this grassy hill near the Liffey was a wooden structure, erected in the early 11th century by the Norse king and Christian convert Sitric. After the Normans arrived, Richard de Clare, better known as '**Strongbow**', instigated the construction of a magnificent new cathedral as a symbol of the new order. All was well until 1871–8, when George Edmund Street restored the cathedral in the then-fashionable Gothic revival style – at such high cost that the distiller who provided the funds for the work went bankrupt. Street's energetic restoration was sometimes too thorough, and whole swathes of the cathedral, including the 14th-century Long Choir and the Chapel of St Mary, were demolished.

The narrow, early Gothic **nave** – which survived Street's interventions – is flanked by aisles. Midway along the south side is the **tomb** popularly believed to be that of Strongbow, who died in 1196; in fact it belongs to a 14th-century earl of Desmond. Strongbow's tomb was destroyed when the south wall, built on a bog, collapsed in the 16th century, but Dublin's landlords hastily found a replacement because they had historically collected their rents on it. There is a curiously truncated figure next to the knight on the tomb, which is said to be the last remains of Strongbow's son, sliced in two by his own father for cowardice on the battlefield.

The 14th-century **choir** with its carved oak stalls also survived Street's well-meaning onslaught, and the nearby **south transept** is one of the oldest sections of the cathedral (currently closed for restoration). From here, steps lead down to the 12th-century **crypt** and the exhibition 'Treasures of Christchurch' (*see* below).

Just off the south transept a small **chapel** contains a grisly relic, the embalmed heart of the 12th-century saint Lawrence O'Toole, one of few such relics to have survived the fires of the Reformation. The ambulatory contains another oddity: the mummified remains of a cat and rat frozen in mid-chase and discovered in the organ pipes.

At the eastern end of the church, the original 13th-century tiles of **St Laud's chapel** provided the inspiration for the tiles which now line the cathedral, including an intriguing one of two foxes – a common representation of the devil in religious imagery of the period – dressed as pilgrims.

Next to it, the **Lady Chapel** contains a beautiful contemporary bronze figure of *Virgin and Child* by Imogen Stuart. There are some original Romanesque capitals close to the north transept, which are now much faded and worn.

The **cathedral choir** is world renowned: it participated in the world's first performance of Handel's *Messiah*, and maintains its tradition of musical excellence to this day. Try to visit for Evensong, usually held at 3.30pm on Sundays and at 6pm on Wednesdays (Girls' Choir) and Thursdays (Full Choir).

Treasures of Christchurch

In the crypt. **Open** *Mon–Fri 9.45–5, Sat 10–4.45, Sun 12.30–3.15; last admission 30 minutes before closing;* **adm** *€3.*

The dank and musty crypt contains a small but glittering collection of ecclesiastical treasures. The most spectacular is the **Royal Plate**, which was presented to the cathedral by William of Orange and Mary after their victory at the Battle of Boyne in 1690. They appointed the cathedral the Chapel Royal, a tradition which continued until the Chapel Royal at Dublin Castle was opened in 1814.

You can also see a short film here recounting the cathedral's history.

'Dublinia' H7

St Michael's Hill, Christchurch, **t** *(01) 679 4611,* **f** *(01) 679 7116, www.dublinia.ie;* **bus** *50, 78A.* **Open** *April–Sept daily 10–5; Oct–March Mon–Sat 11–4, Sun and bank hols 10–4.30;* **adm** *€5.75, students/seniors €4.50, children aged 5–18 €4.25, family ticket €15. Wheelchair accessible. Gift shop. Tea room open June–Aug.*

Dublinia, an expensive, multimedia exhibition on medieval Dublin, is enjoyable (particularly for kids), if a tad tacky. It has lots of touchy-feely exhibits, recreations of medieval homes, the Dublin fair (with an early version of Viagra in the medicine tent) and the trades that prospered at the time. Fact panels give alarming details about the lives of everyday Dubliners in the Middle Ages, when average life expectancy was only 30 years – even before the arrival of the Black Death in 1348. Upstairs is a fascinating model of the city as it looked around 1500, and another section focuses on the excavations of the Viking settlement discovered by the Quays (and now hidden under the monolithic corporation buildings).

The **Synod Hall**, in which 'Dublinia' is housed, was built in 1873 and is a fine example of 19th-century Gothic revivalism, which reaches its height in the timbered Great Hall. From here, a delicate neo-Gothic bridge with pretty stained glass windows links it to Christchurch Cathedral.

St Audoen's Church H7

High Street, **t** *(01) 677 0088;* **bus** *123.* **Open** *May Sat–Sun 9.30–5.30; June–Sept daily 9.30–5.30 (last entry 4.45);* **adm** *€2, children/students €1, family €5.50. Partially wheelchair accessible. Gift shop.*

This winsome church was built in 1190 and dedicated to **St Ouen**, the 7th-century bishop of Rouen and patron saint of Normandy. The ruined Guild Chapel has been restored and contains a small but engaging **visitor's centre** which relates the history of the church. Inside are 17th-century memorials to the Sparke and Duff families, and a medieval tomb with effigies of the church's benefactors. But the most curious monument is the early Christian gravestone in the main porch, known as the **Lucky Stone**, which will bring good fortune to all who rub it.

Squeezed up against the medieval St Audoen's is a 19th-century Catholic church, dedicated to the same saint, where two huge clam shells are used as fonts for holy water at the entrance.

Behind the churches is a small park, unfortunately used by local druggies, which contains a stretch of the Norman walls and gate.

St Werburgh's Church H7

Werburgh St. **Open** *for services on Sunday mornings, usually 11am.*

This church is reputedly the oldest in the city and is named after Werburgh, the abbess of Ely, who died around AD 700. However, the original 12th-century church was destroyed and the current version dates from the mid-18th century.

The spire was removed in 1803 amid fears that someone would climb it to take a potshot at Dublin Castle, but the elegant Georgian interior, with oak panelling and galleries, fortunately avoided any 19th-century meddling because of its unfashionable location.

The church is rarely open, but you can slip in just before the Sunday morning service.

St Patrick's Cathedral H8

St Patrick's Close, **t** *(01) 475 4817,* **f** *(01) 454 6374, www.stpatrickscathedral.ie;* **bus** *49X, 50, 50X, 54A, 56A, 77X, 150.* **Open** *March–Oct daily 9–6; Nov–Feb Mon–Fri 9–6, Sat 9–5, Sun 10–3;* **adm** *€4, students/seniors €3, family €9. Wheelchair access can be arranged with one day's notice. Gift shop.*

According to legend, St Patrick baptized converts from a well on this spot, which was later marked by a small wooden church. It then became the site chosen for Dublin's second great cathedral, built – like Christchurch – by the Anglo-Normans, who had a tradition of erecting magnificent buildings as a way of imposing their dominance. The English-appointed archbishop John Comyn ordered its construction in the 12th century, unwilling to live with the monastic community at Christchurch and be subject to the laws of the City Provosts.

Unlike Christchurch, which lay within the city walls, St Patrick's – then outside the city walls – became a secular cathedral, with a religious and educational purpose. Comyn's building was consecrated on St Patrick's Day 1192, but Comyn's successor, Henri de Loundres, decided it wasn't sufficiently imposing and ordered a grander replacement worthier of an archbishop, which was completed in 1254; the hope clearly was that St Patrick's would replace Christchurch, but the authorities at the latter were understandably reluctant to give up their ancient privileges.

St Patrick's avenged itself with magnificence, becoming the largest medieval church in Ireland, almost 80 feet longer than its rival. And yet it seemed to be dogged by ill fortune: it was gutted by fires in the 14th century, lost its treasures and cathedral status when Henry VIII dissolved the monasteries in 1537 (although the wily dean managed to secure a handsome pension by organizing the surrender of all the cathedral's goods) and reached its lowest point when Cromwell's troops used the nave to stable their horses in 1649. It was **Jonathan Swift**, dean of St Patrick's from 1714, who was largely responsible for its restoration, haranguing his wealthy congregation from the pulpit – and yet, just a century later, much of the building stood in ruins.

Like Christchurch, the cathedral fell victim to enthusiastic Victorian philanthropists in the 19th century, but in this case the restoration was managed with relative sensitivity.

The **nave**, one of the best preserved sections of the cathedral, soars gracefully, light filtering in from the stained glass windows (none of which predates the 19th-century restoration). In the southern aisle, simple plaques embedded in the floor mark the graves of Swift and Stella, and their epitaphs (both written by Swift) can be found on the wall nearby. Stella's reads simply 'Mrs Esther Johnson better known to the world as Stella, under which she is celebrated in the writings of Dr Jonathan Swift, Dean of this cathedral.' Swift's own, translated from the original Latin, reads 'Here is laid the body of/ Jonathan Swift, Doctor of Divinity./ Dean of this Cathedral Church,/ Where fierce indignation can no longer/ Rend the heart./ Go, traveller, and imitate, if you can/ This earnest and dedicated champion of liberty.'

Their simple monument contrasts with the florid **Boyle Monument** at the western end of the church, which was erected by the earl of Cork in memory of his wife and is sculpted with the figures of himself and his family. Opposite, in the northern aisle, there's a statue of John McNeill Boyd, who died trying to save the crew of the *Neptune*, which went down in Dún Laoghaire harbour in 1861. Near it are a pair of carved stones, one with a Celtic cross which covered the ancient remains of St Patrick's well. The northern aisle is lined with tombs and monuments, including one to Turlough Carolan (1670–1738), one of the last wandering musicians in Ireland. He was blinded as a result of smallpox and became one of Ireland's finest composers, harpists and poets.

Leaning against a column close by is the old chapterhouse door, known as the **Door of Reconciliation** after a legend which recounts a moment of peace in the bitter feud between the earls of Ormond and Kildare. Ormond had fled into the church's chapterhouse, refusing to emerge. The earl of Kildare promised a reconciliation, and a hole was cut in the door through which the two leaders were to shake hands. But Ormond feared his arm would be cut off, and it was Kildare who first bravely put his hand through the gap, giving rise to the expression 'chancing your arm'. But the truce was shortlived, and the chronicler Holinshed makes the dry remark that 'all their quarrels for that present rather discontinued than ended'.

The **northern transept** was used as the parish church of St Nicholas Without (meaning outside the city walls) for almost five centuries, almost completely cut off from the rest of the cathedral. Restored and returned to the cathedral during the 19th century, it is lined with memorials to the soldiers who fell in the wars of the last two centuries, and hung with the tragic, tattered regimental colours that accompanied the Irish soldiers into battle. The large **Iveagh Window** which overlooks this part of the church was erected in memory of Lord Iveagh by his children in 1935.

The medieval **choir** also did service as the chapel of the Knights of St Patrick, a chivalric order established by George III in 1783. Each knight was allotted his own stall in the choir, each of which is still carved with their helmet, sword and crest. The Prince of Wales, later Edward VII, was the last to be invested as a knight here. The Duke of Schomberg (1615–90), who fell at the Battle of the Boyne, is buried in the north choir aisle. The south choir aisle contains 16th- and 17th-century brass plaques, a rarity in Dublin, where they were usually melted down for ammunition.

The **Lady Chapel**, at the eastern end of the cathedral, functioned – like St Nicholas Without – almost as a separate church. The chapel was given to the Huguenot refugees fleeing persecution in France as a place of worship, and was used by them from the late 17th to the late 18th centuries. But by 1840 it stood in ruins. The Guinness restoration rebuilt it and returned it to the main cathedral.

The **church choir**, established in 1432, is justly famous, and, along with Christchurch's choir, participated in the first performance of Handel's *Messiah*. The choir perform

Jonathan Swift (1667–1745)

Jonathan Swift's father died before he was born, leaving his mother almost penniless. Swift was raised by his uncles, and educated at Kilkenny School and Trinity, where he was reputed to be a troublesome and badly disciplined student. He moved to England in 1689, and became secretary to Sir William Temple, whose wife was related to Swift's mother. He chafed at his lowly status in the house, but it was here that he met Esther Johnson, the housekeeper's daughter, better known to his readers as **Stella**. The nature of their relationship is still mysterious, although some say that the pair were secretly married, but her importance to Swift is testified by his decision to be buried next to her in St Patrick's Cathedral.

Swift tried to enter politics, becoming editor of the Tory magazine *The Examiner*, but his vitriolic pen got him into trouble; when the Whigs came to power in 1714, he was forced to abandon his political ambitions. He had been ordained in 1695, hoping for a 'a fat deanery or a lean bishopric', but the outrage caused by his religious satire *A Tale of a Tub* dashed any hopes of ecclesiastical preferment in England. He was forced to return to Ireland and the deanery of St Patrick's, which he had been offered in 1713. It felt like banishment, and he wrote moodily 'no man is thoroughly miserable unless he be condemned to live in Ireland'.

Despite this, he continued to champion the Irish in his political pamphlets, advocating economic independence in his *Proposal for the Universal Use of Irish Manufactures* in which he said the Irish should burn all English goods except coal, and denouncing the British government's attitude to Ireland in the series of *Drapier's Letters* (1724). Wealthy Dubliners also came under attack, particularly in *A Modest Proposal* (1729), in which he suggested – with the straightest of faces – that the poor earn money by raising babies to be eaten by the rich. He is probably most famous for *Gulliver's Travels* (1726), one of his most complex satires, which is nonetheless still viewed mainly as a children's book.

Swift had brought Stella to Ireland in 1701, where she died in 1728. He was heartbroken, and finished *Journal To Stella* in the darkened cathedral in the nights following her funeral. Stella was not the only woman whose name was linked to Swift's in society gossip. He had become infatuated with Esther Vanhomrigh, whom he called 'Vanessa', and invited to Dublin in 1714. When Stella discovered this attachment, Swift broke off his relations (whatever they were), and Esther died in 1723 of tuberculosis – or a broken heart depending on which version you believe. Swift himself lived on until 1745, sinking into dementia, perhaps Menière's disease, in his last years. His epitaph is on the cathedral walls. Originally in Latin, it was given a poetic translation by Yeats:

> Swift has sailed into his rest;
> Savage indignation there
> Cannot lacerate his breast.
> Imitate him if you dare,
> World-besotted traveller; he
> Served human liberty.

Evensong at 5.45pm on weekdays and at 3.15pm on Sundays, as well as a traditional carol service on Christmas Eve.

Outside, the broad, grassy lawn of **St Patrick's Park** replaced the miserable tenements and slums which had grown up in the shadow of the cathedral. There are plaques to some of Dublin's famous writers, Vivienne Roche's vast *Liberty Bell* (1988) and a small marker showing the site where St Patrick's Well was located. Along Patrick Street, more slums were replaced by the graceful Arts and Crafts-style Iveagh Buildings (1894), erected by the philanthropic Guinness family, who also commissioned the equally charming Iveagh Baths (1904), located just around the corner on Bride Street.

Marsh's Library H8

*St Patrick's Close, **t** (01) 454 3511, **f** (01) 454 3511, www.marshlibrary.ie; **bus** 50, 54A, 56A. **Open** Mon 10–1, Wed–Fri 10–1 & 2–5, Sat 10.30–1; **adm** €2.50, students/seniors €1.50, children free.*

You almost expect to see Archbishop Narcissus Marsh himself appear in this tranquil library which has survived almost unchanged since the 18th century. Nothing disturbs the peace besides a ticking clock and birdsong drifting in from the gardens. Built in 1701, this was Dublin's first public library, open to 'all graduates and gentlemen', and established by Marsh to dispel the dismal ignorance he found in the Trinity scholars under his charge. The two L-shaped rooms are lined with handsome oak bookshelves, with elaborately curved and lettered gables in green and gold. Jonathan Swift, an early protégé of the Archbishop, became a governor of the library while Dean of St Patrick's; his copy of Clarendon's *History of the Rebellion*, now in the library's collection, is annotated with insulting comments about the Scots and their role in the rebellion. He wasn't much kinder to Marsh, of whom he wrote, 'He is the first of human race, that with great advantages of learning, piety and station, ever escaped being a man'. A case of memorabilia relating to Swift stands opposite the bizarre 'cages' at the furthest corner of the library, where scholars were locked in with the most valuable books and manuscripts. The Swift Case contains his books, his death mask and a photograph of the woman he loved, Esther Johnson, better known as Stella. Rather gruesomely, a cast of her skull is set in one of the cages opposite.

THE LIBERTIES AND KILMAINHAM

In the Middle Ages, the archbishop of Dublin, the abbot of St Thomas' and the abbot of St Mary's acquired the right to try laymen, levy fines and hang criminals on their own gallows. These private '**liberties**' gave their name to the district which spreads west of St Patrick's Cathedral, one of the earthiest and least gentrified neighbourhoods of central Dublin. Huguenot weavers, fleeing France in the late 17th century, settled here, following which the Liberties enjoyed a few brief decades of prosperity. But the introduction of heavy duties on Irish exports to England and the popularity of foreign fabrics drastically undermined their trade. Faced with ruin, bands of unemployed weavers took to accosting ladies of fashion in their street, slashing their dresses of Indian muslin and French silk, and tarring and feathering the tailors who supplied these foreign-made clothes. The Liberties rapidly became a slum, families crammed into stinking tenements and beggars crowding the streets. The slums have long since gone, yet the Liberties remains one of the poorest inner-city districts, its close-knit community still dogged by drug and housing problems. But things are looking up: the arrival of the Massachusetts Institute of Technology's prestigious multimedia research laboratory (www.medialabeurope.org) and the Irish government-sponsored Digital Hub project (www.digitalhub.com) are spearheading the area's development as a centre for digital media and new technologies.

The Liberties G7

Bus 50, 54A, 56A.

There are few reminders of the old Liberties in these streets, but the area hasn't lost its rough-and-ready community atmosphere. The best place to drink it all in is the **Meath Street market**, where the usual ranks of cheap imported tat are sometimes supplemented by a few renegade traders wheeling their wares around in battered prams. **The Coombe** is one of the original thoroughfares of the medieval neighbourhood, and the site of the long-demolished Weaver's Guildhall. The flamboyant gateway from the old Coombe maternity hospital survives, with an odd monument etched with the names of some the Liberties' famous characters. A wealthy widow founded the maternity hospital in 1826, moved by the story of a young woman who died in childbirth on the street on her way to the Rotunda on the other side of the city. **Francis Street** is a little fancier, if still dishevelled, and is the centre of the city's antique trade (the Gallic Kitchen, *see p.195*, is a great lunch-stop). The neoclassical **church of St Nicholas of Myra** on this street was built in the 1830s to celebrate Catholic emancipation, and nearby is the **Iveagh Market**, carved with grinning faces, one of which was said to be modelled on Lord Iveagh himself.

Thomas Street G7

Bus 51B, 78A, 123, 206.

The pungent odour of roasting hops hangs over **Thomas Street**, which leads to the huge Guinness brewery. The ostentatious **Church of Saints Augustine and St John** is one of the gaudiest of the Gothic revival-style churches which sprang up in the late 19th century, its façade a dizzying whirl of granite and red sandstone. The spire (at 30 metres) is said to be the tallest in the city – not a great feat, considering that most of the city's churches ran out of money before they got to building the spires. A small plaque nearby commemorates the capture of Sir Edward Fitzgerald, son of the Earl of Leinster (*see p.71*) and one of the leaders of the Irish Rebellion, who had fled from Leinster House and holed up in the home of a feather-dealer on this street. When the officers of the yeomanry came to arrest him, a fight broke out and Fitzgerald stabbed one to death and wounded the other. But he was shot during the scuffle, and died of his wounds two weeks later in Newgate Prison.

Another rebel came to a sorry end near the elegant Georgian **church of St Catherine**, further down on the southern side of Thomas Street. Robert Emmet was the leader of the short-lived 1803 rebellion, and was hanged and decapitated outside St Catherine's Church on 20 September 1803, aged just 25. His moving speech from the dock ensured him a place in the pantheon of Irish heroes: 'When my nation takes her place among the nations of the earth, then, and not till then, let my epitaph be written'.

Beyond the vast St James's Gate Brewery is **St Patrick's Hospital**, an institution for the treatment of mental illness, which was begun with funds bequeathed by Jonathan Swift – who couldn't resist quipping: 'He gave the little wealth he had,/ To build a house for fools and mad,/ And showed by one satiric touch,/ No nation wanted it so much'.

Guinness Storehouse/ St James's Gate Brewery F6

St James's Gate, **t** *(01) 408 4800,* **f** *(01) 408 4965, www.guinness-storehouse.com;* **bus** *51B, 78A, 123.* **Open** *daily 9.30–5;* **adm** *€13.50, students under 18/seniors €6.50, students over 18 €9, family ticket €28. Wheelchair accessible. Bars, restaurant, shop.*

This is Dublin's biggest attraction, a slick, state-of-the-art operation which rewards the visitor with a complimentary pint of 'the black stuff' in its panoramic Sky Bar. **Guinness** is one of the most profitable businesses in Irish history; its story began in 1759, when Sir Arthur Guinness bought the small Rainford brewery, one of fifty or so in the

> ### The Best Pint of Guinness?
>
> The free pint offered in the Sky Bar at the Guinness Storehouse is often lauded as the best Guinness you'll ever taste. The bar even adjoins a special training section on how to keep and serve Guinness for bartenders from around the world. For quality, the Sky Bar's main rival is Mulligan's on Poolbeg St (see p.204), traditionally regarded as the home of the best pint in town. But, after extensive research, our vote for the best pint of Guinness in Dublin goes to the Bleeding Heart tavern in Howth (see p.134).

area, and began producing 'porter', a beer named for its popularity among the market porters in London. Sir Arthur began a tradition of philanthropism which his descendants were to continue, paying his workers considerably more than the average wage and ensuring they had adequate medical care.

On a visit, the story of how the famous black brew is made is recounted over several floors stuffed with high-tech gimmicks, which manage to explode a few myths along the way. The waters of the Liffey, contrary to legend, have never been used in Guinness; instead it is made with water from the River Dodder, which is fed by springs from St James's Well, 25 miles from Dublin. There are some interesting short films, including a particularly fascinating one showing coopers at work, and an amusing look at the Guinness adverts over the years, from the Toucan to the bizarre Guinness dance which sparked a whole craze (although the actor involved subsequently found himself at the centre of a legal dispute with a dancer who claimed he had stolen the famous moves). The Sky Bar, where you get your free pint complete with shamrock expertly carved into the foam, boasts spectacular 360° views of the whole city.

Kilmainham Gaol C7

Inchicore Road, Kilmainham, t (01) 453 5984, f (01) 453 2037, www.heritageireland.ie; **bus** *51B, 78A, 79.* **Open** *for guided tours only: April–Sept daily 9.30–5; Oct–March Mon–Sat 9.30–4, Sun 10–5;* **adm** *€5, seniors €3.50, children/students €2, family ticket €11. Wheelchair accessible. Café, shop.*

Kilmainham Gaol – long abandoned, now restored as a museum of Irish political history – has hosted a veritable who's who of Irish heroes, from the United Irishmen of 1798 to the leaders of the 1916 Easter Rising.

The prison was opened in 1796 as a replacement for the squalid, overcrowded city gaols, in accordance with Enlightenment ideals. Its first prisoners were the casualties of the failed 1798 rising of the United Free Irishmen led by Wolfe Tone. One of the leaders of the rebellion, Thomas Addis Emmet, was visited here before his execution by his idealistic young brother. Robert Emmet was also imprisoned here after another unsuccessful uprising in 1803 before being led to the scaffold on Thomas Street. Yet more political prisoners poured in after the failure of the rebellion of the Young Irelanders in 1848, but, by that time, the prison was bursting with victims of the Great Famine (1845–9). The convicts' rations were meagre, but at least they weren't starving to death.

By the 1860s, Kilmainham was officially a gaol for political prisoners. In 1879, when the corn crop failed and famine threatened, Michael Davitt formed the Land League of Ireland and was joined by the charismatic politician Charles Stewart Parnell. Parnell was arrested and brought to Kilmainham in 1881, but released in 1882 under the Kilmainham Treaty. The next batch of high-profile prisoners were the leaders of the Easter Rising, who were court-martialled and shot here in 1916. More Republicans were shot during the War of Independence, and one of its last inmates was Eamon De Valera, the future president, who was imprisoned during the Irish Civil War.

The gaol is now a grim memorial to the Irish rebel leaders, the walls etched with graffiti, a chilly wind echoing through the dank chambers. The guided tour begins at the **west wing** (which famously featured in the film *In The Name of the Father*) and continues past the dank cells. Each was supposed to contain a single inmate, yet during the Famine more than 9000 prisoners (including children) were squeezed into 200 cells. The leaders of the Easter Rising were incarcerated in cells leading off a single hall known as the 1916 Corridor. Countess de Markievicz was held here under sentence of death, which was commuted on the grounds of her sex: the countess famously responded, 'I do wish your lot would have the decency to shoot me'. Parnell's former cell, in contrast, is surprisingly light and spacious. The guards would joke that he was given so much freedom that he probably had the key to the front door. Opposite is the cell of Robert Emmet, who was hanged and beheaded at the age of 25. The bodies of such prisoners were buried underneath the flagstones of the exercise courtyards, their decomposition aided by quicklime, although the leaders of the Easter Rising were executed instead in the Stonebreaker's Yard.

A small museum on site contains some horrible mementoes of the jail's bloody history, including the chopping block used to behead Robert Emmet. There's also a calling card belonging to 'William Marwood, Executioner', which he would send to the press after executions.

Irish Museum of Modern Art (IMMA) D7

Royal Hospital, Military Road, Kilmainham, t (01) 612 9900, f (01) 612 9999, www.modernart.ie; bus 26, 51, 79, 90, 123, 51B, 78A, or train to Heuston Station then 5-min walk. Open Tues–Sat 10–5.30, Sun and bank hols noon–5.30; adm free. Wheelchair accessible. Café, bookshop.

The **Royal Hospital** was founded in 1684 as a retirement home for old and wounded soldiers, who, in the style of the Chelsea Pensioners in London, were given a uniform of a 'scarlet coat, and Athlone hat laced with gold lace, and a pair of blue worsted stockings'. It was Ireland's first major classical public building, designed by William Robinson (who was also responsible for Dublin Castle's new look in the early 1700s, and for Marsh's Library) and modelled on the Hôtel des Invalides in Paris. The last soldiers left the Hospital in 1928, which was neglected for 50 years before being extensively restored and re-opened as Ireland's premier gallery for modern and contemporary art. Some elements of the Hospital survive, including the dazzling **Baroque Chapel** (1686), with a delicate floral ceiling, and some fine 19th-century stained glass. Almost nothing has changed in the **Great Hall**, which is still lined with the same royal portraits that were hung here in the early 18th century. Outside, the elegant formal **gardens** have been restored to their manicured Georgian splendour.

The bright and sleekly modern galleries are handsomely arranged around the central courtyard. There is no permanent display, but you can expect to find the works of some of Ireland's most acclaimed modern and contemporary artists on show, including Jack B. Yeats, Louis Le Brocquy, Ciarán Lennon, Sean Scully, Caroline McCarthy and Richard Deacon. The collection also contains works by international artists including Picasso, Bridget Riley, Antoni Tàpies, Gilbert and George, Gillian Wearing and Gary Hume. The **Response Room**, well-stocked with paper and paint, gives children a chance to paint their own answer to the art they have seen. In 2000 the Deputy Master's House was converted to house the **New Galleries**, which feature work from special collections (either the Museum's own or from elsewhere). There's an excellent café where you can linger over the art books and enjoy the garden views.

War Memorial Gardens B7

Island Bridge, off the South Circular Road; bus 51, 61. Open Mon–Fri 8am–dusk, Sat–Sun 10am–dusk; adm free.

These exquisite, sombre and very formal gardens were designed by Edwin Lutyens in 1921 as a memorial to the 49,000 Irish soldiers who died in the First World War. Yet they were not completed or officially opened until 1994: the sacrifice of these men in the service of the British Army sat uneasily with the Irish public and post-independence Irish governments. For years, the great heroes of Irish history in the early 20th century were the martyrs of the Easter Rising, who opposed Irish participation in British wars; those who died on the battlefields of northern France were forgotten. The gardens are now a quiet and reflective space, with graceful terraces, pavilions and rose gardens surrounding a central park where the names of the fallen are inscribed.

Northeast Dublin: Around O'Connell Street

O'CONNELL STREET 102
General Post Office 103
Abbey Theatre 103
Hot Press Irish Music Hall of Fame 104
St Mary's Pro Cathedral 104

PARNELL SQUARE AND AROUND 105
Rotunda Hospital 105
Gate Theatre 105
Hugh Lane Gallery and Francis Bacon's Studio 106
Dublin Writers Museum 107
James Joyce Centre 108
St Francis Xavier 110
Mountjoy Square 110
National Wax Museum 110

THE QUAYS NORTH OF THE LIFFEY 111
International Financial Services Centre (IFSC) 111
Custom House and Visitor Centre 111
Ha'Penny Bridge 112
Millennium Bridge and Boardwalk 112
Grattan Bridge 112

Northeast Dublin: Around O'Connell Street

The north side of the Liffey was where the first great Georgian squares and mansions were built in the early 1700s, enjoying a brief period of glory. Once the exodus began to the newly fashionable neighbourhoods south of the river, however, the northside streets were left to moulder, the once-spectacular mansions stripped of their ornate ceilings and marble fireplaces, and the spacious rooms chopped into tiny flats and sold as tenements. After James Joyce's father had squandered his wealth, the final nail in the coffin of the family's fortunes was to have to move to the shabby neighbourhoods north of the river.

But these days things are finally looking up, and many of the Georgian townhouses are being restored, partly thanks to the efforts of the Irish Georgian Society. One of the finest is now the James Joyce Centre, dedicated to the writer's life and works. Another elegant mansion contains the Dublin Writers Museum, which celebrates the city's literary heritage. Next door, the Hugh Lane Gallery is one of the best municipal art galleries in Europe, with a fine collection of Impressionist paintings and the perfectly preserved studio of Francis Bacon. Even O'Connell Street, which has fallen a

Northeast Dublin: Around O'Connell Street 101

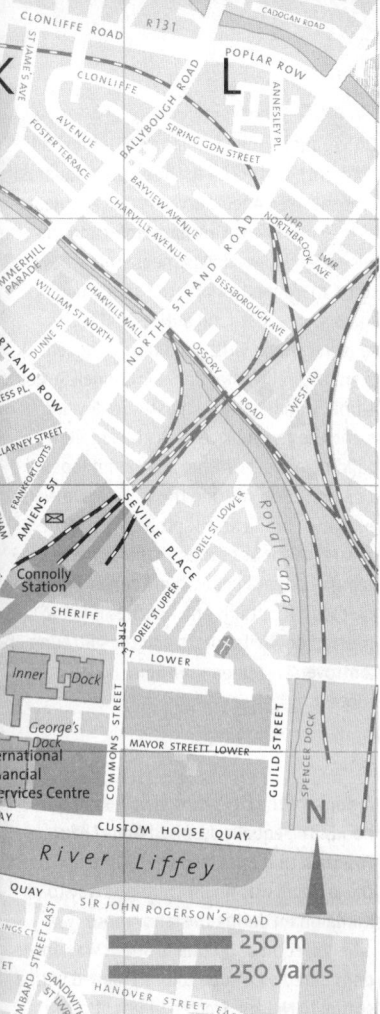

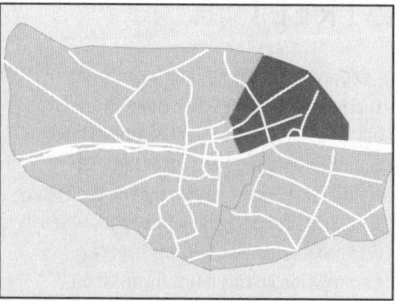

Highlights

Georgian Dublin: Admire the stucco ceilings in the Dublin Writers Museum, p.107
Indoor Dublin: Listen to the Palestrina choir at St Mary's Pro-Cathedral, p.104
Dubliner's Dublin: Explore the scruffy, traditional Moore Street Market, p.103
Green Dublin: Visit the tiny Garden of Remembrance, p.105
21st-Century Dublin: Stroll along Dublin's brand new boardwalk, p.112

1 Lunch

Epicurean Food Hall, *Liffey St Lower.* **Open Mon–Wed 9–7.30, Thurs–Fri 9–8.30, Sat 9–6.30, Sun noon–6.** You'll be spoilt for choice here: choose anything from Thai noodles to Irish seafood at one of the countless indoor stalls.

2 Tea and cakes

The Winding Stair, *40 Lower Ormond Quay,* **t** *(01) 873 3292.* **Open Mon–Sat 9.30–6, Sun 1–6.** This charming bookshop café offers good snacks to go with the bird's-eye views over the Liffey.

3 Drinks

Flowing Tide, *9 Lower Abbey St,* **t** *(01) 874 0842.* **Open Mon–Wed 10.30am–11.30pm, Thurs–Sat 10.30am–12.30am, Sun 12.30–11.** A classic old pub, popular with actors and theatrical types, which is conveniently located opposite the legendary Abbey Theatre.

long way from its heyday as the most elegant thoroughfare in Dublin, is having a facelift, although the towering Millennium Spire – the centrepiece of the renovations – is generally despised. This area is still redolent of the 1916 Easter Rising: bullet holes still mark the statues along O'Connell Street and the pillars of the General Post Office. And nationalism of a different kind is expressed in the famous Abbey Theatre, founded by Lady Gregory and W.B. Yeats as a showcase for Irish drama.

Along the river, the charming, wrought-iron Ha'Penny Bridge has become a symbol of the city, and is now joined by a slim, silvery new pedestrian bridge and a delightful boardwalk suspended above the water.

O'CONNELL STREET

O'Connell Street has had a confusing succession of names over the centuries: it began as Drogheda Street, was renamed Gardiner's Mall – when Luke Gardiner created an elegant square here in the 1740s – and rechristened again in the 1790s when it was broadened by the Wide Streets Commission. In this latest incarnation, Sackville Street (named for the viceroy of the time) became the most fashionable and important thoroughfare in Dublin. It was retitled O'Connell Street – after the 'Great Liberator', 19th-century activist Daniel O'Connell – when Irish independence was won in 1922. Much of the street was blasted to smithereens during the Easter Rising of 1916, which started here in the **General Post Office**, but by then fashionable Dublin had long since fled south to the elegant squares over the river. A few survivors of its opulent past – such as the **Gresham Hotel** and the once-grand **Clery** department store – now stand marooned among the anonymous chain stores, fast-food outlets and tacky souvenir shops. Gritty and traffic-choked, even by Dublin's standards, O'Connell Street is finally undergoing a massive redevelopment, the centrepiece of the Millennium building projects. At the moment it looks like a construction site and the works have worsened the chronic traffic problems, but the ugly renovations of the 1970s and 1980s are being undone, a pedestrian-friendly leafy park with fountains and benches is being inserted down its length and the glittering, if controversial, **Millennium Spire** now looms above it.

O'Connell Street Monuments and Statues

O'Connell Street is packed with statues of Dublin's famous politicians, activists and writers. On O'Connell Street Lower, there's a vigorous bronze of the trade unionist **Jim Larkin**, one of the leaders of the General Strike in 1913. To escape arrest, he was disguised as a priest and smuggled into the Imperial Hotel, which used to share premises with Clery's department store. He famously exhorted the workers from a hotel balcony; the police baton-charged the crowd below, injuring more than 400 people.

The most spectacular and controversial monument is the 130-metre-tall **Millennium Spire**, which missed the celebrations in 2000 and was only completed in 2003 after fighting off a court injunction. Dublin wags – continuing a tradition of attaching rhyming nicknames to city landmarks – instantly dubbed it 'the stiletto in the ghetto'. It is viewed with bemusement or downright contempt by most Dubliners: many say that its needle-like appearance is unconsciously apt, considering the heroin problems still rife in some of the city's run-down neighbourhoods. The equally despised **Anna Livia Fountain** that once stood here ('the floozie in the jacuzzi') was finally shuffled away to Kilmainham during the renovations.

This section of O'Connell Street was once dominated by a huge column topped with a statue to **Nelson**. Erected in 1815, it came under relentless attack as a symbol of British dominance. The IRA finally toppled it in 1966 – the 50th anniversary of the Easter Rising – and the battered remnants of Nelson's head now sit in the Dublin Civic Museum (see p.67).

Even a statue of **James Joyce**, looking dapper with a cane, on the corner of O'Connell Street and Earl Street North, hasn't escaped the locals' penchant for rude rhymes: he is known as 'the prick with the stick'.

Also on this street is a statue of **Matt Talbot**, the 19th-century temperance preacher (see p.110). This is the second version: the first was destroyed by the sculptor's model, who had been dismissed – with poignant irony – for drunkenness.

O'Connell Street

O'Connell Bridge J6

Carlisle Bridge was designed by James Gandon, architect of the Custom House (see p.111), and built in 1790 in order to connect O'Connell Street (then known as Gardiner's Mall) with Trinity College and Parliament Street with the south. It was broadened in 1890 and is now as wide as it is long. Overlooking it on the northern side is a **statue of Daniel O'Connell**, who fought for Catholic emancipation in the early 19th century; it is still pocked with bullet marks from the 1916 Rising.

General Post Office I6

O'Connell St, t (01) 705 7000, www.anpost.ie.
Open Mon–Sat 8–8, Sun 10.30–6.30;
adm free.

> '...We declare the right of the people of Ireland to the ownership of Ireland and to the unfettered control of Irish destinies, to be sovereign and indefeasible...'
>
> Extract from the Proclamation of 1916

Dublin's **General Post Office (GPO)**, an elegant neoclassical building from 1814, still maintains its original function, but is most famous for its association with the terrible events of 1916. On Easter Monday that year, the Volunteers of the Irish Republican Army under Padhraic Pearse and James Connolly seized the GPO. They held out against the British forces here and in other outposts across the city for six days, finally surrendering on 29 April. The leaders of the uprising were sent to Kilmainham, where they were executed (see p.96). The **Easter Rising** would lead to the War of Independence, and eventually to the declaration of the Irish Free State in 1922.

During the uprising, the GPO was destroyed, along with much of O'Connell Street Lower, but was restored and reopened in 1929. A copy of the Proclamation, which had been papered across the city on the morning of Easter Monday, is inscribed on a plaque inside, and at the door stands a moving statue *The Death of Cúchulainn*, commemorating the legendary hero of ancient Ireland.

Clery Department Store J6

18–27 Lower O'Connell St, t (01) 878 6000, www.clerys.com; all buses to O'Connell St.
Open Mon–Wed 9–6.30, Thurs 9–9, Fri 9–8, Sat 9–6.

Clery's was once one of the grandest department stores in Dublin; these days, it is merely reliable and rather old-fashioned. During the Easter Rising, looters ran riot throughout the city, but for some reason were afraid to break into Clery's. Mrs Hamilton Norway, wife of the Irish Postmaster-General and mother of the novelist Nevil Shute, was taking refuge in the Hibernian Hotel at the time, and described the scene in front of Clery's: 'Old women passed up and down gazing longingly at fur coats and silken raiment, and saying sorrowfully, "Isn't Clery's broke yet?" and "Isn't it a shame that Clery's is not broke!"' She adds poignantly, 'Humour and tragedy are so intermixed in this catastrophe.'

Henry Street and Moore Street I5

All buses to O'Connell St.

Off O'Connell Street, pedestrianized **Henry Street** is one of Dublin's major shopping arteries, with department stores, huge shopping centres and all the major chain shops. It's a bland street, indistinguishable from most city shopping streets all over Ireland and the UK. Just off it, the cheerfully scruffy **Moore Street Market** is a good place to pick up fresh fruit and vegetables, with traders yelling in the famously raucous Moore Street accent.

Abbey Theatre J6

Lower Abbey St, t (01) 878 7222, www.abbeytheatre.ie; all buses to O'Connell

*St. See p.212 for box office information. Backstage tours (€6) available Thursdays; call in advance on **t** (01) 887 2223.*

The **Abbey Theatre** was founded in 1904 as the Irish national theatre by William Butler Yeats, Lady Augusta Gregory and Edward Martyn. Between them they managed to revitalize Irish theatre and championed many local playwrights, including the young John Millington Synge, whose early plays *The Shadow of the Glen* and *Riders to the Sea* had been badly received for failing to conform to the idealized notion of rural Ireland expected by Dublin audiences. In 1907, the Abbey Theatre premiered Synge's *The Playboy of the Western World* – it so outraged the audience that a riot broke out partway through, and the play was abandoned. As police surged in waving their batons, Lady Gregory stood calmly to one side, handing out slices of homemade barmbrack to her invitees. Another ruckus broke out during the première of Sean O'Casey's *The Plough and the Stars* in 1926, when the audience took umbrage at the sight of the national flag sharing a stage with a pub and a prostitute.

The Abbey has now settled into the comfortable role of an excellent if largely unchallenging establishment theatre, but the small Peacock Theatre which shares its premises stages some of Dublin's most exciting contemporary drama. The original Abbey buildings were almost completely destroyed by fire in 1951, and a resolutely blank modern replacement by Michael Scott was finally erected on the same spot in 1966.

Hot Press Irish Music Hall of Fame I6

*57 Abbey St Middle, **t** (01) 878 3345; all buses to O'Connell St. **Open** daily 10–7; **adm** adults €8, students/seniors/children €6. Shop, café.*

Indulge here in a multimedia whirlwind tour of Irish music, from traditional to the latest bands. There's also lots of memorabilia, including the (unwashed) T-shirt worn by Bob Geldof at the Live Aid charity concert in 1985.

St Mary's Pro-Cathedral J5

*Cathedral St, **t** (01) 874 5441, www.procathedral.ie; all buses to O'Connell St. **Open daily** 8–6.30; **adm** free.*

'At last an edifice worthy of the loftiness of our creed stands in the centre of the metropolis. Our religion has at last lifted up its proud and majestic head.'

Richard Shiel, at the opening of the Pro-Cathedral in 1814

Before the 1829 Catholic Emancipation Act, Catholics were forbidden to build churches on major thoroughfares. **St Mary's Pro-Cathedral** was originally planned for O'Connell Street, but locals protested vigorously at this, and so Dublin's most important Catholic church is tucked away on a relatively obscure site. It was built in 1814, the finest example of Greek revival architecture in the city, with an imposing façade modelled on the Temple of Theseus in Athens. The interior is no less extravagant, shimmering with marble and scattered with pompous 19th-century statuary. In 1847, the Pro-Cathedral held the funeral rites for the political activist Daniel O'Connell, who died in Genoa on his way to Rome. His coffin arrived in Dublin by steamer and, when it was revealed to the huge crowd assembled on the dockside, everyone dropped spontaneously to their knees. Enormous crowds also attended the funeral of Michael Collins, held here in 1922.

The church's celebrated **Palestrina Choir** was founded by Edward Martyn, one of the founders of the Abbey Theatre along with Yeats and Lady Gregory, and the great tenor John McCormack began his career with the choir in 1902. You can still hear services sung in Latin, usually on Sundays at 11am.

Incidentally, the strange name 'Pro-Cathedral' came about because St Mary's – although the mother church of Dublin's majority Roman Catholic population – has not been granted full cathedral status, unlike the city's two, much more ancient, 'official' cathedrals, Christchurch and St Patrick's.

PARNELL SQUARE AND AROUND

Parnell Square 15

Bus 3, 10, 11, 13, 16, 19, 22.

O'Connell Street culminates in the dignified expanse of **Parnell Square**, once gracious but now rather battered and grimy, and choked, like so much of Dublin, with traffic. It's still surrounded by fine Georgian mansions, many now used as galleries and museums, and dominated by the massive 18th-century Rotunda maternity hospital. At the centre is the small **Garden of Remembrance**, dedicated to those who died for Irish freedom. A grand monument to the Irish nationalist politician Parnell himself stands at the top of O'Connell Street: the plinth is inscribed with the words 'Let no man stop the birth of a nation', and he points – with unintentional irony – at the city's biggest maternity hospital.

Rotunda Hospital 15

Parnell Square South; **bus** 3, 10, 11, 13, 16, 19, 22.

The **Rotunda**, Ireland's first free lying-in hospital, was established in 1745 by Bartholomew Mosse. It was such a success that it soon outgrew its original site on South Great George's Street, and a magnificent new building was commissioned on a site north of Gardiner's Mall (the original incarnation of O'Connell Street). Mosse raised the money for its construction by laying out a walled pleasure garden with tea rooms, and charging admission. The new hospital was designed by Richard Cassels, architect of Leinster House (*see* p.71) which it echoes in appearance, and opened its doors in 1757. It became known as the Rotunda after the domed concert hall (now the Ambassador cinema) which was constructed soon after.

The **Rotunda Chapel** contains some of the finest rococo plasterwork in Ireland – a delicate whirl of garlands and gilt executed by the stucco artist Barthelemy Cramillion. Sadly, Mosse poured so much energy and money into the project that he died worn out and broke, aged just 45.

Dublin babies are still born here, and expectant fathers can traditionally be found drinking a nervous pint in Patrick Conway's pub opposite.

Gate Theatre 15

1 Cavendish Row, Parnell Square South, **t** *(01) 874 4045;* **bus** *3, 10, 11, 13, 16, 19, 22. Box office open Mon–Sat 10–7.*

The **Gate Theatre** was founded in 1928 by Hilton Edwards and Micheal Mac-Liammóir, a pair of flamboyant and openly homosexual English actors who came to Dublin and wholeheartedly embraced Irish literary culture. Mac-Liammóir, originally Michael Wilmore, learned fluent Gaelic, changed his name and would parade around the city in full drag. Their theatre rapidly gained a reputation for showing exciting new drama, and several great actors – including Orson Welles and James Mason – made their names here. One of the first performances was Oscar Wilde's *Salome*, then banned by half the cities of Europe. Mac-Liammóir's one-man show, *The Importance of Being Oscar*, was a massive hit and ran from 1960 until his last Dublin performance in 1975.

Garden of Remembrance 15

Parnell Square East, **t** *(01) 874 3074. Unrestricted access.*

This small garden was laid out in 1966 in commemoration of the 50th anniversary of the Easter Rising. At the centre, Oisin Kelly's beautiful monument *Children of Lir* (1971) soars up from a small pool – according to the much-loved legend, the children of the ancient King Lir were bewitched by their jealous stepmother, who enticed them to Lough Derravaragh and turned them into swans for 900 years.

Hugh Lane Gallery (Dublin City Gallery) and Francis Bacon's Studio 14

Charlemont House, Parnell Square North, t (01) 874 1903, www.hughlane.ie; bus 3, 10, 11, 13, 16, 19. **Open** *Tues–Thurs 9.30–6, Fri–Sat 9.30–5, Sun 11–5;* **adm** *gallery free, Francis Bacon Studio €7, students/seniors €3.50, free on Tues before noon. Free guided tours of gallery Tues 11am, Sun 1.30pm. Lunchtime lectures Wed 1.10pm. Wheelchair accessible. Café, bookshop.*

Charlemont House is one of the grandest survivors of Parnell Square's Golden Age, built by Sir William Chambers in 1762 for the first Earl of Charlemont. Charlemont was one of the leaders of the Volunteer movement of the 1770s, but he, like other moderates among the group, grew alarmed at the increasingly nationalist rhetoric and persuaded the regiments to disband. Edmund Burke described him as 'a man of such polished manners, of a mind so truly adorned... that to see and converse with him, would alone induce me... to pay a visit to Dublin'.

His splendid mansion now contains the **municipal art gallery**, founded in 1908 by **Sir Hugh Lane**, an art dealer and nephew of Yeats's patron, Lady Gregory. Lane offered to bequeath his entire collection to the city on the condition that a suitable location should be found to house them, and then angrily retracted the offer when the city refused to build a special gallery (he favoured a 'gallery-bridge' across the Liffey designed by Edwin Lutyens; *see* p.112). He later relented and added an unwitnessed codicil to his will which gave 39 works 'to the nation'; he was drowned when the *Lusitania* was torpedoed off the Irish coast in 1915. The post-independence Irish and British governments wrangled over the exact meaning of 'the nation' for almost fifty years, finally resolving the issue in the 1980s when half of the collection was allowed to remain in Dublin.

The works are regularly moved for temporary exhibitions, but galleries 1, 2, 3 and 9 contain the **permanent collection**, which is less likely to be shifted about. Highlights of **Gallery 1** include the Impressionist paintings from Lane's bequest for which the gallery is most famous: breezy beach scenes by Eugene Boudin, Bonnard's subdued *Boulevard de Clichy*, Monet's shimmering rendering of *Waterloo Bridge* and, most famously, Renoir's vigorous *Les Parapluies*. There are some fine portraits, including Degas's poignant *Young Woman with a White Headdress*, and another of the sizzling sexpot Eva Gonzalez by Manet. **Gallery 2** contains Irish paintings, including several pieces by Jack B. Yeats: *The Talkers* conveys the emptiness and giddiness of the social scene, and *There is no Night* is a mystical, swirling landscape with a ghostly white horse and rider. There are also some unsettling works by Louis de Brockuy here, such as *Child in a Yard*, in which the pale figure of a child emerges from murky shadows. **Gallery 3** is devoted to late 19th-century works by Irish painters, including a sun-tinged, dusky landscape by Nathanial Hone: *Evening, Malahide Sands*. The adjoining **Gallery 4** contains contemporary Irish art, including works by Dublin-born artists such as Seán Shanahan and Sean Scully. French landscapes by Corot, Courbet and others from the end of the 19th century hang in **Gallery 9**.

Francis Bacon's Studio
Buy tickets from the gift shop in the main gallery.

Francis Bacon turned his back on Dublin as a youth, and it may come as a surprise to many that a man so closely identified with British art was Irish at all. He was born at 63 Baggott Street Lower on 28 October 1909, but when he was 16 his father discovered that he was an active homosexual and threw him out of the house. Bacon left Ireland and travelled to Berlin, Paris, Tangiers and Monte Carlo, doing and trying everything legal and illegal that came along, before eventually settling in London. He never returned to Ireland, and showed almost no interest in

Dublin, which returned the compliment by showing little interest in claiming him until recently.

After Bacon's death in 1992, his partner and sole heir John Edwards donated the artist's London studio to Dublin. Bacon kept his tiny studio in 7 Reece Mews, South Kensington, London for 30 years, and at his death, it was knee-deep in a slurry of magazines, empty champagne boxes, paints, paper, rubbish, books, records and dust. A team of architects carefully documented every inch of the studio, which was found to contain more than 7000 items, and transferred it exactly to Dublin. Even the dust was gathered up, bagged and redistributed. The studio is sealed off, but you can gaze in at it through glass panels, and interactive terminals give lots of information on Bacon's life and works.

The tour begins with a video of Bacon's interview with Melvyn Bragg in 1984, which took place in the artist's studio. Bragg asked him why he worked in such a mess, to which Bacon replied: 'I work much better in chaos. Chaos for me breeds images.' Peering in at the Krug champagne bottles, the torn copies of *Life* magazine opened at a story on the Kennedy assassination, pictures of celebrities and random strangers, more assasination articles, this time on the attempted killings of Pope John Paul II and President Reagan, it's clear that he had no shortage of images to choose from. All the walls and even the door are thickly daubed with rainbow paints, including a toxic silver one that exacerbated Bacon's chronic asthma. On the easel stands a self-portrait, unfinished at his death. Five other unfinished paintings are held in the last surviving space from Lord Charlemont's once-grand library wing, which still has its elaborate stucco ceiling. These belong to the Bacon estate, but the self-portrait on the easel was given to the Hugh Lane Gallery by John Edwards, along with the studio.

Dublin Writers Museum and Irish Writers Centre I4

*18 Parnell Square North, **t** (01) 872 20 77, www.visitdublin.com; **bus** 10, 11, 11B, 13, 13A, 16, 16A, 19, 19A. **Open** Mon–Sat 10–6, Sun 11–5; Sept–May Mon–Sat closes 5; **adm** €5, children €3.50; includes audio-guide. Guided tours available. Café, restaurants, gift shop.*

The north side of Parnell Square was once referred to as 'Palace Row' for its ranks of palatial townhouses. Another lavish Georgian mansion at no. 18 was built for Lord Farnham and still contains its exquisite stucco ceilings, which may have been executed by the celebrated Irish stucco artist Michael Stapleton. Most of the present decoration dates back to the late 19th century, when the house was owned by the Jameson family, who famously made their money in whiskey. Now it contains the **Dublin Writers Museum**, the Living Writers Centre, an excellent bookshop and the Chapter One café and restaurant – one of the best on the north side of Dublin (*see* p.195).

The elegant Georgian salons of the **ground floor** contain a potted history of Irish literature, with miniature biographies of all the Dublin greats from Jonathan Swift to Samuel Beckett. The snappy commentary on the audio-guides doesn't hold back from scathing opinions: Thomas Moore, for example, is condemned for his 'blarneyized' vision of Ireland, and Brendan Behan is described as a 'brawling, boozing exhibitionist'. Cases with some scant possessions – letters, books, diaries, photographs and the typewriter that Behan apparently chucked through the window of a Dublin pub in rage – add a personal touch to the descriptions.

Discount Tickets

The Dublin Writers Museum offers a combined ticket with the James Joyce Museum (*see* p.136), Shaw Birthplace (p.75), Malahide Castle and Fry Model Railway Museum (p.134) – you can choose any two of these attractions for €10 (students/seniors €8, children €5.50, family ticket €28.50).

The staircase, with stained glass depicting the Jameson family's coat-of-arms, sweeps up to the grandest rooms of the house: the former library and ballroom. The **library** contains the works of the authors described on the ground floor, and the ballroom has been renamed the **Gallery of Writers**. Its original pure white stuccoed ceilings were gaudily painted with blue and gold in the 19th-century restoration, and the door panels are inscribed with earnest aphorisms and figures representing the months of the year and the quarters of the day.

Back downstairs, a small Zen garden has been created near the excellent café and bookshop.

Belvedere College I4

6 Great Denmark St, www.belvedere college.ie; bus 3, 10. 11, 11A, 13, 16, 16A, 19, 19A, 22, 22A. No public access.

Belvedere House was built in 1758, but has been a Jesuit boys' school since 1841. It contains some of the finest stucco decoration in the city, executed by Michael Stapleton, including graceful depictions of the deities Diana and Apollo (Venus was removed because the Jesuits considered her improper for a boys' school). The college's most famous former pupil is James Joyce, who describes his schooldays here in *A Portrait of the Artist as A Young Man,* and you can just glimpse the chapel where the famous hell-fire sermon took place, as described by Joyce. Joyce's works were forbidden to students right up until 1960.

James Joyce Centre I4

35 North Great George's St, t (01) 878 8547, www.jamesjoyce.ie; bus 3, 10. 11, 11A, 13, 16, 16A, 19, 19A, 22, 22A. Open Mon–Sat 9.30–5, Sun noon–5; adm €4.50, students/seniors €3.50, family ticket €12.50. Walking tours available. Partially wheelchair accessible. Bookshop and gift shop.

The **James Joyce Centre** is dedicated to the famous author's life and works. It offers excellent guided tours of the city (sometimes led by one of Joyce's descendants, who are involved with the running of the centre), a full programme of lectures and events and a research library for scholars. The house (which isn't directly associated with Joyce himself) stands in an elegant street of restored Georgian mansions, one of very few to have resisted the decay which blights most of the northside's Georgian heritage. It's a quiet, light-filled townhouse, built in 1784 for the Earl of Kenmare and decorated with more creamy plasterwork by the indefatigable Michael Stapleton.

The tour begins with a short video on Joyce's life and Dublin at the turn of the 20th century. The **Maginni room** on the ground floor is named for a professor of dancing, a well-known figure around the city who dressed in 'tight lavender trousers, canary gloves and pointed patent boots' and earned himself a walk-on part in Joyce's *Ulysses*. Professor Maginni was actually Dennis Maginnis, who dropped the 's', affected an Italian accent and adopted colourful clothes in order to entice customers to his dance academy in this room. Upstairs, the former **drawing room** contains a collection of family portraits, which were the pride and joy of John Stanislaus Joyce, James' father. They accompanied him as the family moved into a series of increasingly dingy lodgings, as a reminder of his family's former glory. On his father's death, the portraits passed to James Joyce, who also carted them from one home to the next as he made his equally insolvent way around Europe. These are copies: the originals are at New York State University in Buffalo. The rear drawing room has been converted into a **research library**, with an extensive collection of Joyce-related texts and criticism. The top floors contain a recreation of the Paris apartment of Paul Leon, a friend and admirer of Joyce. This is where they apparently sat and worked out how to make *Finnegans Wake* more difficult. Adjoining this room is a gallery devoted to temporary exhibitions on Joyce-related themes. At the back of the house, the door

James Joyce

'I want to give a picture of Dublin so complete that if the city one day suddenly disappeared from the earth it could be reconstructed out of my book.'

James Joyce was born in the affluent Dublin suburb of Rathgar, on 2 February 1882. His father, John Stanislaus Joyce, came from a wealthy Cork family that initially provided him with enough money from rents, along with his job in the Civil Service, to keep his family in considerable style. However, John Joyce was a genial but improvident loafer; he managed to lose his job and was forced to sell his land to pay off his considerable debts. The family had to move from their last respectable address in Blackrock, and then lived in a succession of increasingly shabby lodgings on Dublin's run-down northside. He managed to wheedle free scholarships for his sons to attend the prestigious Jesuit-run Belvedere College, but, by the time James Joyce entered University College Dublin, the family were poverty-stricken.

Joyce escaped his miserable home life by wandering the city streets, storing up the rich fund of memories that he would draw on in exile. In 1902, he went to Paris, ostensibly to study medicine, and returned to his mother's deathbed a year later. In 1904 he met Nora Barnacle, a chambermaid from Galway who became his lifelong companion. They left for Trieste, at the head of the Adriatic, the same year, and had two children before finally marrying in 1931.

Joyce returned only briefly to Dublin: once in 1909, when he set up the city's first permanent cinema, the Volta, at 25 Mary Street, before tiring of the business and returning to Trieste; and again in 1912, when he attempted to arrange the publication of his first book *The Dubliners*. An argument between Joyce and his publisher culminated with the destruction of the first edition, and Joyce left the next day, never to return. *The Dubliners* was eventually published in London in 1914, with *A Portrait of the Artist as a Young Man* following in 1916. The quintessential exiled writer, Joyce displayed in his books an obsessive attachment to the city of his birth, abandoned but not forgotten.

Joyce and his family took refuge from war-torn Europe in neutral Zurich, where he began work on *Ulysses*, the book which would make his name when it appeared in 1922. The story parallels Homer's *Odyssey*, with Leopold Bloom, a Jewish salesman, figuring as Joyce's unlikely epic hero. The complex narrative is written in a dazzling variety of styles, woven around Bloom's journey through the city on a single day (16 June 1904, now celebrated as 'Bloomsday'). It is regarded as one of the major literary achievements of the 20th century.

In 1920, Joyce moved to Paris, where he began work on *Finnegans Wake*, his most difficult and obscure novel, which took him 17 years. Although Joyce was finally receiving recognition for his writing, this was a difficult period for the family: his eyesight was failing and causing him considerable pain, and his daughter was diagnosed as a schizophrenic. *Finnegans Wake* was published in May 1939. After war broke out, the Joyces fled to Vichy France, and then to neutral Zurich, which had sheltered them once before. On 13 January 1941 – a month after their safe arrival in Switzerland – Joyce died. He is buried in the Fluntern Cemetery in Zurich.

from 7 Eccles Street, the fictional home of Leopold and Molly Bloom, has been preserved in a pretty, glassed-over courtyard. The walls are covered with startling murals depicting scenes from *Ulysses* painted by Paul Joyce, great-grand-nephew of the writer.

James Joyce now enjoys worldwide acclaim as a literary genius, but recognition was late in coming. Out on Great George's Street, a plaque at no. 38 marks the former home of Sir Pentland Mahaffy, provost of Trinity College, who regarded Joyce as proof that 'it was a mistake to establish a separate university for the aborigines of this island, for the corner-boys who spit in the Liffey'.

St Francis Xavier J4

*Gardiner St Upper, **t** (01) 836 3411; **bus** 3, 10, 11, 11A, 13, 16, 16A, 19, 19A, 22, 22A.*

The sombre Jesuit **church of St Francis Xavier** was built between 1829 and 1832, and modelled on the Parisian church of Notre-Dame de Lorette. The gloomy interior is lined with huge, macabre paintings of the martyrs and contains the tomb of the ascetic temperance-preacher Matt Talbot. The church has some Joycean connections, too: the real-life Father Clonmee (who granted the Joyce boys free scholarships to Belvedere) served as its superior, and in *Ulysses* the fictional Father Farley defeated Leopold's efforts to get Molly a place in the church's choir.

Mountjoy Square J4

Mountjoy Square was once one of the most aristocratic addresses in Dublin, linked by Gardiner Street to the brand new Custom House on Beresford Place. It was laid out between 1792 and 1818 by Luke Gardiner, the first Viscount Mountjoy, and grandson of the great landowner who created Henrietta Street (*see* p.118). But fashion abandoned the north side of the river for the grand squares of the southeast, and the once-glorious mansions were ruthlessly divided up into tenements and boarding houses, or simply left to rot. The whole southern side of the square was demolished in the 1970s, although it was replaced with a line of replica Georgian façades and some of the original mansions are now being slowly restored.

According to legend, this area is where Brian Ború established his camp before the Battle of Clontarf in 1014. The playwright Sean O'Casey set *The Shadow of the Gunman* here, and Joyce's impoverished family briefly lived in lodgings around the corner on Fitzgibbon Street.

Beyond the square, you can just make out the grim roof of Mountjoy Prison, where many of the leaders of the Easter Rising were incarcerated, and which Brendan Behan recalled in his play *The Quare Fellow*. When Behan was imprisoned here, the IRA wrote to tell him that he had been court-martialled and condemned to death in his absence. He promptly wrote back, suggesting that they also execute him in his absence.

National Wax Museum I4

*Granby Row, off Parnell Square, **t** (01) 872 6340; **bus** 11, 13, 16, 22, 22A. **Open** Mon–Sat*

> ### Matt Talbot
>
> **Matt Talbot** was born to a poor Dublin family in 1856. His father was a drunk, and young Matt was soon following suit. After a couple of years of schooling, he got his first job in a beer-bottling factory, where he would drink the dregs of the returned bottles. By the time he was in his early 20s, he would run through his wages at O'Meara's Tavern, and beg, borrow or steal when the money ran out. One day in 1884, his former friends refused to lend him any more money. He was shocked into 'taking the pledge' (swearing off drink in front of a priest) for three months, when he began going to church. After three months, he took the pledge for a further six months, and then for life. He then decided to model his life on the early Irish saints, spending hours in prayer, attending Mass daily, fasting, mortifying his flesh by wearing chains under his clothing and allowing himself only four hours' sleep a night. At the timberyard where he worked, nobody knew anything of this other life, although he was considered a generous and charitable man. He suddenly dropped dead of a heart attack in 1925, which was when the chains beneath his clothing were discovered. His story spread rapidly, and now there are Matt Talbot retreats, addiction centres, soup kitchens and hospices as far afield as Sydney and Nebraska. His followers are trying to have him canonized as the patron saint of addiction, but no one has as yet been able to pin down the physical miracle necessary for sainthood.

10–5.30, Sun noon–5.30; *adm* €6, students €5, children €4, family ticket €18.

Back on the other side of Parnell Square, you can't miss Dublin's **Wax Museum**, thanks to the massive Celtic giant apparently scaling the building. Inside it has the usual kitsch collection of dummies, with U2 and Madonna rubbing shoulders with Wolfe Tone and Luke Skywalker. It's neither more nor less bizarre than the average tourist city wax museum, except perhaps for the tableau of Jesus and the apostles reproducing Leonardo da Vinci's *Last Supper*.

Black Church (St Mary's Chapel of Ease) H4

St Mary's Place; bus 11, 13, 16, 22, 22A. No public access.

Built in 1830 of black calp stone, **St Mary's Chapel of Ease** is better known as the '**Black Church**'. It was John's Betjeman's favourite Dublin church, but is now deconsecrated and used for offices. A local legend tells that if you walk 'twice around the Black Church' (some say it has to be done backwards), the Devil will appear.

THE QUAYS NORTH OF THE LIFFEY
International Financial Services Centre (IFSC) K6

Custom House Quay; bus 53, 53A, and all buses to Busáras.

This vast, glass-and-concrete complex is the biggest symbol of the 'Celtic Tiger' phenomenon, the dramatic economic surge which Dublin experienced in the 1990s. Now that the bubble has burst, these offices – which hold the HQs of major corporations, banks, lawyers' offices and accountants – no longer hum with quite the same energy as they used to. Behind is an ugly scramble of roads and railway lines which lead to Dublin's main bus and train stations (Busáras and Connolly station). On the quayside stands a sculpture of emaciated figures, erected in 1987 to commemorate the victims of the Great Famine.

Custom House and Visitor Centre J6

*Custom House Quay, **t** (01) 878 7660; **bus** 53A, 90A; **DART** to Tara St. **Open** Mon–Fri 10–12.30, Sat–Sun 2–5; Nov to mid-March closed Mon, Tues & Sat; adm €1, family ticket €3. Gift shop.*

If the IFSC is a symbol of Dublin's prosperity in the 20th century, the Custom House (1781–91) represents the affluence of the 18th century. Designed by the masterly James Gandon, it is perhaps the most beautiful of the city's neoclassical buildings, its harmonious lines quietly reflected in the River Liffey.

The old Custom House was located upriver in Temple Bar (*see* p.84), on the site where the Clarence Hotel now stands. When plans were mooted to move the Custom House east, there was uproar, both from local traders who didn't want to shift their business and the genteel families on the north of the river who were frightened that unsavoury types would contaminate their neighbourhood. Building had to begin in secret, and Gandon, wary of the ferocious mob, wore his sword to work. The site itself, a half-submerged mudflat, also posed difficulties, which Gandon ingeniously resolved by laying a foundation of wooden planks, to the consternation of many observers. The new Custom House took ten years to build and cost £400,000, an unprecedented sum.

Just nine years later, the building was redundant: with the Act of Union, London became responsible for Dublin's customs and excise. It survived a major fire in 1833, but was targeted by Sinn Féiners in 1921 and the subsequent blaze, fuelled by sheaves of paperwork, continued for several days. In 1926, it was restored at a cost of another £300,000, but by the 1970s it was clear that the restoration works were not sufficiently extensive and there were still problems with cracking stonework and other major flaws. Yet another restoration got underway, from which it emerged pristine in time to celebrate its 200th birthday in 1991.

The best place to admire its expansive façade is from George's Quay on the other side of the Liffey. From here you can make out the figures of Britannia and Hibernia engaged in a cosy chat, while Neptune drives out Famine and Despair. The stone decoration is among the finest of the period in Ireland; symbols of the rivers of Ireland circle the entire building, beginning with a female figure representing the River Liffey above the main doorway and featuring cattle heads (symbolizing the beef trade) and statues of the Four Continents on the northern façade. The huge copper dome is surmounted by an enormous statue of Commerce.

The Visitor Centre offers a history of the building, with original documents and early photographs, and a much less interesting account of the various government offices that have been housed here. However, it does offer the opportunity to see some of the exquisitely carved interior stonework.

Ha'Penny Bridge I6

Bachelor's Walk on the north side; Wellington Quay on the south side. All buses to O'Connell St or Aston Quay.

This winsome, wrought-iron bridge is a much-loved symbol of the city, its delicate twirls and yellow lamps prettily reflected in the river below. For almost two centuries, this was the only pedestrian bridge across the Liffey, and it is still the oldest surviving iron bridge in Ireland. Although its official name is the Liffey Bridge, it is still known as the **Ha'Penny Bridge** after the toll which was once levied on the crossing. The bridge was almost torn down a century ago: Sir Hugh Lane (*see* p.106) wanted to replace it with a gallery-bridge to hold the collection of Impressionist paintings which he donated to the city, but no one wanted to block the view of the Liffey and so the plans never went any further.

On the north side of the river is a contemporary sculpture by Jakki McKenna of two shoppers enjoying a companionable chat; even this hasn't escaped a rhyming nickname, and is known as 'the hags with the bags'.

Millennium Bridge and Boardwalk I6

Ormond Quay Lower on the north side, to Wellington Quay on the south side. All buses to O'Connell St or Aston Quay.

The **Millennium Bridge**, a slinky, pared-down pedestrian bridge, was one of the few architectural plans for the year 2000 that actually met with wholehearted public approval. Silvery, and lit with slick blue lights, it's the antithesis of its frilly 19th-century Ha'Penny neighbour – but every bit as charming. A boardwalk has also been added just below the quay, with coffee kiosks and stalls in summer – even if not quite as Parisian in feel as it wants to be, it is still a delightful spot for a stroll.

Grattan Bridge I6

Ormond Quay Upper on the north side, to Essex Quay on the south side.

The **Grattan Bridge**, a stolid 19th-century construction named after the feisty 18th-century orator and politician Henry Grattan, has also been earmarked for Parisian-style development. A footbridge is planned along the bridge which will function as a book market, and also link up with the Boardwalk.

Northwest Dublin: The Four Courts to Phoenix Park

FOUR COURTS AND AROUND 116
St Mary's Abbey 116
St Michan's Church 117
Dublin Corporation Fruit & Vegetable Market 117
King's Inns 118
Henrietta Street 118

SMITHFIELD 118
Chimney Viewing Tower 119
Old Jameson Distillery 119
Dublin Brewing Company 120
Stoneybatter 120
Collins Barracks 120
Arbour Hill Cemetery 121
Croppies Acre 121
James Joyce Bridge 121

PHOENIX PARK 121
Áras an Uachtárain (President's House) 123
Dublin Zoo 123

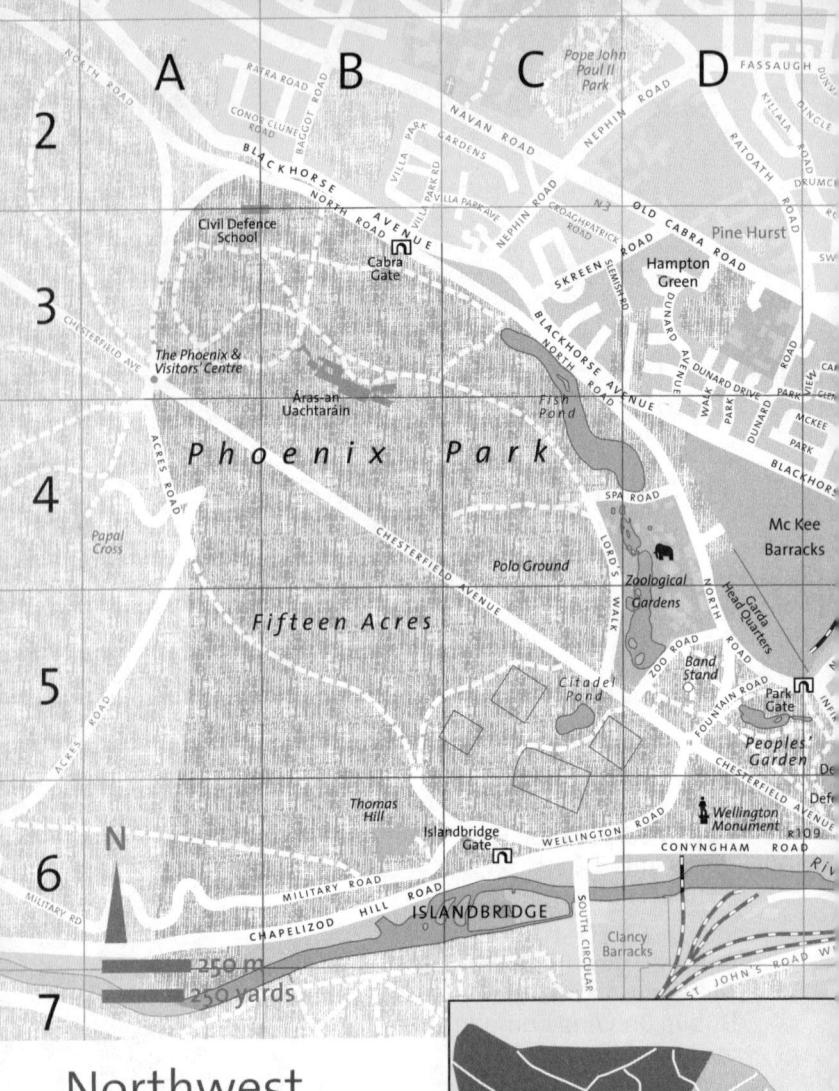

Northwest Dublin: The Four Courts to Phoenix Park

Northwest Dublin has less of a defined identity than other neighbourhoods in the city: workers from the terraced cottages of Stoneybatter rub shoulders with bewigged lawyers near the grandiose Four Courts, and market porters and traders jostle with the trendy young couples buying up pristine flats in newly revamped Smithfield. The mishmash of monuments and sights is equally haphazard: from the imposing neoclassical Four Courts and King's Inns to the curious mummified corpses in St Michan's Church, touched for luck by generations of visitors.

In the Middle Ages, the great Cistercian Abbey of St Mary's owned all this land, but

Highlights

Georgian Dublin: See the pale splendour of the Four Courts reflected in the Liffey, p.116

Indoor Dublin: Visit the excellent Museum of Decorative Arts in Collins Barracks, p.120

Dubliner's Dublin: Make a wish on 'the Crusader's' finger in St Michan's Church, p.117

Green Dublin: Spend the day in glorious Phoenix Park, p.121

21st-Century Dublin: Admire Calatrava's stylish new James Joyce Bridge, p.121

1 Lunch

Kelly and Ping, *Duck Lane, Smithfield Village*, **t** *(01) 817 3840, www.kellyandping.com*. **Open** *daily noon–11*. Light and airy Asian restaurant serving curries and noodle dishes.

2 Tea and cakes

Collins Barracks *(National Museum of Decorative Arts and History), Benburb St*, **t** *(01) 677 7444*. **Open** *Tues–Sat 10–5, Sun 2–5*. An excellent museum café.

3 Drinks

Hughes, *19 Chancery St*, **t** *(01) 872 6540*. **Open** *Mon–Wed 10.30am–11.30pm, Thurs–Sat 10.30am–12.30am, Sun 12.30–11*. Wonderful, old-fashioned pub hidden away behind the Four Courts, offering a well-drawn pint.

the abbey was destroyed during the Reformation and the ruins used to build a city bridge. By the 18th century, the land belonged to wealthy entrepreneurs, who began work on the first of the Georgian townhouses which would soon transform the face of the city. The very first of these lined Henrietta Street, and were the largest and most opulent of all. They suffered when the fashionable families moved south of the river – many were stripped of their sumptuous fittings and chopped into tenements in what would become a familiar tale of greed and neglect. Work has now finally begun on their restoration, as part of a move to smarten up the whole district. This is most evident in Smithfield, where massive redevelopment has created swish new visitor attractions such as the Old Jameson's Distillery and the Chimney Viewing Tower, along with plenty of contemporary loft-style apartments. The vast cobbled expanse of Smithfield marketplace has been cleaned up and renamed Smithfield Plaza; it is flanked with futuristic lighting masts which glow spectacularly on Saturday nights. Further west is the excellent National Museum of Ireland's decorative arts collection, set in the beautifully restored Collins Barracks. But the jewel of northwestern Dublin is Phoenix Park, a glorious and much-loved open space which stretches for several miles, within which stands the home of the Irish president.

FOUR COURTS AND AROUND

Four Courts H6

Inns Quay; bus 10, 10A. **Open** *when courts are sitting;* **adm** *free.*

James Gandon, architect of the splendid Custom House up-river (*see* p.111), was also responsible for this stately neoclassical edifice on the banks of the Liffey. Built between 1786 and 1802 as the seat of the High Court of Justice, it exudes authority and majesty, and many a prisoner must have quaked in his or her boots on entering its magnificent columned portico. It cost £200,000 – just half the cost of the Custom House, but still a sufficiently substantial sum for locals to complain of the 'contemptible vanity' of lawyers who required 'the grandest building in Europe, in the world, to plead in'.

Moses and statues of the Legal Virtues sit gravely above the portico and, inside, traditionally bewigged and berobed lawyers scuttle across the vast hall, which is topped with a 64-foot-wide rotunda. The Four Courts were occupied by anti-treaty Republicans in 1922, and besieged by government forces for almost two months before a huge explosion cracked the great rotunda and fire whipped through the building. Before they escaped, the Republicans mined the adjoining Public Records Office, destroying many of Ireland's irreplaceable historic documents. Sean O'Casey described 'all the foolish wigs and gowns of Dublin sailing up into the sky; with all the records of the country... and all the hereditaments chronicled since Strongbow came to Ireland, flying up after the wigs and gowns, to come fluttering down, scorched and tattered, into every Dublin back-yard and front garden'.

After major restoration, which enlarged the rotunda but whittled off part of the façade to accommodate traffic, the building has opened again for its original function, and the curious can attend the courts when they are in session.

St Mary's Abbey H6

Chapter House, Meetinghouse Lane, off Capel St, **t** *(01) 872 1490; all buses to Middle Abbey St.* **Open** *mid-June to mid-Sept Sat–Sun 10–5;* **adm** *€1.50, seniors €1, children/students €0.75. Guided tours can be arranged in advance on* **t** *(01) 833 1618.*

Virtually nothing remains of **St Mary's Abbey**, once one of the largest and wealthiest Cistercian abbeys in Ireland. It was here in 1534 that 'Silken Thomas' Fitzgerald furiously renounced his oath of loyalty to Henry VIII of England and began his short-lived and unsuccessful rebellion (see p.22). In 1539, the abbey was destroyed during the Reformation, when all its 'popist trappings' were burnt and its lands surrendered to the King. In 1681, what little remained was picked over and the stones used to build Essex Bridge, the precursor of O'Connell Bridge. Now, only the **Chapterhouse** and **slype** (a narrow covered passage) survive; for years, the Chapterhouse was used for storage, but it has now been restored by the Heritage Council and contains a small but interesting exhibition on the abbey's history.

St Michan's Church H6

*Church St; **bus** 25, 26, 37, 39, 67, 67A, 68, 69, 79. **Open** Mon–Fri 10–12.45 and 2–4.45, Sat 10–12.45; **adm** €3.50, students/seniors €3, children €2.50. Gift shop.*

This church was built in 1095, on the site of an older church dedicated to the Danish saint **Michan**, but it underwent major renovations in the 17th and 19th centuries. It was once one of Dublin's most fashionable churches, and the handsome interior contains an 18th-century organ enclosed by an unusual carved wooden panel depicting musical instruments, as well as a fine pulpit with an elaborately wrought staircase. Wrongdoers were forced to kneel at the Penitents' Pew and publicly apologize for their misdeeds.

But while the church is interesting, what really draws the crowds to St Michan's are the **mummified bodies** in the crypt. This visit is definitely not for the squeamish, and the tour guides delight in making the crowds shiver with fascinated horror. There are four bodies which, owing to a combination of temperature, limestone (to absorb humidity) and methane emissions from the ground, have been strangely well preserved. The coffins which once contained them have long since rotted, and the bodies lie gruesomely exposed. Their identity is unknown: one, missing his feet and his right hand, may have been a criminal; another is thought to be a nun, over 100 years old at the time of her death, with long curling toenails and brittle hair. But the most famous is 'the Crusader', so-called because his legs are crossed in the traditional manner of those who fought in the Crusades. At more than six feet six inches tall, he would have been a giant in his day, and his legs have been broken and tucked under him, perhaps to make him fit inside the coffin. It is an ancient tradition that touching his hand will bring good luck ('shaking hands with the Crusader'), and his fingers are worn smooth with centuries of fortune-making.

The adjoining crypt contains the bodies of some of the great Dublin landowners, dating back to the years when this church was the only one north of the Liffey. A corridor is lined with individual vaults, some still in use: the Lords of Leatrim have the fanciest coffins, but the most famous belong to John and Henry Sheares, who were hanged, disembowelled, beheaded and quartered for their role in the unsuccessful 1798 rebellion. Two other 1798 rebels, Oliver Bond and the Reverend William Jackson, are buried in the graveyard: Bond, a wealthy merchant whose home was a regular meeting place for the United Irishmen, took poison and died before sentence could be carried out, and the Reverend died of a fever in jail. Another rebel leader, Robert Emmet – who led an equally ill-fated rebellion in 1803 – is also rumoured to be buried in the church graveyard. He was hanged outside St Catherine's Church (see p.95), but his body was spirited away and no one knows for sure where his remains lie.

Dublin Corporation Fruit and Vegetable Market H6

*Mary's Lane; **bus** 25, 26, 37, 39, 67, 67A, 68, 69, 79. **Open** Mon–Fri 6am–3pm.*

The delightful **Fruit and Vegetable Market** was built in 1892, a fanciful and multi-coloured affair with delicate wrought iron, red and yellow brickwork and terracotta panels. It's mainly a wholesale market, but

King's Inns H5

Constitution Hill and Henrietta St, t (01) 874 4840, www.kingsinns.ie; bus 25, 26, 37, 39, 67, 67A, 68, 69, 79. No public access.

The **King's Inns** was begun in 1795, and was the last great public building designed by James Gandon. Like its predecessors, the Four Courts (*see above*) and the Custom House (*see p.111*), it was plagued by delays and difficulties, and Gandon finally resigned, worn out, in 1808. Construction was completed by his partner and pupil Henry Aaron Baker. The dining room is one of the few surviving interiors by Gandon in the whole of Dublin, but unfortunately, you won't be able to see it, as this is still the home of Dublin's legal profession and closed to visitors.

Henrietta Street H5

Henrietta Street was one of the first and finest of the new Georgian streets of the 18th century. It was laid out in the 1720s by Luke Gardiner, a wealthy banker and the first of the great private landlords who were to transform the face of Dublin so thoroughly. Henrietta Street was his masterpiece: its elegant succession of mansions were the largest and most opulent in the city, boasting fine stuccowork and rich panelling. The street was quickly nicknamed 'Primate Hill' after its legion of high-ranking inhabitants. Mary Wollstonecraft once lived at no. 5, as governess to Lord Kingsborough, but was dismissed for contaminating his children with her radical feminist ideas.

When the north side lost its battle with the south for more fashionable neighbourhood, Henrietta Street slipped quickly into decline. The houses were divided up into tenements, the ceilings and panelling stripped out, the marble fireplaces and carved balustrades sold, and the airy rooms divided into tiny boxes for unscrupulous landlords: at one point, no. 7 was home to 70 people. Until relatively recently, the street was a slum and a definite no-go area. Now it is still shabby and rundown, but pockets of restoration work have been undertaken, and, with the change in attitude towards the preservation of Dublin's architectural heritage and determined efforts on the part of the Irish Georgian Society, Henrietta Street's prospects are finally looking up.

SMITHFIELD

The **Smithfield** area was long one of Dublin's most rundown neighbourhoods, but is now experiencing a 21st-century revamp. It's still very much a work-in-progress despite being more than a decade into redevelopment, and the new buildings sit uneasily in a sea of tiny, red-brick terraces. New loft-style apartment buildings are being erected around the expansive cobbled square at the centre of the district, which has been rechristened Smithfield Plaza and given a row of 12 tall, futuristic lighting masts. These are usually lit on Saturday nights in summer – a spectacular sight, with huge blue flames leaping against chrome canopies. The square, which was used for livestock markets for four centuries, has been cleaned up and pedestrianized (even the cobbles were dug up, cleaned and returned); it's still the site of a monthly, rough-and-ready horse market (*see* box), and is occasionally used for outdoor concerts. One of Dublin's best old pubs, Cobblestones (*see p.207*), has survived the redevelopment and remains a good place to catch some traditional Irish music.

Smithfield Village G6

Smithfield Square; bus 25, 26, 37, 67, 67A, 68 69, 79.

Adjoining Smithfield Square is the modern development of **Smithfield Village**, which incorporates existing warehouses and factories, along with a huge hotel (Chief O'Neills, *see p.182*), a few shops, bars and restaurants,

Dublin Cowboys

The cobbled square in Smithfield was laid out as a marketplace in the mid-17th century, a tradition which continues today with the monthly horse fair. This is no romanticized tourist event, but a throwback to a grittier past which has all but vanished under the glossy effects of the boom years of the 1990s. Clumps of sharp-eyed farmers haggle over horseflesh as kids from the sink estates race skittish ponies with makeshift bridles. There are more than 3,500 ponies living on the mouldering council estates which circle Dublin. Ballymun – probably the poorest and most desperate of them all – is a prime example of 1960s planning gone horribly wrong. Its high-rise concrete towers are slated for demolition, but this has been delayed by the discovery of asbestos. In the meantime, the children of Dublin's poorest families pour their time and energy into their ponies, which crop peacefully in the incongruous concrete surroundings of the tower blocks. The monthly horse market at Smithfield is their chance to show off, and the kids make the five-mile trek on their ponies to the city centre at dawn. They career through the crowds, bareback, oblivious to annoyed yells and whistles of the more sedate, each trying to outdo their friends with their speed and dexterity. The Smithfield horse market was officially moved out of the plaza in 2001, but old traditions die hard and it has edged its way back. Its future remains uncertain as the gentrification of central Dublin continues apace.

the Old Jameson Distillery for whiskey fans and the Smithfield Chimney with panoramic views. The Village is the least successful element of the Smithfield redevelopment; despite the flow of tourists, it feels strangely disconnected from the neighbourhood.

Chimney Viewing Tower G6

Smithfield Village, t (01) 817 3800, www.chiefoneills.com; bus 25, 25A, 67, 67A, 68, 69, 79. Open Mon–Sat 10–5.30, Sun 11–5.30 (times may vary according to the season); adm by tour only (approximately hourly) €5, students/seniors/children €3.50, family ticket €10. Purchase tickets in the gift shop of the Chief O'Neill's Hotel. Bar, restaurant, gift shop in complex.

The **chimney** – 185 feet (56m) tall – which dominates the Smithfield Plaza was once a working part of the Old Jameson distillery, but has been revamped to contain a glass lift that will whoosh you up to a viewing platform for 360° views over Dublin (although whether the view is worth the hefty admission price is debatable). A guided tour points out the highlights of the city, from Phoenix Park in the east right around to the Millennium Spire to the west, and, once you are up there, you can linger as long as you like. Having said that, if you've already made it to the panoramic Gravity Bar at the top of the Guinness Storehouse (see p.95), you won't see anything new here.

Old Jameson Distillery G6

Bow St, t (01) 807 2355, f (01) 807 2369; bus 67, 67A, 68, 69, 79, 90. Open daily 9.30–6, last tour at 5.30; adm €7, students/seniors €5.75, children €3, family ticket €18. Restaurant, gift shop.

One of Dublin's most popular tourist attractions, the **Old Jameson Distillery** is really a slick marketing campaign masquerading as an historical tour. Still, it's reasonably interesting for anyone who wants to know more about whiskey (a name derived from *uisce beatha*, Gaelic for 'water of life') – and there's always the bonus of a tasting at the end. The tour begins with a short video, which gives a potted history of the distillery's beginnings back in 1780 and the story of Irish whiskey (which takes an 'e', unlike its Scottish cousin). But the main theme is established early on with constant reference to the World's Preferred Whiskey (Jameson's of course) – only the beginning of the hard-sell approach which dominates the visit. A series of small rooms illustrate the process of producing whiskey, from the roasting of the barley to its maturation in oak casks. A stuffed cat called Smith, a great ratter in his day, still stands guard over the grain store, and there is a fascinating collection of century-old distillation vessels (Irish whiskey is distilled three times, Scotch whisky twice and bourbon once). The whiskey matures for at least five years in oak casks; during this time, a portion of the alcohol – known, rather charmingly, as 'the angels' share' – evaporates. At the end of the tour, volunteers get to compare some of Jameson's best brands, while everyone else makes do with a standard 7-year-old.

Dublin Brewing Company G5

141–146 North King St, t (01) 872 8622, www.dublinbrewing.com; bus 67, 67A, 68, 69, 79, 90. Open Mon & Wed–Sun noon–6.

As an antidote to the blatant self-aggrandisement of world-famous companies like Guinness and Jameson's, Dublin does have its own microbrewery just around the corner from Smithfield Village. There is no bar on the premises, but you can taste their range of excellent beers in some of the city's pubs, including nearby Cobblestones (*see* p.207).

Stoneybatter E5

Bus 10, 10A, 16.

Stoneybatter, a small neighbourhood with neat rows of identical terraces, was built around 1900 for the workers at the Guinness factory. This once deeply working-class district was the last area of Dublin where Irish was spoken. Now it's the latest city-centre neighbourhood to be gentrified, with rising house prices and new restaurants springing up.

Collins Barracks (National Museum of Decorative Arts and History) F6

Benburb St, t (01) 677 7444, www.museum.ie; bus 25, 25A, 66, 67. Open Tues–Sat 10–5, Sun 2–5; adm free. Guided tours available, tour times vary: call in advance or check listings magazines. Wheelchair accessible. Café, gift shop.

The newest addition to the National Museum of Ireland (*see also* p.68), **Collins Barracks** have been crisply restored to house the national collection of decorative arts and history. Originally built as the Royal Barracks in 1701, it was renamed after Michael Collins in 1922. It's an austere yet handsome complex set around a vast arcaded square, and able to accommodate 5000 soldiers. One of the largest purpose-built barracks in the world, it had also become the oldest in continuous use when it was finally demilitarized in 1992.

It contains an enjoyable magpie collection, spanning everything from furniture and ceramics to weaponry and scientific instruments, as well as anything that wouldn't quite fit in the main museum in Kildare Street. The themed exhibitions are laid out in large, light galleries with plenty of interactive terminals and information panels, and there's a good café and gift shop. The most interesting exhibits can be found in the **Curator's Choice** section, which contains its most famous treasures – few of which, oddly, are Irish. The star exhibit is the Fonthill Vase, the earliest documented piece of Chinese porcelain in Europe, but other highlights include a 2,000-year-old Japanese ceremonial bell and the decorative gauntlets worn by King William at the Battle of the Boyne. There is an extensive collection of Irish furniture, from the ornate pieces of the Georgian period to Eileen Gray's sleek chrome table; lots of Irish silverwork, ceramics and glassware; a fabulous collection of historic

Arbour Hill Cemetery F5

Arbour Hill, t (01) 605 7700; bus 25, 25A, 66, 67. Open daily 9–5.

This small, unadorned military cemetery behind Collins Barracks is the final resting place of 14 of the leaders of the 1916 Easter Rising, who were court-martialled and shot at Kilmainham Gaol (see p.96). Among those remembered here are Padraig Pearse, Joseph Plunkett, James Connolly and Thomas MacDonagh; a copy of the Proclamation of 1916 is inscribed on a cenotaph. The cemetery is often used for public ceremonies, with political and republican leaders commemorating the events of 1916.

Croppies Acre F6

Wolfe Tone's Quay; bus 25, 25A, 66, 67.

Croppies Acre, a small green field next to Collins Barracks, is where the soldiers of the 1798 rebellion are buried – although 'buried' is too formal a term for the pit, or 'Croppy Hole' into which their remains were flung. Few of these unnamed soldiers were identified, but two of the leaders, Bartholomew Teeling and Matthew Tone, who were hanged at the Provost Prison on Arbour Hill, are known to have been buried here. The soldiers of the United Irishmen were nicknamed Croppies after their short haircuts (a style adopted along with revolutionary principles from the French), which made it difficult for them to escape detection in the Dublin crowds once it was clear that the rebellion had failed. The Guild of Lamplighters refused to light the lamps on the bridges, quays and main thoroughfares to help them evade Crown forces, but several of the lamplighters were hanged as a result. It was also here that a huge soup kitchen was opened during the time of the Great Famine, which fed almost 9,000 people each day.

James Joyce Bridge G6

Blackhall Place; bus 10, 10A.

The newest of the Liffey Bridges, this was designed by the fashionable Spanish architect Santiago Calatrava and opened in 2003. A cool, white, uncompromisingly modern bridge, it's named for James Joyce who set his famous story *The Dead* (from *The Dubliners*) in a 'dark, gaunt house' across the river at 15 Usher's Island. John Huston used the exterior of the house in his haunting 1987 film of the story.

Another of Calatrava's signature spare white bridges is planned for the docklands, further east – designed to swing open to allow ships up river. It is unlikely to be completed before the end of 2005.

PHOENIX PARK

Phoenix Park is Europe's largest enclosed park – a vast green expanse filled with paths and manicured lawns, cricket grounds and polo pitches, flower gardens and lakes, monuments and historic houses. There's nowhere better to leave the chaotic city behind and stroll or picnic in peace – although it's inadvisable to linger after dusk.

The name comes not from the mythical bird, but from a corruption of the Gaelic *fionn uisce*, meaning 'clear water', which referred to a nearby well (now long gone) that supplied healing waters. The park was created by the Duke of Ormond in 1663, acting on instructions from King Charles II, and has changed very little since then. It was enclosed and stocked with deer, became a favourite retreat for visiting royalty and dignitaries and, in 1747, was presented to the City of Dublin by the Earl of Chesterfield. There are two entrances: the main one on Parkgate Street; and another off the North

> ### The Phoenix Park Murders
>
> On 6 May 1882, Lord Cavendish, the chief secretary of Ireland and nephew of the British prime minister Gladstone, and Cavendish's under-secretary Thomas Burke were stabbed to death by four men within sight of the Viceregal Lodge. It was discovered to be the work of the Invincibles, a Fenian splinter group, but the assassination shocked the public both at home and in Britain, and set back the nationalist cause dramatically. Charles Stewart Parnell, the leader of the Home Rule party, had been released from Kilmainham Gaol just four days before. He was appalled and offered to resign in order to forestall any suspicion, but Gladstone urged him not to. Forged letters later appeared in the London *Times* which attempted to throw blame on Parnell, but the forgery was discovered and the man responsible shot himself while trying to escape arrest. The murdered men are remembered by a plaque near the Polo Grounds, and their assassins are commemorated in Glasnevin Cemetery (*see* p.129).

Circular Road that is more convenient for the Visitor's Centre and the upper reaches of the park.

A Tour of the Park A4

Phoenix Park; **bus** 10, 10A, 37.

The best-known formal garden in Phoenix Park is the **People's Park**, close to the main entrance. These prim and primped Victorian gardens were laid out in 1864, and are full of meticulously weeded flower beds, willow-fringed ponds and leafy paths.

Beyond is the **Wellington Monument**, a tall pillar of Wicklow granite which, at 63 metres, is Ireland's tallest monument. It was designed in 1817, but not erected until 1861, and the proposed statue of the man himself (a Dubliner) on horseback never materialized owing to lack of funds. The friezes depict scenes from famous battles in India and at Waterloo, which were cast from melted-down cannons captured at Waterloo itself. Close by is **The Hollow**, a peaceful glade of oaks and elms with an old-fashioned bandstand, with the Phoenix Park Tea Rooms on hand for refreshments and Dublin Zoo just beyond (*see* opposite).

Chesterfield Avenue, which cuts for two and a half miles through the park to the Phoenix Monument at its centre, is bordered on one side by the grassy expanse of Nine Acres (used for polo matches) and the Áras An Uachtárain (the President's House, *see* opposite), and on the other by the cricket ground and wooded areas where you might glimpse some of the park's 500 or so deer. The infamous Phoenix Park murders (*see* box) were committed by the Polo Ground, where the two men who died are commemorated with a small plaque.

The **Phoenix Monument** at the centre of the park was erected by Lord Chesterfield, then Lord Lieutenant of Ireland, in 1747. The area north of the monument belongs to the former Chief Secretary's Lodge and Demesne, which is now the residence of the US ambassador. The USA were quick to give their support for the Irish nation after it won independence in 1922, and the ambassador was granted the right to reside here in return for a peppercorn rent in recognition of American support.

To the west of the Phoenix Monument is the **Papal Cross**. This grass mound marked with an enormous cross commemorates Pope John Paul II's visit in 1979, and offers wonderful views down across the grassy fields of Fifteen Acres (named for an ancient enclosure, which predated the park's current layout and which presently covers more like 200 acres). This part of the park used to be used for duels and military exercises, but now the most exertion that you'll see is the odd game of football.

To the north stretches the **Oldtown Wood**, one of the most extensive wooded areas in the park and a fabulous spot for a ramble but not somewhere you should hang around after dark. In the northeastern corner of the

> *Little and Large*
>
> A famous duel took place between two lawyers on Fifteen Acres, one very large and one very small. When the big man complained that he couldn't see his opponent, the latter responded vigorously: 'Let his second get a bit of white chalk, and draw my exact size and shape on that huge carcass of his; and any bullet of mine that hits outside that white line shall not count.'

park, near the pretty **Glen Pond**, Neolithic and early Bronze Age tombs have been discovered which pre-date the famous passage tombs at Newgrange, Dowth and Knowth (*see* p.160). You can find out more about them at the Phoenix Park Visitors' Centre.

Phoenix Park Visitors' Centre A3

*Phoenix Park, **t** (01) 677 0095, www.heritageireland.ie; **bus** 37. Open Nov to mid-March Sat–Sun 10–5, mid-March to end-March daily 10–5.30, April–Sept daily 10–6, Oct daily 10–5; **adm** €2.75, seniors €2, children/students €1.25, family ticket €7. Ground floor is wheelchair accessible. Café, gift shop.*

Phoenix Park's useful **Visitors' Centre** has exhibitions on the park's history and wildlife, plus lots of activities for children, as well as plans of the park and leaflets showing some of its highlights. It also has a reconstruction of the Knockmaree cist grave discovered in the park's northeastern corner in 1838.

Admission includes a visit to the 17th-century Ashtown Castle. This miniature tower house was found inside the walls of a later building (demolished due to dry rot), and has been carefully restored. Its defences include a 'murder hole' – an unexpected hole in the ceiling above the entrance, through which the tower's inhabitants would pour boiling water or oil on unwanted visitors' heads – and a 'trip step' on the spiral staircase leading to the family apartments.

The Visitors' Centre is also where you can pick up the free tickets (which are limited in number, so get there early) to Áras An Uachtaráin (the President's House, *see* below).

Áras an Uachtaráin (President's House) B3

*Phoenix Park, **t** (01) 677 0095, www.heritageireland.ie; **bus** 37. Open Sat 10.30–4.30; **adm** free, by hourly guided tour only.*

The current home of the Irish president was built between 1751 and 1754 by Nathaniel Clements, the famously strict Ranger who 'ensured that every impropriety [within the park] was rigorously expelled'. It was later enlarged to become the viceregal residence by Francis Johnston in 1816. A luxurious hideaway surrounded by good hunting grounds, it was a favourite with visiting royals – including Queen Victoria who stayed here in 1849, and whose letters home never once mentioned the appalling horrors of the Great Famine. Winston Churchill spent his first three years in the Little Lodge, a stone's throw from the Viceregal Lodge, and remembered being given a drum by Mr Burke, who was later killed in the Phoenix Park murders. The tour guides you through the lavish State Reception Rooms and the President's Office.

Dublin Zoo D4

*Phoenix Park, **t** (01) 474 8900, **f** (01) 677 1660; **bus** 10, 25, 26. Open March–Sept Mon–Sat 9.30–6, Sun 10.30–6; Oct–Feb Mon–Sat 9.30–dusk, Sun 10.30–dusk; last admission one hour before closing; **adm** €10.10, children/seniors €6.30, unwaged €7.70, family ticket €30.*

Dublin Zoo, the second oldest zoo in Europe, has risen to the challenge of modernization; it has widened its enclosures and added new buildings and educational facilities. Thirteen acres of the lands adjoining the president's house were donated, allowing the zoo to double in size and build the new African Plains exhibition. But it is still a city zoo, and, despite the changes, the animals remain cramped. The zoo famously raised Caibre the lion, who roars in the opening sequence of all MGM movies, and is now focused on conservation and education work carried out in conjunction with other zoos across the world.

All the zoo favourites are here, from elephants to giraffes, penguins and polar bears, and there's a petting zoo to please the younger children.

Outside the Centre

SOUTH OF THE CENTRE 126
Pearse Museum 126
Rathfarnham Castle 128
Drimnagh Castle 128
Dillon Garden 129

NORTH OF THE CENTRE 129
Glasnevin Cemetery (Prospect Cemetery) 129
National Botanic Gardens 130
Croke Park: the GAA Museum 131
Casino at Marino 131

THE COAST AROUND DUBLIN BAY 132
Bull Island Nature Reserve 132
Malahide 132
Howth 134
Dún Laoghaire and Sandycove 135
Dalkey and Killiney Bay 136
Bray 138

Scattered around the edges of Dublin are some of the city's quirkiest sights: in the south, you can visit a couple of fairy-tale castles (including one with a moat), explore a celebrity garden and see the school established by Pádhraic Pearse, hero of the 1916 Easter Rising. In the north, the most famous nationalist heroes of the Irish struggle are laid to rest in Prospect Cemetery in Glasnevin, and nearby you can relax in the graceful Botanic Gardens. The beautiful Casino at Marino is an exquisite 18th-century pavilion which unfolds magically once you get inside, and at the hi-tech GAA museum you can try your hand at Gaelic sports. A stroll along the strands at Bulls Island will clear the head after a night on the town.

While immersed in the city, it's easy to forget that Dublin sits on the coast, but the string of seaside resorts which line Dublin Bay are a short and easy journey on the DART, the city's excellent suburban rail line which hugs the coastline from Malahide in the north to Bray and beyond in the south. Joyce fans will want to make the pilgrimage to the Joyce Tower in Sandycove, but there are also castles, spectacular cliff walks, coves and beaches, country houses with formal gardens and plenty of great pubs and restaurants.

SOUTH OF THE CENTRE

Pearse Museum

St Enda's Park, Grange Road, Rathfarnham, t (01) 493 4208; bus 16. Open daily Nov–Jan 10–4, Feb–April and Sept–Oct 10–5, May–Aug 10–5.30; adm free; free guided tours available on request. Café.

This quiet, stone mansion set in beautiful leafy grounds was once the boys' school of St Enda's, established by the revolutionary hero Pádhraic Pearse in 1908 and continued by his mother and sister until 1935. As a young man, Pádhraic was steeped in the heroic Irish tales recounted by his mother, and dreamed of Irish freedom brought about through education and culture. He thought of St Enda's as 'the Eton of Ireland', where the future leaders of the country would be taught their own culture in their native tongue. The school crest depicted the legendary hero Cúchulainn, and the boys were taught in Irish and played ancient Gaelic games such as hurling. Four of the teachers at the school were executed after the Easter Rising: Pádhraic himself, his younger brother Willy, Thomas McDonagh and Colum Colbert. The house was give to the state on the death of Pearse's sister in 1968, in accordance with his mother's wish that it be kept as a memorial to her two sons. Parts of the house, including the uncomfortable dormitories, look much as they would have done during Pearse's time, and cabinets full of photographs, letters, books and mementoes give a moving and very personal account of Pearse's progressive views on education, as well as the events leading up to the Easter Rising.

Out in the peaceful extensive gardens, another rebel is remembered in Emmet Walk: Robert Emmet (see p.95) strolled here with his lover Sarah Curran, who would be the unwitting cause of his capture when he returned to her house instead of fleeing when the rebellion proved unsuccessful.

Pádhraic Pearse

Patrick Henry Pearse was born in Dublin in 1879. His father was an English stonemason who had come to Ireland to find work, and his mother was a native Irish speaker from County Meath who loved to tell her children Irish folk tales. Patrick, who later changed his name from the anglicized version to Pádhraic, began learning Irish at the age of 11, and joined the Gaelic League five years later. A fervent supporter of home rule, he initially believed that education would open the door to Irish independence. But his politics became increasingly revolutionary, and in 1913 he joined the Irish Volunteers, precursor of the Irish Republican Brotherhood (IRB). In 1914, at a famous speech at the graveside of a Sinn Féin revolutionary, he proclaimed, 'While Ireland holds these graves, Ireland unfree shall never be at peace.'

When war broke out in Europe, and almost 50,000 Irish soldiers went to their deaths in the service of the British Army, the IRB was split between those who wanted to take advantage of the British military involvement in Europe and those who wanted to wait until the men had returned. Pádhraic Pearse was one of those who felt the time for an uprising was right, and secretly began preparations for a rebellion planned for 1916. On Easter Monday, he and his men took up their posts across the city, with their HQ in the General Post Office on O'Connell Street. They held out for nine days against 20,000 soldiers of the British Army, before finally surrendering on 29 April. The leaders of the rebellion were led through the city streets, where, to their shock, their countrymen hissed and spat at them – some were angry at the damage inflicted on their homes and businesses, while others felt that Ireland should stand with Britain in the war which was devastating Europe. The rebel leaders were court-martialled, condemned to death in secret by a British military court and, on 3 May 1916, were taken to the Stonebreaker's Yard in Kilmainham Gaol and executed by firing squad. The public were horrified by this heavy-handed response, and opinion immediately swung behind the rebels, who were fêted as martyrs. It was the beginning of the end for the British administration, and the fuse was lit for the war of independence that would culminate in the declaration of the Irish Free State in 1922. On the evening before he was shot, Pádhraic wrote to his mother: 'This is the death I should have chosen if God had given me a choice of deaths – to die a soldier's death for Ireland and for freedom.'

Rathfarnham Castle

*Rathfarnham, **t** (01) 493 9462, www.heritageireland.ie; **bus** 16, 16A, 17, 75A. **Open** May–Oct daily 9.30–5.30; times are subject to change – call to check in advance; **adm** €2, seniors €1.25, children/students €1, family ticket €5.50. Partial access for wheelchair-users. Café.*

Rathfarnham Castle is either wildly romantic or a building site, depending on your point of view. Once the grandest castle in the whole of Dublin, it suffered terrible neglect and remains in a very dilapidated state. And yet the peeling walls and battered stucco ceilings hint poignantly at its former opulence, and it's not hard to believe in the ghosts which are said to haunt it.

The castle was built in the 1580s for Adam Loftus, an ambitious Yorkshireman who arrived in the city as chaplain to the Earl of Sussex and went on to become the Archbishop of Dublin, Lord Chancellor of Ireland and first provost of Trinity College. It remains the only Elizabethan building in Dublin, built as a fortified house with sturdy defensive towers. It was one of the first castles in Dublin and certainly the most luxurious; Oliver Cromwell was among its many guests. The original battlements were removed in the 18th century, when it was turned into a fashionable Georgian residence by Henry Loftus. He commissioned the most fashionable architects of the day, including William Chambers (who designed Trinity's Chapel and Examination Hall), to remodel it completely. Chambers was responsible for the opulent **Great Hall**, with its Doric columns and glowing stained glass windows. The **Dining Hall**, with its thick walls (built, so it was said, to 'keep the heat in and the Irish out'), has particularly fine plasterwork, with a delicate tracery of acorns spiralling sinuously across the ceiling. Upstairs are the most sumptuous chambers, including an ornate **reception room** and a magical **ballroom** with a surviving stucco ceiling designed by Chambers. Only two decades after Henry's death the castle was abandoned and its collections dispersed. It was lived in sporadically in the 19th century, and taken over by the Jesuits in the early 20th century (they put in the terrible religious panels in the Long Gallery). Finally, the city bought it back in the 1980s and have undertaken a painstaking renovation. Plans show the extent of the estate when it was first built, but most of the lands have been taken over by a golf course. A tiny section of the formal **gardens** has survived, with an ornamental pond and some decidedly modern, council-issue benches.

Drimnagh Castle

*Long Mile Road, Drimnagh, **t** (01) 450 2530; **bus** 56A. **Open** April–Sept Wed, Sat & Sun noon–5; Oct–March Wed noon–5 and Sun 2–5; last tour at 4pm; **adm** €4, students/seniors €3.50, children €2.*

Rising dramatically from a grey suburban sprawl of pebble-dashed terrace houses and an industrial estate, **Drimnagh Castle** looks like something from a story book. It is the only castle in Ireland with a flooded moat, the only medieval castle in Dublin and one of the oldest in Ireland to be continually inhabited. It was built as a tower house in the 13th century for a powerful Anglo-Norman family, the Barnewalls, who kept an eye on their extensive lands from the lookout turrets (Captowers). The castle was meticulously restored from ruins in the 1980s, using medieval crafts. Accurate replicas of the original oak roofs were made on site by hand, and the stonework was carved without the use of modern tools. An original '**murder hole**' survives above the entrance, through which unsuspecting invaders would have been doused with boiling water. Staircases were built to favour sword hands, and, as Sir Hugh Barnewall was left-handed, the castle's **staircase** spirals anti-clockwise. It leads to the **Great Hall** at the heart of the castle, where one of the magnificent Irish oak ceilings created during the Restoration is slowly beginning to darken with age. No nails were used in its assembly, and each piece was hand-carved (some of the craftsmen have been commemorated in the carved effigies). The floor would originally have been strewn with rushes, but it is now tiled with the Barnewall family's heraldic emblems, echoed in the windows; the chandeliers were bought from the set of *Excalibur*, which was filmed around the Powerscourt Estate (*see* p.170). Outside is an exquisite formal **garden** from the 17th century, with a small kitchen garden and a poultry run.

Dillon Garden

*45 Sandford Road, Ranelagh, **t** (01) 497 1308, www.dillongarden.com. **Open** March and July–Aug daily 2–6, April–June and Sept Sun only 2–6; **adm** €5, children not admitted unless by prior arrangement.*

Helen Dillon, one of Ireland's best-known gardeners and TV personalities, has taken 25 years to create this stunning city garden, with clematis-draped arches, borders filled with flowers, sweet-smelling lilies and wild flowers and roses. She recently ripped out the lawn to replace it with a modern canal set in sleek limestone, which has become the garden's most striking feature.

NORTH OF THE CENTRE

Glasnevin Cemetery (Prospect Cemetery)

*Fingals Road, **t** (01) 830 1133, www.glasnevin-cemetery.ie; **bus** 40, 40A, 40C, 40D. **Open** daily 8.30 to dusk; **adm** free. Free guided visits available; check listings guides for times, or call for information.*

This vast Catholic cemetery in the quiet suburb of Glasnevin was opened in 1832. Before that, Catholics had to bury their dead in Protestant cemeteries because of restrictions on Catholic services enforced by the repressive Penal Laws. After a Protestant sexton scolded a Catholic priest for performing a limited version of a funeral Mass, Daniel O'Connell, the 'Great Liberator', took up the cause and proved that there was no legal obstacle to prevent Catholics praying over their dead in a graveyard. Nine acres of land were purchased in Glasnevin (now expanded to 120 acres) and the first Catholic burial took place here in 1832.

The cemetery is contained by a medieval-style stone wall, with carved figures by James Pearse, the father of Pádhraic Pearse. Watchtowers were added in the late 19th century to deter bodysnatchers (*see* box on p.130). Among the million or so buried here are some of the most famous names in Irish history, including Daniel O'Connell himself. The **O'Connell Monument** stands right at the entrance to the cemetery, a round tower that deliberately recalls the early Christian era in Ireland before the Anglo-Norman invasion. O'Connell died in Genoa in 1849; his heart was given to Rome, as he had instructed, and the rest of his body was returned to Ireland. The crypt beneath the round tower where O'Connell's remains were finally laid in 1869 is decorated with traditional Celtic ornamentation, and an inscription reads 'My body to Ireland, my heart to Rome and my soul to Heaven'. In front of the tower, a new monument commemorates nine men who were hanged and buried at Mountjoy Prison 80 years ago, and whose bodies were finally transferred here in 2001. The most famous of these was Kevin Barry, a member of the Irish Republican Army who was only 18 when he was captured during a raid on the British Army in 1920; he was hanged on 1 November, despite pleas for clemency on account of his age. Barry rapidly became a popular hero, and his exploits were recorded in dozens of still-famous traditional ballads, including one which begins: 'Another martyr for old Erin/ Another murder for the crown/ The British laws may crush the Irish/ But cannot keep their spirits down'. These songs became so well known that one little girl apparently asked her mother 'What used they to sing before Kevin Barry?'

The other great Nationalist leader to be buried here is **Charles Stewart Parnell**. He

> ### *The Bodysnatchers*
>
> Bodysnatchers, also known as 'sack-em-ups' or 'resurrectionists', plied a brisk trade in Dublin from the late 18th century. From 1791, the bodies of executed murderers were regularly donated for dissection by medical students, but, as the numbers of medical schools rose, there were not enough fresh corpses to go around and bodysnatchers saw a gap in the market. They would steal the corpses from fresh graves by hooking them under their chin and dragging them up (the Ghost Bus tour run by Dublin Bus, see p.45, gives a gruesome demonstration), or sometimes they just removed the teeth and hair from cholera victims. The public grew increasingly alarmed, and eventually night watchmen known as 'Charlies' were employed to keep an eye on graveyards. The five towers built into the walls of Glasnevin were erected for armed guards who ensured that the bodysnatchers stayed outside the walls. The practice gradually faded after the 1832 Anatomy Act, which legalized the donation of bodies for medical research.

asked to be buried in a mass grave, and his body lies in the Cholera Mound alongside his mother Delia. A granite boulder from his Wicklow estate, simply inscribed with his name, serves as his gravestone. This monument is the simplest in the cemetery, which has a sea of beautiful Celtic stone crosses with intricate, interlocking ornamentation, plenty of lavish 19th-century Gothic revival headstones and even some flamboyant neoclassical mausolea. The most outrageous of these is for **John Philpott Curran** – an exact replica of an ancient Roman tomb, to be found in Curran's Square, the oldest part of the cemetery. Other famous graves include those of the **Countess de Markievicz**, who held the College of Surgeons during the Easter Rising; **Maud Gonne McBride**, revolutionary and muse to W.B. Yeats; James Joyce's father, **John Stanislaus Joyce**; **Gerald Manley Hopkins** (in an unmarked Jesuit grave); and the playwright **Brendan Behan**.

The back gate of the cemetery is now closed, but it's worth taking a stroll around the perimeter to find Kavanagh's pub on Prospect Square which faces the former back entrance to the graveyard. Better known as 'The Gravediggers', this wonderful pub has barely changed in the last 180 years, and even the yellow light filtering through the windows seems to come from another era.

National Botanic Gardens

Off Botanic Road, Glasnevin, **t** *(01) 837 7956;* **bus** *19, 19A, 13, 134.* **Open** *summer Mon–Sat 9–6, Sun 11–6; winter Mon–Sat 10–4.30, Thurs until 3.15, Sun 2–4.15;* **adm** *free. Glasshouses usually shut one hour before closing, and most are also closed 12.45–2. Guided tour (€2) usually offered on Sundays at 2.30 – call in advance to check. Partially wheelchair accessible. Café, shop, visitor centre.*

Dublin's tranquil, elegant **Botanic Gardens** were laid out by Dr Walter Wade and John Underwood between 1795 and 1825 for the Royal Dublin Society. The highlights are the immaculate Victorian glasshouses, including Richard Turner's spectacular Curvilinear Range which have recently emerged from a sparkling restoration. At the centre is the Great Palm House, built in 1884, which contains giant palms along with figs, bananas, bamboo, camellias and lillies. The comparatively modest Aquatic House contains a limpid pool with a huge Amazonian lily and delicate creepers curling prettily around the ironwork of the roof. Beyond the glasshouses is Yew Walk, also known as Addison's Walk, which dates back to 1740; it is all that remains of an earlier garden which existed here before the public gardens were opened. To the west are the delicately scented Rose Gardens, close to a small river with a weir, and beyond are extensive woodlands. It's one of the most beautiful, peaceful and relaxing spots in the city, and a perfect retreat from the city clamour.

Croke Park: the GAA Museum

*Croke Park, t (01) 855 8176, www.gaa.ie; bus 3, 11, 11A, 16, 16A, 123. Open Mon–Sat 9.30–5, Sun noon–5; stadium tours at 12.30 and 3; **adm** €5.50, or €8.50 including tour, students/ seniors €3.50 or €6 with tour, children €3 or €5 with tour. On match days, only those with spectator tickets are admitted to the museum. Café, shop.*

Croke Park is the home of Ireland's ancient national games of hurling and football, and the legendary stadium has recently been completely overhauled to emerge as one of the most modern in Europe. It is owned by the **Gaelic Athletics Association (GAA)**, which was founded in the 1880s at the height of the Gaelic revival in order to promote Gaelic sports, as well as all other aspects of Gaelic culture. The main instigator behind the establishment of the GAA was Michael Cusack, who liked to be known as 'Citizen Cusack', earning himself a walk-on part as the 'Citizen' in Joyce's *Ulysses*. The GAA became a focus for nationalists, and was even briefly taken over by the Irish Republican Brotherhood (IRB). Members of the Irish Royal Constabulary and British soldiers and sailors were banned from the Association, and in 1902 GAA members were forbidden to play soccer or rugby. The Irish Volunteers, founded in 1913, regularly drilled using their hurling sticks as mock rifles.

In 1920, the stadium was the scene of the 'Bloody Sunday Massacre', an incident sparked after Michael Collins ordered the execution on 21 November 1920, of the 'Cairo Gang' – 14 British officers who had infiltrated the IRB. The following day Tipperary played Dublin at the Croke Park stadium, and the British army – who had information that the men responsible for the executions were among the crowd – machine-gunned the stands. Fourteen were killed and dozens injured.

To this day, the rules of the GAA still forbid the playing in the stadium of 'foreign games' (any which weren't played by the ancient Gaels); the atmosphere at a big hurling or Gaelic football final is hard to beat. Both sports are fast, exciting and pretty rough, and both have a huge and enthusiastic following. As part of the stadium's major overhaul, a state-of-the-art **museum** has been built, with lots of imaginative exhibits to keep kids happy and adults absorbed. On the ground floor, the history of the Gaelic sports of hurling and football and the establishment of the GAA are outlined with touch-screen information screens, colourful panels and exhibit cases (one contains a cast of a 15th-century grave slab, complete with carved sword and a hurley and ball). Upstairs, you can watch match highlights on special video screens, or, best of all, try out your agility, reflexes, balance and co-ordination in specially constructed booths.

> ## Gaelic Sports
>
> **Gaelic football** (roughly speaking, a cross between rugby and association football) and **hurling** (which resembles hockey) date back thousands of years, and the modern versions are fast and furious. (Camogie is a version of hurling played by women.) Both games are played on the same pitch, both last 70 minutes and both field teams of 15. The aim is to get the football or the slíothar – the ball used in hurling – over the crossbar to gain points.
>
> Dublin may have the national stadium, but its teams are usually outshone by other counties in both sports. If you don't manage to see a match in the Croke Park stadium, there are games held on sports fields all around the city. The tourist information office can tell you what's on where.

Casino at Marino

Off Malahide Rd, Marino, t (01) 833 1618; bus 20A, 20B, 27, 27A, 42, 42C, 123; DART to Clontarf Rd. Open for guided tours only: Feb–March & Nov Sun & Thurs noon–4; April Sun & Thurs noon–5; May & Oct daily 10–5; June–Sept daily 10–6; last admission 45 minutes before closing time; **adm** €2.75, seniors €1.25, children/students €1.25, family ticket €7. Limited wheelchair access.

The **Casino** (Italian for 'little house' – and nothing to do with roulette and blackjack) at Marino is considered one of the finest neoclassical buildings in Ireland. It was built between 1750 and the 1770s as a garden pavilion for the Earl of Charlemont (*see* p.106) who had recently inherited an estate with extensive lands (all now submerged by modern housing estates). He began construction of his pavilion in order to 'attach myself to my native land... Without some attractive employment, I doubted whether I should have resolution to become a resident'.

The Casino is the only survivor of the Earl's estate, which was demolished in the 1920s, although the entrance gates have recently been re-erected. It was designed by William Chambers, the principal architect of the 18th-century classical revival, with suggestions from Charlemont himself, who was a notable classical scholar. It's an extraordinarily ingenious construction in which nothing is quite what it appears. From the exterior, it looks like a tiny classical temple and appears to contain just one storey, but inside it magically unfolds like a Chinese box to reveal 16 rooms set over three floors. All kinds of clever devices are used to trick the eye, beginning with the imposing portico, in which the actual doorway is only half-size. Even the windows are cleverly masked to conceal the fact that they illuminate two levels. Inside, hidden doorways, staircases, sky-blue domes and *trompe l'oeil* carvings add to an impression of space. The most extravagant of the main reception rooms is the **Saloon**, with an exquisite stucco ceiling, the original patterned marquetry floor and an adjoining library and music room. A hidden staircase leads up to the state room, with a canopied bed tucked behind a rank of gilded columns. There are beautiful views from the rooftop, with two large urns which, ingeniously, double as chimneys.

Near the Casino, look out for Marino Crescent, better known as **Ffoliot's Revenge**; it is named for an artist and landowner who deliberately built the crescent in order to spoil the Earl's view from the Casino.

THE COAST AROUND DUBLIN BAY
Bull Island Nature Reserve

*North Bull Wall, Clontarf Rd, **t** (01) 833 1859; **DART** to Raheny then 30-min walk, or **bus** 130 to Dollymount then 30-min walk. Opening hours of interpretive centre vary; call for times; **adm** free.*

Bull Island is really an overgrown sandbank, formed from the sand which accumulated behind the North Bull Wall after it was built in 1821 in order to prevent Dublin's harbour from silting up. Now a UNESCO biosphere reserve, its sandflats and mud banks are home to thousands of migratory birds, including a substantial population of Brent geese. Over 300 species of plants also have been recorded, including some rare and officially protected species, and the grasslands are home to badgers, rabbits and the hares.

The windswept strand of **Dollymount Beach** is a popular spot to walk off a hangover, and there are a couple of golf courses (the Royal Dublin Golf Club and St Anne's Golf Course, *see* p.221) if you are looking for birdies of a different kind.

Malahide

*There are regular **DART** trains (journey time 30min) to Malahide: make sure you are on the right train, as the line splits at Howth Junction. **Bus** 42 leaves from Talbot St and takes 45 minutes – longer if the traffic is bad. Tourist information is at Malahide Castle, **t** (01) 845 0490.*

Malahide is a pretty, chi-chi little seaside

resort with a straggle of old-fashioned tearooms and antique shops and a long, sandy beach. To the southwest of the village and not marked from the train station – turn left and cross the bridge away from the village) is Malahide Demesne, with a 12th-century castle set in extensive grounds and a host of smaller attractions tucked into the outbuildings.

Malahide Castle

Malahide Demesne, Malahide, t (01) 846 2184 or 846 2516; bus 42 from Talbot St; DART to Malahide. Open April–Oct Mon–Sat 10–12.45 & 2–5, Sun 11–6; Nov–March Mon–Fri 10–5, Sat–Sun 2–5; adm €6, seniors/students €5, children €3.50, family tickets €16.50; includes guided tour and audio-guide. Café, craft shop. Botanic Gardens open May–Sept daily 2–5; guided tours (€3) of walled garden on Wed at 2; t (01) 816 9910.

> ### Discount Tickets
> Malahide Castle and the Fry Model Railway Museum offer a special combined ticket with the Dublin Writers Museum (*see* p.76), Shaw Birthplace (*see* p.76) and the James Joyce Museum (*see* p.136) – you can choose any two of these attractions for €10 (students/seniors €8, children €5.50, family ticket €28.50).

The Talbot family lived in **Malahide Castle** for almost eight hundred years, and the original medieval Anglo-Norman tower house has been added to and expanded throughout the centuries. The result is a delightfully eccentric hotchpotch of styles, which trace the castle's transformation from fortress to private home. The castle passed to the city on the death of Lord Milo, the last Talbot, in 1973, and a part of the National Portrait Collection is now housed here. The Boswell Papers, a collection of documents and travelogues by Johnson's companion James Boswell, were discovered here in a croquet box in the 1920s.

The first room on the tour is a 16th-century style panelled room in the heart of the original **tower house** which forms the core of the castle. Every inch is carved with elaborate floral and plant decoration, and there's a 16th-century Flemish carving of the Coronation of the Virgin which was always considered lucky by the Talbots (who were Catholic until the 18th century). The 18th-century **apartments**, which were tacked onto the medieval tower house, are large and light, with sumptuous rococo stucco ceilings and a fine collection of Irish furniture and portraits. There's a charming circular **reading room**, where the family could sit and admire the views over the gardens. There are even better views from the upstairs apartments; the ladies' bedroom is stuffed full of fans and other trinkets; the children's room has some charming old-fashioned toys; and the main bedroom has some disconcerting 1960s-style shop mannequins modelling the Lord's ermine-trimmed robes. The **Great Hall**, the only surviving medieval hall in Ireland, was built around 1475, and it was here that 14 members of the family ate breakfast before going to their deaths at the Battle of the Boyne on 1 July 1690. A small arched doorway is known as **Puck's Doorway**, after the castle's resident ghost. Puck is said to have been a family servant who fell asleep when invaders arrived and hanged himself in shame. He appears whenever there are changes that he doesn't agree with, and he was last seen in 1975, when the castle and its contents were being auctioned.

The castle is surrounded by extensive **gardens**, including some beautiful **Botanic Gardens** which were largely created by Lord Milo Talbot between 1948 and 1973. They contain thousands of species, many of them exotic plants from the southern hemisphere.

Tara's Palace and Museum of Childhood

Malahide Demesne, t (01) 846 3779; bus 42 from Talbot St; DART to Malahide. Open April–Sept Mon–Sat 10–1 & 2–5; suggested donation €2 (children €1).

The former stable block has been converted into a craft courtyard, with a few shops selling local crafts from woodwork to jam.

Also here is **Tara's Palace and Museum of Childhood**, with a small collection of antique dolls and toys on the ground floor, an extraordinary doll's house collection upstairs. Among the dolls' houses is one dating back to around 1700, which is possibly the oldest in the world; it was donated by Graham Greene's wife, Vivian. There's also a Georgian dolls' house which belonged to Oscar Wilde's mother's family. Upstairs is Tara's Palace, a magnificent and still unfinished dolls' house which is an amalgam of some of Ireland's greatest mansions – Castletown House, Leinster House and Carton. The detail is astonishing, with miniature versions of famous portraits, replica Chippendale furniture and tiny porcelain tea sets. There's also a huge and very odd collection of dressed-up dolls, their feather boas and jewellery sitting very oddly with their blank, babyish faces.

Fry Model Railway Museum

Malahide Demesne, t (01) 846 3779; bus 42 from Talbot St; DART to Malahide. **Open** *April–Oct Mon–Sat 10–5, Sun 2–6; Oct–March Sat–Sun 2–5;* **adm** *€6, seniors/students €5, children €3.50, family ticket €16.50. Shop.*

This is an odd, old-fashioned little museum, which seems more geared towards elderly model enthusiasts than children – who are allowed to watch but not touch. The handmade models were built by Cyril Fry, a railway engineer and draughtsman in the 1930s. They are laid out on a track which passes many miniaturized Dublin landmarks, including Heuston station and the River Liffey with all its bridges, trams, barges and boats. The meticulous detailing goes as far as replicating original signs inside the carriages, including this one from 1949: 'Please do not spit in the carriages. It is offensive to other passengers and is stated by the medical profession to be a source of serious disease.'

Howth

There are regular **DART** *trains to Howth station (the line splits at Howth Junction, so be sure to get the right train), or you can take* **bus** *31 or 31B from Lower Abbey St. The DART takes about 25 minutes, the bus can take substantially longer because of the traffic.*

The seaside town of **Howth** (rhymes with 'both') sprawls around the base of the Head of Howth, a rugged peninsula which closes off Dublin Bay to the north. Yachts and a smattering of brightly painted fishing boats bob in the small harbour, with the village clustered tightly behind it.

The town's name comes from the Old Norse *hofuth*, meaning 'promontory', and a ruined abbey in the centre of the village recalls the establishment of the first church on the spot by the Danish king Sitric in 1042. The present ruins date back to the 15th and 16th centuries, and contain a small, windswept graveyard with the 15th-century tomb of Christopher St Lawrence, 13th Baron of Howth, whose family were given these lands after the Anglo-Norman conquest.

Howth has views across to the tiny island of **Ireland's Eye**, a mile out to sea, which you can reach by boat from the harbour during the summer. Its name comes from a corruption of *Inis Eireann*, 'Island of Eire', and the old stone church on the island is all that is left of a 6th-century monastery. The island is now a bird sanctuary, and has some beautiful wild beaches which are perfect for summer picnics. Beyond Ireland's Eye is the hazy outline of **Lambey Island**, which is now a private bird sanctuary.

The famous **Howth Cliff Walk** snakes steeply out of the southern end of the village beyond the Martello Tower and towards the Baily Lighthouse, passing secluded coves and rugged gorse-packed banks, and offering fabulous views across Dublin Bay. The walk is about five miles, but if you don't want to do the whole thing you can cheat and hop on the 31B bus, which runs parallel to much of it. It's also possible to extend the hike and make the climb up to the Ben of Howth for more spectacular views. W.B. Yeats would come up here, swallow a pellet of hash, then lay his head on the ground and listen to the 'heartbeat of the earth'. In the last section of

Joyce's *Ulysses*, Molly Bloom stands here gazing across the bay.

Howth Castle Demesne

If you turn right out of the DART station, you'll come to **Howth Castle Demesne**, which still belongs to the St Lawrence family. According to legend, the famous 16th-century pirate queen Grace O'Malley was once refused admittance to the castle because the family were eating. Outraged, she snatched Lord Howth's infant son and heir and sailed away with him to Mayo. The child was returned on condition that the castle gates remained open at mealtimes and that a place would always be set for the head of the O'Malley clan, a custom that is apparently still kept today. The dour castle, an odd mish-mash of architectural styles coated with peeling grey plasterwork, is private, but the extensive grounds contain the smart Deer Park Hotel and Golf Links (*see* p.184), and a stunning glade of wild rhododendrons reached by a small path behind the hotel – a blaze of scarlet, pink and white in May and June.

National Transport Museum

Howth Castle Demesne, t (01) 848 0832, www.nationaltransportmuseum.org. Open June–Aug Mon–Sat 10–5, Sun and bank hols 2–5; Sept–May Sat–Sun and bank hols 2–5; adm €2.

The Howth Castle grounds also contain the fascinating **National Transport Museum**, which provides many of the vehicles for the dozens of period films shot in Ireland every year. A series of huge sheds contain this fascinating collection of old fire engines, trams, coaches, buses and everything else that ever rolled on an Irish road.

Dún Laoghaire and Sandycove

*There are regular **DART** trains to Dún Laoghaire, which take about 20 minutes. **Bus** 7, 7A and 8 from O'Connell St are frequent, but can take up to an hour because of the traffic.*

Tourist information is at the New Ferry Terminal, t 1850 230330; open all year.

Dún Laoghaire (pronounced 'dunleary') is a brisk seaside town named for the 5th-century High King of Ireland, who was converted by St Patrick in the 5th century. It still exudes the cheerful air of a Victorian seaside resort, despite the presence of a major ferry port and the glassy new shopping centres and harbour-side developments which have been popping up in the last decade or so. Smart, red-brick terraced houses with well-polished railings line the seafront, where families still take the air around what was the largest artificial harbour in the world when it was constructed in the early 19th century. Along the East Pier, there's a bandstand and a smattering of statues and monuments, and you can sometimes spot seals from the less glitzy West Pier. Dún Laoghaire is an important yachting centre, and some of Ireland's snootiest yachting clubs are clustered around the harbour.

At the centre of the harbour is a pompous monument to George IV, which Thackeray described in his *Irish Sketchbook* as 'a hideous obelisk, stuck upon four fat balls, and surmounted with a crown on a cushion'. It commemorates the king's departure from the town in 1821 – he should have arrived here, too, but his boat ended up at Howth instead, and the king rolled off in a drunken stupor. Despite this, Dún Laoghaire chose to rename itself Kingstown after the event, and its original name wasn't restored until 1921.

Just inland from the harbour, the **National Maritime Museum** is housed in the Mariner's Church on Haigh Terrace, but it has been closed indefinitely for some time because of serious structural problems. Near it is Andrew O'Connor's striking statue *Christ the King*, which met with disapproval from the Church authorities when it was first purchased in 1929 and sat in storage for years before being secretly erected in 1979.

From the harbour, a gentle **beach walk** crosses coves and rocky outcrops to the adjoining village of **Sandycove**, which has been swallowed up by its sprawling neighbour. The Martello Tower on the headland is unmissable, and contains the James Joyce Museum. Next to it is Geragh, a sleek, white private villa which was built in the 1930s by Michael Scott, one of Ireland's foremost modern architects.

James Joyce Museum

Joyce Tower, Sandycove, t (01) 280 9265, joycetower@dublintourism.ie. **Open** *April–Oct Mon–Sat 10–1 & 2–5, Sun 2–6; Nov–March by prior arrangement only; call to check times in advance, as longer opening hours are currently being discussed;* **adm** *€6, students/seniors/under 18s €5, children under 12 €3, family tickets €16.50.*

In 1904 James Joyce discovered that Sandycove's Martello Tower, built during the Napoleonic Wars, was available for rent. He promised Oliver St John Gogarty that he would cover the rent if Gogarty would furnish it. Gogarty and another friend, Samuel Chevenix Trench, moved in, but relations between the three were tense, and Joyce's stay in the tower was short-lived – less than a week. But, by setting the first chapter of *Ulysses* here, Joyce granted the place immortality, and it remains a shrine for all Joyce fans.

The **ground floor** contains a small museum with photographs, papers, first editions, a beautiful copy of *Ulysses* illustrated by Matisse and Joyce's death mask. There are a lot of letters begging for loans: money was always tight for Joyce, until Ezra Pound stepped in and helped him find wealthy patrons. The steep, winding stone staircase leads up to the **Round Room**, which, as the principal room in the tower, was where the three young men slept and ate. The museum has recreated the scene here which forced Joyce to leave, and which then figured in the first chapter of *Ulysses*: on the night of 14 September 1904, Trench had a nightmare about a black panther, fired some shots into the fireplace and fell back asleep. Gogarty then took the gun, shouted 'leave him to me' and shot down the saucepans on the shelf above Joyce's bed. Relations between Joyce and Gogarty were already tense: Joyce found Gogarty smug, and Gogarty wrote of Joyce (with a touch of the condescension that Joyce found so irritating) 'He is planning some sort of novel that will show us all up and the country as well: all will be fatuous except James Joyce'. Joyce's pointed revenge was to make Gogarty appear as the splendidly awful Buck Mulligan in *Ulysses*. You can climb all the way to the **roof**, where Joyce and his companions used to sunbathe.

> ### Discount Tickets
>
> The James Joyce Museum offers a special combined ticket with the Dublin Writers Museum (*see* p.76), Shaw Birthplace (*see* p.76), Malahide Castle and Fry Model Railway Museum (*see* p.133) – you can choose any two of these attractions for €10 (students/seniors €8, children €5.50, family ticket €28.50).

Just beside the tower is the **Forty Foot Pool**, where, in *Ulysses*, Buck Mulligan had a morning dip into the 'snotgreen scrotumtightening sea'. Made for the 40th Foot infantry regiment, it was traditionally a nude, men-only bathing spot, but now you have to wear a bathing suit (although you can still get away without one before 9am). Women made a point of swimming here some years ago, but few bother now. People take to the water all year round, rain or shine, but only experienced swimmers should try it.

Dalkey and Killiney Bay

Regular **DART** *trains from Dublin's city centre take about 25 minutes to Dalkey and Killiney.*

Dalkey and Killiney are the most exclusive areas of the Dublin coastline, home to celebrities from Bono to Neil Jordan, and boasting some of the most expensive property in Ireland. **Dalkey** was the port of Dublin in the 15th and 16th centuries, and the main street, Castle Street, still has a smattering of fortified mansions and a medieval castle

The Dalkey Gold Rush

In 1834, one Etty Scott claimed to have a recurrent dream about a hoard of Viking gold hidden in a cave on White Rock beach in Dalkey. He managed to raise the money to hunt for the stash, but the story precipitated an extraordinary gold rush: workers at the quarry and at the docks downed tools and flocked to the cave in the hopes of finding the treasure. Then a group of local jokers daubed some stray cats with luminous paint and released them into the cave, where their ghostly forms caused enormous panic. The treasure-seekers slunk back to their jobs and the gold was never found.

now a heritage centre). It's a swanky little village of smart restaurants, organic delis and sleek beauty parlours, with a popular, if pebbly, beach and a small harbour. In summer you can hire boats from the harbour out to Dalkey Island, where there is a Martello Tower and the ruins of St Begnet's Oratory.

South of the village the Vico road, a coast road which is often fancifully compared with the Amalfi Coast in Italy winds dramatically towards the beautiful, curved expanse of **Killiney Bay**. It passes Sorrento Terrace, the poshest address in Ireland, lined with spectacular mansions. From Sorrento Point, a pleasant stroll from the village centre, there are stunning views across the coastline, the Sugar Loaf Mountains and the elegant sweep of Killiney Bay itself. A steeper climb up Killiney Hill offers even more spectacular views, and there's a wishing stone at the top where you can pray that the descent will be less arduous.

Dalkey Castle and Heritage Centre

Goat Castle, Castle St, **t** (01) 285 8366, www.dalkeycastle.com. **Open** April–Dec Mon–Fri 9.30–5, Sat–Sun and bank hols 11–5; Jan–March Sat–Sun and bank hols 11–5; guided tours daily at 3; **adm** €7, students/seniors €5, children €4, family ticket €18.

Of the seven castles that guarded Dalkey when it was the most important port of Dublin (from the Middle Ages to the late 17th century), **Goat Castle** is the only survivor, apart from the ruins of Archibald's Castle just behind it. The building got its odd name from the original Anglo-Norman residents, the Cheevers family: 'Cheevers' was a corruption of *chèvre* (the French for 'goat') and the family coat-of-arms features three of the animals.

The history of the castle and Dalkey is recounted by the area's famous resident author, Hugh Leonard. When it was built, it was within the Pale, but it was continually attacked by the Irish tribes from outside the Pale. At the entrance is a '**murder hole**', a secret opening through which oil, stones or boiling water were poured down on unsuspecting invaders. On the **first floor**, there's a model of medieval Dalkey with its seven castles all intact: it remained Dublin's most important port until Oliver Cromwell's decision to land at Ringsend instead of Dalkey in 1649 signalled the end of the town's importance. Money finally began rolling in again in the 19th century, when the quarry opened.

A small **exhibition** with old photos, models and plans relates the history of the train and tram lines that connected Dublin with Dalkey during the 1800s. The world's first 'atmospheric' passenger railway connected the city with the port, powered by an elaborate vacuum system, but it only lasted 10 years because rats kept eating the leather cylinders. The railway closed in 1844, but a tram line replaced it between 1879 and 1949.

Just off the main hall, there's a **garde-robe** (or medieval toilet) where the medieval occupants of the castle hung their clothes above the smelly latrines so that the fumes would kill off the fleas and lice resident in the cloth. From the **battlements**, you can enjoy views across the pretty village and out to sea, and down to the ruins of Archibald's Castle and a small church dedicated, like the ruined church on Dalkey Island, to St Begnet. These are the only known churches dedicated to this obscure saint: Begnet was a local princess given a bracelet by an angel, who asked her to devote her life to God. After she refused the king of Norway's petition to marry his son, Begnet fled to Northumberland and founded her own abbey.

A large, modern **extension** to the castle contains exhibitions by local artists, lots of old maps, photographs of famous residents like Joyce and contemporary authors such as Maeve Binchy and the playwright Hugh Leonard. Joyce briefly taught at a school here, which appears in the second chapter of *Ulysses*, and also on view is the delightful illustrated story *The Cat and the Devil*, which Joyce wrote for his four-year-old grandson.

Bray

*Regular **DART** trains from Dublin city centre take about 35 minutes.*

Bray, well south of Dublin in County Wicklow, is a down-to-earth seaside resort with none of the upmarket charm of Dalkey and Killiney but plenty of cheerful seaside attractions, from amusement arcades to an aquarium. Bright blue railings line its long pebbly beach, and it has a bracing cliff walk around the rocky bluff which rounds off the bay. The walk climbs steeply over Bray Head, where the summit is topped with a cross and offers extraordinary views of the Sugar Loaf mountains and the coastline, and continues to Greystones, another modest resort on the leeward side of the Head. A few miles south of Bray is Kilruddery House, with some of the oldest and most extensive 17th-century gardens in Ireland.

National Sea Life Centre

*Strand Road, Bray, **t** (01) 286 6939, www.sealife.ie. **Open** Mon–Fri 10–4, Sat–Sun 10–5; reduced hours in winter, call for times; **adm** €8, children €5.50.*

This is a small aquarium with a strong educational and conservationist bias – it's also very entertaining, particularly for younger kids. There are tanks full of Irish marine life, sharks, seals and special attractions such as the 'Lair of the Octopus' and the 'Kingdom of the Seahorses', along with – best of all – lots of pools where kids can pick up starfish and crabs.

Killruddery House and Gardens

*Off Greystones Road, Bray, **t** (01) 286 3405, www.killruddery.com. House **open** May, June & Sept daily 1–5, gardens open April–Sept daily 1–5; **adm** €8, students/seniors €6, children €3; gardens only €5, students/seniors €4, children €2. Information on summer concerts: info@musicingreatirishhouses.com.*

Kilruddery House was built in 1651 for the Brabazon family, the earls of Meath, to whom it still belongs. It was substantially remodelled in the early 19th century by the fashionable architect Richard Morrison, and then considerably reduced in the 1950s. It has a gentle, faded charm which has earned it plenty of film roles, including appearances in *My Left Foot* and *Angela's Ashes*.

The **gardens** are the star attraction of the Killruddery estate, and are among the oldest and earliest formal gardens to survive in their original style in Ireland. They were laid out in the 1680s in the French classical style by the leading landscape architects of the age, including Bonet, a pupil of Le Notre who had worked at Versailles. The central features are the Long Ponds – two slim sparkling canals known as the *miroirs d'eaux*, which were once used to stock fish for the house. The oldest part of the gardens contains elegant *parterres*, walks flanked by beech hedges and avenues of birch and poplar trees. Behind the Beech Hedge Pond are the 19th-century gardens, including a very pretty rose and lavender garden with a fountain in the centre. The most unusual feature is the romantic Sylvan Theatre laid out in the classical style with a high bay hedge and terraced banks. It is still used for occasional performances, and the house itself usually features in the 'Music in the Great Houses of Ireland' concert series in June.

Walks

A LITERARY WALK 141
VIKING AND MEDIEVAL DUBLIN 143
THE DOCKS AND THE GRAND CANAL 149

A LITERARY WALK

Dublin is famous for the legions of extraordinary writers it has produced, and almost every square and certainly every pub seems to be associated with one of them. James Joyce, who lived in exile for most his life, was the most obsessive mapper of the cityscape, and once wrote, 'I want to give a picture of Dublin so complete that if the city one day suddenly disappeared from the earth it could be reconstructed out of my book'. This walk touches in parts on the one-day odyssey of Leopold Bloom in *Ulysses*, but committed Joyce fans who want to recreate the full journey should contact the excellent James Joyce Centre (*see below*) which has maps and runs the best Joycean walking tours.

The best place to begin a literary walk around Dublin is the **Dublin Writers Museum**, which is set in a handsome, 18th-century mansion on **Parnell Square**. It offers a good introduction to the city's major writers – a stellar list which numbers three Nobel prize winners (Shaw, Yeats and Beckett), countless drunkards and one tee-totaller, and there's an excellent café and bookshop here, too. The adjacent Writers Centre caters to Dublin's living writers, and it's always worth inquiring about the lecture programme (*see p.107*).

Turn left as you leave the museum and cross the street towards **Great Denmark Street**. Continue down Great Denmark Street and on the left you'll pass Joyce's former school, **Belvedere College**, at no. 6, which features in *A Portrait of the Artist as a Young Man*. Turn right down **North Great Georges Street** to find the James Joyce Centre on the left at no. 35 (*see p.108*), set in an immaculately restored Georgian mansion and containing a library of Joyce-related texts, a recreation of the room in which he considered how make *Finnegans Wake* even more obscure and the original door from 7 Eccles Street, the fictional home of Leopold and Molly Bloom in *Ulysses*. Almost opposite, the

> **Start:** Dublin Writers Museum, Parnell Square
> **Finish:** Shelbourne Hotel, St Stephen's Green
> **Walking time**: One and a half hours, not including museum, lunch or drinks stops.
> **Cafés and lunch stops**: Chapter One (in the Dublin Writers Museum), p.195; Cobalt Café, p.198; The Flowing Tide, p.207; Mulligan's, p.204; Davy Byrne's, p.203; The Bailey, p.203; Bewley's Oriental Café, p.192; Toner's pub, p.204; Horseshoe Bar, p.204.
> **Suggested start time**: This walk presupposes a relaxed attitude to afternoon drinking! Line your stomach with a good lunch at the Chapter One restaurant at the Dublin Writers Museum (museum closed Sun) and totter off for the remainder of the walk around 2.30pm.

Cobalt Café is a relaxing, arty little café if you are ready for a cup of coffee.

Retrace your steps up North Great Georges Street, and turn right onto **Gardiner Place** (the extension of Great Denmark Street). This leads to **Mountjoy Square**, which was one of the most fashionable Georgian squares in its prime, but became one of the most notorious slum districts on the north side of the river. Still faded and run-down, work has begun on a piecemeal restoration. Mountjoy Square was home to the playwright Séan O'Casey (1880–1964), who set his tragi-comic play *The Shadow of the Gunman*, about a poet who might be an IRA soldier, here. Brendan Behan was born a few minutes' walk away at **14 Russell Street**.

From Mountjoy Square, turn down Gardiner Street, following the route taken by Leopold Bloom in *Ulysses*. **Railway Street** on the left is where Bella Cohen's brothel can be found in the same book (Joyce's alter-ego Stephen Dedalus confronts his mother's ghost here), and if you turn right down **Talbot Street** a statue of Joyce himself at the corner of O'Connell Street.

Turn left down **O'Connell Street**, where until recently you might have admired (or sneered at, as most Dubliners did) a fountain dedicated to Anna Livia, Joyce's personification of the River Liffey. The **General Post Office**, on the right, recalls Yeats' moving poem on the 1916 Easter Rising.

Turn left again down **Abbey Street** to find the **Abbey Theatre**, founded by Lady Gregory and W.B. Yeats and still the most prestigious of Dublin's theatres. Yeats and Lady Gregory spearheaded the Irish literary revival at the turn of the 20th century, which galvanized all aspects of the arts in Ireland, and founded the Irish Literary Theatre, which became the Abbey, as a means of bringing new work to Dublin audiences. Not all their choices met with audience approval, and some premières, such as Synge's *The Playboy of the Western World* in 1907 and Séan O'Casey's *The Plough and the Stars* in 1926, so disgusted the audience that riots erupted and the police had to be called in. The original theatre burned down in 1951, but the modern replacement still contains a legion of photographs of famous dramatists and theatrical personalities. The Flowing Tide pub, opposite the theatre at 9 Lower Abbey Street, is a favourite with local thespians and has a wonderful collection of posters.

Turn right at the end of **Lower Abbey Street** and head down to **Eden Quay**, where you can cross the Liffey along **Butt Bridge**. The first street on the right is **Poolbeg Street**, where Mulligan's pub (also on the right) has survived unchanged since Brendan Behan would drink himself into a stupor on their beautifully poured Guinness (traditionally considered the best in the city), and probably looks much as it did when Joyce's characters in *Dubliners* 'went round to Mulligan's'.

As you emerge from Mulligan's turn right to the end of Poolbeg Street, and left down **Hawkins Street** which emerges at **College Green**.

Flanking the gates of **Trinity College** which overlook College Green are two statues of the university's famous literary alumni, Oliver Goldsmith (1728–74) and Edmund Burke (1729–97); other alumni include Oscar Wilde and Samuel Beckett.

Keeping the entrance to Trinity on your left, head straight up **Grafton Street**. Just off this busy street on the left is **Duke Street**, where Davy Byrne's at no. 21 is probably the most famous literary pub in Dublin. It gets a mention in *Ulysses*, and the lunch which Leopold Bloom enjoyed here – a gorgonzola sandwich and a glass of Burgundy – is a regular feature of modern Bloomsday celebrations. The lunches here are very good, particularly the seafood. Across the street, the Bailey is now a slick, ultra-modern bar, but was once another favourite watering hole of Brendan Behan and Patrick Kavanagh. It used to contain the original doorway from 7 Eccles Street (fictional home to the Blooms), now kept at the Joyce Center (*see* p.141), but dramatic renovations have stripped out all reminders of the past.

Return to Grafton Street and continue walking until you reach **Bewley's** on the left, with its glittering Art Deco façade. This café was built on the site of Samuel Whyte's Academy which educated Thomas Moore (1779–1852), a romantic, lyrical poet who is now very unfashionable, and his friend Robert Emmet, whose short-lived rebellion in 1803 ended on the scaffold.

At the top of Grafton Street, the Gaiety Theatre on the right just down **South King Street** staged the first play written in the Irish language in 1901. The author was Douglas Hyde (1860–1949) who, with Yeats and Lady Gregory, had founded the Irish Literary Theatre, and who went on to become president of Ireland.

Grafton Street opens up onto **St Stephen's Green**, a delightful public park which is scattered with monuments to the city's literary heroes. Walk through the entrance to the park which almost faces you and continue along the path until you reach the ornamental pond. Circling the pond to the right, up the steps near a pagoda-style shelter, is an intriguing, abstract sculpture of W.B. Yeats, and further around the pond is a bust of the Dublin poet James Clarence Mangan. A path leads to the southern side of St Stephen's Green, where a statue of James Joyce stands opposite his alma mater,

Newman House, which belongs to University College Dublin. Newman House, which is formed from two sumptuous adjacent Georgian mansions, has been spectacularly restored and its gorgeous interior is now open to the public (see p.73). The house is also connected with the English poet Gerard Manley Hopkins, who came to teach at the Catholic university, died of typhoid and is buried in a Jesuit plot in Glasnevin Cemetery.

As you emerge from Newman House, turn right and continue down **Leeson Street** when you reach the edge of St Stephen's Green. A left on Pembroke Street will bring you to quiet, graceful **Fitzwilliam Square**, where W.B. Yeats lived at no. 42 in the 1930s.

Continue up Pembroke Street until it meets **Lower Baggot Street**, and turn left. Toner's pub at no. 139 (see p.204) is a delightfully old-fashioned establishment; it is apparently the only pub that Yeats ever patronized in Dublin. Turn right up **Merrion Street**, which leads onto **Merrion Square**, the most aristocratic of all the Georgian squares south of the river.

Many of Dublin's literary luminaries are associated with Merrion Square and almost every house bears a commemorative plaque: famous residents include Joseph Sheridan Le Fanu (1814–73), W.B. Yeats and Oscar Wilde (1854–1900), whose statue sprawls languidly at the corner of the park facing his former family home at no.1. Wilde, whose plays include *Lady Windermere's Fan* and *The Importance of Being Earnest*, was the son of the flamboyant Sir William and Lady Wilde (who wrote under the pen name Speranza). Oscar was the toast of London when he was convicted of homosexual offences and sentenced to two years' imprisonment. Wilde described his experience in the poignant *Ballad of Reading Gaol*, but the time in prison broke his health and he died in Paris, where he is buried.

Oscar Wilde was born just off Merrion Square at **21 Westland Row**, and at the corner of **Lincoln Place** the façade of Sweny's Chemist at no. 1 has been preserved just as it was when Leopold Bloom bought the fragrant lemon soap for Molly: 'Mr. Bloom raised a cake to his nostrils. Sweet lemony wax'. Joyce fans can still pick up a bar or two as gifts.

Continue along **Lincoln Place** and head down **Kildare Street** until you find yourself back at St Stephen's Green. A fitting end to a literary tour of Dublin is the historic **Shelbourne Hotel**, where the Horseshoe Bar has long been one of literary Dublin's most established watering holes.

VIKING AND MEDIEVAL DUBLIN

Almost nothing of Viking or medieval Dublin survives today, all swept away in the great building frenzy of the 18th century and the development boom of the 1990s. There were a couple of settlements on the banks of the Liffey in Celtic times, but Dublin's importance really began with the arrival of the Vikings at the end of the 8th century. It was a sizeable settlement by the time the Anglo-Normans – led by Strongbow – arrived at the end of the 12th century, and began to build cathedrals and fortresses in the continental style. Little has survived of this first big building boom, but the city's beginnings are still recalled in street names describing the ancient trades, such as Winetavern and Fishamble Streets, and in the imposing pair of medieval cathedrals, Christchurch and St Patrick's.

Start: Steyne Monument, College Green
Finish: Dublinia, Christchurch Cathedral
Walking time: One hour, not including museum, drink or lunch stops.
Café and lunch stops: Queen of Tarts, p.195; Silk Road Café, p.87; Old Dublin Restaurant, p.193; Gallic Kitchen, p.195; Brazen Head, p.205; Porterhouse Pub, p.206.
Suggested start time: This walk can be done at any time, although note that the cathedrals and other attractions close around 4.30–5pm.

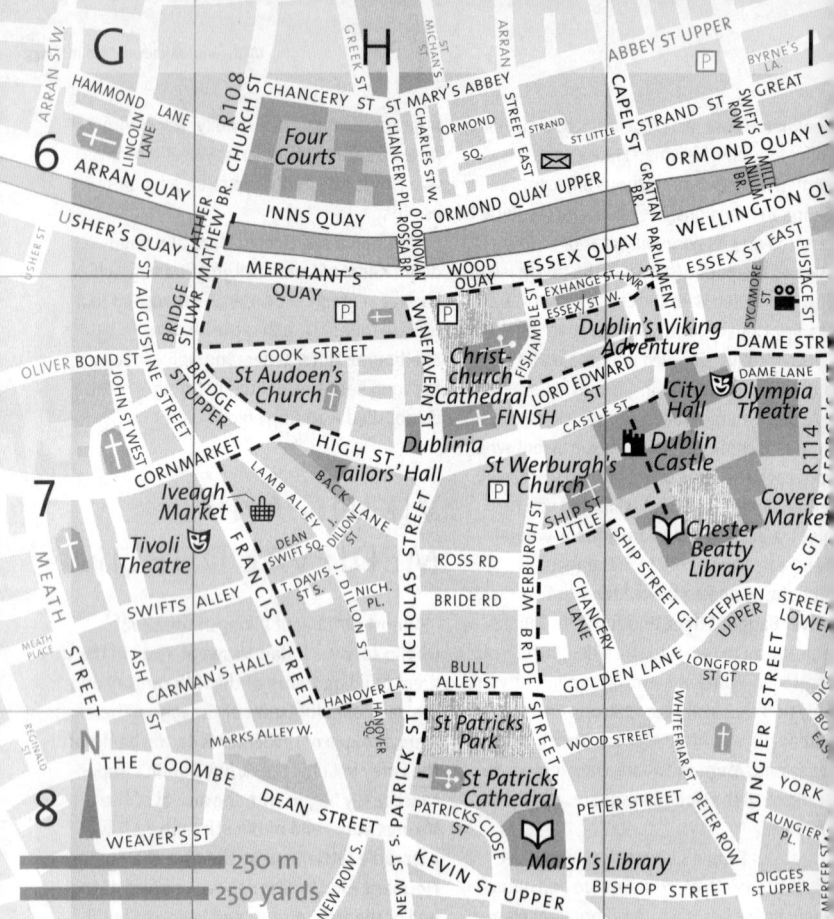

On **College Green** the *Steyne Monument*, a modern statue erected in the 1980s, marks the spot where the Vikings first berthed in Dublin in 795 and erected the original *steyne* which stood here right up until 1794. Twelve hundred years ago, the waters of the Liffey would have covered much of this area.

Take a peek into the courtyard of **Trinity College** on your left, where the mid-19th century Campanile marks the centre of the medieval priory of All Hallows, one of many monastic complexes which were clustered in this area from the 6th century onwards. It was destroyed and stripped of its lands during the Reformation, and the site was used for Trinity College, Ireland's first university, which received its charter from Queen Elizabeth in 1592.

Keep the gates of Trinity College behind you and continue along **College Green**, which was called Hoggen Green (from the Scandinavian word for 'mound') until the 1600s. The Vikings built their 'thingmote' or assembly place on high ground between this street and Suffolk Street, which was only levelled in the 17th century.

College Green becomes **Dame Street**, which derives its name from the medieval convent of St Mary del Dame that once stood on this land, and which got its name in turn from the nearby crossing point of the River Poddle.

Dublin's imposing **City Hall**, gleaming like new after a major restoration, overlooks the junction of Dame Street with **Parliament Street** and contains an engaging, imaginatively displayed exhibition of the city's history called 'The Story of the Capital'. On show are copies of medieval charters and seals, including the charter granted by Henry II in 1171 which gave the city of Dublin to the people of Bristol – thereby checking

Viking and Medieval Dublin | 145

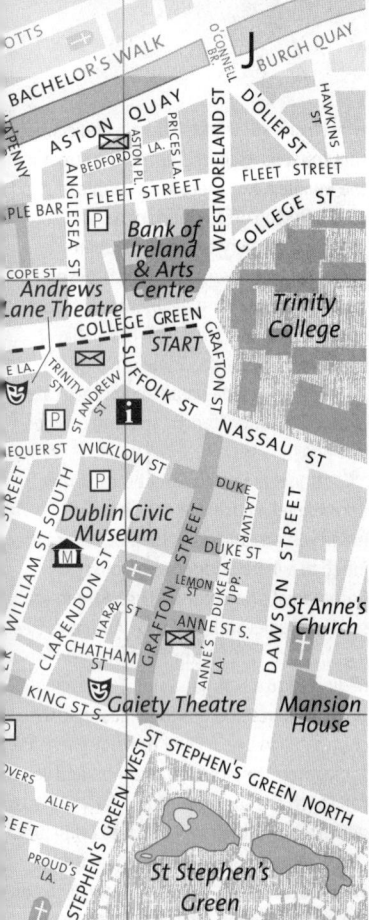

Strongbow's ambitions and opening up new trade links. There's a branch of the excellent patisserie Queen of Tarts in the City Hall, or you can visit the main shop right across the road.

Almost next to the City Hall is the entrance to **Dublin Castle**, which was built by the Anglo-Normans in the early 1200. The castle, symbol of the British domination of Ireland until it was finally handed over to the Free State in 1922, was feared and hated for centuries. In the Middle Ages, it would have been surrounded by a moat (formed by the River Poddle which now runs underground) and the gateway would have been lined with the spiked heads of traitors.

If you pass through the archway, you'll reach the **Lower Yard** (there's a craft shop and tea rooms on the right if you are ready for a coffee break). The **Record Tower**, which stands to the left of the entrance to the Upper Yard, is virtually all that remains of the original Anglo-Norman castle, and even that has been substantially rebuilt. Red Hugh O'Donnell, the 15-year-old son of the Prince of Tyrconnell, was kidnapped and brought to the castle as a hostage to ensure the good behaviour of the Irish lords. He made a daring escape from the Record Tower in 1591, letting himself down by a long rope from a window in the privy at the top of the tower. He fled to the Wicklow mountains and his journey is still commemorated with a Christmas hike through the mountains.

The remains of another medieval tower, the **Gunpowder Tower**, which flanked the other side of the entrance to the Upper Yard, were discovered during excavations in the 1980s; these also uncovered parts of the Viking defences. You can see them as part of the Dublin Castle tour (see p.87).

Pass through the entrance and into the **Upper Yard**, now an elegant square surrounded with Georgian buildings, but formerly the site of the original Anglo-Norman castle. The statue of Justice holding her scales aloft above the archway on your left stands with her back to the city – indicative, said pre-Independence Dubliners, of what the Irish could expect from the British justice system.

Retrace your footsteps to the Lower Yard, and pass the Chapel Royal on your right to reach the **Dubh Linn Gardens**. These formal gardens were laid out on the site of a dark pool (dubh linn in Irish) which gave its name to the modern city. They are now overlooked by the wonderful **Chester Beatty Library**, which contains a magnificent collection of manuscripts, paintings and artefacts (see p.87), as well as the excellent Silk Road Café, an ideal lunch stop.

Leave the castle grounds by the **Ship Street** exit, behind the Chester Beatty Library. Ship Street was the medieval Sheep Street, whose name has evolved with the passage of time. At the end of Ship Street you'll reach **Werburgh Street**, named for a medieval church dedicated to a Scandinavian saint; it was replaced by the present building (which you can see to your right) in the 18th century.

Turn left down Werburgh Street, which becomes **Bride Street**, named after St Bride's Church. This pre-Viking church was demolished as part of the Iveagh Trust Scheme in the late 1800s, which aimed to replace the terrible slums that once blighted this part of the city. (You can see the handsome, copper-domed, Art Nouveau-style **Iveagh Baths**, now a Listed Building, which were part of the Scheme on Bride Road, to the right off Bride Street.) You are now entering the area called **The Liberties**, which got its name because it lay outside the city walls and was not subject to their laws.

Bride Street flanks **St Patrick's Park**, an attractive grassy lawn with benches and a few scattered monuments. A plaque marks the site of a Holy Well, where St Patrick is said to have baptized the early Christian converts in the 5th century. The **Cathedral** itself was built soon after the Anglo-Normans arrived, and was consecrated on St Patrick's Day, 1192. It has suffered fires, neglect and the attentions of over-enthusiastic restorers ever since, and little of the original construction survives. Nonetheless, it remains one of Dublin's most impressive monuments, and, even rebuilt, it isn't hard to imagine how magnificent it would have looked to medieval Dubliners. **Jonathan Swift**, who is buried here next to his adored Stella, was Dean of St Patrick's during the early 18th century. In the early 16th century, it was the scene of a legendary reconciliation between feuding Geraldines and Ormonds, when the Earl of Kildare 'chanced his arm' by thrusting it through a hole hacked out of a door in order to assure the Earl of Ormond that his promise of a truce was genuine. The door still survives in the cathedral.

Hanover Lane leads off Patrick Street, which runs along the edge of St Patrick's Park. Follow Hanover Lane to **Francis Street**, whose name recalls a long-demolished Franciscan friary. Francis Street, one of the major thoroughfares of medieval Dublin, is now known for its antique and junk shops, which echo some of the bustle and clamour that must have characterized the street in the Middle Ages. There are a couple of good places to stop off for lunch or a snack, including the very smart Old Dublin Restaurant, at nos. 90–91, which, despite its name, serves a menu of Oriental and East European dishes (*see* p.193). The Gallic Kitchen, at No.49, has some good Irish home baking (soda bread and potato cakes) along with fancy French tarts and quiches (*see* p.195).

Continue up Francis Street until it meets **Cornmarket**, which was the site of a medieval corn and grain market. Across the junction, where Bridge Street joins Cornmarket and becomes **High Street**, you'll see the medieval church of **St Audoen's** (*see* p.90), which was first built in 1190 and is dedicated to a Norman saint. The original tower survives and it is the oldest parish church still in use in Dublin. Inside there are some interesting medieval tombs, and you can touch the Lucky Stone (an early Christian gravestone) in the main porch to bring luck.

Turn right outside the church up **Bridge Street**, which leads past the Brazen Head on the left, reputedly Dublin's oldest pub and built on the site of a 12th-century tavern. The **Father Mathew Bridge** which crosses the Liffey was built on the site of the original ford that gave Dublin its Gaelic name: *Áth Cliath*, the ford of the hurdles. A settlement existed here in Celtic times, straddling the junction of four major roadways, and the ford – the only crossing over the Liffey – was made by placing mounds of rocks at regular intervals and connecting them with logs and tree branches.

Walk back a short way along Bridge Street and turn down **Cook Street**. Dublin was once surrounded by a double ring of solid walls, studded with 32 watchtowers and several fortified gates. Along Cook Street, you'll see a lonely stretch of the original medieval walls which date back to 1275, and **St Audoen's Gate**, the sole surviving city gate. Cook Street leads to **Winetavern Street**, whose name needs no explanation, and which was lined with taverns, ale houses and caskmakers until well into the 19th century.

Turn left up Winetavern Street, passing on your left the church of **St Francis of Assisi**, – it was founded on the site of a tavern which contained an underground church in the days when Catholics were being severely persecuted. The present church is still known as 'Adam and Eve's' after the old tavern, and makes an oblique appearance in Joyce's *Finnegans Wake*: 'riverrun, past Eve and Adam's, from swerve of shore to bend of bay'.

Turn right along **Wood Quay**, which was built on reclaimed land and gets its name from the wooden stakes used to stabilize the shifting ground. This area marks the northern limits of the Viking and Norman settlement, and it was here that the most extensive Viking remains outside Scandinavia were discovered by chance in the 1960s. The site had been cleared for the construction of new headquarters for the Dublin Corporation when the diggers came across the ruins, but, despite a huge public outcry, the city decided to go ahead with the construction of the new buildings (*see* p.89). The excavations revealed the remains of about 200 wattle-and-daub Viking buildings, and threw up an extraordinary number of artefacts including tools, coins, leather shoes, combs and weapons, many of which are on display at the National Museum on Kildare Street (*see* p.68).

Turn right down **Fishamble Street**, the main thoroughfare from the Viking port to High Street, which was once lined with fish stalls known as 'shambles'. A modern sculpture of a longboat is a reminder of the presence of the Viking port. The Liffey once reached to the junction with **Essex Street West**, which became a slipway near the point at which it now joins Fishamble Street. Turn left down Essex Street West and walk down it until it meets **Parliament Street**. Opposite, you'll see the Porterhouse Pub, which brews its own beer and offers sophisticated pub grub (*see* p.206). A plaque opposite the pub marks the location of the Essex Gate, one of the main entrances to the medieval city.

Turn right down Parliament Street, and right again onto **Lord Edward Street**, which was built in the 19th century to link Dame Street with the old city. It becomes **Christchurch Place**, which was formerly known as Skinner's Row and was the centre of the skinning industry in medieval Dublin. It was here that the old Tholsel, a kind of predecessor of City Hall, was established in 1308 (now long demolished) and is where the mayor held court and customs duties were paid. During the Reformation, it was also the site of an enormous bonfire of relics from the dissolved Catholic churches and monasteries. The nearby **High Street** was the main trading centre of Viking Dublin and was where leather goods were bought and sold in the Middle Ages.

Christchurch Cathedral, Dublin's earliest and grandest cathedral, rises above Christchurch Place (*see* p.89). It was built by Richard de Clare, better known as Strongbow, in the late 12th century, but was, like so many of Dublin's churches, so thoroughly restored in the 19th century that little remains of the original construction. It replaced a wooden church on the same site, and the crypt, the choir, the transepts and some faded Romanesque stone carving are almost all that survives from the medieval church. Strongbow was buried here, but the tomb that supposedly contains his last remains in fact belongs to a 14th-century earl. Dublin landlords collected their rents on Strongbow's tomb, and when it was destroyed by a collapsing wall, they hastily found a replacement.

A neo-Gothic bridge connects Christchurch with the 19th-century Synod, which contains **Dublinia**. This entertaining multimedia exhibition outlines the city's medieval history and contains a model of Dublin during the Middle Ages.

The Docks and the Grand Canal   149

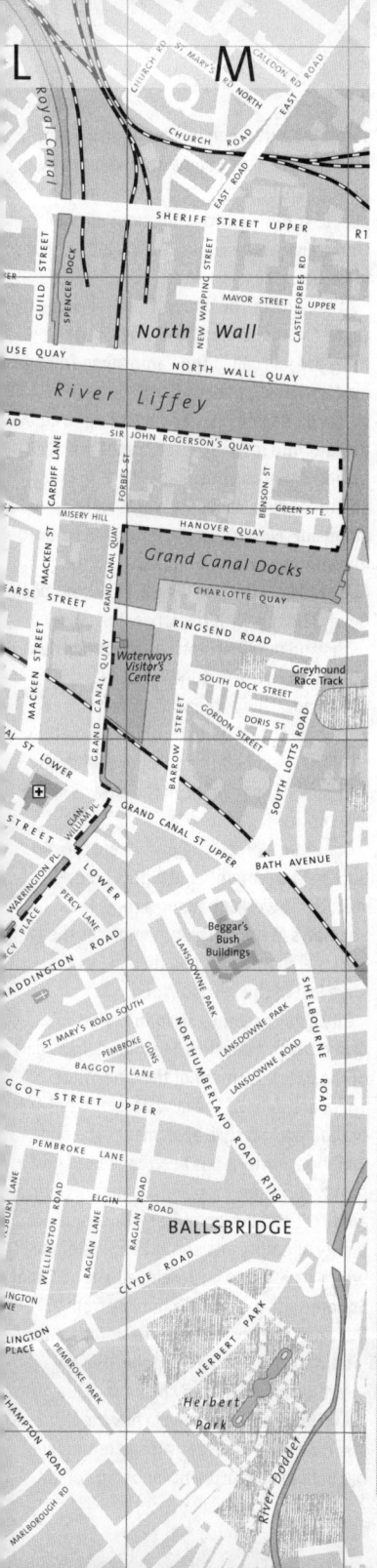

THE DOCKS AND THE GRAND CANAL

This watery walk skirts the fringes of the modern city, from the splendid Custom House on the banks of the Liffey, through the glossy 21st-century developments in the Docklands, and along the tranquil towpath of the Grand Canal to the old Jewish quarter in Portobello. It will take you out of the touristy heart of town and into quieter, more relaxed neighbourhoods which both reveal the city's changing face and recall its recent past.

The best place to admire Dublin's **Custom House** (see p.111) is from the opposite side of the river on **George's Quay**, near the southern end of Butt Bridge. It's one of Dublin's finest Georgian buildings, a magnificent neoclassical edifice designed by James Gandon.

Cross **Butt Bridge** and turn right onto **Custom House Quay** for a closer look. The old Custom House was located upriver in Temple Bar, and no one was happy with the decision to build a new one further down the Liffey: the traders didn't want to move their businesses and the wealthy residents near the proposed site of the new building were early 'nimby'-ists ('Not In My Back Yard') who were concerned about the effects on their neigh-

> **Start**: Custom House
> **Finish**: Slattery's, Lower Rathmines Road.
> **Walking time**: Two hours, not including museum, drink or lunch stops.
> **Cafés and lunch stops**: Harbour Master, p.198; The Canteen, p.151; Slattery's, p.208.
> **Suggested start time**: This is a good Sunday afternoon walk (note that in winter the Jewish museum is open on Sun only, and the Waterways Visitor Centre is closed on Mon and Tues). Begin around midday, and work up an appetite to enjoy a good lunch at The Canteen.

bourhood. Despite their objections, the mob who attacked the building site and the technical problems which plagued construction, the new Custom House was finally completed in 1791 for the unprecedented sum of £400,000. The smart residents were right about the neighbourhood: for one thing, thousands of cattle were now driven along the docks, soiling the streets and causing traffic chaos. The rich upped and left, and the area rapidly became a notorious slum.

Outside the Custom House is a **memorial** to the victims of the Great Famine (1845–7), a group of emaciated figures sculpted by Rowan Gillespie and placed here in 1997, the 150th anniversary of the famine. When the potato crop failed, thousands of desperate rural Irish made their way to Dublin – so many, indeed, that guards were posted on the edge of the city to turn away as many as possible. The lucky ones scraped together the fare to emigrate, and were crammed onto the overcrowded and disease-ridden ships which left from the major ports, including the Dublin docks. The Custom House became the Irish headquarters of the Poor Law Commissioners, who were largely responsible for providing relief during the famine years.

Continuing along Custom House Quays, the glassy green **International Financial Services Centre (IFSC)** was the flagship building of the 'Celtic Tiger' economy of a couple of decades ago. The boom years may be over – at least according to a dramatic pronouncement in 2001 from the Ireland's Central Bank – but IFSC is still the focus of the city's financial industry and is always humming with activity. The complex contains lots of coffee shops and restaurants, including the Harbour Master bar and brasserie (see p.198).

After the IFSC, turn right and cross the river on the **Matt Talbot Memorial Bridge**. Matt Talbot (see p.110) was an alcoholic who gave up drinking and took to going to church, fasting and praying. No one knew about his secret life, but when he died, it was discovered that he wore chains around his body to mortify his flesh. He has become an icon for people suffering with addictions all over the world, and yet he is surprisingly little known in his home city.

At the end of the bridge, turn left onto **City Quay**. The quays along this stretch of the Liffey are still called the Campshires, from an old Norman word describing the ancient method of using piles and boarding to create a quay. Until recently, huge cranes travelled up and down the river banks here, loading and unloading the boats which were moored alongside. Nowadays, most freight is moved in containers, and the cranes – and the Campshires – fell into disuse. They have been newly laid out with trees, benches, cycle paths and public sculpture, reflecting the huge shift in the fortunes of Dublin's Docklands. Things are still a little too new and shiny to feel quite comfortable, but it's nonetheless a breezy and enjoyable stroll, and provides a relief from the crowds in the city centre.

Continue along City Quay, where the old dockers are remembered with a bronze **statue** of a worker hauling a rope. The **Seaman's Memorial** commemorates the 13 Irish merchant ships and their crews that were lost in the Second World War.

City Quay becomes **Sir John Rogerson's Quay**, which has yet to be spruced up as part of the redevelopment of the Campshires. There are signs of the new development – brand new loft-style apartments, the odd warehouse which has been converted into a trendy furniture shop and plaques denoting architect and design offices – but there are plenty of empty lots and shabby warehouses which have yet to be developed. **Grand Canal Square**, with a red brick chimney from a Victorian factory at the centre, is one of the landmark developments in the area.

At the end of Sir John Rogerson's Quay, turn down **Britain Quay**, where a few Irish 'tinkers' still have their caravans, an odd reminder of old Ireland in a futuristic landscape of glittering new apartment complexes. The path continues along the water's edge, past a few mouldering old warehouse buildings to **Grand Canal Quay** which overlooks the Grand Canal Basin – one of the most developed parts of the new docklands. Cross the modern **MacMahon Bridge** towards the new buildings and continue until you reach the **Waterways Visitor Centre** on the left.

Known as 'the box in the docks', this elegant, glassy building houses an excellent exhibition on the city's canals. The two main canals, the Grand to the south and the Royal to the north, were built in the 1760s and, traditionally, true Dubs are born somewhere between them. The network of canals were widely used for trade and public transport until the railways took away most of the passenger business in the late 19th century.

The **Grand Canal** closed to commercial traffic in 1960, but is still used by pleasure craft and barges. The former towpath has been renovated, and a very pleasant walking path has been laid out along the grassy, tree-lined canal banks. It feels a world away both from the busy city centre, and from the aggressive new developments in the docklands. There are ducks and swans to feed, a scattering of benches to relax on and a series of charming 18th-century stone bridges offering some delightful views of the canal.

As you stroll along the path, the leafy Victorian suburb of **Ballsbridge** unfolds to the south of the canal. At the corner of **Northumberland Road**, a former school has been converted into a charming hotel, The Schoolhouse (see p.183), which also contains an excellent restaurant in a wonderful beamed hall. It's called The Canteen, but, rather than stodgy school dinners, it serves a delicious menu featuring contemporary Irish cuisine (see p.199).

Cross the next small stone bridge to find a stone **monument** with an Irish inscription which recalls the Easter Rising in 1916. Key buildings across the city were taken by the Irish Volunteers, most famously the GPO on O'Connell Street, but the rebel army also held a warehouse on the edge of the canal.

The next stretch of the canal is one of the prettiest, edged with handsome 19th-century houses and overlooked by **Huband Bridge**, which offers picture-book views of the whimsical cupola of the **Peppercanister Church** (see p.80).

The novelist Elizabeth Bowen (1899–1973) was born in **Herbert Place**, which overlooks the canal on your right, and just beyond the next bridge, you'll find a statue of the journalist and poet Patrick Kavanagh (1904–67) sitting on a bench and gazing at the canal. Kavanagh's poetry often evokes the deprivation of rural life in his home county of Monaghan, but he was disillusioned with Dublin and his writing was often bitterly satirical. He would regularly escape to the leafy towpath, described in his poem *Canal Bank Walk* which opens 'Leafy-with-love banks and the green waters of the canal/ Pouring redemption for me'.

Continue your stroll along the canal, passing Eustace Bridge and Charlemont Bridge until you reach **Portobello Bridge**, built in 1791. **Portobello House** (1807), overlooking the northern end of the bridge, is now handsomely restored as a private college, but used to be the Grand Canal Hotel, the most popular of five hotels which once lay along the canal banks, as it stood right at the passenger terminus. The introduction of the railways spelled the end for passenger boats, the last of which were withdrawn in the mid-19th century, but freight continued to be carried right up until 1960.

Keep walking along the northern edge of the canal, which flanks **Portobello Harbour** (which was filled in when the last of the trade boats were withdrawn in 1960) and **Portobello Road**. This area of Dublin was known until relatively recently as 'Little Jerusalem' and was home to Dublin's small Jewish community, which had been swelled by refugees from Russia and eastern Europe. A pair of terrace houses on **Walworth Street** (signposted from the canal) have opened as the fascinating Irish Jewish Museum (*see* p.74). Nearby, the excellent kosher bakery at 1a Lennox Street has delicious freshly baked breads and bagels.

Continue east along **Lennox Street** until it meets **South Richmond Street**, where you can either hop on a bus or make the 15-minute walk back across Portobello Bridge and down **Lower Rathmines Road**. At no. 217, Slattery's is an excellent, traditional pub, which is well off the tourist trail and is always buzzing with locals. If you are lucky, you might stumble on one of its regular traditional music nights, held upstairs.

Day Trips

THE COAST NORTH OF DUBLIN 155
Swords 155
Donabate 155
Skerries 156

THE VALLEY OF THE BOYNE 157
Drogheda 157
Slane 159
Brú na Boinne: Newgrange, Knowth & Dowth 160
Hill of Tara 162
Trim 163
Kells 164

SOUTHWEST TO KILDARE 165
Celbridge 165
Kildare Town 166

THE WICKLOW MOUNTAINS 167
Glendalough 167
Powerscourt Estate 169
Blessington Lakes 171

THE COAST NORTH OF DUBLIN

Swords

Swords, a small village about 16km north of Dublin, was named for a **holy well** founded by St Columba with curative waters. The name comes from *Sord* or *Surd*, meaning 'clear' or 'pure', and the magical well still exists (the waters are said to be especially good for curing eye problems). The ancient abbey which once stood near the well was destroyed in Viking raids, but a single round tower still stands. **Brian Ború's** body was brought to the abbey after he was killed at the Battle of Clontarf in 1014, when his armies beat the Vikings. The archbishop of Dublin built a fortified **palace** here (open daily 9am–dusk) in the 12th century, gradually modified through the ages.

Donabate

Donabate is a manicured commuter town by the sea, with a popular beach backed by sand dunes. There's a wild fowl reserve on the peninsula which divides the town from nearby Portrane, but the local seal sanctuary was forced to close in 2002 after the government reneged on its promise to provide funding. The major attraction here is **Newbridge House**, one of the finest and most authentically maintained Georgian manors in Ireland, which even runs its own farm according to 18th-century techniques.

Getting There

For Donabate and Newbridge House, take the Suburban Rail service from Connolly or Pearse train stations in Dublin city centre to Donabate (hourly; takes 30mins). Alternatively bus 33B leaves Eden Quay every 30 minutes, but takes an hour or more depending on traffic, and you may have to change at Swords.

Tourist Information

www.donabateportrane.com

Lunch

The tea rooms at Newbridge House, *see* opposite, do tasty light lunches and teas.

Getting There

For Swords, take bus 33 from Eden Quay, which takes about 50 minutes.

Lunch

Old Schoolhouse Restaurant, *Church Road, Swords,* **t** *(01) 840 2846*. **Moderate–Expensive**. Set in a restored 18th-century stone school building, this is a delightful restaurant down by the river which serves local seafood and other dishes, including wild boar.

In summer, you can dine in the garden or conservatory.

Newbridge House and Traditional Farm

Newbridge Demesne, Donabate, **t** *(01) 843 6534.* **Open** *April–Sept Tues–Sat 10–1 & 2–5, Sun 2–6; Oct–March Sat–Sun 2–5;* **adm** *house €6.20, students/seniors €5.20, children €3.70, family ticket €17;* **adm** *farm €3, children €2, family ticket €8. Café, shop.*

Newbridge House was built around 1737 for Archbishop Cobbe, and extended in 1760 by his socialite daughter-in-law **Lady Elizabeth Beresford** to display her husband's art collection. The house was sold to the local council in the 1980s, but the Cobbes have retained a private apartment. The interior is particularly opulent, thanks to Lady Elizabeth, who took her social responsibilities very seriously and ensured that her home became one of the most glamorous of the era. She commissioned fashionable architects and stucco artists – including the society favourite, Robert West – and added a new wing containing the spectacular Red Drawing Room.

Tours of the house begin with the **Dining Room**, with a lavish rococo stucco ceiling by West, and an intriguing **Museum of Curiosities** in an adjoining hall that displays all kinds of curios and oddities, many gathered from the family's journeys in India. Out on the stairway is a portrait of one of Swift's great loves – but no one knows whether it is Stella or Vanessa.

The **Red Drawing Room** is dazzling, entirely covered with crimson damask wallpaper, drapes and carpet, which have survived intact since the last major redecoration in 1828. A bowed window looks out over the gardens, and the elaborate stucco ceiling was executed by Richard William, a pupil of the celebrated Robert West.

The **kitchens** are equally authentic, with huge dressers piled up with gleaming jugs and dishes and all kinds of contraptions including a whiskey still and a duck press (used for squeezing out the poultry juices).

In the adjoining **laundry**, there are some early washing machines and even one of the first vacuum cleaners.

Out in the **cobbled yard**, there's a dairy with marble niches for the cheeses to mature, a worker's kitchen, a blacksmith's forge and a carpenter's shop. In the coach house is the state carriage made in London in 1790 for 'Black Jack' FitzGibbon, Lord Chancellor of Ireland, who was related to the Cobbes. It had been painted completely black, probably for the funeral of Queen Victoria, before finally being restored to its original shimmering gold in the 1980s.

The estate **farm** is run as a self-sufficient 18th-century agricultural holding, and there are lots of animals to delight children.

Skerries

Skerries is a quiet seaside town with long sandy beaches, a resident seal colony and a clutch of tiny islands which are good for swimming. According to legend, St Patrick came to one of these islands when he was chased out of Wicklow. He left his goat on the island while he went off to preach to the people of Skerries, but, while he was gone, the people stole it, roasted it and ate it. When St Patrick discovered that his goat was missing, he made two giant strides from his island, leaving footprints (which you can still see) on Red Island and Colt Island, and angrily confronted the locals. They began to lie about what had happened, but suddenly found that they were bleating like goats; their real voices weren't restored until they finally started telling the truth. The people of Skerries have been known as 'goats' ever since.

There's a good **cliff walk** to the south of the town, with spectacular views of rocky coves – and you might glimpse the local seals.

Skerries Watermill and Windmills Industrial Heritage Centre

*Skerries, t (01) 849 5208. **Open** daily 10.30–5.30; Oct–March closes 4.30; **adm** €5, seniors/students €4, family ticket €10. Café, shop.*

The biggest attraction in town (besides the beach) is a group of 17th-, 18th- and 19th-century windmills and watermills, which were immaculately restored at the end of the 1990s and can be seen in action at the heritage centre.

> ### Getting There
> Suburban trains from Dublin's Connolly station to Skerries take around 30 minutes. Bus 33 from Eden Quay runs more frequently, but the journey takes an hour – more if the traffic is bad.
>
> ### Lunch
> **Red Bank House**, *5–7 Church St, Skerries, t (01) 849 1005, f (01) 849 1598, www.redbank.ie.* **Expensive**. One of the finest restaurants in the area, this serves up excellent contemporary Irish cooking in handsome, traditional surroundings. There's a set lunch for €28, and the desserts here are legendary. It also has guestrooms (*see p.184*).
>
> For something cheaper, the tea rooms at the **Skerries Heritage Centre** and at **Ardgillan Castle** offer delicious home-baked goods, soups and sandwiches.

The first windmills on this site were built for the Priory of Canons Regular of St Augustine of Holmpatrick in the 16th century, and a bakery was established here in 1840. It managed to survive right up until the 1980s, despite the decline of stone-ground milling. There is a watermill, a five-sail and a four-sail windmill and a mill pond; you can see them all in action, have a go at grinding yourself, and then sample some homebaked goods in the pretty tearooms.

Ardgillan Castle and Demesne

Balbriggan, **t** *(01) 849 2212. House* **open** *July–Aug daily 11–6; April–June and Sept Tues–Sun 11–6; Oct–March Tues–Sun 11–4.30;* **adm** *€4, students/seniors/children €3. Park open daily 10–dusk; free. Guided tours of Ardgillan Gardens: Thurs 3.30. Café.*

Just outside Skerries village on the way to Balbriggan is the handsome Ardgillan Demesne, with extensive woods and gardens overlooking the bay of Drogheda.

Ardgillan Castle has a perfect setting, poised above a deep blue bay and surrounded by woodland and formal gardens. The name Ardgillan comes from the Irish *Ard Choill*, which means 'high wood', and the land was first cleared by ex-soldiers and itinerant workers in return for a penny a day plus sleeping accommodation and one meal. The house itself is not really a castle, despite its crenellations, but a comfortable country mansion, built in 1738 by Robert Taylor. The ground floor apartments have been restored and are furnished in an elegant mixture of Georgian and Victorian styles. The upper apartments contain changing art exhibitions, and are regularly used for lectures and talks; there is also a permanent exhibition of maps, including the 17th-century 'Down Survey of Ireland', on which Robert Taylor's grandfather had collaborated. There is a delightful Victorian formal garden with a profusion of perfumed, old-fashioned roses and a pretty conservatory, and a walled kitchen garden full of herbs and vegetables. There's also a peculiar Fruit Wall, with special alcoves for growing delicate fruits such as peaches and nectarines.

The extensive **park** lands are now a nature reserve, with five miles of woodland walks, offering sudden, spectacular views over the bay and the impossibly blue sea.

THE VALLEY OF THE BOYNE

Drogheda

Drogheda, an unassuming, rather shabby town on the banks of the River Boyne, has a tranquil atmosphere that belies its violent history. It was founded by the Vikings in 911, and became one of the four largest and most important cities in Ireland under the Anglo-Normans, who constructed massive, defensive walls. In 1641 these walls – a mile and half long, 20 feet high and 6 feet thick – kept out rebellious Catholic forces, who then tried to starve the city into submission – only to be thwarted by the arrival of a government food ship into Drogheda harbour. In

Getting There

From Dublin's Connolly station to Drogheda, there are ordinary trains (50min) and Intercity trains (30min). There are also buses from Dublin's main bus station – either local bus 100 or 101 (1hr 15mins) or express bus 1 (1hr).

Tourist Information

West Street, Drogheda, **t** *(041) 983 7070; open June–mid-Sept.*

Lunch

Buttergate Restaurant and Wine Bar, *Millmount, Drogheda,* **t** *(041) 983 4759.* ***Moderate***. This is a relaxed restaurant offering simple but well-prepared dishes made with local produce.

Borzalino, *Mell, Drogheda,* **t** *(041) 984 5444.* ***Inexpensive***. A bright, modern Italian serving decent pizza and pasta dishes.

1649, Cromwell's army famously besieged the city and massacred 2,000 inhabitants, including many who had taken refuge in St Peter's Church, in one of the bloodiest episodes of his time in Ireland. Sir Arthur Aston, the defeated leader of the garrison in Drogheda, had confidently pronounced 'He who could take Drogheda could take Hell!' but was clubbed to death with his own wooden leg when the Cromwellian armies took the town. (Apparently, it was believed that the leg was filled with gold.)

The walls have long been destroyed, but a pair of gates survive, of which **St Lawrence's Gate**, a twin-towered, four-storey gate on the Baltray road, is the better preserved. There are two churches dedicated to St Peter nearby: the Protestant church, built in 1753, is the grander, but the Catholic church is worth a visit to see the embalmed head of St Oliver Plunkett, Archbishop of Armagh. He became innocently embroiled in 'The Popish Plot' fabricated by Titus Oates in 1678, and was martyred in 1681. He was canonized in 1975, the first new Irish saint since St Lawrence O'Toole, more than 700 years ago. On a motte overlooking the town, an 18th-century Martello tower and military barracks have been converted into a fascinating museum of local history.

About 10km northwest of Drogheda are the dreamy ruins of **Mellifont Abbey**, the first Cistercian abbey in Ireland, and a few miles east of it is another evocative monastic ruin at **Monasterboice**. Local buses from Drogheda can drop you off at both sites.

Millmount Museum

Millmount Square, Drogheda, **t** *(041) 983 3097, www.millmount.net.* **Open** *Mon–Sat 10–6 (last tour at 5.30), Sun 2.30–5.30;* **adm** *€4.50, children/seniors €2.50, students €3, family ticket €11.50.*

This quirky museum has all kinds of exhibits including a 19th-century kitchen, a recreated post office, the only collection of 18th-century guild banners outside the National Museum in Dublin, medieval floor tiles and lots of historical information relating to the dramatic events in the town's history. The complex also contains a craft centre, where local designers create and sell everything from jewellery to ceramics.

Battle of the Boyne Heritage Centre

Oldbridge Estate, Donore, **t** *(041) 988 4343.* **Open** *May–Sept daily 10–6;* **adm** *free.*

About 3km north of the tiny village of **Donore**, close to Drogheda, a heritage centre has been set up on the site of the **Battle of the Boyne**, which took place here in 1690. It was the largest battle on Irish soil, with more than 60,000 troops clashing on the banks of the River Boyne. The Catholic king James II had been deposed from the throne of England by his Protestant daughter Mary and her husband William of Orange. James decided to win back his crown in Ireland, where he could count on the support of the Irish Catholics, and the war in Ireland had already been raging for a year by the time William arrived in Belfast in June 1690 with reinforcements. James's ragged, exhausted and ill-trained army was no match for William's superior forces, and the battle ended in a rout. More than 1,500 were slain on the battlefield, and James fled to France.

The centre runs very interesting guided tours of the battlefield, or you can take a self-guided tour along the river bank or around the Oldbridge Estate. A small exhibition area relates the history of the battle and displays some replica weaponry. Between June and September, there are special events every Sunday as part of the 'Living History' activity series, which include 17th-century cavalry and weaponry demonstrations.

Mellifont Abbey

Tullyallen, **t** *(041) 982 6459; Nov–April call* **t** *(041) 988 0300 instead.* **Open** *April–Oct 10–6;* **adm** *€2, seniors €1.25, children/students €1, family ticket €5.50. Partial wheelchair access. Visitor centre.*

Ireland's first Cistercian monastery was founded here in 1142 by St Malachy of Armagh, who was horrified at the corruption of the local religious orders and invited in an austere band from France to shake things up. The French failed to bond with the locals and returned to France within a decade, but the abbey grew to become the largest and most substantial in Ireland, with more than 20 smaller monasteries under its rule. You can still pick out vestiges of its former splendour in the remnants of a Romanesque cloister, a 14th-century Chapter House and the unusual octagonal lavabo, used for washing and the best-preserved of the surviving buildings. The Visitor Centre has some intriguing displays on medieval stonemasonry, including examples of their craft.

Monasterboice

Off the N51 road; site open daily during daylight hours.

These magical 5th-century ruins are all that is left of an early Christian abbey. Within the grounds is the stunning high cross of Muiradach, which is over a thousand years old and thickly encrusted with biblical scenes, a sermon in stone from before the days of mass literacy. There's another striking cross and a battered round tower, erected as protection from Viking raids.

Slane

Slane is a small, attractive town of slate-roofed houses built as part of the Slane Castle estate. The four identical houses which mark each corner of the crossroads in the centre of the village were apparently built for four spinster sisters who refused to speak to each other but couldn't bear to be parted. The Hill of Slane, silhouetted beyond the town, is supposedly where St Patrick lit the Paschal (Easter) fire in AD 433 as a direct challenge to the High King of Tara. Easter coincided with the pagan festival of Beltane and the spring equinox, and the laws of the day decreed that no fires should be lit in the vicinity of the Hill of Tara (which can be seen from the Hill of Slane) while a festival fire was blazing. The High King thundered over in his chariot, but St Patrick managed to calm

> ### Getting There
> To Slane, buses 32, 33 or 36 run about five times a day from Dublin's main bus station (takes 45mins). Alternatively you can take the train to Drogheda and catch a local bus (three daily) from there.
>
> ### Lunch
> **Poet's Rest**, *Chapel Street, Slane,* **t** *(041) 24579.* **Moderate–Inexpensive**. A traditional, welcoming little spot, with a varied menu of Irish and European dishes and a decent wine list.
>
> **Boyles Tea Rooms**, *Main Street, Slane,* **t** *(041) 24195.* **Inexpensive**. Cosy tea rooms serving home-made soups, sandwiches and fine afternoon teas. It's on the tourist trail, but charming all the same. Open daily until 11pm.

the angry king with his eloquence. The ruins of a 16th-century Franciscan monastery which replaced an earlier church and a statue of the saint can be found on top of the hill, which offers commanding views across the whole valley.

Slane Castle

Slane Castle Demesne, **t** *(046) 988 4400, www.slanecastle.ie.* **Open** *April–Oct daily noon–5;* **adm** *€7, students/seniors/children €5, family ticket €20.*

The current version of **Slane Castle** was built in the 1780s for the Conyngham family, who still live here. The most fashionable architects of the day worked on it, including James Gandon (who designed the Four Courts and Custom House in Dublin), James Wyatt and Francis Johnston. It was gutted by fire in 1991, but reopened to visitors after a ten-year restoration. The glorious interior features stunning stucco ceilings, original furnishings, magnificent crystal chandeliers and some fine stained glass. Highlights of the guided tour include the famous King's Room where George IV stayed in 1821 with his mistress (and hostess) Lady Elizabeth, the 1st Marchioness Conyngham; and the neo-

Gothic Ballroom which was especially commissioned to impress the king on his visit. The extensive gardens and parkland were landscaped by Capability Brown.

The castle is probably best known for the enormous outdoor pop concerts staged in the grounds – in 2001 Irish rock band U2 played here, while in 2004 Madonna headlined as part of her world tour.

Brú na Boinne: Newgrange, Knowth and Dowth

Brú na Boinne, meaning 'Palace of the Boyne', is the name given to a stretch of land between Drogheda and Slane which contains some of the most spectacular prehistoric monuments in the world. This area, which includes the celebrated passage tombs of **Newgrange**, **Knowth** and **Dowth**, has been declared a World Heritage Site by UNESCO.

Admission to the tombs is by guided tour only, organized from the heritage centre near Donore. These can be a frustratingly bureaucratic affair: you'll be forced to queue, slapped with a stick-on badge giving your tour time and shipped off in a coach. However, when you get inside the tombs, the guides provide an excellent and enthusiastic commentary which constant repetition doesn't seem to dull.

Arrive early, try to avoid summer weekends and – better yet – come with a tour, such as the one run by Mary Gibbons (*see* p.45), which will give you a chance to ask questions in your own time.

Brú na Boinne Visitor Centre

Donore, **t** *(041) 988 0300, brunaboinne @ealga.ie.* **Open** *Nov–Feb daily 9.30–5; March, April & October 9.30–5.30; May & mid-Sept to end-Sept 9.30–6.30; June to mid-Sept 9–7;* **adm** *Visitor Centre only €2.75, seniors €2, children/students €1.50, family ticket €7;* **adm** *Visitor Centre plus tour of Newgrange €5.50, seniors €4.25, children/students €2.75, family ticket €13.75;* **adm** *Visitor Centre plus tour of Knowth €4.25, seniors €2.75, children/students €2.50, family ticket €10.50;* **adm** *Visitor Centre plus tour of Newgrange and Knowth €9.75, seniors €7, children/students €4.25, family ticket €24.25. Wheelchair access to visitor centre but not to tombs, which have steps. Café, shop, regional tourist information centre.*

The **Brú na Boinne Visitor Centre** is a huge, slick affair full of multimedia exhibits, including touch screens, recreations of Neolithic huts, explanatory videos and excellent descriptions of the layout and significance of the tombs. About 40 passage tombs have been discovered in the Boyne area, which date back to around 3200 BC – making them more than five hundred years older than the Pyramids of Egypt, and about a thousand years older than Stonehenge. They probably took around sixty years to build, at a time when the average life expectancy was only 25 years. The tombs display exceptional artistic and engineering skills, even though their construction predates the invention of the wheel or metal tools. Almost 200,000 stones were used to

> ## Getting There
> The easiest way to get to Brú na Boinne is by taking a guided tour from Dublin (*see* p.45); alternatively you can take the train to Drogheda and then a local bus (about six daily 10am–4pm).
>
> ## Tourist information
> There's a regional tourist information office in the Visitor Centre, *see* opposite.
>
> ## Lunch
> **Newgrange Farm and Coffee Shop**, *near Slane,* **t** *(041) 982 4119.* **Inexpensive**. A delightful spot, run by a charming and very welcoming couple, which is close to the Newgrange tomb and serves excellent home-made soups and sandwiches. There are also lots of puppies and farmyard animals for kids to play with.
>
> There is an adequate **café** in the Visitor Centre.

build the Newgrange tomb alone, including the glistening white quartz which must have been transported from the Wicklow mountains more than fifty miles away. And the Knowth tomb, even bigger than the one at Newgrange, contains about a quarter of all the Neolithic art in the whole of Europe. The monuments were clearly meant to endure and had a number of functions: as a burial place for some members of the population, as a reminder of the continuing presence of the ancestors and as territorial markers (most are prominently placed on hill-tops). Much of their significance remains a matter of speculation – it isn't even universally accepted that their primary function is burial sites – and many of the discoveries from inside the tombs also throw up questions. Some of the bones found within the tombs, for example, have a small, disk-shaped hole bored into the skull. It's possible that this was done to release the evil spirits within, but no one really knows.

Newgrange

For admission details see above.

The vast stone and turf mound of the **Newgrange** tomb cuts a stark arc against the sky. This is the best known of Ireland's prehistoric tombs, and the only one which is completely accessible to visitors. According to early Irish myth, Newgrange was the burial place of the prehistoric kings of Tara, and also the home of a race of Irish supernatural beings known as *Tuatha de Danann*, meaning 'the people of the goddess Danu'. It got its modern name of Newgrange during the Middle Ages, when the area formed part of the farm lands ('grange' was another word for farm) of Mellifont Abbey. The tomb was discovered by accident in 1699, and was generally believed to be the work of the Vikings, as no one then believed that the Neolithic peoples had the skill to create such extraordinary buildings.

The mound is about 85m (280ft) in diameter and 13.5m (44ft) high, and surrounded by a stone circle. This stone circle was built about a thousand years after the original structure, probably during the Beaker period, but no one knows why the circle was erected, nor why those responsible chose not to build any settlements in the area. There are almost one hundred large stones around the base of the mound, inscribed with swirling spirals, circles and lozenges. The most spectacular of these huge stones is the great kerbstone, which sits right at the entrance to the passage tomb. The swirling double circles have given rise to scores of interpretations, from the perplexing – for example, these circles are often described as the ancient Celtic symbol of life and yet these patterns were carved three millennia before the arrival of the Celts – to the downright ludicrous (it has been suggested they are a map for spaceships). The sparkling white quartz which has been used to circle the mound with such dazzling effect is a recreation and has caused controversy: the stones were found on the ground, forcing archaeologists to guess at their original position, and this has upset the purists. Much more extraordinary is their provenance: the nearest source of quartz is the Wicklow mountains more than fifty miles away, and it is hard to imagine how these Neolithic builders would have transported the heavy rocks over such a distance. The remains of at least three, and possibly four, smaller tombs have been discovered close by.

Inside, the claustrophobically narrow passage is lined with tall standing stone slabs, and leads to a domed chamber, the heart of the tomb and the greatest feat of engineering. (The only major damage that these tombs have suffered in the five thousand years since they were constructed is the recent appearance of a kind of algae on the roof, caused by the breath of visitors.) The dome is created by spiralling stones, with a massive cap stone in the centre. The chamber is cruciform, with stone basins in each of the three recesses, which bear a distinctive symbol at the entrance and more elaborate carving within. The stone basins are marked with shallow dents, and were probably used to cremate bodies. Five cremated bodies have been found, which are currently undergoing DNA testing.

The most spectacular discovery was made in the 19th century, and scientifically proved during the 1960s: every year at the winter solstice, sunlight shafts in through an ingenious roof box above the entrance, bounces off an S-shaped column and gradually fills the entire tomb.

The guide recreates the spectacle with a weak yellow torch, but even that can bring you out in goose bumps. If you want to witness the real thing, the current waiting list is already ten years long. This discovery proved beyond doubt that the Neolithic builders had unexpectedly sophisticated astronomical knowledge, and confirms Newgrange as the earliest solar observatory in the world.

Knowth

For admission details see above.

Knowth is less well known than Newgrange, even though it is bigger and contains two passages. The tour doesn't allow access into the passages, which some have claimed – although this is not accepted by the academic community – are aligned with the position of the rising and setting sun at the two equinoxes.

The tomb contains a spectacular array of Neolithic art, including the spiral and circle designs found at Newgrange (and at Neolithic sites across Europe) as well as more unusual diamond designs. Several of the smaller satellite tombs, along with beautiful examples of the incised stones, are open to visitors.

Dowth

No public access.

The Dowth tomb was plundered in the 19th century by Victorian souvenir hunters, and it is still being excavated. It's closed to visitors, although you can look at the exterior (it lies about 3 miles east of Newgrange, off the N51).

Hill of Tara

*Information centre in St Patrick's Church, Hill of Tara, **t** (046) 25903; in winter (Nov–April) call **t** (041) 988 0300 instead.* **Open** *mid-May to mid-Sept daily 10–6;* **adm** *to information centre €2, seniors €1.25, children/student €1, family ticket €5.50. The site is accessible at any time, and admission is free.*

The mythical **Hill of Tara** was the political and spiritual centre of Celtic Ireland, and the seat of the High Kings until the 11th century. It's a low hill, and the ancient monuments are hard to discern, and yet it still exudes a powerful aura. Daniel O'Connell cannily tapped into its mythical significance for the Irish when he held a huge rally for Home Rule here in the 1840s.

When the Celts arrived in Ireland around 500 BC, they divided Ireland into provinces, each ruled by a petty king who was answerable to the *Ard Ri*, or High King, who held court on the Hill of Tara. Although the Hill of Tara reached the height of its power and importance during the first centuries AD, the hill had been inhabited long before that: a 4,000-year-old Stone Age passage tomb has been discovered, and in ancient Irish mythology it was known as a sacred dwelling place of the gods, and the entrance to the Otherworld.

Getting There

The Hill of Tara is easiest to get to by car. If you don't have your own transport, take the Navan bus 109 or 110 from Dublin and ask to be dropped at Tara Cross, about 1km from the site.

Tourist Information

Information on the site only is at the Visitor Centre, *see below*.

Lunch

There is a small **café** on the edge of the site selling sandwiches and coffee and not much else, so pick up some picnic supplies before you arrive.

A church on the edge of the site has been converted into a small **visitor centre**, with a short film describing the history of the site and the archaeological excavations. In the churchyard are two standing stones: the taller of the two is possibly a representation of the Celtic fertility god Cernunnostso, similar to the Sheela na Gig symbols found across Ireland, and the other is the Admnán's stone, with some weatherbeaten carving, which commemorates an early Christian saint. The stones recall an early legend which relates that candidates for the High Kingship of Tara had to drive their chariots full-pelt at a pair of adjacent standing stones, which would only part for the rightful king.

At the brow of the windswept hill, it's hard to make out the shapes of the early settlements – although their form is clearly discernible when viewed from the air (there are photographs in the visitor centre). The wooden buildings have long since disintegrated, and all that remains are grassy undulations. The hill may be low, but the views are breathtaking, with lush green pastureland unfolding for miles in all directions. You can even glimpse the glint of the white quartz at the entrance to the Newgrange tomb, and the outline of the Hill of Slane where St Patrick angered the High King by daring to light his Easter bonfire. At the very peak of the hill, a circular ditch marks the boundaries of the **Ráth na Ríoch**, or Royal Enclosure, a hill fort which encompasses the Teach Cormaic (Cormac's Seat), the adjacent Forradh (Royal Seat) and the Dumha na nGiall, the Stone Age passage tomb which was used for habitation, ritual and burial for many centuries. The **Lia Fáil**, or Stone of Destiny, stands at the top of the mound known as Cormac's House, and was used to crown the ancient kings. A statue of St Patrick commemorates the saint's visit to the court of King Laoire, when it's said that he used the shamrock to explain the Christian notion of the Holy Trinity, but this is actually a 19th-century story which gained currency during the Gaelic revival.

A rectangular, shallow dip marks the boundaries of the famous **Banqueting Hall** which is often mentioned in the early sagas.

Trim

Trim lives up to its name: it's a very trim little town on the banks of the River Boyne, scattered with medieval ruins and famous for its picture-book castle, which has appeared in countless films including *Braveheart*. It's one of the largest Anglo-Norman castles in Ireland and, although most of it still lies in ruins, parts have been renovated to contain a heritage centre.

Across the river from the castle are the atmospheric ruins of the 12th-century **Abbey of St Mary**. The abbey was rebuilt a century later after being destroyed by fire, and the ruins are overlooked by the curious Yellow Steeple (so-called because of the way the sunlight catches one side of it). To the east lie more medieval ruins: the remnants of St Patrick's cathedral, the cathedral of Saints Peter and Paul, Newtown Abbey and the Crutched Friary which sits next to one of the oldest bridges in Ireland.

Trim Castle (King John's Castle)

Castle St, Trim, t (046) 38619. **Open** *Easter–Oct daily 10–6, Nov–Easter Sat–Sun 10–5, last admission 45mins before closing;* **adm** *€1.50,*

Getting There

Take bus no. 111 (roughly hourly) from Dublin's Busáras, which takes about 1hr 10mins.

Tourist Information

Mill St, Trim, t (046) 37111.

Lunch

Bounty Bar, *Bridge St, Trim, t (046) 31640.* **Inexpensive**. This ancient pub (the oldest in the county) serves bar snacks and a good pint.

Haggard Inn, *Haggard St, Trim, t (046) 943 1110.* **Inexpensive**. Decent pub grub (including veggie options) in this traditional inn.

seniors €1, children/students €0.75, family ticket €4.25; **adm** including guided tour of keep €3.50, seniors €2.50, children/students €1.25, family ticket €8.25.

This vast castle dominates Trim, and is still a dramatic sight despite its dilapidated state. It was built by Hugh de Lacy and his son Walter at the end of the 12th century, as a defence against Richard de Clare, better known as Strongbow. It stood beyond the Pale, and was in the front line in the Anglo-Norman struggle against the Irish kings. The town gate was the main entrance to the castle, and the spiked heads of traitors once lined the gate as a deterrent to would-be invaders (ten headless bodies were discovered within the castle grounds in the 1970s). De Lacy left the castle in the hands of Hugh Tyrell, who set fire to it rather than allow it to fall into the hands of Roderick O'Connor, King of Connaught, whose armies had taken the town. It was patched up and used during the rebellion of 'Silken Thomas' in the early 16th century, and again by Lord Fennick and the Cromwellites in the 17th century, but was abandoned after the English Civil War.

The extraordinary 20-sided **keep** at the centre of the castle grounds replaced an earlier wooden structure and was protected by a ditch, curtain wall and moat. The bottom part of the curtain wall was known as the 'battered wall', and was deliberately built so that stones dropped from above would bounce off the surface and hit the enemy with maximum force. Raiding parties would 'sally' out from the sally gates which pock the impressive outer walls, still ringed with five sturdy towers.

Butterstream Gardens

Kildalkey Road, Trim, t (046) 36017. **Open** *May–Sept daily 11–6;* **adm** *€4, children/students €2. Wheelchair accessible. Café.*

These imaginative modern gardens sit on the edge of Trim, and were laid out in the early 1970s by Jim Reynolds. They are deliberately designed as a series of 'rooms', edged with hedges of beech, thorn and yew, with spectacular colour schemes and a theatrical layout.

Kells

Almost every visitor to Ireland will make time to see the magnificent illuminated Book of Kells, which is kept in Trinity College Dublin (*see* p.62), but the quiet village of **Kells** in the wooded valley of the Blackwater – where it was kept for centuries – is much less visited. In the 6th century, Diarmuid, High King of Ireland, granted these lands to St Columba, who established a monastery here. Monks fleeing the Viking raids on their community at Iona arrived in the early 9th century, bringing their extraordinary Book with them. The 18th-century **church** which now stands on the monastery lands contains a fascinating history of the religious community and the celebrated manuscript. A roofless, thousand-year-old **round tower** still survives nearby, along with an imposing array of high crosses, including the well-preserved 9th-century South Cross. If you can get in (it's rarely open), **St Columba's House** is

Getting There

For Kells, take bus 30 or 108 from Dublin's main bus station; the journey takes about one hour.

Tourist Information

Tourist office is in the heritage centre; *see* opposite.

Lunch

Vanilla Pod, *Headfort Place, Headfort Arms Hotel, Kells, t (046) 40063, www.headfort-arms.com.* **Expensive–Moderate**. This is one of the best restaurants in town; it's usually open for dinner only, but it also does a fine Sunday lunch.

Jack's Railway Bar, *Athboy Road, Kells, t (046) 40215.* **Inexpensive**. A traditional Irish pub with log fires in winter and a walled garden to sit out and sip a pint in the summer. There are reasonable pub lunches, including a daily carvery.

a tiny, steep-roofed stone oratory which still stands after a thousand years. A 10th-century **High Cross** was placed in the centre of town and used as a gallows during the 1798 rebellion, but it was damaged by a car in 1996 and has been moved to the Kells Heritage Centre.

Kells Heritage Centre

Old Courthouse, Headfort Place, Kells, **t** *(046) 47840.* **Open** *May–Sept Mon–Sat 10–6, Sun and bank hols 1.30–6; Oct–April Tues–Sat 10–5, Sun and bank hols 10.30–6; last adm 45mins before closing;* **adm** *€4, children €3. Limited wheelchair access. Café, shop.*

Kells' graceful early 19th-century courthouse has been remodelled to house an interesting **Heritage Centre**. Its main attraction is the battered High Cross which did grim duty as a gallows during the 1798 rebellion. It has an interesting audio-visual display on the town's history which runs every 45 minutes, plus a smattering of local artefacts; it also recounts the history of the Book of Kells.

SOUTHWEST TO KILDARE
Celbridge

The busy little town of **Celbridge** was built as part of the estate of Ireland's most spectacular Georgian country mansion: **Castletown House**, the largest and most significant Palladian building in Ireland.

If you've had your fill of Georgian mansions, nearby **Celbridge Abbey** is a great place to take the kids, with a model railway, adventure playground and some delightful walking trails. It's run by the St John of God religious order, who offer special family events all year round.

Castletown House

Celbridge, **t** *(01) 628 8252.* **Open** *mid-April to Sept Mon–Fri 10–6, Sat–Sun 1–6, last adm one hour before closing;* **adm** *€3.50, seniors €2.50, children/students €1.25, family ticket €8.25. Wheelchair accessible. Café.*

This extraordinary mansion was built for the speaker of the Irish House of Commons, William Conolly, who was, at the time, the richest man in Ireland. Conolly commissioned the Italian architect Alessandro Galilei (1691–1737) to prepare plans for the house, although much of the construction was overseen by Edward Lovett Pearce, who was deeply influenced by Palladio's love of classical forms. Pearce created the signature sweeping twin ranks of colonnades which connect the kitchen and stables to the main house. The house was remodelled in the late 18th century, possibly to designs by William Chambers (who had a hand in dozens of Ireland's grandest homes without ever actually setting foot on the island). The house stayed in the Conolly family until the 1960s, when it was auctioned off to property developers. For a few tense months, it looked as though the mouldering mansion would be torn down, but Desmond Guinness stepped in at the last moment and bought it. It became the headquarters of the Irish Georgian Society, who began to restore it, and eventually passed to Dúchas, who have spent €6.5 million bringing it back to its former glory.

The **guided tour** will take you around spectacular **drawing rooms** decorated with exquisite original 18th-century furnishings and elaborate stucco ceilings, some created by the celebrated Lafranchini brothers; the only surviving **print room** in Ireland, which dates back to the brief fashion for pasting engravings and mezzo tints onto walls; a lavish **Long Gallery** lined with Pompeii-style

---

Getting There

Buses 67 and 67A leave Middle Abbey Street in Dublin for Celbridge, with a stop at the gates of Castletown House.

Lunch

There are tea rooms at Castletown House. There is also a pleasant restaurant and café at Celbridge Abbey.

friezes; and, best of all, the **dining room**, where it is said that Tom Conolly entertained the devil. The story goes that he met the devil out hunting and invited him home, before realizing the stranger's true identity when he removed his boots to reveal hairy feet shaped like cloven hooves. A priest was called, who threw his breviary at the devil, but missed him and cracked the mirror instead. The devil took fright and disappeared up the chimney, leaving behind the split hearthstone and cracked mirror which you can still see today.

In the castle grounds, Tom Conolly's widow commissioned an eccentric folly (**'Conolly's Folly'**) as a monument to her husband and as a means of providing work for the local people after a particularly harsh winter. It was designed by the eminent architect Richard Cassels (architect of Leinster House in Dublin), and is an extraordinary pile of superimposed arches topped off with a huge obelisk.

Celbridge Abbey
Clane Road, Celbridge, t (01) 627 5508. **Open** *Mon–Sat 10–6, Sun noon–6;* **adm** *€3.50, students/seniors/children €2, family ticket €8. Wheelchair access. Shop, café.*

Celbridge Abbey was built in 1690 for Bartholomew Van Homrigh, who became Lord Mayor of Dublin. Jonathan Swift was smitten with his daughter Esther Van Homrigh, whom he called 'Vanessa', and regularly came to visit her here (*see* box p.93). When Vanessa died of tuberculosis at the age of 35, the abbey came into the possession of Lord Chief Justice Thomas Marly, grandfather of the famous politician and orator Henry Grattan. Grattan wrote many of his greatest speeches here, and claimed to be inspired by the spirit of Swift. He wrote his famous speech 'The Declaration of Rights' (which led to legislative independence for Ireland) in Vanessa's Bower.

The St John of God Order, who care for and educate people with learning difficulties, have developed the grounds as a public attraction, and they now boast a model railway, guided historical walks, trails, playgrounds, tea rooms and a garden centre.

Kildare Town

Kildare Town is a charming market town set around a pub-lined square, and is famous throughout Ireland for its horse-breeding and racing. There are countless private stud farms on the outskirts of the town, but only one, the National Stud Farm, is open to visitors. The town itself is dominated by the imposing St Brigid's Cathedral, overlooked by a battered and roofless round tower.

St Brigid's Cathedral
St Market's Square, Kildare, t (045) 521299. **Open** *May–Oct Mon–Sat 10–1 & 2–5, Sun 2–5;* **adm** *donation requested.*

This church commemorates one of Ireland's most famous saints, St Brigid, who founded a religious community here in 490. According to legend, the king promised to grant her whatever land she could cover with her handkerchief, whereupon it miraculously expanded to cover a swathe large enough for her convent. The present building dates back

Getting There
There are regular trains to Kildare from Heuston station in Dublin, which take about 35 minutes. There is also a regular bus service, but it takes about one hour.

Tourist Information
Heritage Centre, *Market House, Market Square, t (045) 530672.*

Lunch
Kristiannas Bistro, *Market Square, Kildare, t (045) 522985.* **Moderate**. A popular breezy bistro, serving good local dishes with the emphasis on seafood.

Castle View Farm, *Lackaghmore, Kildare, t (045) 521816.* **Inexpensive**. A pretty whitewashed working dairy farm, located 4km from Kildare, which offers fine home-cooking; particularly good if you are travelling with children.

to the 13th century, and although it was considerably restored in the 19th century, the architects managed to stick largely to the original design. Inside, a three-light west window depicts scenes from the lives of Ireland's three most important saints – Patrick, Brigid and Columba – but the most curious sight is an ancient fire temple, in which a sacred fire was kept burning until the dissolution of the monasteries in 1537. There were no early Christian martyrs in Ireland, and Christianity seemed to be adopted peacefully by the local people: part of the reason for this was the early adoption of pagan deities into the Christian canon, and some believe that St Brigid herself was a Celtic goddess whose story was adopted by the early Christians.

National Stud and Japanese Gardens

Tully, **t** *(045) 522963, www.irish-national-stud.ie.* **Open** *daily mid-Feb to mid-Nov 9.30–6; guided tours daily usually at 11, noon, 2, 3 and 4;* **adm** *€8.50, students/seniors €6.50, children €4.50, family ticket €18. Restaurant, shop, playground.*

The lands around Tully have a history of horse-breeding which dates back to the 14th century, when horses were bred here for the Knights of Malta. The first formal stud farm was established here by Colonel William Hall-Walker, later Lord Wavertree, in 1900. Between 1904 and 1914, seven classic winners were bred at Tully, including Minoru (the Colonel's favourite), Prince Palatine and Cherry Lass. He presented the stud-farm to the Crown in 1915 when he left for England, and it passed to the Irish Free State in 1943. The Colonel was a decided eccentric, who had some odd ideas about how horses should be raised. On the guided tour, the unusual skylights which he had installed in the stables will be pointed out to you; a firm believer in astrology, he wanted the stars to exert their influence on his horses to the full. Another of his passions was Japan, and he commissioned the landscape architect Tassa Eida and his son Minoru to lay out a spectacular Japanese-style garden with an exquisite tea house and miniature village. The path through the gardens traces the journey of a soul from Oblivion to Eternity, and it is one of the most beautiful Japanese gardens in Europe. A new garden, dedicated to the patron saint of gardeners St Fiachra, was created to celebrated the millennium. It is a beautiful expanse of woodlands, wetlands, lakes and islands with beautiful ferns and orchids, and some dramatic modern lighting to give it a very contemporary feel.

THE WICKLOW MOUNTAINS

Glendalough

Glendalough is a spellbinding ancient monastic site in the shadow of the Wicklow mountains. The name means Valley of the Two Lakes – St Kevin, in the tradition of the early Christian monks, came to live in a cave on the edges of the Upper Lake in the 6th century. His fame spread, and gradually other monks joined him until finally a monastery

Getting There

The easiest way to get to Glendalough is by guided tour (see p.45), but there is also a daily bus, run by St Kevin's Bus Service, **t** (01) 281 8119, which departs from outside the Royal College of Surgeons on St Stephen's Green in Dublin at 11.15am. It returns from Glendalough at 4.15pm.

Tourist Information

Local information in the Visitor Centre (see p.169).

Lunch

Mitchell's, *Laragh, Glendalough,* **t** *(0404) 45302.* **Moderate.** A traditional restaurant in a converted schoolhouse about a mile from Glendalough, serving Irish dishes such as delicious Wicklow lamb, and excellent afternoon teas.

The Wicklow Way

The **Wicklow Way** was the first Waymarked Way in Ireland and remains one of the country's most popular walking routes.

It begins in Marlay Park on the southern outskirts of Dublin, and winds for 80 miles (130km) through some of the most beautiful scenery in the country to its culmination in the village of Clonegal, County Carlow. Much of the route lies over 1600ft (500m), offering glorious views over loughs, rivers and historic remains including the spellbinding monastic site of Glendalough; and the lower paths twist through forests and farmland along the flanks of the Wicklow mountains. The full walk takes about a week (but many people make do with a single section), and you should come prepared for changeable weather and rain-sodden paths.

Useful guides include *The Complete Wicklow Way* by J.B. Malone; *Way Marked Trails of Ireland* by Michael Fewer; and *The Wicklow Way* by Jacquetta Megarry. The best maps are published by Ordnance Survey Ireland; those covering the relevant area are nos. 50, 56 and 62.

---

was established on the shores of the Lower Lake. St Kevin died in 618, reputedly at the age of 120, but the monastery continued to flourish for another six centuries, becoming a famous centre of scholarship. Most of the surviving remnants date from the 10th-to-12th centuries, a haunting huddle of semi-ruined churches, Celtic crosses and ancient, leaning gravestones. (Many people wanted to be buried in a graveyard which contained the last remains of a saint, and the Glendalough graveyard is still in use today.) When Christchurch Cathedral was built in Dublin and the dioceses of Glendalough and Dublin were united, the monastery's importance diminished, and the Anglo-Normans reduced the settlement to rubble in 1398. Nonetheless, it has continued to be a place of pilgrimage, contemplation and retreat ever since.

The **gateway** is the only one of its kind still standing in Ireland, and is over a thousand years old. It would originally have had two storeys, capped with a wooden roof. Just within it is a stone inscribed with a faded simple cross: this delineated the monastery proper which offered sanctuary within its borders.

A stony path leads to the **Round Tower**, one of the finest in the country. A lightning-strike in the late 1800s almost split it in two; a local man, Sam Kennedy, apparently danced a hornpipe around the edge of the roof during the repairs. The tower, about 100 feet tall and with walls at least 3 feet thick, had several functions: as a watchtower to keep an eye out for Viking raids; as a belltower to call the monks to prayer; and as a storehouse for the most important treasures. A door is set about 12 feet up its length; when raiders arrived, the monks would pile into the tower and draw the ladder up after them.

Beyond the tower are the lofty ruins of the **cathedral church of Saints Peter and Paul**, one of the largest early Christian churches in Ireland. Bishops sat here until the construction in the 13th century of Christchurch Cathedral in Dublin (*see* p.89), which became the new cathedral church of Glendalough. St Lawrence O'Toole, whose heart is preserved in Christchurch, was abbot of Glendalough in the 12th century, before becoming Archbishop of Dublin. The ruins, now strewn with worn gravestones, date back to the 12th and 13th centuries and incorporate parts of an earlier church. The walls would originally have been painted, and monks would pray here for eight hours at a time, lying prone with their arms outstretched. The window at the east end is especially fine, and the remnants of a baptismal font can be made out underneath the southern window of the Chancel.

Just outside the cathedral, a huge granite Celtic cross, known as **St Kevin's Cross**, is said to mark the burial site of St Kevin. According to legend, if you put your arms around it, make a wish and link your fingers, the wish will come true. Near it is a tiny building called the 'Priest's House' which was rebuilt from ruins and is another rumoured burial place of St Kevin. Its original function is unknown, although it may once have held relics associated with the saint, and it gets its modern name from the practice of burying priests there in the 18th and 19th centuries.

St Kevin's Church, curiously known as 'St Kevin's kitchen', is the only one remaining in Glendalough with a roof, and is where St Kevin is said to have prayed, worked and slept when he wasn't in his cave. Only official guides have access to the church (you can arrange tours with the Visitor Centre, *see opposite*), and inside you can make out a tiny cruft, a little sleeping hole built into the stone roof of the church.

It's a short but delightful walk to the **Lower Lake**, and another 20 minute-stroll to the shores of the **Upper Lake** where St Kevin lived in his cave. On the way, you'll pass a gushing waterfall, and the remnants of a strange, stone-walled, circular enclosure called the Caher. The cave, known as '**St Kevin's Bed**', has been hacked into the cliff about 8 metres above southern side of the lake, close to the ruins of an ancient church and is accessible only by boat. The saint is said to have stood at the water's edge absorbed in prayer for so long that birds built nests in his outstretched arms. Another famous legend says that St Kevin, whose Gaelic name *Coemhagen* means 'fair-born', was astonishingly handsome, and attracted a lot of attention from love-struck young women: one, called Kathleen, followed him up to his cave and tried to seduce him, and he angrily threw her into the lake where she drowned. The walk is part of the Wicklow Way, one of the most scenic long-distance footpaths in the country (*see box opposite*).

In 2001, a 29-kilometre **pilgrimage path** was re-established, which follows the line of the ancient pilgrim trail called St Kevin's Road. Scattered along it and around the Glendalough monastic site are about thirty curious boulders with shallow, artificial hollows. They are called Ballaun stones, and were probably originally used for grinding grain or pigments for illuminating manuscripts. In later centuries, local people came to believe that the water which gathered in these hollows could cure warts, a tradition which persists.

Glendalough Visitor Centre

Glendalough, t (0404) 45325. Open daily 9.30–6, mid-Oct to mid-March closes 5; last adm 45mins before closing; adm €2.75, seniors €2, students €1.25, family ticket €7. Wheelchair access.

The modern **visitor centre** is a five-minute walk to the east of the monastery complex. It contains a fascinating exhibition, which includes an audio-visual presentation that outlines the history of the site and recounts the legends surrounding St Kevin. The centre organizes excellent guided tours of the complex, which include entrance into some of the monuments normally closed to visitors.

Powerscourt Estate

Enniskerry, Co. Wicklow, t (01) 204 6000, www.powerscourt.ie. Gardens and house exhibition open daily 9.30–5.30; adm gardens €6.50, students €5.50, children €3.50; adm house €2.50, students €2.20, children €1.60; adm waterfall €4, students €2.20, children €3.

Getting There

Powerscourt Estate is tricky to reach without your own transport, so consider taking one of the tours (see p.45). Bus 44 from Dublin bus station goes to Enniskerry, about 3km from Powerscourt, or take the DART to Bray and then bus 85 from the station to Enniskerry.

Lunch

There's an excellent restaurant and café run by Avoca on the grounds, and a delicatessen if you want to pick up picnic supplies.

Partially wheelchair accessible. Café, restaurants, shopping centre.

Powerscourt House was built by the eminent Palladian architect Richard Cassels for the Wingfield family around 1740, and incorporated the remains of a medieval castle. The estate has a breathtaking location on the fringes of the Wicklow mountains, and the beautiful façade was deliberately designed to echo the Sugar Loaf which looms in the distance. The mansion was one of the finest country houses in Europe, with a spectacular interior of dazzling opulence. Unfortunately, it was burned to a shell by a fire which broke out on the very night of a party celebrating the completion of renovations in 1974. Although most of the house is still closed to the public, the extravagant ballroom has been restored and is regularly used for society weddings and other events. Admission to the **house exhibition** includes a glimpse of the ballroom, with its slim colonnades, sumptuous walnut marquetry floor, double height ceiling and dazzling gilded detailing. Part of the house has been converted into an upmarket, if touristy, shopping centre, with an outpost of Avoca, with beautiful fabrics and crafts, an excellent deli, several giftshops and even a couple of furniture shops. There's also a very good café and restaurant.

But the star attraction at Powerscourt remains the splendid **gardens**, which were first created by Cassels when the house was built in the early 18th century. The seventh Viscount of Powerscourt commissioned the eccentric landscape architect Daniel Robertson to improve and extend the gardens in the mid-19th century. Robertson, a gouty alcoholic, was pushed around the estate in a wheelbarrow clutching a bottle of sherry. When the bottle was finished, he would down tools and go home.

Whatever his state of inebriation, Robertson had a magical touch. The first sight of the gardens, a series of formal terraces spilling downhill to the **Triton Lake**, with the Sugar Loaf mountains in the background, is startlingly beautiful. Statues of classical deities line the upper terrace, and the view of the lake is framed by a pair of rearing winged horses. Vivid green lawns flank the central path, which is intricately patterned with Wicklow granite and pebbles from the beach at Bray. At the centre of the lake, Triton (based on Bernini's statue in the Piazza Barberini in Rome) sends a jet of water from his conch shell soaring 100 feet into the air. The views back up to the house are magnificent.

Beyond the Triton Lake are the **Japanese Gardens**, laid out in 1908, overlooked by a charming pagoda and scattered with miniature bridges and stone lanterns. The colours are glorious, a riot of deep reds from the Japanese maples, blazing pink rhododendrons, and delicate pink cherry blossom. Behind it is the Killing Hollow, where the first Viscount of Powerscourt apparently killed the last member of the O'Toole clan.

Tucked away in woodland beyond the Triton Lake is the pet cemetery, where the family pets are laid under affectionately inscribed headstones. Along with Jyp and Tim, two Irish terriers who were 'faithful friends for 12 years', are more unusual pets, like Eugenie, a much-loved cow, who had 17 calves and produced 100,000 gallons of milk. Tommy, a Shetland pony, is buried with 'his wife', Magic.

Heading back toward the house, the quiet **Dolphin Pond** has a pretty central fountain made of four leaping dolphins, and beyond it lie the extensive **Walled Gardens**. At the end of the garden is the Bamberg Gate, an extravagant 18th-century wrought-iron gateway from the cathedral at Bamberg in Bavaria.

A beautiful 6km walk through woodland and banks of wild rhododendrons leads to the spectacular **Powerscourt Waterfall**, which cascades for almost four hundred feet from a rock-shelf into the river and glints like gold if the sun shines. The area around the waterfall is a deer park, and criss-crossed with attractive walking trails.

Blessington Lakes

Russborough House and Gardens

Blessington, t (045) 865239. Open June–Aug daily 10.30–5.30, April–May and Sept Sun 10.30–2; adm main rooms €6, students €4.50, children €3; adm bedrooms €3.50. Café, shop.

Russborough House is another spectacular Palladian mansion designed by Richard Cassels for the first Earl of Milltown, Joseph Leeson, who inherited a fortune from his brewer father. Begun in 1741 and completed a decade later, it is made from local silvery-grey granite and boasts an imposing façade with curving graceful colonnades topped by a rank of Baroque urns. The house is set in a beautiful 300-acre demesne with shady walking trails and a spectacular maze, surrounded by the soft silhouettes of the Wicklow mountains. In 1951, the house was bought by Sir Alfred and Lady Beit, who used it to house their art collection, one of the most prestigious in Ireland. Much of it was bequeathed to the National Gallery on Sir Alfred's death (one of the wings of the Gallery bears his name), but plenty of masterpieces remain in the house and can be briefly admired on the whirlwind tour.

The sumptuous interior features delicate stuccowork ceilings probably carried out by the famous Lafranchini brothers, elaborately inlaid marquetry floors, glistening marble staircases and chimney-pieces. The grandest room of all is the Saloon, which was used by rebels during the 1798 Rebellion. They managed to leave it without a mark, but the government troops were so careless that an outraged Lord Milltown reportedly challenged Lord Tyrawley to a duel 'with underbusses and slugs in a sawpit'. There's a handsome rococo ceiling, and the walls are covered in rich-red velvet which forms a sumptuous backdrop for the collection of Dutch and Flemish paintings.

Dwyer McAlister Cottage

Derrynamuck, Knockanarrigan, t (0404) 45325. Open mid-June to mid-Sept daily 2–6; adm free.

With your own transport, this tiny thatched, whitewashed cottage makes for a pleasant detour, just beyond the lovely Hollywood Glen, a couple of miles south of Russborough. It's named for Michael Dwyer and Sam McAlister, two of the United Irishmen who fought in the rebellion of 1798. On a snowy night in February 1799, the cottage was surrounded by government forces and a vicious gun battle ensued. McAlister died, but Dwyer made a daring escape and fled into the snow-covered mountains. It took the authorities another four years to capture him. The cottage was reduced to rubble, but was restored in the 1940s, in a style typical of the late 1800s.

Russborough's Notorious Art Thefts

The architecture, the authentic 18th-century décor and the dazzling art collection make Russborough one of the most spectacular country houses in Ireland, but it's most famous for a series of daring art thefts. The first major robbery happened in 1974, when an IRA gang (which included British heiress Rose Dugdale) stole 19 paintings at a value of £8m, including a Vermeer, a Goya, two Gainsboroughs and three Rubens. They were subsequently recovered in a cottage two weeks later. In 1986, a well-known Dublin thief stole £30m-worth of paintings, and in 2001 another two paintings were pinched when thieves drove a Jeep through the front door. Security, as you might expect, is now particularly tight, and the 45-minute guided tours are closely watched.

Getting There

Blessington Lakes is not easy to reach with public transport. Bus 65 leaves Eden Quay in Dublin roughly every 2 hours and takes about 90 minutes.

Lunch

The tea rooms at Russborough House offer a decent range of snacks, sandwiches and cakes.

Where to Stay

Southeast Dublin 173
Southwest Dublin and Temple Bar 178
Northeast Dublin 179
Northwest Dublin 182
Outside the Centre: Dublin Suburbs 182
Outside the Centre: Dublin Bay 184

Dublin has the full range of **accommodation**, from chic designer hotels to family-run B&Bs. The *grandes dames* of the city's hotel trade, the historic Shelbourne and the Gresham, are still going strong, or you could plump for a quirky guesthouse or an opulent Georgian mansion. There are dozens of hostels, many of which are great for families or groups on a budget.

As a (very) general rule, much of the more expensive accommodation is in on the **south side** of the river, and many of the cheaper guesthouses on the **north** side. Prices also vary depending on location, with the same thing often costing more on the south side. The divisions between the north and south are lessening all the time – although that doesn't stop the terrible jokes such as 'Why do southside girls go out with northside men? To get their handbags back'.

Many hotels and guesthouses can be found in the elegant suburban district of **Ballsbridge**, which, although a 20-minute walk from the centre, is a good choice if you are looking for peace and quiet. Anywhere in **Temple Bar** suffers from noise, so either come here looking to party or pack your ear plugs. There are plenty of delightful places to stay **around Dublin Bay**, from where the convenient DART train makes getting into town very easy.

Hotels generally have the highest level of amenities, although some of the best **guesthouses** offer equally good services. Guesthouses at the bottom end of the scale are little more than **B&Bs**, but most are friendly and welcoming. B&Bs also vary, from simple rooms in family homes to luxurious Georgian townhouses. **Breakfast** is usually included in the rates for guesthouses and always at B&Bs; the traditional Irish breakfast, a high-cholesterol affair comprising (at least) bacon, sausage, egg and potato bread, is often excellent.

The **tourist office** has a brochure on where to stay, and it also has an accommodation-booking service (also available online). Many hotels offer **discounts** for stays between Sunday and Thursday. There are also hundreds of websites offering discounts, and you should check the website of the particular hotel you're interested in to see if has any online deals. Book well in advance during the summer, or around big events such as St Patrick's Day.

All the hotels listed take **credit cards** unless otherwise stated; Visa and Mastercard are most widely accepted, Amex less so.

Price Categories

Price categories for a double room in high season are as follows:

Luxury	Over €250
Expensive	€180–250
Moderate	€120–180
Inexpensive	€70–120
Cheap	Under €70

Southeast Dublin

Luxury

Conrad Dublin J8
Grafton St, t (01) 602 8900, f (01) 676 5424, www.conradhotels.com; wheelchair accessible.

A smart, modern hotel in a fine location opposite the national concert hall. The top-hatted doormen are perhaps the cheeriest in the city. Rooms are large and well-equipped, with windows framing fabulous views, and a great selection of bathroom goodies. Facilities include a gym and two restaurants.

Le Meridien Shelbourne I8
27 St Stephen's Green, t (01) 663 4500, f (01) 661 6006, www.shelbourne.com.

Overlooking St Stephen's Green, this is the most traditional hotel in Dublin, with oodles of charm and a delightfully old-fashioned atmosphere. High tea is a treat, with trays of sandwiches and cakes and silver pots of tea laid out on crisp white cloths. The bar, with its sumptuous leather armchairs, is a favourite with well-heeled Dubliners. Rooms are very comfortable, with overstuffed furniture, antiques and thick drapes, and the hotel also has a health and fitness centre with a small pool.

Merrion Hotel K8
Upper Merrion St, t (01) 603 0600, f (01) 603 0700, www.merrion-hotel.com; wheelchair accessible.

One of the most luxurious hotels in the city, occupying four restored Georgian townhouses (one of which was home to the Duke of Wellington) set around manicured gardens. Rooms in the Garden Wing are cheaper, but have views over the gardens; those in the older part retain original features. There are two restaurants, including the celebrated Patrick Guilbaud, and a pool, gym and spa.

Self-Catering Options

The tourist office has a long list of self-catering accommodation. The following all operate a range of self-catering properties in the city centre:

Active Ireland, *t (01) 478 2045, f (01) 478 4327, www.activeireland.com.* Immaculate two-bedroomed apartments in an elegant complex in the smart Ballsbridge suburb. They are available by the night or for longer periods for €150–250 per night.

Dial a Short Let, *80 Haddington Rd, Ballsbridge, t (01) 667 2541, f (01) 668 5911, www.dialashortlet.com.*

Dublin Self-Catering Accommodation Association, *32 Lower O'Connell St, t/f (01) 269 1535, www.dublin-accommodation.com.*

Express Accommodation, *3 Lower Abbey St, t (01) 878 2100, f (01) 878 2850, accexpress@eircom.net.*

Short Term Solutions, *85–86 Grafton St, t (01) 679 2222, f (01) 668 5911, www.shorttermsolutions.com.*

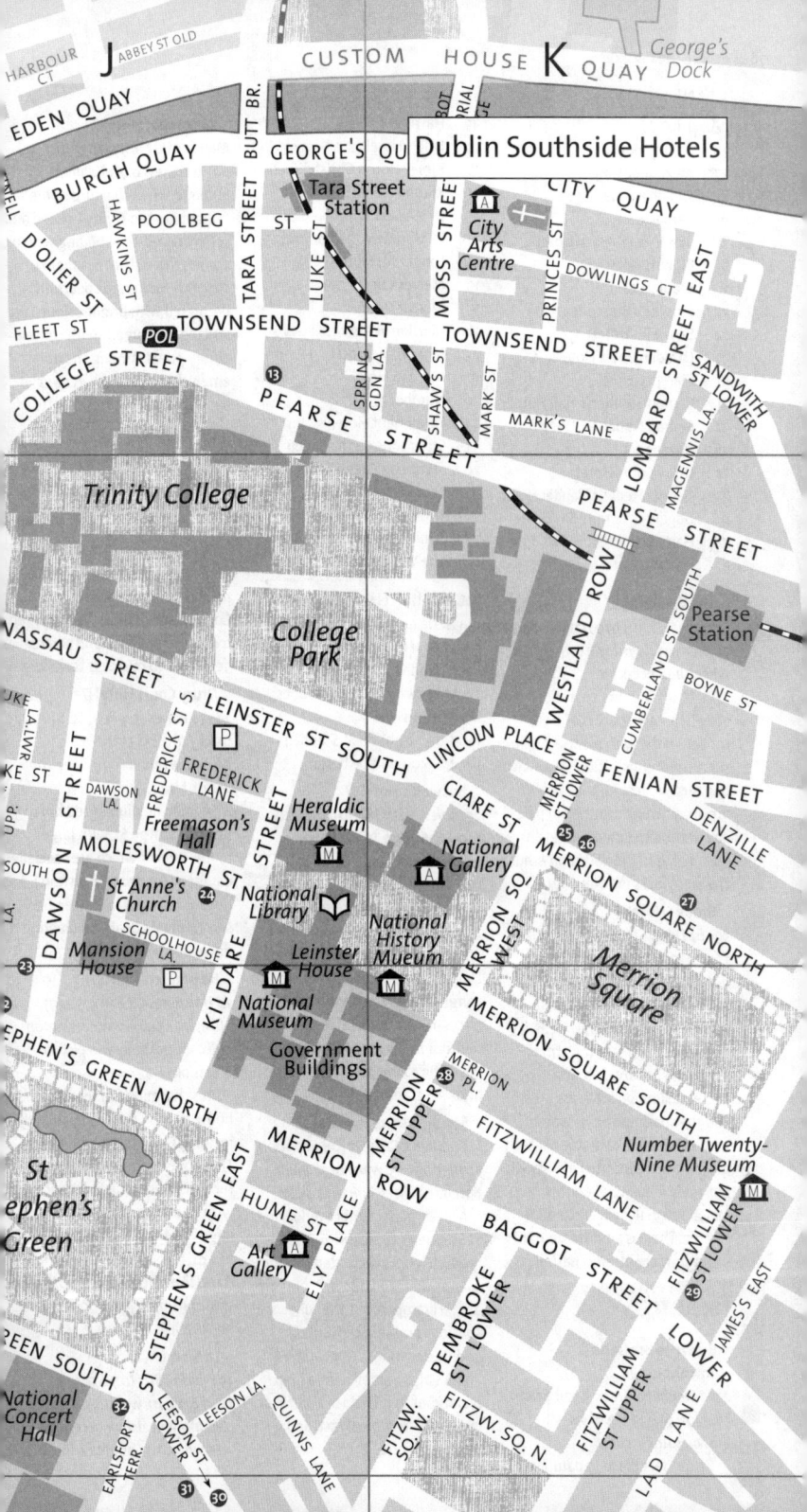

Where to Stay

Map Key

#	Name	#	Name
36	Albany House	35	Harrington Hall
27	Alexander Hotel	14	Kellys Hotel
18	Avalon House	1	Kinlay House Christchurch
6	Barnacle's	37	Kilronan Guesthouse
12	Bewley's Principal Hotel	23	La Stampa
8	Blooms Hotel	21	Le Meridien Shelbourne
16	Brooks Hotel	29	Longfields Hotel
22	Browne's Brasserie	19	Mercer Court
24	Buswell's Hotel	19	Mercer Hotel
37	Camden Court Hotel	28	Merrion Hotel
5	Clarence Hotel	25	Mont Clare Hotel
31	Clarion Stephen's Hall Hotel	10	Morgan Hotel
32	Conrad Dublin	4	Number 31
26	Davenport	33	Parliament Hotel
17	Drury Court Hotel	20	Stauntons on the Green
2	George Frederic Handel Hotel	11	Stephen's Green Hotel
9	Gogarty's Temple Bar Hostel	7	Temple Bar Hotel
34	Harcourt Hotel	13	Trinity Arch Hotel
3	Harding Hotel	15	Trinity Capital Hotel
			The Westbury

The Westbury J7
Grafton St, t (01) 679 1122, f (01) 679 7078, www.jurysdoyle.com; wheelchair acessible.

Right off Dublin's best shopping street, the Westbury is a large, modern hotel with plenty of luxurious trimmings, including a swish bar and two restaurants. Rooms are attractively furnished in pale colours and the mod cons even include TVs in the bathrooms, but the place lacks individuality.

Brooks Hotel I7
59–62 Drury St, t (01) 670 4000, f (01) 670 4455, www.sinnott hotels.com; wheelchair accessible.

This elegant hotel is tucked away on a quiet central street. It has tried to recreate the atmosphere of a private club, and succeeds: lounge areas are plush, and the spacious rooms (some with plasma TVs and other hi-tech gadgets) are decorated in a stylish but traditional way. Services include a small gym and a mini-cinema. There is a fine restaurant – and staff are utterly charming.

Expensive

Brownes Brasserie & Townhouse J8
22 St Stephen's Green, t (01) 638 39 39, f (01) 638 39 00, www.brownesdublin.com.

The perfect place to pamper yourself, the celebrated Brownes Brasserie restaurant (see p.186) now has 11 luxurious guestrooms. Each is individually designed and furnished with the best fabrics and fittings. The location – right on St Stephen's Green – couldn't be better.

Buswell's Hotel J7
25 Molesworth St, t (01) 614 0500, f (01) 676 2090, www.quinnhotels.com.

This 18th-century townhouse has been a hotel since 1921, and is a favourite among Dubliners – particularly politicians from the Dail just around the corner, who congregate in the popular public bar. It has a comfortable, clubby feel, but manages to avoid stuffiness. The rooms are comfortable and very traditional.

Stephen's Green Hotel I8
St Stephen's Green, t (01) 607 3600, f (01) 661 5663, www.ocallaghan-hotels.ie; wheelchair accessible.

A sleek, glassy hotel overlooking St Stephen's Green, with crisply modern rooms decorated in bright colours and bold prints. Rooms are a little cramped, but the suites are spacious and very comfortable, and the location is unbeatable. There's also a small gym, a fine restaurant (which does a particularly good Irish breakfast) and a business centre.

Alexander Hotel K7
Merrion Sq, t (01) 607 3700, f (01) 661 5663, www.ocallaghan hotels.ie; wheelchair accessible.

Right next to Trinity College and set in an unusual building with a domed tower. The reasonably spacious rooms are cheerfully decorated with bright colours and striking bedspreads with contemporary prints. Among the many amenities are a small gym, valet parking and a business centre.

Davenport K8
Merrion Sq, t (01) 607 3500, f (01) 661 5663, www.ocallaghan hotels.ie; wheelchair accessible.

An elegant hotel set in a 19th-century building with an imposing neoclassical façade painted primrose yellow. Comfortable, classically furnished rooms, a small gym and an area dedicated to business travellers.

Drury Court Hotel I7
28–30 Lower Stephens St, t (01) 475 1988, f (01) 478 5730, www.drurycourthotel.com; wheelchair accessible.

Friendly, medium-sized hotel just off Grafton St, with large rooms (two of which are specially equipped for disabled visitors), a restaurant and bar. It often has special online deals which bring it down one price category.

Harrington Hall I8
70 Harcourt St, t (01) 475 3497, f (01) 475 4544, www.harrington-hall.com; partially wheelchair accessible.

This charming family-run guesthouse is set in two immaculately restored Georgian townhouses. The rooms are traditionally furnished with quiet elegance, with sweeping drapes on the large windows and spacious bathrooms. The staff try hard to make it feel like a home-from-home; it is unsurprisingly very popular, so book well in advance.

La Stampa J7
35 Dawson St, t (01) 677 4444, f (01) 677 4411, www.lastampa.ie; partially wheelchair accessible.

Pared-down, but luxurious

décor in these gorgeous guestrooms above one of the city's most celebrated restaurants (see p.187). Each is individually styled, but all feature sumptuous fabrics and furnishings.

Moderate

Albany House I8
*84 Harcourt St, **t** (01) 475 1092, **f** (01) 475 1093, www.byrne-hotels-ireland.com.*

A very comfortable guesthouse in a lovingly restored Georgian mansion around the corner from St Stephen's Green. The rooms are decorated with traditional prints and dark antiques, and prices include an excellent breakfast.

Camden Court Hotel I9
*Camden St, **t** (01) 475 9666, **f** (01) 475 9677, www.camdencourthotel.com.*

It's a good ten-minute walk to Grafton St from this large, modern hotel, but this is reflected in the very reasonable prices. The décor is what you might find in any international chain hotel, but the rooms are large and bright, and there's a bar, restaurant, gym and fabulous pool. The staff are extremely helpful.

> ### University Dorms
> Dublin's colleges and universities offer summer accommodation in their student housing, usually available from early June until mid-September.
> **Dublin City University**, *Glasnevin, **t** (01) 700 5736, **f** (01) 700 5777, campusresidence@dcu.ie.* 50 double and 220 single rooms. €35–41 per person sharing.
> **Trinity College**, ***t** (01) 608 1177, **f** (01) 671 1267, reservations@tcd.ie.* 589 rooms, of which 261 are ensuite. €38–60 per person. These are the most central and therefore the most popular of the university dorms: book early.
> **UCD Village**, *Belfield, **t** (01) 269 7111, **f** (01) 269 7704, ucd.village@usitworld.com.* 1200 rooms. From €33 per person, €600 per unit per week (sleeps 3–5).

Clarion Stephen's Hall Hotel & Suites J9
*The Earlsfort Centre, Lower Leeson St, **t** (01) 638 1111, **f** (01) 638 1122, www.premgroup.com; partially wheelchair accessible.*

This unusual hotel offers 34 suites in place of regular hotel rooms; choose from standard rooms with kitchenettes, or one- or two-bedroom suites with a living room and fully fitted kitchen. All are equipped with modern furniture and fittings (including modem points and CD players), and you'll get fantastic views from the top-floor rooms.

Harcourt Hotel I8
*60 Harcourt St, **t** (01) 478 3677, **f** 478 1557, www.harcourthotel.ie.*

The Harcourt is a decent moderately priced option close to the centre, with reasonably comfortable rooms and cheerful staff. If you are in Dublin for the *craic*, you might enjoy the downstairs pub – a great venue for traditional music – and the slightly tacky nightclub. But if you're after peace and quiet, look elsewhere.

Kilronan Guesthouse J9
*70 Adelaide Rd, **t** (01) 475 5266, **f** (01) 478 2841, www.dublinn.com.*

This welcoming guesthouse is set in a whitewashed 19th-century townhouse, about a ten-minute walk to the main sights and shopping areas. It's on a quiet, leafy street, and the impeccable rooms (all with orthopaedic beds) still have many of their original features. The staff have won awards for their charming service, and the hearty Irish breakfasts are among the best in the city.

Longfields Hotel K8
*9–10 Fitzwilliam St Lower, **t** (01) 676 1637, **f** (01) 676 1542, www.longfields.ie.*

Another delightful small hotel, set in a pair of restored Georgian townhouses. The handsome rooms are individually decorated with antique furniture and traditional fabrics, and some deluxe rooms have four-poster beds. It's

home to Kevin Arundel's Number 10 Restaurant (*see p.186*), one of the finest in Dublin.

Mercer Hotel I8
*Lower Mercer St, **t** (01) 478 2179, **f** (01) 478 0328, www.mercerhotel.ie; wheelchair accessible.*

Small, intimate and perfectly located, the Mercer combines trendiness with tradition in its small but stylish rooms. Staff are well-intentioned.

Mont Clare Hotel K7
*Merrion Sq, **t** (01) 607 3800, **f** (01) 661 5663, www.ocallaghanhotels.ie; partially wheelchair accessible.*

A medium-sized traditional hotel with pretty rooms. Standard rates are overpriced, but there is almost always a special offer available. It is run by the same people who have the Davenport across the street, and guests can use the Davenport's gym.

Number 31 K9
*31 Leeson Close, **t** (01) 676 5011, **f** (01) 676 2929, www.number31.ie.*

One of the most unusual places to stay in the city. The elegant bedrooms are in the Georgian house, which is linked to an ultra-modern annexe designed by Sam Stephenson. You can sink into the conversation pit in the lounge area, surrounded by unusual modern art, and breakfast is served on a delightful patio.

Stauntons on the Green I8
*83 St Stephen's Green, **t** (01) 478 2300, **f** (01) 478 2263, www.stauntonsonthegreen.ie.*

For a taste of the country in the city, you can't do better than this: a beautiful Georgian mansion with views over St Stephen's Green, and a private garden at the back leading into the magical Iveagh Gardens. Airy, elegant rooms feature large windows (including some for families), and there's a relaxed bar area.

Trinity Capital Hotel J6
*Pearse St, **t** (01) 648 1000, **f** (01) 648 1010, www.capital-hotels.com*

A modern hotel located very close to Trinity College, which is reasonably priced for the facilities on offer. The rooms are not large, but they are all crisply furnished in contemporary style. Some of the lower rooms suffer from noise from the adjoining nightclub.

Inexpensive

Kellys Hotel I7
36 South Great George's St, t (01) 677 9277, f (01) 671 3216, www.kellyshtl.com.

A small, cheerful, family-run hotel with spotless rooms painted in sunny colours. It's good value for its excellent city-centre location, and offers a range of rooms, including family rooms.

Mercer Court I8
Lower Mercer St, t (01) 474 4120, f (01) 672 9926, www.mercercourt.ie. Open mid-June to late Sept.

Mercer Court is used as a student residence during the academic year, but during the summer break they offer affordable accommodation (B&B or self-catering apartments). Situated right next to St Stephen's Green in the heart of the city centre, and run by the much swisher Mercer Hotel next door.

Cheap

Avalon House I8
55 Aungier St, t (01) 475 0001, f (01) 475 0303, www.avalon-house.ie.

This is a very popular hostel in an old redbrick building in a great central location. There is a mix of rooms – twins and quadruples – and dorms sleeping between 10 and 26. The café is open to 10pm.

Southwest Dublin and Temple Bar

Luxury

Clarence Hotel I6
6–8 Wellington Quay, Temple Bar, t (01) 407 0800, f (01) 407 0820, www.theclarence.ie.

Famously owned by the rock band U2, this is one of the most luxurious hotels in Dublin. No austere minimalism here: each room is individually designed with a stylish mixture of traditional and contemporary furniture. Everything feels wonderful: plump down duvets and pillows, soft leather chairs, extra-fluffy robes and a great range of goodies in the marble bathrooms. For a real treat, opt for the Pentagon Suite (€2100), a favourite with visiting rock stars. Services include a fitness and beauty centre for some serious pampering. The Tea Room (see p.193) is one of the best restaurants in Dublin, and the Octagon Bar (see p.206) is the favoured hangout of the fashion pack. Staff are highly efficient, competent and friendly.

Expensive

Morgan Hotel J6
10 Fleet St, Temple Bar, t (01) 679 3939, f (01) 679 3946, www.themorgan.com.

Very sleek, chic, boutique hotel in the purest minimalist style. Standard rooms are on the small side, but feature crisp white cotton bedding, abstract art and 21st-century essentials like wireless broadband Internet. You can pamper yourself with a massage or aromatherapy treatments, or work out in the fitness room, and the black and white bar is one of the places to see and be seen.

Moderate

Bewley's Principal Hotel J6
19–20 Fleet St, Temple Bar, t (01) 670 8122, f (01) 670 8103, www.bewleysprincipalhotel.com.

Sitting above the former café, this is a friendly hotel which has been recently refurbished. The rooms are comfortable and modern but lack individuality. The prices are very reasonable for the location and service though.

Blooms Hotel I6
6 Anglesea St, Temple Bar, t (01) 671 5622, f 671 5997, www.blooms.ie.

A modern hotel with simple, unexceptional rooms, but a good location if you want to enjoy the nightlife of Temple Bar. And you won't have to go far: it has got its own nightclub, Club M, in the basement and offers discounts in other bars and clubs in the area.

George Frederic Handel Hotel H7
16–18 Fishamble St, t (01) 670 9400, f (01) 670 9410, www.handelshotel.com.

The first recital of Handel's *Messiah* apparently took place on the spot now occupied by this modern hotel, alongside Christchurch Cathedral. The rooms are decorated in an unmemorable chain-hotel style, and prices are high for the facilities. But online deals can bring the prices down considerably, making it a good bargain for the central location.

Parliament Hotel I7
Lord Edward St, Temple Bar, t (01) 670 8777, f (01) 670 8787, www.regencyhotels.com.

These bedrooms are among the frilliest and flounciest in town, but reasonably spacious. The central location is both good and bad: all the sights are on your doorstep, but so is the nightlife – which means plenty of noise.

Temple Bar Hotel I6
Fleet St, Temple Bar, t (01) 677 3333, f (01) 612 9290, www.towerhotelgroup.com.

Reasonably priced for the facilities and location – but, like most places in Temple Bar, very noisy. Rooms are spick and span, if blandly decorated. Give breakfast a miss – you'll eat much better at local restaurants. The bar, Buskers, is one of the liveliest in the area.

Trinity Arch Hotel I7
46–49 Dame St, Temple Bar, t (01) 679 4455, f (01) 679 4511, www.trinityarchhotel.com.

A relatively small hotel (29 rooms) set in a handsome 19th-century mansion on the edge of Temple Bar, with tasteful rooms decorated in warm colours. Best for folk out to enjoy the nightlife, as street noise can be bad.

Inexpensive

Harding Hotel H7
*Copper Alley, Fishamble St, **t** (01) 679 6500, **f** (01) 679 6504, www.hardinghotel.ie.*

A modern, red brick hotel tucked between Christchurch and Temple Bar, with spacious rooms and a popular bar with traditional music. Prices are very reasonable for the location and facilities.

Cheap

Barnacle's I6
*Temple Bar House, 19 Temple Lane, Temple Bar, **t** (01) 671 6277, **f** (01) 671 6591, www.barnacles.ie.*

A bright, colourful hostel with rooms and dorms, and cheerful staff. Facilities include laundry, kitchen and free breakfast.

Gogarty's Temple Bar Hostel I6
*18–21 Anglesea St, **t** (01) 671 1822, **f** (01) 671 7637, www.olivergogartys.com.*

A favourite with backpackers who want to be in the middle of Temple Bar, Gogarty's offers dorm accommodation (rooms from 3–10 people), plus twin rooms with or without ensuite bathrooms. Other facilties include kitchen, laundry, TV room and no curfew.

Kinlay House Christchurch H7
*2–12 Lord Edward St, **t** (01) 679 6644, **f** (01) 679 7437, www.kinlayhouse.ie.*

A slightly old-fashioned hostel, Kinlay House is a city institution, with twin and double rooms (with and without bathrooms) and dorms sleeping 4–6. Good facilities include a kitchen and café.

Northeast Dublin

Luxury

Gresham Hotel J5
*23 Upper O'Connell St, **t** (01) 874 6881, **f** (01) 878 7175, www.gresham-hotels.com; partial wheelchair access.*

This is one of the most historic hotels in the city, a classic early 19th-century establishment that dates back to the heyday of O'Connell Street. It still exudes an air of old-fashioned gentility, but, despite recent refurbishment, it doesn't offer the kind of services you might expect for the price or its four-star rating. The bar is a popular watering hole for affluent Dubliners, and there's an excellent restaurant, '23' (see p.198).

Morrison Hotel I6
*Ormond Quay, **t** (01) 887 2400, **f** (01) 878 3185, www.morrison-hotel.ie; wheelchair access.*

The fashionistas flock to the Morrison, a temple to sleek, modern design. The interior was styled by the celebrated Irish designer John Rocha, and the immaculate rooms feature his beautiful fabrics. If you really want to push the boat out, there are a handful of suites and a penthouse for the latest in *über*-cool luxury. There are two restaurants, and the Lobo bar is a popular spot with Dublin's beautiful people.

Expensive

Arlington Hotel J6
*23–25 Bachelors Walk, **t** (01) 804 9100, **f** 804 9112, www.arlington.ie.*

A large, stylish hotel set in a converted auction house right on the river. It's a great location, and each of the spacious rooms is decorated with sumptuous blue, gold and ochre fabrics. There's a popular bar with traditional music and Irish dancing nightly, and a relaxed, elegant restaurant.

Clarion Hotel K6
*Excise Walk, IFSC, **t** (01) 433 8800, **f** (01) 433 8801, www.clarion-hotelifsc.com; wheelchair access.*

Huge, luxurious and ultra-modern hotel within the Financial Services Centre, with hi-tech rooms and large bathrooms. There's a gym with an 18-metre pool. A smart bar serves Asian food, and a smarter restaurant, Sinergie, features refined European cuisine and an excellent wine list, including wines specially bottled for the restaurant.

Moderate

Hotel Capri I6
*58–59 Middle Abbey St, **t** (01) 872 0361, **f** (01) 872 0392, www.hotel-ireland.com/hotel-capri.*

A small, welcoming hotel in an 18th-century Georgian townhouse. The décor is chintzy and overstuffed, which makes it cosy in a rather old-fashioned way. Hospitable staff and a great location make this a bargain.

Caulfield's Hotel I4
*18–19 Dorset St, **t** (01) 878 1550, **f** (01) 01 878 1650, caulfieldshotel @eircom.net; partially wheelchair accessible.*

A simple, friendly hotel with small but comfortable rooms and a very decent Irish breakfast. Traditional music is on offer at the pub downstairs – but the noise does waft up to the rooms.

Lynams Hotel J5
*63–64 O'Connell St, **t** (01) 888 0886, **f** (01) 888 0890, www.lynams-hotel.com.*

Tucked behind a smart Victorian façade, Lynams offers spacious traditionally decorated rooms and a pleasant lounge. Some rooms suffer from street noise.

The Townhouse J5
*47–48 Lower Gardiner St, **t** (01) 878 8808, **f** (01) 878 8787, www.townhouseofdublin.com.*

One of the city's quirkiest and most original places to stay. Each guestroom has a different theme and style, named after the works of the two writers who once lived here: Lafcadio Hearn (1850–1904) and Dion Boucicault (1829–90), whose histories are recounted in the memorabilia-crammed lobby. Plump for the Rip Van Winkle honeymoon suite, which boasts a four-poster bed and red velvet drapes. There's also a Japanese garden and a restaurant.

Waltons Hotel I4
*2–5 North Frederick St, **t** (01 878 3131, **f** (01) 878 3090, www.waltons-hotel.ie.*

This hotel sits above Waltons music shop, which specializes in

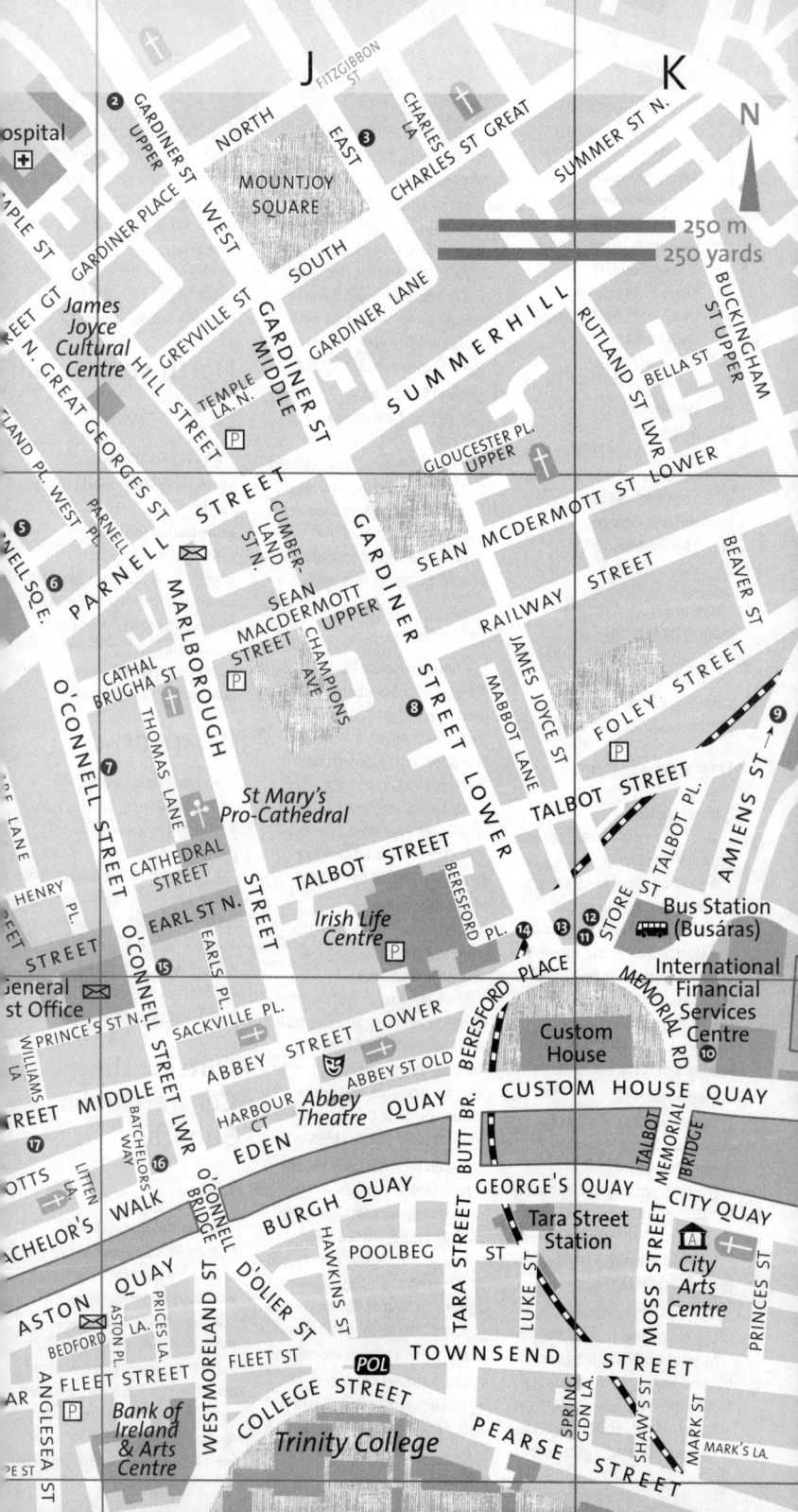

Map Key

8	Abraham House
16	Arlington Hotel
17	Hotel Capri
1	Caulfield's Hotel
6	Charles Stewart
10	Clarion Hotel
3	Dublin Int'l Youth Hostel
7	The Gresham
12	Hotel Isaacs
11	Isaacs Hostel
15	Lynams Hotel
13	Maple Hotel
2	Marian Guest House
18	Morrison Hotel
9	The Old Dubliner
5	Hotel St George
14	The Townhouse
4	Waltons Hotel

traditional Irish music. It's a modest budget hotel, set in Georgian townhouses (although few original features have survived). Rooms are plain but spotless, and the staff are friendly.

Inexpensive

Hotel Isaacs K5
Store St, t (01) 855 0067, f (01) 836 5390, www.isaacs.ie.

A medium-sized hotel set in a converted wine warehouse around the corner from the main bus station. Rooms are simple but crisply furnished, and all have TVs and ensuite bathrooms. There's a mad Italian restaurant, with over-the-top décor, which does decent food at a moderate price.

Maple Hotel J5
75 Lower Gardiner St, t (01) 874 0225, f (01) 874 5239, www.maplehotel.com.

This is a central and welcoming family-run hotel set in a Georgian townhouse. Traditional, if rather plain, rooms and friendly staff make it a reliable choice.

Marian Guest House J4
21 Upper Gardiner St, t (01) 874 4129.

More of a B&B than a guesthouse, this is run by a charming family. There are just six rooms, all with bathrooms and TVs, and the price is exceptionally good value.

The Old Dubliner K5
62 Amiens St, t (01) 855 5666, f (01) 855 5677, www.olddubliner.ie.

Set in a listed Georgian building, this is a relatively new guesthouse with fourteen en suite rooms and courteous staff. There are some beautiful original features, and care is taken over extras like bathroom goodies and tea and coffee-making facilities.

Hotel St George J5
7 Parnell Sq, t (01) 874 5611, f (01) 874 5582.

A small, personal hotel close to the Writers Museum and Hugh Lane Gallery. All rooms, which are functional but more than adequate, are ensuite, and there's a private car park for guests.

Cheap

Abraham House J5
82–83 Lower Gardiner St, t (01) 855 0600, f (01) 855 0598, abraham@indigo.ie.

A popular choice with backpackers, this fun and friendly hostel is situated close to Busaras and Connolly station. There's a mix of accommodation in 23 bedrooms and 10 dorms.

Charles Stewart J5
5–6 Parnell Sq, t (01) 878 0350, f (01) 878 1387, www.charlesstewart.ie.

The birthplace of Irish author Oliver St John Gogarty, this B&B is set in a restored Georgian building. Rooms sleeping two to four are available, and prices include breakfast. One room has full access for the disabled.

Dublin International Youth Hostel J4
61 Mountjoy Sq, t (01) 830 1766, f (01) 830 1600, www.anoige.ie.

A large and slightly impersonal hostel, with 22 singles, doubles and triples, and 22 dorms. Location is reasonably central, and there's a laundry, games room and Internet.

Isaacs Hostel K5
2–5 Frenchman's Lane, t (01) 855 6215, f (01) 855 6574, www.isaacs.ie.

Just around the corner from the main bus station, this big backpacker's hostel has single, double, twin and triple rooms, dorms and facilities including a kitchen and cybercafé. Its smarter sister hotel is next door, and it also runs the Jacob's Inn Hostel close by on Talbot St (21–28 Talbot St, t (01) 855 5660, f (01) 855 5664).

Northwest Dublin

Expensive

Chief O'Neill's Hotel G6
Smithfield Village, t (01) 817 3838, f (01) 817 3839, www.chiefoneills.com.

A large modern hotel in the Smithfield Village complex, this has an impersonal chain-hotel feel, but the rooms are bright, stylish and spacious and the suites on the top floor have their own roof terrace balconies.

Inexpensive

Phoenix Park House E6
38–39 Parkgate St, t (01) 677 2870, f (01) 679 9769, www.dublinguesthouse.com.

A good choice if you want some peace and quiet, this guesthouse is right outside the gates of Phoenix Park, but just a ten-minute walk to the centre. Rooms are comfortable if a little old-fashioned, and offer value for money.

Outside the Centre: Dublin Suburbs

Luxury

Herbert Park Hotel M10
Herbert Park, Ballsbridge, t (01) 667 2200, f (01) 667 2595, www.herbertparkhotel.ie.

A huge, modern hotel geared towards business travellers, overlooking the lovely green expanse of Herbert Park. It is slick and well designed, and the contemporary rooms have all kinds of amenities from interactive TVs with email to

PlayStation. The excellent Pavilion restaurant serves modern Irish cuisine and has a pretty terrace.

Radisson SAS St Helen's Hotel
OFF MAPS
Stillorgan Road, t (01) 218 6000, f 218 6030, www.radissonsas.com.

This immaculate 18th-century mansion has been spectacularly converted into one of Dublin's most luxurious hotels. Sadly, the bedrooms are in a modern adjoining annexe which doesn't have the same atmosphere as the grand house itself, but the long list of amenities – fine restaurants, formal gardens, fitness room and health and beauty clinic – will dispel any disappointment. And there's a great view across Dublin Bay to Howth.

Schoolhouse Hotel L8
2 Northumberland Rd, Ballsbridge, t (01) 667 5014, f (01) 667 5015, www.schoolhousehotel.com.

Right on the Grand Canal, this charming hotel is housed in a restored former primary school which dates back to 1861. There are 31 rooms, each handsomely decorated with a mixture of traditional and contemporary fittings, and there's a very popular bar, the Inkwell.

Expensive

Butlers Townhouse OFF MAPS
44 Lansdowne Rd, Ballsbridge, t (01) 667 4022, f (01) 667 3690, www.butlers-hotel.com; wheelchair accessible.

A charming guesthouse in the quiet residential suburb of Ballsbridge, with traditionally decorated rooms featuring floral prints and four-poster beds (in some rooms). Amenities include air-conditioning, power showers, multi-channel TV and modem connection. Breakfast is served in the airy conservatory.

Hibernian Hotel OFF MAPS
Eastmoreland Place, Ballsbridge, t (01) 668 7666, f (01) 660 2655, www.hibernianhotel.com.

A handsome Victorian private mansion has been beautifully converted to house this chic little hotel. It still manages to convey the sense of a private home, and the spacious, elegant rooms are kitted out with every modern amenity (including a fantastic array of treats in the bathroom). The Patrick Kavanagh Room is a fine, if expensive, restaurant.

Pembroke Townhouse
OFF MAPS
90 Pembroke Rd, Ballsbridge, t (01) 660 0277, f (01) 660 0291, www.pembroketownhouse.ie.

Another of the luxurious Georgian-style town houses in Ballsbridge which are hotels in all but name: this one is particularly delightful, with individually decorated rooms featuring contemporary Irish art, and a fine breakfast menu.

Moderate

Aberdeen Lodge OFF MAPS
53 Park Ave, Ballsbridge, t (01) 283 8155, f (01) 283 7877, www.halpinsprivatehotels.com.

An excellent four-star guesthouse in a grand Edwardian house, with large, elegant bedrooms, some with four-poster beds and Jacuzzis. Linger in the graceful drawing room, and admire the landscaped gardens.

Merrion Hall OFF MAPS
54–56 Merrion Rd, Ballsbridge, t (01) 668 1426, f (01) 668 4280, www.halpinsprivatehotels.com.

An award-winning small guesthouse set in a delightful, creeper-clad Edwardian house, offering spacious rooms with all the amenities you would expect of a smart hotel, from satellite TV to bathrobes. Some rooms have four-poster beds and Jacuzzis.

Mespil Hotel K9
50–60 Mespil Rd, t (01) 667 1222, f (01) 667 1244, www.mespil-hotel.com; wheelchair accessible.

A large, modern and rather anonymous hotel close to the Grand Canal, which offers one of the best deals in the city. Rooms are spacious and stylish, and it is just a ten-minute walk to St Stephen's Green. They have family rooms, rooms equipped for disabled travellers and non-smoking rooms.

Raglan Lodge M9
10 Raglan Rd, Ballsbridge, t (01) 660 6697, f (01) 660 6781.

An elegant and intimate guesthouse in the leafy suburb of Ballsbridge, with seven charmingly furnished rooms. The fine Irish breakfasts are legendary.

Waterloo House X00
8–10 Waterloo Rd, Ballsbridge, t (01) 660 1888, f (01) 667 1955, www.waterloohouse.ie.

Two Georgian town houses have been combined to create this elegant guesthouse, close to the RDS and Lansdowne Road stadium. A delightful conservatory and private gardens make it feel very much like a home from home and the spacious rooms have every modern convenience.

Inexpensive

Abrae Court OFF MAPS
9 Zion Rd, Rathgar, t (01) 492 2242, www.longfields.ie.

Rathgar is one of a string of former villages which have been swallowed up by the Dublin sprawl and yet retain a cosy village atmosphere. This is a relaxed but charming guesthouse with 14 well-appointed rooms and a warm welcome. It also serves a great traditional Irish breakfast.

Bewley's Hotel OFF MAPS
Newlands Cross, Naas Rd, t (01) 464 0140, f (01) 464 0900, www.bewleyshotels.com.

This large modern hotel offers great value for money, particularly for families. Spacious, modern rooms have all amenities: at this price, you won't mind that it feels like an airport terminal.

Egans House OFF MAPS
7–9 Iona Park, Glasnevin, t (01) 830 3611, f (01) 830 3312, www.eganshouse.com.

Handy for Dublin's gorgeous Botanical Gardens or the Gaelic

sports at Croke Park stadium, this refined guesthouse is located in a terrace of smart Edwardian houses. There are 23 traditionally decorated bedrooms, all with en suite bathrooms, TVs, hairdryers and tea-making facilities.

Cheap

Brewery Hostel F7
22–23 Thomas St, **t** *(01) 458 8600, f 453 8616, breweryh@indigo.ie.*

Next to the huge Guinness brewery, this is a small and fairly new hostel offering accommodation in double rooms and dorms. Family-run, with lots of good amenities including a big lounge, kitchen and barbecue area. It does operate a curfew, though.

Outside the Centre: Dublin Bay

Luxury

Clontarf Castle Hotel OFF MAPS
Castle Avenue, Clontarf, **t** *(01) 833 2321, f (01) 833 0418, www.clontarfcastle.ie.*

This picture-book castle, dating back to the 12th century and just three miles from the city centre, is now a luxurious hotel. Tapestries and roaring fires give it a medieval feel, but the sumptuous rooms have every 21st-century convenience including ISDN and voicemail. There's a gym, a couple of bars and a bistro. It is next to Clontarf golf course; fishing and horse-riding can be arranged.

Fitzpatrick Castle OFF MAPS
Killiney, **t** *(01) 230 5400, f (01) 230 5430, www.fitzpatrickcastle.com.*

Another converted castle, this one is set in upscale Killiney. Surrounded by elegant, landscaped gardens, it has spacious rooms with all the luxury extras plus a health and fitness area with pool, Jacuzzi and spa. It is largely geared towards businesspeople, but it's also a big favourite with golf fans: there are five championship courses nearby.

Grand Hotel OFF MAPS
Malahide, **t** *(01) 845 0000, f (01) 816 8025, www.thegrand.ie; wheelchair accessible.*

A wonderful, old-fashioned seaside hotel in the picturesque village of Malahide. Many of the beautiful rooms have sea views, and there's an excellent new leisure complex with pool, Jacuzzi and gym. It is set in its own grounds, and can arrange golfing, tennis and fishing.

Expensive

Deer Park Hotel OFF MAPS
Howth, **t** *(01) 832 2624, f (01) 839 2405, www.deerpark-hotel.ie.*

Set in the vast parklands of Howth Demesne, with panoramic views across Dublin Bay, this is a great place to get away from it all. The hotel is modern and not especially atmospheric, but it has great facilities for sports fans, including Ireland's largest golf complex, pool, tennis courts and some wonderful nearby hikes.

Gresham Royal Marine Hotel OFF MAPS
Marine Rd, Dún Laoghaire, **t** *(01) 280 1911, f (01) 280 1089, www.gresham-hotels.com.*

The *grande dame* of the seafront, retaining its Victorian opulence and splendour, particularly in the suites. These enjoy harbour views, four-poster beds and antiques, but standard rooms are disappointingly bland. The afternoon teas in the Bay Lounge are an institution.

Moderate

Red Bank House OFF MAPS
5–7 Church St, Skerries, **t** *(01) 849 1005, f 849 1598, www.redbank.ie.*

This fine restaurant (see p.156) also offers accommodation in a dozen charming guestrooms: if you've eaten too much to move – the desserts here are legendary – at least it's an easy step to bed. Unsurprisingly, a particularly good Irish breakfast is included in the price.

Inexpensive

Cumberland Lodge OFF MAPS
54 York Rd, Dún Laoghaire, **t** *(01) 280 9665, f (01) 284 3227.*

A charming, family-run guesthouse in a superbly refurbished 19th-century mansion. The rooms are furnished with antiques, and you can enjoy a fine breakfast.

Eating Out

Southeast Dublin 186
Southwest Dublin and Temple Bar 193
Northeast Dublin 195
Northwest Dublin 199
Outside the Centre: Dublin Suburbs 199
Outside the Centre: Dublin Bay 200

Irish cuisine has long shaken off its old-fashioned image of stewed bacon and cabbage: the Dublin culinary scene has utterly changed since the early 1990s. Award-winning chefs such as Patrick Guilbaud, Kevin Thornton, Adrian Roche and Kevin Arundel are at the forefront of this gastronomic revolution. As Dublin has opened up to international influences, a host of new cuisines are now available, from US-style brunches to outstanding East Asian fare. Dubliners have become more discerning, and there is a new emphasis on quality produce, including Dublin Bay oysters, local cheeses, Irish breads, fresh fish and organic meat. You'll still find many of the traditional dishes such as **Irish stew** (mutton stewed with vegetables), **coddle** (stew made with sausages, rashers, onions and potatoes) and **boxties** (stuffed potato pancakes) – but they are no longer boiled grey, and the meat and vegetables will be the freshest available.

These are often found in pubs, which usually focus on traditional Irish dishes. The classic partnership is **Guinness and oysters** – Davy Byrne's pub is just one great place to try it. Some traditional staples should not be messed with, and Dublin's **fish and chips** (particularly the legendary Leo Burdock's) are the best. **Irish breakfasts** haven't changed: the greasy but delicious 'fry' of rashers, black pudding, egg and soda bread or potato cakes will set you up for the day.

Many of the smartest places offer a **fixed-price lunch menu**, which will give you the chance to try out some of the best that is on offer at a reasonable price.

Don't miss out on the Irish cakes and breads like fruity barmbrack, soda bread and scones, best washed down with a cup of tea (of which the Irish drink more than any other nation). The fanciest afternoon teas are at the Shelbourne Hotel, but Bewley's and the Avoca café are also good spots to sample traditional baking.

Major credit cards are accepted at all these establishments unless otherwise noted. Note that Diners Club cards are rarely accepted.

Price categories

Price categories at restaurants – for a meal for one person – are as follows:

Luxury	Price no object
Expensive	Over €65
Moderate	€32–65
Inexpensive	Under €32

Southeast Dublin

Luxury

Restaurant Patrick Guilbaud K8
21 Merrion St Upper, **t** *(01) 676 4192, www.merrionhotel.ie.* **Open** *Tues–Sat 12.30–2.15 and 7.30–10.15.*

One of the finest restaurants in Dublin, with two Michelin stars to prove it, is Patrick Guilbaud's eponymous restaurant. The outstanding cuisine is French, with a touch of Irishness in some of the ingredients. Set in a Georgian town house (the main house of the grand Merrion Hotel), the dining room is the epitome of refined elegance, with Irish paintings on the wall, and a terrace overlooking landscaped gardens in summer. There's an excellent-value fixed menu (€28) at lunchtimes.

Thornton's I8
128 St Stephen's Green, **t** *(01) 478 7008.* **Open** *Tues–Sat 12.30–1.45 and 7–10.30.*

Kevin Thornton has rapidly become one of the most renowned chefs in Ireland – and deservedly so. His elegant restaurant high above St Stephen's Green serves some of the finest and most imaginative modern Irish cuisine in Dublin, using the best local produce. A set lunch is available for €29, but consider pushing the boat out for the Surprise Menu which features eight heavenly courses prepared specially for each table.

Expensive

Brownes Brasserie J8
22 St Stephens Green, **t** *(01) 638 3939, www.brownesdublin.com.* **Open** *Mon–Sat 12.30–2.45 and 6.30–10.30, Sun 12.30–2.30 and 6.30–10.*

One of the best-known and most stylish restaurants in town, this is set in a handsome Georgian townhouse (which also has guestrooms). It features a varied menu of international dishes – always with plenty of choice for vegetarians – accompanied by an excellent wine list.

Fadó J7
Mansion House, Dawson St, **t** *(01) 676 7200, www.fado.ie. Wheelchair accessible.* **Open** *Mon–Sat noon–11.*

A spectacular restaurant in the *fin-de-siècle* former supper room of the Mansion House, the Lord Mayor's official residence. Modern Irish cuisine is expertly prepared and served by attentive staff, and there's a fine children's menu. Dine on the terrace in fine weather.

Jacob's Ladder J7
4 Nassau St, **t** *(01) 670 3865, www.jacobsladder.ie.* **Open** *Tues–Fri 12.30–2.30 and 6–10, Sat 12.30–2 and 6–10.*

One of the city's new breed of fine restaurants, Jacob's Ladder is spacious and stylish. Excellent modern Irish cuisine is on offer, including seafood and a good vegetarian selection. Adrian Roche is a chef to watch, reinventing classic Irish recipes with flair. There is a good early dinner set menu for €20 (available 6–7pm).

Kevin Arundel @ Number 10 K8
Longfields Hotel, 10 Fitzwilliam St Lower, **t** *(01) 676 1367.* **Open** *Mon–Fri 12.30–2.30 and 6.30–10.30, Sat–Sun 6.30–10.30.*

Tucked into the cosy basement of the charming Longfields Hotel, 'Number 10' is one of Dublin's most celebrated restaurants. Chef Kevin Arundel prepares exquisite contemporary French cuisine using the finest ingredients, and the wine selection is among the best in the city. The feast culminates with particularly good desserts. Set lunchtime menu for €26, or Tasting Menu for €60.

La Stampa J7
*35 Dawson St, **t** (01) 677 8611, www.lastampa.ie. **Open** Mon–Fri 12.30–2.30 and 5.30–midnight, Sat 6.30–12.30am, Sun 6.30–11.30pm.*

This fashionable brasserie is set in the magnificent former Guildhall, crammed with gilded mirrors, statues and candelabra. The menu changes frequently, but you can always rely on fresh, beautifully prepared international cuisine. The slightly cheaper 'Tiger Becs' in the basement serves spicy Southeast Asian food in colourful souk-like surroundings.

L'Ecrivain K8
*109a Lower Baggot St, **t** (01) 661 1919, www.lecrivain.ie. **Open** Mon–Fri noon–2 and 7–11, Sat 7–11.*

This is a truly delightful restaurant, light, bright and airy, serving highly imaginative cuisine which fuses the best of traditional French and modern Irish cuisine. Impeccable touches include a complimentary *amuse-bouche* at the beginning of the meal, and staff are unfailingly attentive and professional. It does a special lunchtime menu for €27–35.

One Pico J7
*5 Molesworth Place, Schoolhouse Lane, **t** (01) 676 0300, www.onepico.com. **Open** Mon–Sat 12–3 and 7–11.*

Chef Eamonn O'Reilly has been cooking up a storm since moving to these larger premises: the menu, which takes its inspiration from around the world, remains as adventurous as ever. It's extremely popular, both with critics and Dubliners, and reservations are essential. The set lunch menu is a modest €22, but you can could also go the whole hog on the Tasting Menu (€70).

Moderate

Bang Café L8
*11 Merrion Row, **t** (01) 676 0898, www.bangrestaurant.com. **Open** Mon–Sat noon–3 and 6–10.30.*

This stylish, minimalist restaurant is a big hit with Dubliners, offering fine food, attentive service and generous portions at a reasonable price. It serves imaginative Irish cuisine which you can watch being prepared in an open kitchen, and, although the menu leans slightly towards seafood, there's always a good choice. Save room for the excellent desserts. The set lunch menu is €30, and there's also a €40 dinner menu.

Bleu Bistro Moderne J7
*Joshua House, Dawson St, **t** (01) 676 7015, www.onepico.com/bleu. **Open** daily noon–11.*

The latest venture of the people behind the successful One Pico and Pacific, and already a winner of several awards, thanks to its slick combination of pared-down contemporary décor, market fresh food and very reasonable prices. There are three menus – lunch, afternoon and dinner – featuring anything from fish and chips to corn-fed chicken with chorizo.

Bruno's J8
*21 Kildare St, **t** (01) 662 4724, www.brunos.ie. **Open** Mon–Sat 6.30am–10.30pm.*

The upmarket sister of Bruno's in Temple Bar, this swish, contemporary restaurant is set in original wine cellars. It serves up excellent, imaginative modern Irish dishes with a French influence, prepared by acclaimed chef Garrett Byrne. There are great desserts to follow. Set lunch or early dinner for €18.50.

Café Mao I7
*Chatham Row, **t** (01) 679 4899, www.cafemao.com. Wheelchair accessible. **Open** Mon–Thurs noon–11, Fri–Sat noon–11.30, Sun noon–10.*

A super-trendy spot that doesn't take reservations: get there early. On the menu, you'll find all the Southeast Asian favourites from Indonesian nasi goreng to spicy Thai curries.

The Chilli Club J7
*1 Anne's Lane, South Anne St, **t** (01) 677 3721. **Open** Mon–Sat 12.30–2.30 and 6–11, Sun 6–11.*

This tiny, welcoming restaurant was Dublin's first authentic Thai and it remains as popular as ever for its seriously good cooking – the lemongrass soups have a real kick, whilst the curries vary in spiciness. Booking advisable.

Citron I8
*Fitzwilliam Hotel, St Stephen's Green, **t** (01) 478 7000. Wheelchair accessible. **Open** daily noon–10.*

The sleek, yellow-and-grey dining rooms at the Fitzwilliam Hotel offer reliable if not particularly inventive Mediterranean cuisine and slick service.

The Commons Café J8
*National Concert Hall, Earlsfort Terrace, **t** (01) 475 0060, www.thecommonscafe.ie. Wheelchair accessible. **Open** daily 9.30am–11pm (until 6pm when there are no concerts).*

Big, whitewashed and airy, this is an excellent café linked to the smart Commons restaurant in Newman House. It serves a simple menu of soups, pastas and fancy fish and chips, prepared with the finest local ingredients. It's worth timing your visit to avoid the pre- and post-concert rush.

Coopers Restaurant J9
*62 Lower Leeson St, **t** (01) 676 8615. Wheelchair accessible. **Open** Mon–Thurs 12.30–3 and 6–11, Fri 12.30–3 and 6–11.30, Sat 6–11.30, Sun 6–10.*

A charming restaurant located in a handsomely restored old coach house. Reliable international cuisine is on offer, made with fresh local ingredients.

Diep Le Shaker K8
*55 Pembroke Lane, **t** (01) 661 1829, www.diep.net. **Open** Mon–Fri 12.30–2.30 and 6.30–11, Sat 6.30–11.*

A smart and fashionable restaurant which draws big crowds of affluent Dubliners, and serves an interesting menu of classy Thai and Chinese cuisine.

Dobbins Wine Bistro L8
*15 Stephens Lane (off Mount St Lower), **t** (01) 661 3321. **Open** Mon 12.30–3, Tues–Fri 12.30–3 and 7.30–11, Sat 7.30–11.*

Smart, convivial and friendly,

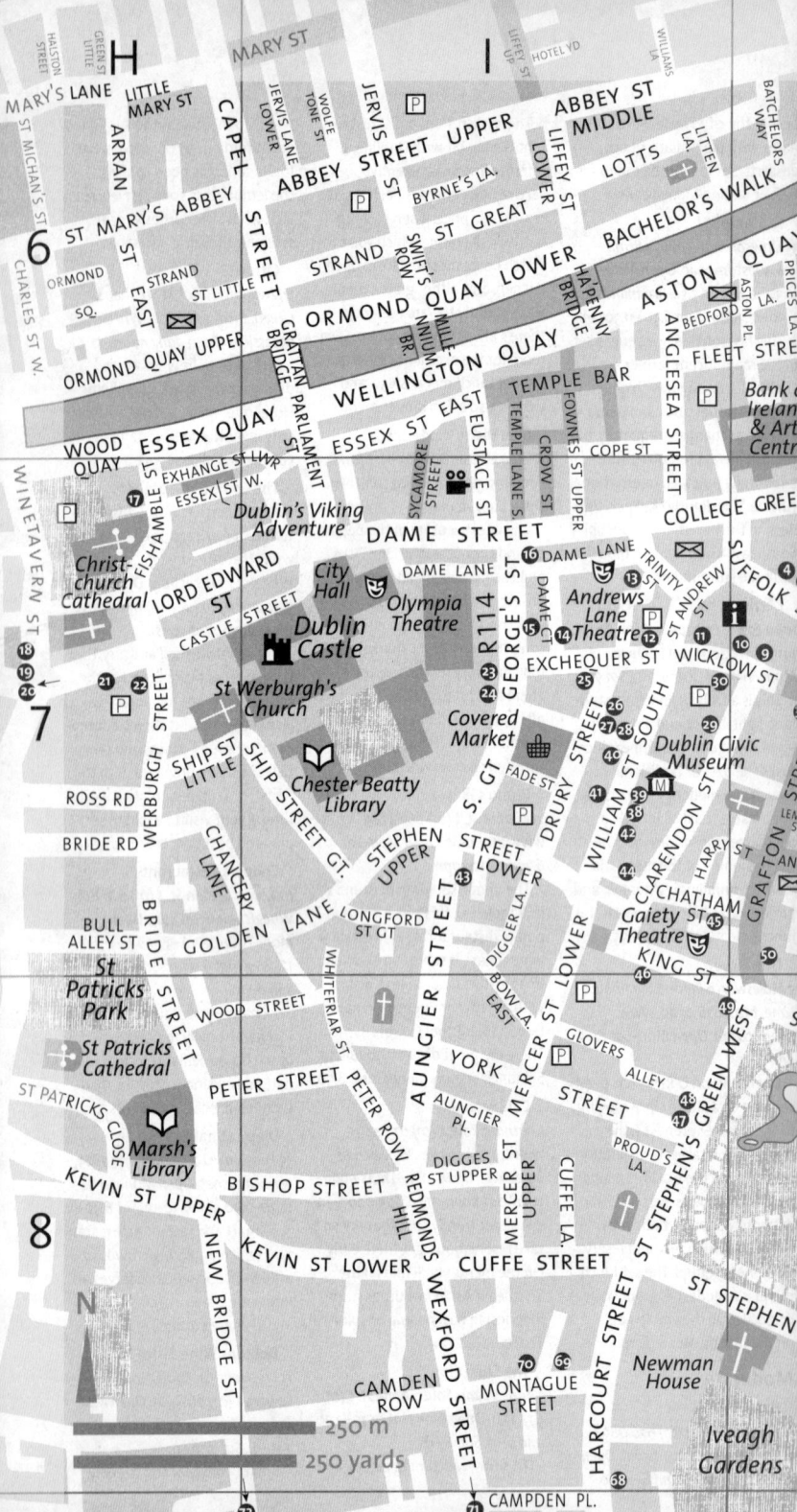

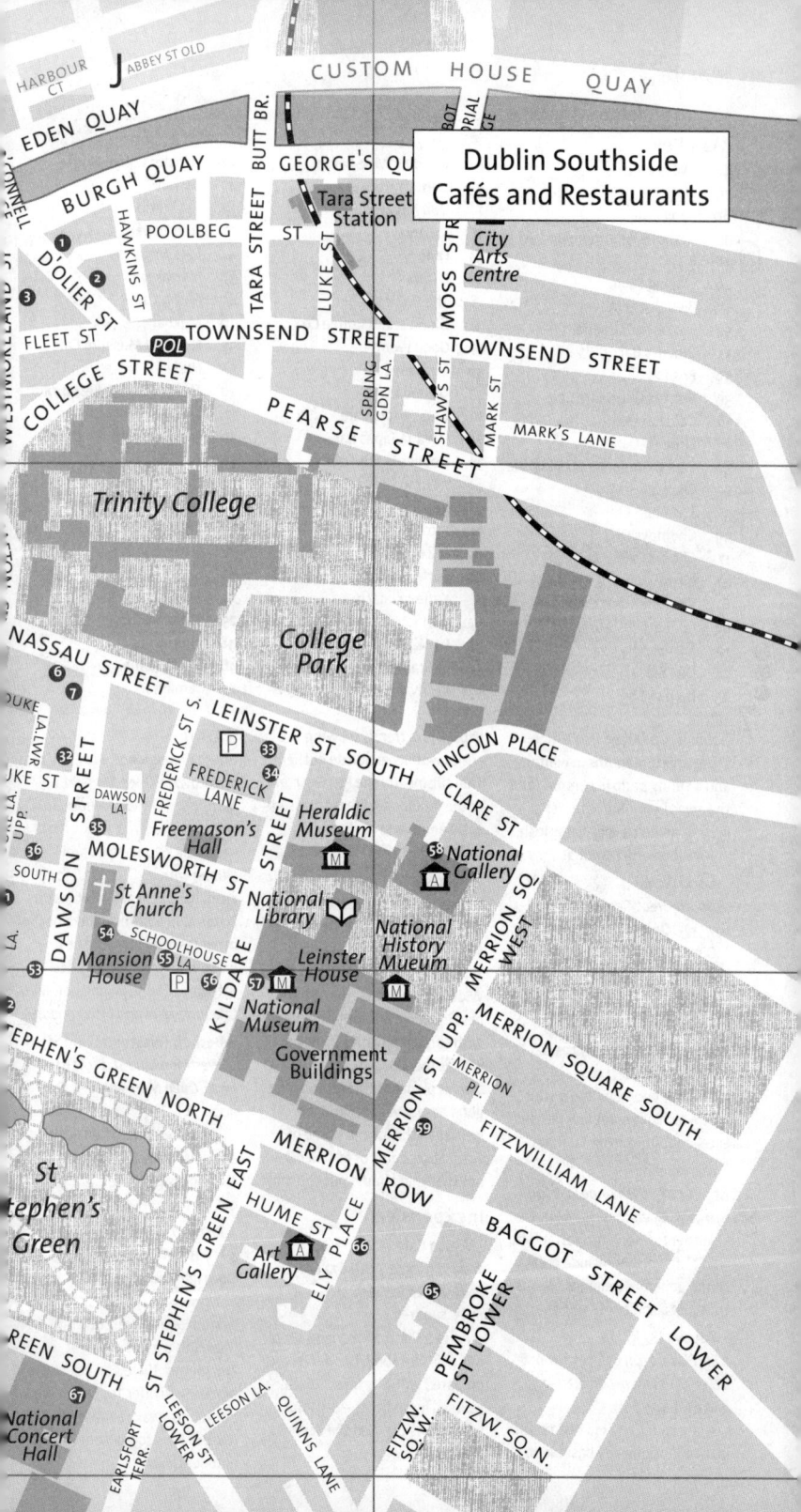

Eating Out

Map Key

4	Avoca Café	61	Dobbins Wine Bistro	33	Leinster Coffee House
29	AYA	49	Dome	42	Lemon
60	Bang Café	1	Don Angel	22	Leo Burdock's
3	Beshoff (Westmoreland St)	11	El Bahia	21	Lord Edward
28	Bistro	54	Fadó	44	Café Mao
26	Blazing Salads	58	Fitzers	37	Marrakesh
35	Bleu Bistro Moderne	18	The Gallic Kitchen	40	Metro Café
52	Brownes Brasserie	38	Gloria Jean's Coffee Co	70	Milkbar
31	Brown's Bar	15	Good World	57	National Museum Café
56	Bruno's	36	Gotham Café	5	Nude
30	Butler's Chocolate Café	43	Govinda's	20	The Old Dublin Restaurant
16	Café Bar Deli	19	Grass Roots Café	12	The Old Stand
7	Caife Trí-D	71	Havana Tapas Bar	55	One Pico
50	Captain America's Cookhouse	32	Hodges Figgis Café	72	Pad Thai
2	Chez Jules	69	Il Primo	66	Papaya
51	The Chilli Club	9	Imperial	45	Pasta Fresca
39	Chompys Deli	6	Jacob's Ladder	59	Restaurant Patrick Guilbaud
17	Chorus Café	23	Juice	13	Rio Coffee Bar
47	Citron	41	Kaffe Moka	68	Saagar
67	The Commons Café	8	Kaffee Klatsch	14	The Stag's Head
64	Coopers Restaurant	62	Kevin Arundel @ Number 10	25	Stone Wall Café
10	Cornucopia	27	La Maison des Gourmets	48	Thornton's
34	Dail Bia	53	La Stampa	46	Wagamama
65	Diep Le Shaker	63	L'Ecrivain	24	Yamamori

Dobbins is a Dublin institution. There are cosy booths in winter and a sunny patio in summer, and the award-winning wine list is accompanied by very classy Irish cuisine. Booking essential.

Good World I7
18 South Great Georges St, t (01) 677 5373. Open daily 12.30pm–3am.

Dim sum is served every day, but it's a Sunday institution at this smart and cheerful Chinese.

Imperial J7
12a Wicklow St, t (01) 677 2580. Open daily 12.30–11.30.

Another good Chinese restaurant which offers set lunches and excellent dim sum on Sundays.

Marrakesh J7
1st floor, 28 South Anne St, t (01) 670 5255. Open Tues–Sat 6–11.

Authentic Moroccan restaurant. Traditional dishes include great soups, generous helpings of couscous and a choice of tagines.

Papaya J8
8 Ely Place, t (01) 676 7077 or 676 0044. Open Mon–Sat 12.30–2.30 and 6–11, Sun 6–11.

A charming, relaxed restaurant in a lofty-ceiling airy basement, Papaya is currently wowing the critics with its exquisite authentic Thai cuisine. Try the Penang curry or the fabulous sea bass dressed with lemon and chilli.

Saagar I8
16 Harcourt St, t (01) 475 5060, www.saagarindianrest.com. Wheelchair accessible. Open Mon–Fri 12.30–2.30 and 6–11, Sat–Sun 6–11.

Widely regarded as one of the best Indian restaurants in Ireland, with some innovative dishes as well as the old favourites. There's always plenty of choice, and it's a good bet for vegetarians. It's located in the former home of Bram Stoker, author of *Dracula* – not that that should put you off.

Inexpensive

Avoca Café J7
11–13 Suffolk St, t (01) 672 6019, www.avoca.ie. Open Mon–Sat 10–5, Sun 11–5.

An excellent café serving simple but delicious food. The dishes are prepared with the finest, locally sourced ingredients – organic where possible. And the desserts are legendary.

AYA I7
49–52 Clarendon St, t (01) 677 1544, www.aya.ie. Open Mon–Fri 8am–11pm, Sat 10am–11pm, Sun 11am–10pm.

This slick, funky spot provided Dublin with its first conveyor belt sushi bar. There are great bento boxes at lunchtimes, and a host of other tasty Japanese dishes (which can push it up a price category). The adjoining deli sells take-out sushi and other goodies.

Beshoff (Westmoreland St) J6
14 Westmoreland St, t (01) 677 8026. Open Mon–Sat 11–11, Sun noon–11.

There are times when nothing beats fish and chips, and Beshoff's are reliably good. Take it away or opt for the self-service restaurant.

Bistro I7
4–5 Castle Market, t (01) 671 5430. Open daily noon–11.

A handy location close to Grafton St and cheerful staff make this a great choice at lunchtimes. There's an eclectic mix of dishes on offer, from wok-fried chicken to steak sandwiches. Get there in time to grab one of the outdoor tables in summer.

Café Bar Deli I7

12–13 South Great George's Street, t (01) 677 1646, www.dublin.cafebardeli.com. Open Mon–Sat 12.30–11, Sun 2–11.

With décor as pared down as its name, Café Bar Deli offers simple fresh cooking – great pizza, pasta and salads – prepared with unusual ingredients. Stylish and relaxed, it's popular with trendy Dubliners, who appreciate its good value for money.

Captain America's Cookhouse J7

1st floor, Grafton Court, Grafton St, t (01) 671 5266. Open Mon–Sat 8–6.

Always a hit with kids, this joint serves burgers and milkshakes to a loud soundtrack.

Chez Jules J6

D'Olier St, t (01) 677 0499. Open daily noon–11.

One of a reliable chain of French-style bistros, this has all the trappings, including gingham tablecloths and wooden floors. The food is reasonable if unimaginative.

Chompys Deli I7

U22 Powerscourt Townhouse Centre, Clarendon St, t (01) 679 4552. Open Mon–Sat 8–6.

An institution for its big American-style breakfasts – great pancakes, bagels and eggs benedict.

Cornucopia I7

19 Wicklow St, t (01) 677 7583. Open Mon–Sat 8.30–8 (Thurs until 9pm).

One of the oldest vegetarian restaurants in town, cosy little Cornucopia has been slightly eclipsed by the arrival of trendier places. Nonetheless, it continues to dish up reliably good food accompanied by delicious breads. It also caters for people on restricted diets (such as wheat- or gluten-free). Usually it is self-service, but there is table service in the evenings at weekends.

Dome J8

2nd floor, St Stephens Green Shopping Centre, t (01) 478 1287. Open Mon–Sat 9.30–5.30.

Located right at the top of the St Stephens Green Shopping Centre, this self-service café does decent light meals and snacks for a very reasonable price. The homemade cakes are not to be missed: munch away and enjoy the views.

Don Angel J6

7 D'Olier Street, t (01) 679 3859, www.donangel.ie. Open Mon–Sat noon–10, Sun 5–10.

Cheerful, lively, Spanish-owned tapas bar serving a fabulous array of tapas and other dishes (including a very decent paella). There's a great selection of Spanish wines, excellent ultra-strong coffee and live flamenco guitar on Wednesday evenings.

El Bahia I7

37 Wicklow St, t (01) 677 0213. Open daily 6pm–midnight.

Hidden behind a gilded, pink Moroccan door is this charming little restaurant. Relax onto a cushion-covered bench as your hands are rinsed with rose water, and choose from a good, well-priced menu of Moroccan dishes.

Gotham Café J7

8 South Anne St, t (01) 679 5266. Open Mon–Sat noon–midnight, Sun noon–10.

A hit with Dublin's youth, trendy Gotham has a buzzy atmosphere and a decent selection of pizza, pasta and the like. It's a popular place for weekend brunch.

Govinda's I7

4 Aungier St, t (01) 475 0309. Open Mon–Sat noon–9.

A friendly, peaceful little Hare Krishna vegetarian restaurant, with a cosy atmosphere. It serves lots of good soups, curries and baked goods. No smoking.

Juice I7

73 South Great George's St, t (01) 475 7856. Open Mon–Fri noon–11, Sat–Sun 6–11.

Modern vegetarian restaurant serving unusual dishes and great juices and smoothies. It feels like a cool bar, with art on the walls and a hip young clientele watching the world go by through the big windows. There's a special lunch deal for €7.50, and an 'early bird' dinner menu for €12.95.

The Old Stand I7

37 Exchequer St, t (01) 677 7220. Open for food noon–9. American Express and Diners Club not accepted.

The Old Stand claims to be Ireland's oldest pub, but the décor is quietly modern. It's very handy for the shopping on Grafton St and serves up better-than-average pub grub including great steaks and simple fish and pasta dishes.

Pad Thai I9

30 South Richmond St, t (01) 475 5551. Open Mon–Tues 6–11, Wed–Fri 12.30–3 and 6–11, Sun 6–10.

Popular with students, Pad Thai is noisy and cheerful, and the food is cheap but very tasty. There's an 'early bird' menu (6–7.30pm), and it also does take-aways. There is another branch in Howth.

Pasta Fresca I7

2–4 Chatham St, t (01) 679 2402, www.pastafresca.ie. Open Mon–Sat 10am–11pm, Sun 12–10.

Crowded fresh pasta shop which serves its own produce at a limited number of tables. You can also pick up pasta and other goodies from the deli counter.

The Stag's Head I7

Dame Court, t (01) 679 3701. Open Mon–Wed 10.30am–12.30am, Thurs–Sat 12.30pm–1.30am, Sun 12.30–midnight; food available lunchtimes only.

A fine traditional pub, with stained glass, mahogany, stuffed deer heads and a great atmosphere. The pub lunch menu is as traditional as the surroundings, serving up dishes such as Irish stew or boiled bacon and cabbage.

Stone Wall Café I7

187 Exchequer St, t (01) 672 7323. Open daily 11–5 and 6–11.

Pasta and salads during the day, European and Asian food at night.

Wagamama I7

South King St, t (01) 478 2152. Open daily noon–11.

Dine communally at this vast canteen-style restaurant with long, stripped wood tables and benches. It deftly serves up fresh and healthy noodle dishes. Part of the popular British chain, it offers good set menus, a selection of Japanese beers and fresh juices.

Yamamori I7
71–75 South Great George's St, t (01) 475 5001. Open daily 12.30–11.30.

Cheap, trendy and always buzzing, it's a huge favourite with Dublin hipsters. There's a good menu of Japanese noodle dishes and it does a cheap lunch special.

Cafés

Butler's Chocolate Café I7
24 Wicklow St, t (01) 671 0591, www.butlerschocolates.com. Open Mon–Sat 8–7, Sun 11–6.

The perfect combination: excellent coffee and gorgeous handmade chocolate. Also at 51 Grafton St and elsewhere.

Blazing Salads I7
42 Drury St, t (01) 671 9552, www.blazingsalads.com. Open Mon–Fri 10–4, Sat 9–5.

A great vegetarian café serving imaginative dishes including soups, salads and stir fries. It also caters for dietary restrictions, and serves organic wines and a range of fresh juices. There's a deli and bakery for take away.

Brown's Bar J7
88–95 Grafton St, t (01) 605 6666. Open Mon–Sat 9–6 (Thurs until 8), Sun noon–6.

Join the ladies who lunch at the smart café in Dublin's most upmarket department store, Brown Thomas. Refuel on cakes, coffee and sandwiches before heading back out to the shopping fray on Grafton St.

Caife Trí-D J7
3 Dawson St, t (01) 474 1050, www.tri-d.ie. Wheelchair accessible. Open Mon–Fri 7.30am–8.30pm, Sat 9–5, Sun noon–5.

This Irish-speaking cafe serves a huge range of great snacks, from posh sandwiches to bagels, muesli and croissants for breakfast.

Fitzers K7
In the National Gallery of Art, Merrion Sq, t (01) 661 4496. Open Mon–Sat 10–5 (Thurs until 7.30), Sun 2–5.

Good salads, pasta dishes, quiches, cakes and much more in this airy gallery café.

Gloria Jean's Coffee Co I7
12 Powerscourt Townhouse Centre, Clarendon St, t (01) 679 7772. Open Mon–Sat 8–7 (Thurs until 8), Sun 10.30–6.

Fabulous selection of good, if rather expensive, coffees. You can also buy from the amazing array of freshly roasted beans here.

Hodges Figgis Café J7
57 Dawson St, t (01) 677 4754. Open Mon–Sat 9.30–6, Sun 12.30–5.30. No credit cards.

Hodges Figgis is one of the best bookshops in Dublin, and this is one of the first bookshop-cafés. It offers a selection of good sandwiches and cakes.

Kaffe Moka I7
39 South William St, t (01) 679 8475. Open Mon–Wed 8am–1.30am, Thurs–Fri 8am–4am, Sat 10am–4am, Sun 10am–1.30am.

Lively, popular café with a huge selection of teas and coffees and a menu of light meals and snacks – soup, sandwiches and salads. It fills up with shoppers on Saturdays and in the evenings when the pubs close. The service can be erratic and harassed at busy times. There is another branch in the Epicurean Food Hall.

Kaffee Klatsch I7
Unit 7, Westbury Mall (off Grafton St), t (01) 670 7056. Open Mon–Fri 7.45–5, Sat 9–5, Sun 11–5.30.

If you've been hard at work shopping on Grafton St, take a break at this airy café. Delicious coffee, full Irish breakfast and a range of snacks are available.

La Maison des Gourmets I7
15 Castle Market, t (01) 672 7258, www.gourmetmaison.com. Open Mon–Fri 9–6, Sat–Sun noon–6.

One of the best patisseries in town. The cakes here are authentically French and mouthwatering. There's a fine selection of breads, and they do great light lunches. Also a tiny little salon upstairs.

Metro Café I7
43 South William St, t (01) 679 4515. Open daily 10am–11pm.

Great coffee (ground to order), bagels and cakes at this relaxed, boho-chic spot near the Powerscourt shopping centre.

Lemon I7
66 South William St, t (01) 672 9044. Open Mon–Fri 8–7.30 (Thurs until 9.30pm), Sat 9–7.30, Sun 10–6.30.

A wonderful, multi-coloured café serving delicious French-style crêpes – light, paper-thin and utterly delicious. Be restrained and choose the classic with lemon, or pig out on chocolate and banana, or great breakfast crêpes with sausage and egg. Fresh juices and good coffee, too.

Leinster Coffee House I8
17 Leinster St South, t (01) 676 4356. Open Mon–Fri 7–7, Sat 9–6, Sun 10–6.

A lively, buzzy student café, with good coffee and snacks.

Milkbar I8
18 Montague St, t (01) 478 8450, www.milkbar.ie. Open Mon–Fri 7.30–4.

A sleek, contemporary café serving great soups, salads and sandwiches, plus smoothies.

National Museum Café J8
Kildare St, t (01) 602 1269. Open Tues–Sat 10–5, Sun 2–5.

Simple and tasty coddle, salads and cakes.

Nude I7
21 Suffolk St, t (01) 676 1367. Open Mon–Sat 8am–10pm, Sun 11–7.

A very popular little café serving soups, sandwiches and wraps, plus fresh juices. It uses Fairtrade products where possible, and you can eat in or take out. There's another branch, Nude To Go, at 203 Lower Leeson St (just off St Stephen's Green) mainly for take-out.

Rio Coffee Bar I7
15 Trinity St, t (01) 677 1060. Open Mon–Fri 7.30–7 (Thurs until 8pm), Sat 10–8, Sun 10–6.

A relaxed, light, white-painted coffee shop, with high wooden tables and stools, and friendly waitresses. It does great coffee, accompanied by good cakes and pastries (including very nice scones) as well as fresh juices.

Southwest Dublin and Temple Bar

Luxury

Clarence Hotel Tea Room I6
Clarence Hotel, 6–8 Wellington Quay, Temple Bar, t (01) 407 0800.

The dining room of the celebrated Clarence Hotel is as stylish and fashionable as you would expect. Light-filled and elegant, it serves impeccable modern Irish cuisine, exquisitely presented. There are some very good value set meals, including lunch for a bargain €14, dinner for €40 and a fabulous 'tasting menu' for €70.

Expensive

. Brunos I6
30 East Essex St, Temple Bar, t (01) 670 6767. **Open** *Mon–Thurs 12–2.30 and 6.30–10.30, Fri 12.30–5 and 6.30–10.30, Sat 6.30–10.30.*

It's generally agreed that the sister branch on Kildare Street serves the finer cuisine, but Brunos in Temple Bar is also a good choice for imaginative contemporary Irish fare. There's always plenty of buzz, and reservations are essential. Make sure you save room for the excellent selection of desserts.

Eden I7
Meeting House Square, Temple Bar, t (01) 670 5372. **Open** *Mon–Fri 12.30–3 and 6–10.30, Sat–Sun noon–3 and 6–10.30.*

An elegant, ultra-minimalist designer restaurant in the heart of Temple Bar, which serves equally stylish contemporary Irish cuisine. Organic produce is used wherever possible, and it does a good-value set lunch for €18. There's a wonderful outdoor terrace, and the Sunday brunch is a Dublin institution.

Les Frères Jacques I7
74 Dame St, t (01) 679 4555, www.lesfreresjacques.com.
Open *Mon–Fri noon–2.30 and 7.15–10.30, Sat 7.15–10.30.*

Head off to *fin-de-siècle* Paris at this romantic restaurant that serves lovingly prepared French cuisine. The menu leans towards fish and seafood (the lobster ravioli is particularly good), and the desserts are heavenly. The lunchtime €20 menu is a bargain.

The Old Dublin Restaurant H7
90–91 Francis St, t (01) 454 2028.
Open *Mon–Fri noon–2 and 6–10.30, Sat 6–10.30.*

A refined setting for this popular, traditional restaurant. A very appealing and well-presented menu inclines towards the Oriental and East European – mainly Scandinavian and Russian. They serve lovely kasha barley or savoury rice; and vegetarian satsiv, crispy curried fresh vegetables.

Pacific I7
Sycamore St, t (01) 677 9144. **Open** *Mon–Sat 12–3 and 5.30–11, Sun 12–3 and 5.30–9.30. Bar open Thurs–Sat from 8pm.*

Sister restaurant to One Pico, Pacific is one of the top places to see and be seen in Dublin – refined, contemporary cuisine, a sociable, ultra-stylish bar area, and elegant, sleek surroundings to go with the elegant, sleek clientele.

Moderate

Gallagher's Boxty House I6
20–21 Temple Bar, t (01) 677 2762.
Open *daily noon–11.30.*

Yes, the place is touristy, but the food is authentically Irish and, more importantly, reliably good. A boxty is an Irish potato cake, and these are among the best you'll taste. Other traditional classics include Irish stew and boiled bacon with cabbage (which is better than it sounds).

Mermaid Café I7
69–70 Dame St, t (01) 670 4911, www.mermaid.ie. **Open** *Mon–Sat 12.30–3.30 and 6.30–11, Sun 12.30–3 and 6.30–9.*

A cool, stylish restaurant with crisp modern décor and an imaginative mid-Atlantic menu which features now-legendary crab cakes and a very fine pecan pie, plus an array of dishes prepared with fresh local ingredients. The vegetarian choices are among the most creative in the city, and the desserts and cheeses exceptional. A classic for Sunday brunch.

Il Primo I8
16 Montague St, t (01) 478 3373.
Open *Mon–Fri 12.30–3 and 6–11, Sat 6–11.*

Consistently reliable Italian food, accompanied by a vast selection of Italian wines. There are pizzas with unusual gourmet toppings, all kinds of handmade pasta served with delicious sauces, plus deftly prepared meat and seafood dishes. It's very popular and always busy, so book in advance.

Lord Edward H7
Christchurch Place, t (01) 454 4280.
Open *Mon–Fri noon–3 and 6–10.30, Sat 6–10.30.*

Dublin's oldest seafood restaurant is housed in a tall, narrow building overlooking Christchurch Cathedral. Deeply traditional and oblivious to the fashion frenzy taking over many of the city's restaurants, it dishes up popular favourites and has a few non-fish dishes on the menu, including Irish stew.

Inexpensive

Alamo Café I6
22 Temple Bar, t (01) 677 6546.
Open *daily noon–11.30.*

All the usual Tex-Mex fare on the menu at this colourful, fun restaurant in Temple Bar. Its most famous dessert is the deep fried ice-cream.

Bad Ass Café I6
9–11 Crown Alley, Temple Bar, t (01) 671 2596, www.badasscafe.com.
Open *daily noon–11.30.*

Diner-style spot for pizza, chops and burgers, that became famous because the singer Sinead O'Connor used to waitress here. It's a good place to take the kids, who will enjoy the food as well as the pulley system that whips orders into the kitchen. Good set menu for less than €15.

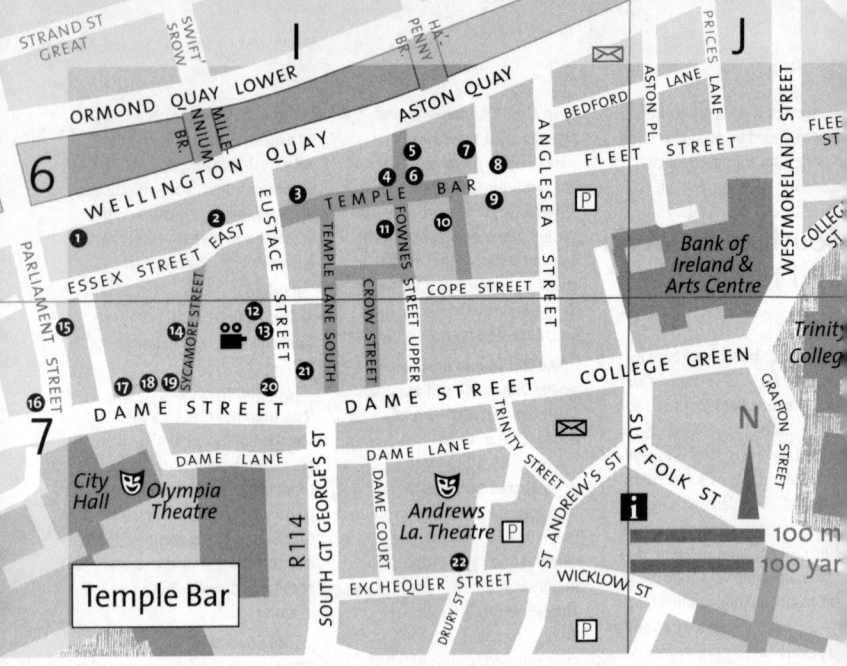

Map Key	
9	Alamo Café
10	Bad Ass Café
2	Brunos
22	Boulevard Café
5	The Chameleon
1	Clarence Hotel Tea Room
16	Da Pino
12	Eden
6	Elephant and Castle
11	Fitzers
8	Gallagher's Boxty House
7	Café Gertrude
18	Gruel
4	Café Irie
13	Irish Film Centre
3	The Joy of Coffee
20	Les Frères Jacques
17	Mermaid Café
21	Monty's of Kathmandu
14	Pacific
19	Queen of Tarts
15	Zaytoon

The Chameleon I6
1 Lower Fownes St, t (01) 671 0362. Wheelchair accessible. **Open** *Tues–Sun 6–11.*

A delightful, intimate Indonesian restaurant specializing in *rijsttafel* (a grand sampler of lots of tasty dishes), with low tables and silk cushions. It's at the bottom end of this price category, and does an excellent 'early-bird' menu for €20.

Da Pino I7
38–40 Parliament St, Temple Bar, t (01) 671 9308. **Open** *daily noon–midnight.*

Da Pino may look like a bit of a tourist trap, but Dubliners still recommend it for the classic Italian food at very reasonable prices. The crispy pizzas (which you can watch emerge sizzling from the oven) are particularly good, and there's a great weekday lunch available for €7.

Elephant & Castle I6
18 Temple Bar, t (01) 679 3121. **Open** *Mon–Fri 8am–11.30pm, Sat 10.30am–11.30pm, Sun noon–11.30.*

Very popular, relaxed restaurant serving up burgers, omelettes and spicy chicken wings (kids always love it). Always busy, and good for brunch on Sundays.

Fitzers I6
42 Fownes St, Temple Bar, t (01) 679 0440, www.fitzers.ie. **Open** *daily noon–11.*

There are several Fitzers around the city, all providing good fresh and simple cuisine. This branch is the most popular, and it is always packed out for Sunday brunch.

Gruel I7
68a Dame St, t (01) 670 7119. **Open** *daily 8am–9.30pm.*

Small, arty and relaxed, with deliberately mismatched tables, a big blackboard showing the day's specials and friendly staff. It's cool in a theatrical sort of way, and is a favourite with the acting crowd. The food is good, well priced and very tasty, and the atmosphere is laid-back and welcoming.

Havana Tapas Bar I9
3 Camden Market, Grantham St, t (01) 476 0046, www.havana.ie **Open** *Mon–Wed 10–10, Thurs–Sat 10am–11.30pm.*

Buzzy, cosy and atmospheric, this is a chic wine bar serving up some very good tapas, accompanied by an excellent range of sherries. The coffee (all Fairtrade) is good, and if you like the soundtrack, you can buy their own CDs of salsa and merengue.

Leo Burdock's H7
2 Werburgh St, t (01) 454 0306. **Open** *Mon–Sat noon–midnight, Sun 4–midnight.*

Consistently voted the best 'chipper' (fish and chip shop) in town, this is always heaving – particularly when the pubs close. It's also had its fair share of celebrities, including Tom Cruise and Naomi Campbell.

Monty's of Kathmandu I7
28 Eustace St, Temple Bar, t (01) 670 4911. Wheelchair accessible. **Open** *Mon–Sat noon–2.15 and 6–11.30, Sun 6–11.*

Small, relaxed little Nepalese restaurant, which serves up truly excellent cuisine at very modest prices – and it's got plenty of awards to prove it.

Zaytoon I7
14–15 Parliament St, Temple Bar, t (01) 677 3595. **Open** *daily noon–4am.*

This restaurant gets packed at pub-closing time: choose from the menu of illuminated photographs above the counter, and then squeeze onto a big wooden table. Reasonable kebabs, and fresh bread baked daily in a clay oven.

Cafés

Boulevard Café I7
27 Exchequer St, Temple Bar, t (01) 679 2131. **Open** *daily 10am–midnight.*

A pretty, blue-painted café tucked down a side street. It serves good breakfasts and a very decent cup of java. In the evenings nosh on simple dishes such as pasta and grilled meats and seafood.

Café Gertrude I6
3–4 Bedford Row, Temple Bar, t (01) 677 9043. **Open** *Mon–Wed 10.30–6, Thurs–Sun 10.30am–11pm.*

A little off the beaten track in Temple Bar, this pretty bistro serves light meals during the day and a fuller menu in the evenings.

Cafe Irie I6
11 Upper Fownes St, Temple Bar, t (01) 672 5090, www.cafeirie.web.com. **Open** *Mon–Sat 9–8, Sun noon–6.*

A hugely popular, hippyish café with homemade bread and cakes, plus tasty soups and sandwiches.

Chorus Café H7
7 Scarlet Row, Fishamble St, t (01) 616 7088. **Open** *Mon–Fri 7–5, Sat 10–6. No credit cards.*

A great little café for lunch in the Christchurch area, this serves great soups, sandwiches and cakes (including delicious scones), as well as fabulous breakfasts.

The Gallic Kitchen H7
49 Francis St, t (01) 454 4912. **Open** *Mon–Sat 9–5.*

This is another of the excellent bakeries which Dublin does so well: it offers fantastic soda bread and potato cakes, delicious quiches and pies, and some of the most delectable cakes in town. It's the perfect spot to pick up picnic goodies, although you can also eat in at the handful of small tables.

Grass Roots Café D7
Kilmainham Hospital (Irish Museum of Modern Art), t (01) 612 9000. **Open** *Tues–Sat 10–5.30, Sun noon–5.30. Amex not accepted.*

This bright, self-service museum café overlooks gardens. It serves good salads, sandwiches, soups and quiches, and is a relaxed and mellow spot for a coffee.

Dail Bia J7
46 Kildare St, t (01) 670 6079. **Open** *Mon–Fri 7.30–6, Sat 9.30–5.*

A good, Irish-speaking basement café serving traditional favourites such as potato cakes, mussels and good homemade soups.

Irish Film Centre I7
6 Eustace St, t (01) 679 5744. **Open** *daily noon–11.30.*

Relaxed arty café with big wooden tables, serving a decent range of sandwiches, burgers and other snacks. It's the kind of place where people sit for hours over the papers, and is a welcome respite from the hubbub of Temple Bar.

The Joy of Coffee I6
25 East Essex St, Temple Bar, t (01) 679 3393. **Open** *Mon–Thurs 8.45am–10.30pm, Sat 9am–11pm, Sun 10–10.*

Trendy hangout with expensive but excellent coffee to linger over while reading the paper.

Queen of Tarts I7
Dame St, t (01) 670 7499, and also in City Hall. **Open** *Mon–Fri 7.30–6, Sat 9–6, Sun 10–6.*

This pretty little café has sunny décor and wooden tables, but best of all is the smell of fresh baking. Heavenly cakes, tarts and quiches, Irish soda bread and potato cakes are among the selection on offer. The coffee is top-notch, too.

Northeast Dublin

Luxury

Halo I6
Morrison Hotel, Ormond Quay Lower, t (01) 878 2421, www.morrisonhotel.ie. **Open** *daily 7.30–10.30am, 12.30–2.30pm, 7–10.30pm.*

Soaring ceilings and John Rocha's sleek interior design are the setting for the restaurant at the Morrison Hotel. Divine French-inspired cuisine with an Asian twist is exquisitely presented on vast white platters, and the desserts are miniature works of art. There is an excellent-value set lunch menu, which at €25 for two courses, or €29 for three, is one of Dublin's best culinary bargains.

Expensive

Chapter One I4
Dublin Writers Museum, 18 Parnell Sq, t (01) 873 2266, www.chapteronerestaurant.com. **Open** *Tues–Fri 12.30–2.30 and 6–11, Sat 6–11.*

One of the first smart restaurants north of the Liffey, Chapter One continues to serve an excellent French and contemporary Irish menu in the atmospheric, vaulted basement of the Writers Museum. Fresh, locally sourced produce including particularly good game in season, and delicious desserts. Handy for the Gate Theatre, and there's a pre-theatre menu available (6–7pm) for €28.

No. 23 J5
Gresham Hotel, 23 O'Connell St, t (01) 874 6881, www.ryanhotels.com. **Open** *Mon–Sat 12–2.30 and 5.30–10.*

This fine restaurant in the setting of one of Dublin's oldest and most traditional hotels has got off to a good start. Elegant, crisp décor and beautifully

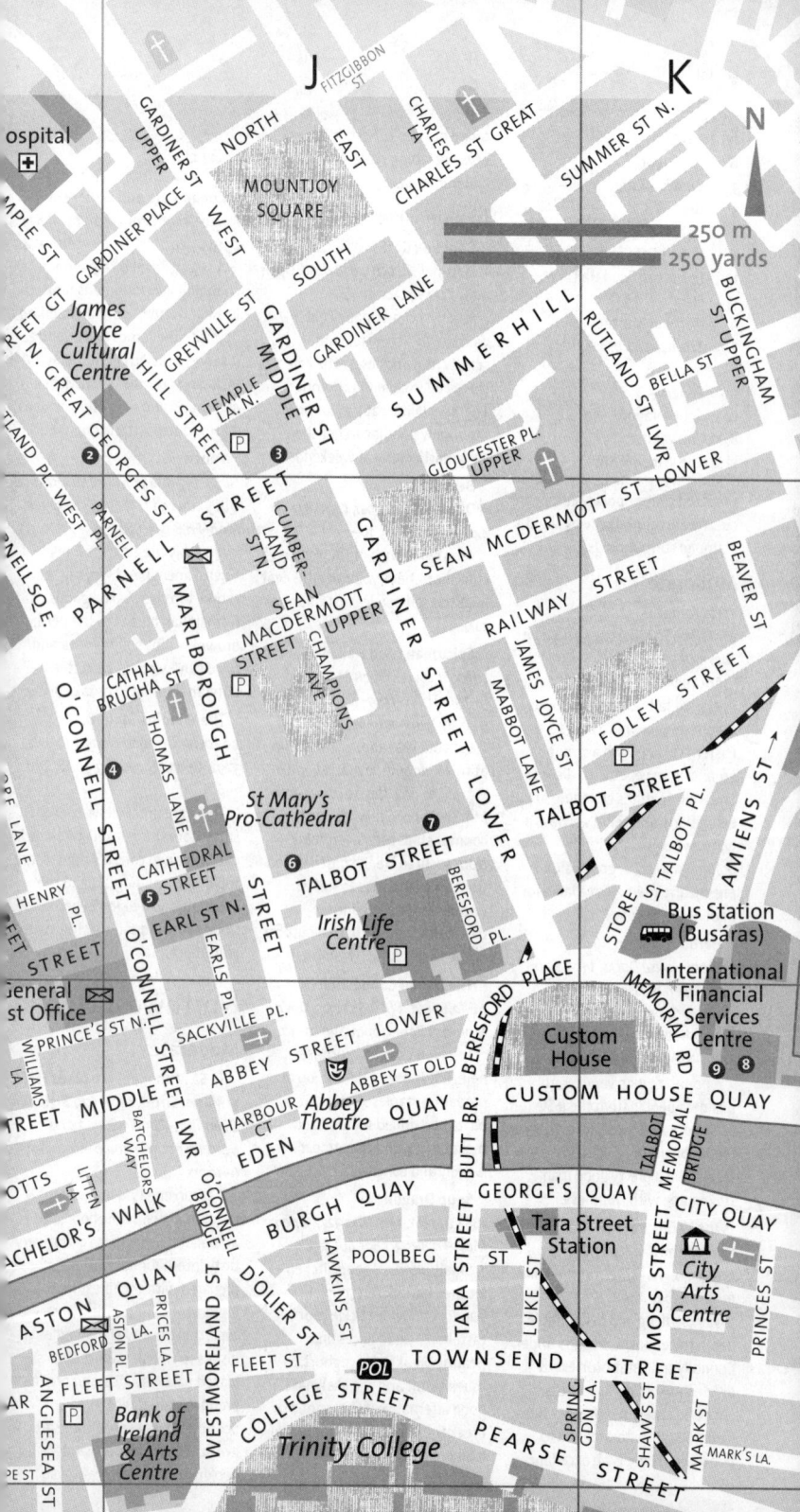

Map Key

6	101 Talbot
3	Bangkok Café
5	Beshoff's
1	Chapter One
2	Cobalt Café and Gallery
10	Epicurean Food Hall
13	Halo
9	Harbour Master
7	The Italian Connection
4	No. 23
11	Panem
14	Soup Dragon
8	The Vaults
12	The Winding Stair

prepared contemporary European cuisine are marred only by slightly cramped surroundings.

Moderate

101 Talbot J5
*101 Talbot St, t (01) 874 5011. **Open** Tues–Sat 5–11.*

Another favourite with theatre-goers, 101 Talbot offers delicious Mediterranean and Middle Eastern cuisine with a strong emphasis on vegetarian dishes. The walls features changing art exhibitions, and there's always a warm welcome and mildly bohemian buzz. A good value pre-theatre menu is available for under €20 (5–8pm).

Harbour Master K6
*Custom House Docks, t (01) 670 1688. **Open** brasserie Mon–Fri noon–9, Sat noon–10, Sun noon–7; bar Mon–Wed noon–11.30, Thurs–Sat noon–12.30am.*

A popular lunch venue with business people from the IFSC, with a great canal setting. The food is bistro fare, including pasta, steaks and a pretty good Irish stew made with Guinness.

The Vaults K6
*Harbourmaster Place, IFSC, t (01) 605 4700, www.thevaults.ie. **Open** for food daily noon–8.*

Vast, striking and fashionable bar in the enormous vaults under Connolly train station, cleverly divided up into distinct areas, each decorated in different styles from the ultra-streamlined to boho-chic. There is an excellent range of simple, fresh food on offer, including pizza, pasta, grills and homemade ice-cream.

Inexpensive

Bangkok Café J4
*106 Parnell St, t (01) 878 6618. **Open** daily 5.30–10.30.*

Run by a charismatic Thai woman, this cheerful, rather scruffy (but spotless) little café serves up excellent authentic Thai specialities at a great price. It's hugely popular, so get there early, particularly at weekends.

Beshoff's J5
*6 O'Connell St Upper, t (01) 872 4400. **Open** daily 10–10.*

Another branch of the fish and chip shop chain: you can either eat in at the self-service restaurant, or take away.

Epicurean Food Hall I6
*Liffey St Lower. **Open** Mon–Wed 9–7.30, Thurs–Fri 9–8.30, Sat 9–6.30, Sun noon–6.*

Eat your way around the world at this indoor food market (with entrances on Liffey St Lower and Middle Abbey St), where dozens of counter stalls offer everything from sushi to French pastries, and from Spanish tapas to Turkish sweets. Make a beeline for Caviston's Seafood bar, an outpost of the excellent fish restaurant.

The Italian Connection J5
*96 Talbot St, t (01) 878 7125. **Open** Mon–Sat 8am–10pm, Sun 10–10.*

You won't get any surprises here, but it does a decent job of preparing staples such as pizza, pasta and grilled seafood and meat dishes, and the atmosphere is lively and convivial.

Soup Dragon I6
*168 Capel St, t (01) 872 3277. **Open** Mon–Fri 8–5.30, Sat noon–5.*

Small, informal soup kitchen – let the Thai chicken soup or haddock chowder tickle your tastebuds. Good juices and healthy breakfasts (yoghurt, muesli, fruit and the like) make a good alternative if you want a break from the greasy traditional Irish breakfasts.

Cafés

Cobalt Café and Gallery I4
*North Great George's St, t (01) 873 0313. **Open** Mon–Fri 10–5, Sat 11–4.*

A smart, relaxed café with changing art exhibitions housed in a handsome Georgian building opposite the James Joyce centre. It serves delicious light meals, including gourmet sandwiches and soups, and in winter you can warm yourself at the open fire.

Panem I6
*Ha'penny Bridge House, 21 Ormond Quay Lower, t (01) 872 8510. **Open** Mon–Fri 8–5.30, Sat 9–5.*

Probably the tiniest bakery in town, Panem has a very big reputation: top class baked goods, from Italian breads to the perfect brownies, plus soups, pasta and filled sandwiches. The coffee is outstanding. Eat in or take away.

The Winding Stair I6
*40 Lower Ormond Quay, t (01) 873 3292. **Open** Mon–Sat 9.30–6, Sun 1–6.*

There are great views over the Liffey from this relaxed, two-level, old-fashioned café. It's right at the top of the 'winding stair' in this eccentric and delightful bookshop. Good soup and sandwiches, cakes and crêpes.

Northwest Dublin

Moderate

Tá Sá Mahogani Gaspipes F5
*17 Manor Street, t (01) 679 8138. **Open** Tues–Thurs noon–3 and 6–10, Fri noon–3 and 6–10.30, Sat 6–10.30.*

A surprising find in this largely residential neighbourhood, this is a small but lively spot serving very tasty international cuisine prepared with the finest local ingredients. The menu spans everything from Asian noodle dishes to French classics such as glazed pork calvados, and organic produce is used wherever possible. At weekends there are live jazz performances, and booking in advance is always advisable. In summer, there are outdoor tables overlooking a pretty garden.

Inexpensive

Chief O'Neill's Café Bar G6
Smithfield Village, t (01) 817 3818.

Bright and modern, if rather lacking in atmosphere, this hotel café-bar offers sophisticated traditional and contemporary Irish bar food. It's accompanied by live Irish music at weekends – although if you're genuinely interested in traditional music, the Cobblestones pub just around the corner is the place to go.

Kelly and Ping G6
Duck Lane, Smithfield Village, t (01) 817 3840, www.kellyandping.com. **Open** *daily noon–11.*

Right opposite the entrance to Old Jamesons Distillery is this bright, colourful Asian restaurant with good curries and noodle dishes which can be spiced according to taste. There's a good range of Asian beers, and a reasonable wine list, too.

Mero Mero F5
57a Manor St, Stoneybatter, t (01) 670 7799. **Open** *Mon–Fri 9–7, Sat 9–5.*

A delightful miniature café serving spicy and authentic Mexican in the up-and-coming district of Stoneybatter. It's always packed, and with good reason: the food is very tasty and very cheap.

Still Room Restaurant/1780 Bar G6
Old Jameson Distillery, t (01) 807 2355, www.whiskey-tours.com. Wheelchair access. **Open** *restaurant daily noon–7, bar open for food daily noon–3.*

The slick operation which is the Old Jameson Distillery has two eating options: decent traditional Irish food, including stews and bacon and cabbage soup, in the informal surroundings of the Still Room Restaurant; or lighter pub grub in the bar.

The Hole in the Wall C3
Blackhorse Ave, Phoenix Park, t (01) 838 9491. **Open** *for food noon–6.*

This classic Irish pub gets its name from the old tradition of passing pints through a hole in the wall to soldiers garrisoned in nearby Phoenix Park. They do a good carvery lunch, along with old favourites such as coddle and Irish stew, and there's a simple bar menu available all day.

Outside the Centre: Dublin Suburbs

Luxury

Locks H10
1 Windsor Terrace, Portobello, t (01) 454 3391. **Open** *Mon–Fri 12.15–2.15 and 7–11, Sat 7–11.*

This refined, cosy restaurant overlooking the Grand Canal is the perfect place to linger over exquisitely prepared Irish food. No slave to fads, it offers assured, adventurous cuisine, prepared with organic produce from County Wicklow. A good set lunch menu is €26, or set dinner €46.

Expensive

Ernie's OFF MAPS
Mulberry Gardens (off Morehampton Rd), Donnybrook, t (01) 269 3300. **Open** *Tues–Fri 12.30–2.30 and 7.15–10.30, Sat 7.15–10.30.*

A wonderful, long-established family-run restaurant, where you'll find refined, ungimmicky Irish cuisine served with aplomb. The walls are covered with art, and there's a fine wine list. The set lunch is just €15, or set dinner €35.

The Lobster Pot OFF MAPS
9 Ballsbridge Terrace, t (01) 660 9170. **Open** *Mon–Fri 12.30–2.30 and 6.30–10.30, Sat 6.30–10.30.*

This is a very fine seafood restaurant, where the fish (several daily specials) is served with real flair. It also has a reasonable selection of meat dishes and an extensive wine list. It's refined and deeply traditional in the best sense, with impeccable service: the charming staff are always happy to make recommendations.

Moderate

Bijou OFF MAPS
47 Highfield Road, Rathgar, t (01) 679 0043. **Open** *Mon–Sat 5–11, Sun noon–3.*

You will definitely have to book a table at this cosy neighbourhood bistro. It's set over two floors, and has an excellent and wide-ranging menu which always offers plenty of choice. The seafood is particularly good.

The Canteen L8
Schoolhouse Hotel, 2–8 Northumberland Rd, t (01) 667 5014, www.schoolhousehotel.com. **Open** *daily 12.30–2.30 and 6.30–10.*

Modern European bistro-style food, served in an airy hall.

Dish K10
146 Upper Leeson St, t (01) 664 2135, www.dishrestaurant.net. **Open** *daily noon–4 and 6–11.*

A real favourite, Dish serves modern Irish cooking prepared with the ingredients including organic locally reared meat. The surroundings are coolly stylish and it well deserves its fine reputation. Booking advisable.

Ocean M7
Charlotte Quay Dock, t (01) 668 8862. **Open** *daily for food 12.30–10.*

Huge bar and restaurant with great views of the canal. The food is simple bistro fare, but made with good quality ingredients and attractively served. A good place to go with kids during the day.

Roly's Bistro OFF MAPS
7 Ballsbridge Terrace, t (01) 668 2611. **Open** *daily 12–3 and 6–11.*

This is one of Dublin's best-loved restaurants: it's smart, stylish and vibrant, and chef Colin O'Daly produces much-lauded contemporary Irish cooking. While this is probably the best place in town to try Dublin prawns, you won't be disappointed with anything on the adventurous menu. The set lunch is a modest €18. Reservations are essential. There's a branch in Dún Laoghaire.

Ryan's OFF MAPS
28 Parkgate St, t (01) 671 9352.

Open Mon–Wed 10.30am–12.30am, Thurs–Sat 12.30pm–1.30am, Sun 12.30–midnight; food available lunchtimes and evenings.

A classic Dublin pub with stained glass, ornate woodwork and plenty of Victorian frills. It serves tasty pub grub in the bar at lunchtimes, but there's a separate restaurant upstairs for more substantial traditional Irish fare.

Le Panto/Talavera OFF MAPS
*Radisson SAS St Helen's Hotel, Stillorgan Road, **t** (01) 218 6000. **Open** Le Panto: Tues–Sat 7–10, Sun 12.30–3; Talavera: Mon–Sat 12.30–2.30 and 6.30–10.30, Sun 6.30–10.30.*

The Radisson SAS St Helen's Hotel is the setting for the formal restaurant Le Panto (expensive), but tucked away in the basement of the 18th-century mansion is the intimate Italian restaurant Talavera. A huge circular table groans with a spectacular selection of antipasti – marinated artichokes, chargrilled peppers, and tomato and mozzarella salads among them. On Fridays, they serve market fresh seafood specialities.

Tribeca OFF MAPS
*65 Ranelagh, **t** (01) 497 4174. **Open** daily noon–11.*

Hip restaurant that takes its inspiration from New York – the weekend brunches are massively popular. There's a wide-ranging menu offering everything from standards such as burgers and salads (all prepared with the finest ingredients) as well as spicy Asian noodle dishes, but they don't take bookings – get there early.

Inexpensive

Punjab Balti House OFF MAPS
*15 Ranelagh Village, **t** (01) 497 9420. **Open** Sun–Thurs 5.30–11.30, Fri–Sat 5.30–midnight.*

This is a cheap and cheerful balti house where you can bring your own wine, which helps to keep the costs down. The menu holds no surprises, but it's all good stuff.

Cafés

Café Java OFF MAPS
*2 Upper Leeson St, Ranelagh, **t** (01) 660 0675. **Open** Mon–Fri 7.30–5, Sat 8–5, Sun 11–5.*

An outpost of a small coffee shop chain, this comfortable, relaxed spot serves muffins, bagels and a few simple dishes.

Expresso OFF MAPS
*1 St Mary's Rd, Ballsbridge, **t** (01) 660 0585. **Open** Mon–Fri 7.30am–9.30pm.*

More than a café, this bright, laid-back joint is best known for its mouthwatering breakfasts and weekend brunches. The pancakes are heavenly.

Nectar Juice Bar OFF MAPS
*53 Ranelagh Village, **t** (01) 491 0934. **Open** daily 9am–4pm and 5–10pm.*

There are several outposts of this juice bar around Dublin, which all do good coffee, cakes and snacks besides the delicious range of juices and smoothies.

Outside the Centre: Dublin Bay

Expensive

The King Sitric OFF MAPS
*Howth, **t** (01) 832 5235, www.kingsitric.com. **Open** Mon–Sat 6.30–10.*

A handsome, long-established harbourside restaurant with huge windows overlooking the pretty bay in Howth. The speciality is fish, landed daily on Howth pier and beautifully and classically prepared. For a real treat, try the lobster which is caught by their own fishermen in Balscadden Bay, washed down with a selection from the award-winning wine list. Reservations are advisable.

Bon Appetit OFF MAPS
*9 James Terrace, Malahide, **t** (01) 845 0314, www.bonappetit.ie. **Open** Mon–Fri 12.30–2 and 7–10, Sat 7–10.*

A welcoming brasserie with restful blue and cream décor, tucked away in the basement of a Georgian townhouse. On the menu, you'll find skilfully prepared local seafood and Wicklow lamb, along with some more surprising dishes such as ostrich. A good set lunch is under €25, set dinner €44.

Kish OFF MAPS
*Coliemore Rd, Dalkey, **t** (01) 285 0377, www.kishrestaurant.ie. **Open** Wed–Sun 7–10.30, Sun noon–3.30.*

An expansive, fashionable restaurant with huge windows looking over the bay, Kish offers delicious French-inspired cuisine to match the beautiful views. There is a set lunch available on Sundays (€38). Book in advance.

Moderate

Abbey Tavern OFF MAPS
*Abbey St, Howth, **t** (01) 839 0307, www.abbeytavern.ie. **Open** Tues–Sat 7–10.30.*

This 16th-century tavern and restaurant serves old-fashioned fish dishes – right down to prawn cocktails with marie-rose sauce – but what they lack in imagination, they make up for in freshness: the tavern is a stone's throw from the harbour. Live, traditional Irish music is offered in the evenings.

Aqua OFF MAPS
*West Pier, Howth, **t** (01) 832 0690, www.aqua.ie. **Open** Tues–Sat 5–10.30.*

A big, bright modern restaurant on the harbour in Howth with spectacular sea views, serving contemporary cuisine with the emphasis on local seafood.

Avoca Handweavers OFF MAPS
*Kilmacanogue, Bray, **t** (01) 286 7466, www.avoca.ie. **Open** Mon–Fri 9.30–5, Sat 10–5, Sun and bank hols 10–5.30.*

The Avoca craft centre is probably the best place to pick up stylish Irish gifts, but it's equally famous for its fine café and food hall. The company's headquarters are located on a beautiful garden estate south of Bray. Sit out on the terrace in summer and enjoy excellent cakes, quiches, salads and light meals.

Barracuda OFF MAPS
*Strand Rd, Bray, **t** (01) 276 5686, www.barracuda.ie.* ***Open*** *daily 11–11.*

A big, shiny modern restaurant and bar complex right on the seafront with spectacular views. Enjoy a drink in the bar, or dine on reliable if unexceptional fish, steaks and other standards in the upstairs restaurant.

Bloody Stream OFF MAPS
*Howth DART station, Howth, **t** (01) 839 5078.* ***Open*** *Mon–Wed 10.30am–12.30am, Thurs–Sat 12.30–1.30am, Sun 12.30–midnight.*

A classic Irish pub which serves one of the best pints of Guinness in the region. It has a restaurant upstairs, serving a no-nonsense menu featuring uniformly excellent steak and seafood. Dine on lighter fare in the bar downstairs.

Brasserie Na Mara OFF MAPS
*Railway Station, 1 Harbour Rd, Dún Laoghaire, **t** (01) 280 6767.* ***Open*** *Mon–Sat 12.30–3 and 6.30–10, Sun 6.30–10.*

Excellent modern Irish cooking in a former railway station. Prices are at the top end of this category.

Dali's OFF MAPS
*63–66 Main St, Blackrock, **t** (01) 278 0660.* ***Open*** *Tues–Fri 12–3 and 6–10.30, Sat 6–10.30.*

A reliably good restaurant serving contemporary Irish cuisine with a quirky international flavour. There's a good value set lunch menu for around €15.

Eagle House OFF MAPS
*18 Glasthule Rd, Dún Laoghaire, **t** (01) 280 4740.* ***Open*** *for food 12.30–10.*

An excellent, traditional Irish pub serving good bar meals (inexpensive). Upstairs is Duzy's Café, a stylish restaurant (moderate) with live jazz at the weekends, which serves contemporary cuisine from locally sourced produce.

Forty Foot OFF MAPS
*The Pavilion, Dún Laoghaire, **t** (01) 284 2982.* ***Open*** *Mon–Thurs 6–10, Fri and Sat 6–10.30.*

The Pavilion shopping and entertainment complex is the location for this big, bistro-style restaurant. With huge windows offering great harbour views, and an outdoor terrace on summer days, it has a perfect setting. The service is equally top-notch, and the only quibble is that the extensive menu carries a slightly inflated price tag.

P.D.'s Woodhouse OFF MAPS
*1 Coliemore Rd, Dalkey, **t** (01) 284 9399.* ***Open*** *Mon–Sat 6–11, Sun 4–9.30.*

This remains a big favourite in Dalkey by sticking to what it does best: providing great friendly service and succulent oak wood barbecued steaks.

Purty Kitchen OFF MAPS
*Old Dún Laoghaire Rd, Monkstown, **t** (01) 284 3576.* ***Open*** *for food noon–10.*

Sophisticated bar food with the emphasis on seafood (great chowder) served in one of Dublin's oldest pubs (established 1728).

Inexpensive

Caviston's of Sandycove OFF MAPS
*59 Glasthule Rd, Sandycove, **t** (01) 280 9120, www.cavistons.com.* ***Open*** *Tues–Sat noon–5.*

Caviston's is so popular that diners must opt for one of three lunch sittings: noon to 1.30pm, 1.30 to 3pm or 3.30 to 5pm. Linked to their shop (selling all kinds of gourmet treats), the restaurant serves some of the finest and freshest seafood in the region.

El Paso OFF MAPS
*10 Harbour Rd, Howth, **t** (01) 832 3334.* ***Open*** *daily 6–10 (Fri–Sat to 11).*

Big, colourful Mexican restaurant near the harbour, with all the usual Tex-Mex dishes. A good family option.

Mao Café Bar OFF MAPS
*The Pavilion, Dún Laoghaire, **t** (01) 214 8090, www.cafemao.com.* ***Open*** *daily noon–11.*

Good Asian noodle dishes with a sliding scale of spiciness. An airy, modern setting and a cheerful young crowd.

nosh OFF MAPS
*11 Coliemore Rd, Dalkey, **t** (01) 284 0666, www.nosh.ie.* ***Open*** *Tues–Sun noon–4 and 6–11.*

A stylish, minimalist place appealing to Dalkey's surprisingly big fashion pack. Simple, tasty food and excellent brunches. At dinner, it goes up a price bracket.

The Queens OFF MAPS
*12 Castle St, Dalkey, **t** (01) 285 8345.* ***Open*** *pub Mon–Wed noon–midnight, Fri–Sat noon–12.30am; restaurants Mon–Sat 6–11.*

Dalkey's oldest pub, serving good sandwiches, light meals and seafood chowder. There are also two restaurants here: La Romana, for inexpensive Italian food, or the smarter Vico upstairs, for contemporary cuisine in more formal surroundings (moderate).

Cafés

Malahide Castle OFF MAPS
*Malahide, **t** (01) 846 3027.* ***Open*** *April–Oct Mon–Sat 10–12.45 & 2–5, Sun 11–6; Nov–March Mon–Fri 10–5, Sat–Sun 2–5.*

Try out the lovely, rather old-fashioned tea rooms in Malahide Castle, which serve homemade soups and sandwiches, cakes and reasonable coffee.

Gresham Royal Marine Hotel OFF MAPS
*Marine Rd, Dun Laoghaire, **t** (01) 280 1911.* ***Open*** *daily for tea.*

This grand Victorian hotel overlooking the bay is the perfect spot for old-fashioned afternoon tea.

Nightlife

Pubs and Bars 203
Clubs 208

Dublin's pubs are legendary. The cliché of the wood-panelled traditional bar with a line of regulars stooped over their pints of Guinness still survives, although in ever-decreasing numbers. The boom years of the 1990s saw the appearance of a new breed of 'superbars' – huge, generic, slickly designed bars with DJs and minimalist furnishings, where you could be in any city in Europe. Dublin's youth seemed eager to shake off the city's cosy but parochial image and replace it with something more exciting and international. Old-fashioned pubs came under pressure to modernize in order to keep the punters, and some revamped completely (like The Bailey, mentioned in Joyce's *Ulysses*, but now ultra-fashionable and utterly unrecognizable).

However, not all the old-style pubs have disappeared: The Long Hall and the Old Stand, for example, still retain their burnished Victorian interiors and courteous old-fashioned service, and Kavanagh's – better known as The Gravediggers – up by Glasnevin Cemetery, hasn't changed in centuries and doesn't look like it ever will. And while many of the superbars are nothing more than slickly packaged theme bars, some of them are genuinely stylish and mix as good a cocktail as you'd get in any fancy New York or London bar.

Dublin's clubbing scene is equally mixed: there's a lot of tawdry tourist tat, particularly around Temple Bar, but there are also some very hip clubs which pull in some of the best international DJs around. For the best clubbing listings, pick up a copy of *Hot Press*, *InDublin* or *The Event Guide*, all of which list the best club nights at each venue.

Pubs and Bars
Southeast Dublin

AKA I7
6 Wicklow St, **t** *(01) 670 4220.* **Open** *Mon–Tues 4–11.30, Thurs–Sat 4–2.30, Sun 4–11.*

A long, stylishly minimalist bar, with a mellow atmosphere and chill-out music during the week. It gets packed out for DJ sessions at weekends.

The Bailey J7
2 Duke St, **t** *(01) 670 4939.* **Open** *Mon–Sat 11.30–11.30, Sun 4–11.*

The big, slightly snooty Bailey was mentioned in *Ulysses*, but contains no vestige of the pub that Joyce would have known. It's now full of ultra-modern black and white furnishings, too-cool staff dressed in black, and lots of contemporary art and photographs. Full of fashionably dressed locals, it's a popular place to pose and there's usually the odd celebrity hanging about. There's a small (heated) pavement terrace, much sought after in summer.

Café En Seine J7
39–40 Dawson St, **t** *(01) 677 4576 or 677 4369.* **Open** *Mon–Wed 9am–12.30am, Thurs–Sat 9am–2.30am.*

This huge bar could double as a set for the film *Moulin Rouge*, recreating turn-of-the-century Paris beautifully. Large, light and spacious, it's full of quirky corners filled with huge palms and ferns, and crammed with lavish chandeliers and Art Nouveau-style mirrors and lamps. At the centre is an opulent curving marble bar, and it serves good food including a great jazz brunch on Sundays.

The Chocolate Bar I8
Hatch St Upper, Harcourt St, **t** *(01) 478 0166.* **Open** *Mon–Thurs 5–11.30, Fri 5–1, Sat 6–1, Sun 6–11.*

One of Dublin's trendiest bars, the Chocolate Bar is where the city's bright young things warm up for the long night ahead (often not getting any further than Pod or Redbox next door). There's a great cocktail list and a 'happy hour' on weeknights 5.30–8pm.

Cocoon J7
Royal Hibernian Way, Duke Lane, **t** *(01) 679 6259, www.cocoon.ie.* **Open** *Mon–Wed noon–11.30, Thurs–Sat noon–12.30am, Sun noon–11.*

Another slick, minimalist bar and cocktail lounge decked out largely in black and white, Cocoon is a favourite with the well-dressed office crowd. It's got big, deep sofas and comfortable armchairs, and plasma screens show fashion TV and music videos. From Thursday to Saturday, live DJs keep it hopping until late.

Davy Byrne's J7
21 Duke St, **t** *(01) 677 5217, www.davybyrnespub.com.* **Open** *daily 11am–12.30am.*

James Joyce made Davy Byrne's famous, by having Leopold Bloom take lunch there in *Ulysses* (see p.66). It successfully combines modernity and tradition, and serves delicious pub food, including particularly good seafood.

Dawson's Lounge J7
24 Dawson St, **t** *(01) 677 5909.* **Open** *Mon–Thurs and Sat noon–11.30, Fri noon–12.30am.*

Dublin's smallest bar, this inevitably cosy space is tucked in a cellar close to St Stephen's Green. If you are on the hunt for the perfect pint of Guinness, you may well find it here.

Doheny & Nesbitt K8
5 Lower Baggot St, **t** *(01) 676 2945.* **Open** *Mon–Wed 10.30am–11pm, Thurs–Sat 10.30am–12.30am, Sun 12.30am–11pm.*

A Dublin institution, this gloriously old-fashioned pub is a favourite with lawyers and well-heeled Dubs who tuck themselves away in the cosy snugs. There's always a great atmosphere, and it sometimes has traditional music on Sundays.

Hartigan's J9
100 Lower Leeson St, **t** *(01) 676 2280.* **Open** *Mon–Wed 10.30am–11.30pm, Thurs–Sat*

10.30am–12.30am, Sun 12.30pm–11pm.

A scruffy, student favourite, this old-fashioned spartan pub was mentioned in Flann O'Brien's *At Swim Two Birds*.

Horseshoe Bar J8
Shelbourne Hotel, St Stephen's Green, **t** *(01) 676 6471.* **Open** *Mon–Wed 10.30am–11.30pm, Thurs–Sat 10.30am–12.30am, Sun 12.30–11.*

One of the most traditional and best-known bars in the city, the comfortable Horseshoe is set in the historic Shelbourne Hotel. Old-fashioned leather armchairs, a roaring fire and a lively crowd of politicians, journalists, actors and smart shoppers set the scene.

Inn on the Green J8
Fitzwilliam Hotel, St Stephen's Green, **t** *(01) 478 7000.* **Open** *daily 10.30am–11.30pm.*

A slick, ultra-modern bar in the Fitzwilliam Hotel, this is popular with local office-workers and the business crowd. Good cocktails, lunches, but a slightly anodyne atmosphere.

James Toner's K8
139 Lower Baggot St, **t** *(01) 676 3090.* **Open** *Mon–Wed 10.30am–12.30am, Thurs–Sat 12.30pm–1.30am, Sun 12.30–midnight.*

Toner's is one of the few Dublin pubs to resolutely resist modernization and is all the better for it. Relaxed, traditional and reputedly the only pub W.B. Yeats ever visited, it's one of the best places for a quiet pint.

Kehoe's J7
9 South Anne St, **t** *(01) 677 8312.* **Open** *Mon–Wed 10.30am–11.30pm, Thurs–Sat 10.30am–12.30am, Sun 12.30–11.*

This is one of Dublin's classic old-fashioned bars, full of Victorian fittings and blessed with cosy snugs. It serves a very fine pint of Guinness and packs out in the evening, but it's also a great place to linger over a quiet pint during the day.

The Long Stone J6
10–11 Townsend St, **t** *(01) 671 8102, www.thelongstone.com.* **Open** *Mon–Wed noon–11.30, Thurs–Fri noon–1.30am, Sat 4–12.30am, Sun 4–11.*

A big, traditional pub which takes its name from the Norse stone or *steyne* which the Vikings used to mark the location of their first berthing in Dublin. There's a strange fireplace in the shape of the Viking God of Light, but otherwise it's a pretty regular pub which is packed and friendly.

McDaid's I7
3 Harry St, **t** *(01) 679 4395.* **Open** *Mon–Wed 10.30am–11.30pm, Thurs–Sat 10.30am–12.30am, Sun 12.30–11.*

Firmly on the tourist literary route, this is nonetheless a great Dublin bar. Old-fashioned and wood-panelled, its walls are lined with old whiskey and Guinness posters and there's a welcoming and enjoyably mixed crowd of locals and tourists.

Mulligans J6
8 Poolbeg St, **t** *(01) 677 5582, www.mulligans.ie.* **Open** *Mon–Wed 10.30am–11.30pm, Thurs–Sat 10.30am–12.30am, Sun 12.30–11.*

Mulligan's has long enjoyed a reputation as the home of the best pint of Guinness in Dublin. A gloriously untouched and old-fashioned bar, it's a peaceful retreat during the day, but packs out in the evenings.

Neary's I7
1 Chatham St, **t** *(01) 677 8596.* **Open** *Mon–Wed 10.30am–11.30pm, Thurs–Sat 10.30am–12.30am, Sun 12.30–11.*

A wonderful Edwardian bar, full of shiny brass and wood panelling, which is close to the Gaiety Theatre and popular with the theatre crowd (both audience and actors). It does excellent bar food, including delicious oysters.

Odeon I8
Old Harcourt St Station, 57 Harcourt St, **t** *(01) 478 2088.* **Open** *Mon–Wed 10.30am–11.30pm, Thurs 10.30am–12.30pm, Fri–Sat 10.30am–3am (cover charge applies Sat from 10pm).*

This huge, modern bar is set in an old train station and heaves at weekends with students and a young crowd dancing to predictable chart music. Early in the evening it's a great spot to linger in one of the big, comfortable seats and there's also a summer terrace. It does good food, and is the perfect spot for a relaxed Sunday brunch.

O'Donoghues K8
15 Merrion Row, **t** *(01) 676 2807.* **Open** *Mon–Wed 10.30am–11.30pm, Thurs–Sat 10.30am–12.30am, Sun 12.30–11.*

This classic pub is famously associated with bands like The Dubliners and U2, and it regularly features impromptu music sessions. It's very popular and consequently often overcrowded.

O'Dwyers L8
7–8 Lower Mount St, **t** *(01) 676 1718, www.capitalbars.com.* **Open** *bar Mon–Wed 11am–11.30pm, Thurs–Fri 11am–2.30am, Sat 5pm–2.30am; nightclub Thurs–Sat only.*

This is a big and trendy theme pub, which has opted for a slight stagey traditional look. There's also a club upstairs and regular live music.

The Old Stand I7
37 Exchequer St, **t** *(01) 677 7220, www.theoldstandpub.com.* **Open** *daily 11am–12.30am.*

One of Dublin's oldest pubs, the Old Stand has modernized, but continues to serve a good pint accompanied by decent traditional bar food. It's perfectly placed to take a breather from shopping on Grafton St, and the bar staff are uniformly charming.

O'Neills I7
2 Suffolk St, **t** *(01) 679 3656, www.oneillsbar.com.* **Open** *Mon–Wed 10.30am–11.30pm, Thurs–Sat 10.30am–12.30am, Sun 12.30–11.*

A big traditional bar which is popular with Trinity students and handy if you've just been visiting the tourist office. It does reasonable and inexpensive bar food (see p.199).

Peter's Pub I7
1 Johnston Place, **t** (01) 677 8588. **Open** Mon–Wed 10.30am–11.30pm, Thurs–Sat 10.30am–12.30am, Sun 12.30–11.

A quiet, modern little bar off the trendy shopping street of South William St. Good light bar meals and tables outside in the summer.

SamSara J7
35–36 Dawson St, **t** (01) 671 7723. **Open** daily 4pm–midnight (Thurs–Sat until 2.30am).

Part of the fashionable La Stampa hotel and restaurant (see p.176 and p.187), this is a very trendy Moroccan-style bar. Media luvvies and fashionistas lounge under chandeliers, and check out each other's designer clothing. DJs play an eclectic mix of dance, ambient and rock music at weekends.

Solas I8
31 Wexford St, **t** (01) 478 0583, www.solas-bars.com. **Open** Mon–Wed noon–11.30, Thurs–Sat noon–12.30; food served Mon–Fri noon–8, Sat noon–7.

Funky, laid-back bar that manages to be stylish without being posey. There are candle-lit tables, retro-look globe lights, comfortable booths and a good mixed crowd. Regular DJ sessions. It does simple food (pasta, salads, sandwiches) during the day.

Sosume I7
64 South Great George's St, **t** (01) 478 1590, www.capitalbars.com, **Open** Mon–Fri 5–2.30, Sat 2pm–2.30am, Sun 4–1.

Another of the huge superbars that have sprung up in Dublin over the last decade or so, Sosume has funky, Oriental-style décor and attracts big crowds at the weekends.

Thing Mote J7
15 Suffolk St, **t** (01) 677 8030. **Open** Mon–Wed 10.30am–12.30am, Thurs–Sat 12.30pm–1.30am, Sun 12.30–midnight.

This welcoming little bar is a bit too crowded in the evenings, but it's a good place to stop off after some shopping, when it's quieter.

Southwest Dublin and Temple Bar

Auld Dubliner I6
17 Anglesea St, Temple Bar, **t** (01) 677 0527. **Open** Mon–Thurs 10.30am–11.30pm, Fri–Sat 10.30am–12.30am, Sun 12.30–11.

This traditional pub in the heart of Temple Bar is always full of tourists, but isn't a bad alternative to the bland superbars if you come early in the evening.

Bob's Bar I6
35–37 East Essex St, **t** (01) 677 5482. **Open** Wed–Fri 4pm–2.30am, Sat–Sun noon–2.30am.

As big, brash superbars go, this is no better or worse than the average. It's a huge venue with a club in the basement, and is popular with tourists on the pull. Live music on Sunday nights.

Brazen Head H7
20 Lower Bridge St, **t** (01) 679 5186. **Open** daily 10.30am–12.30am.

The Brazen Head claims to be the oldest bar in Dublin, and attracts a good crowd of locals and lawyers from the Four Courts across the river. There are regular live folk music sessions.

Brogan's I7
75 Dame St, **t** (01) 679 9570. **Open** Mon–Thurs 10.30am–11.30pm, Fri–Sat 10.30am–12.30am, Sun 12.30–11.

A decent, down-to-earth bar crammed with Guinness memorabilia on the edge of Temple Bar, which has a mixed crowd of slightly older Dubs. On Tuesday nights it's hosts the Poetry Slam night, an open mic session where aspiring poets get up on stage to compete for the title of Grand Slam Poet.

Bruxelles I7
7–8 Harry St, **t** (01) 677 5362. **Open** daily 10.30am–1.30am, Thurs–Sat until 2.30am.

Bruxelles is a loud, vaguely trendy and very noisy bar on two levels, with regular live music, including good jazz sessions. The late licence makes it a reliable bet for late-night drinking.

Buskers J6
Fleet St, Temple Bar, **t** (01) 677 3333. **Open** bar Mon–Wed 11.30–11.30, Thurs–Sat 11.30am–12.30am, Sun 11.30–11; Boomerang nightclub Wed–Sat only.

One of the Temple Bar superbars, this has the usual crowd of boozing and sharking tourists at weekends, and a very popular nightclub, Boomerang, downstairs, playing chart and dance music.

Dakota I7
9 William St South, **t** (01) 672 7696. **Open** daily 3–midnight, Fri–Sat until 3am.

Another huge, blandly stylish bar, with a relaxed feel before the crowd trickle in after about 9pm. It's got plenty of couches and comfy armchair, low tables and booth areas which are good for groups. It turns into a club on Thursday to Saturday nights.

4 Dame Lane I7
4 Dame Lane, **t** (01) 679 0291. **Open** daily 5pm–2.30am (Sun until 1am).

A hip, chrome-filled hangout with a great range of music nights from guest and resident DJs.

Doyle's of College Street J6
9 College St, **t** (01) 671 0616. **Open** Mon–Thurs noon–1am, Fri–Sat noon–2.30am, Sun 4pm–1am.

A boozy traditional hangout favoured by students.

The Duke J7
9 Duke St, **t** (01) 679 9553. **Open** Mon–Wed 11.30–11.30, Thurs–Sat 11.30am–12.30am, Sun noon–1am.

Another haunt of Dublin's literary set, this is a relaxed and welcoming place to stop off for a quick pint.

Eamonn Dorans I6
3a Crown Alley, Temple Bar, **t** (01) 679 9114, www.eamonndorans.com. **Open** bar daily 11am–3am; nightclub 8pm–3am.

A popular tourist haunt in Temple Bar with live traditional

music nightly, and a surprisingly decent nightclub with good guest DJs.

Farringdon's I6
*27–29 East Essex St, Temple Bar, **t** (01) 671 5135.* **Open** *Mon–Wed 11am–11.30pm, Thurs–Sat 11am–12.30am, Sun 11–11.*

One of the better pubs in Temple Bar, still with some of its traditional ambience despite the tourist crowds.

Fireworks J6
*Old Central Fire Station, Tara St, **t** (01) 648 1099, www.capitalbars.com.* **Open** *Sun–Tues 4pm–midnight, Wed–Sat 4pm–2.30am.*

A huge venue in a converted fire station, with several bars, dance floors and cheerful office parties making the most of happy hour.

Foggy Dew I6
*1 Upper Fownes St, Temple Bar, **t** (01) 677 9328.* **Open** *Mon–Tues noon–11.30pm, Wed noon–12.30am, Thurs noon–1am, Fri noon–2am, Sat 1pm–1am, Sun 1–11pm.*

A favourite in Temple Bar, this has no airs or pretensions and attracts a good crowd of regulars.

The Globe I7
*11 South Great George's St, **t** (01) 671 1220.* **Open** *Mon–Wed 11am–11.30pm, Thurs–Sat 11am–12.30am, Sun 11–11.*

Trendy young things predominate in this hip bar, which is always buzzing. Excellent DJs and live jazz on Sundays.

Grogan's Castle Lounge I7
*15 South William St, **t** (01) 677 9320.* **Open** *Mon–Wed 11am–11.30pm, Thurs–Sat 11am–12.30am, Sun 11–11.*

A refreshingly unchanged pub on an increasingly fashionable street, Grogan's is stuck in the 1970s. It's another arty haunt, with lots of writers and artists escaping the bland superbars, and you can get a great toastie to go with your beautifully pulled pint.

Hogan's I7
*35 South Great George's St, **t** (01) 677 5904.* **Open** *Mon–Wed 10.30am–11.30am, Thurs 10.30am–12.30am, Fri–Sat 10.30am–2.30am, Sun 12.30–11.*

A big trendy bar with huge windows which display posing fashion victims gearing up for the night ahead. There's a small club in the basement.

The Long Hall I7
*51 South Great George's St, **t** (01) 475 1590.* **Open** *Sun–Wed 10.30am–11.30pm, Thurs 10.30am–12.30am, Fri–Sat 10.30am–2.30am.*

A fabulous old pub with old prints, shining brass taps and polished wooden fittings. One of Dublin's best traditional boozers, with a line of regulars along the bar that look as though they haven't moved in decades.

Messrs Maguire J6
*1–2 Burgh Quay, **t** (01) 670 5777.* **Open** *Sun–Tues 10.30am–12.30am, Wed–Sat 10.30am–2.30am.*

This big pub has a microbrewery on the premises, and boasts all kinds of nooks and crannies leading off a spectacular staircase.

The Morgan Bar J6
*10 Fleet St, Temple Bar, **t** (01) 679 3939, www.themorgan.com.* **Open** *Mon–Wed 10.30am–11.30pm, Thurs–Sat 10.30am–12.30am, Sun 12.30pm–11pm.*

The Morgan bar is as sleekly designed as the boutique hotel to which it is attached. A good spot for a cocktail to kick off the evening, but not that's about it.

Octagon Bar I6
*Clarence Hotel, 6–8 Wellington Quay, Temple Bar, **t** (01) 670 9000.* **Open** *Mon–Sat 11–11, Sun 12.30–10.30.*

Still one of the best places to see and be seen, the gorgeous Octagon Bar attracts everyone from wide-eyed tourists hoping to spot Bono to media celebrities and pop stars. It's pricey, but oozes glamour.

O'Sullivan's Bar J6
*Westmoreland St, **t** (01) 635 5451.* **Open** *Sun–Wed 10.30am–11.30pm, Thurs 10.30am–12.30am, Fri–Sat 10.30am–2.30am.*

A handsome Victorian bar which serves a good pint of Guinness and offers live traditional music every evening.

The Palace Bar J6
*21 Fleet St, **t** (01) 671 7388.* **Open** *Mon–Wed 10.30am–11.30pm, Thurs–Sat 10.30am–12.30am, Sun 12.30–11.*

The Palace Bar is one of Dublin's best unreconstructed traditional pubs, with a great skylit snug and lots of frosted glass and gilt mirrors. It's been popular with writers and journalists for generations.

The Porterhouse I6
*16–18 Parliament St, **t** (01) 679 8847, www.porterhousebrewco.com.* **Open** *Mon–Wed noon–11.30pm, Thurs noon–12.30am, Fri–Sat noon–2.30am, Sun 12.30–11.*

A huge, multi-levelled bar with its own microbrewery, this is a very popular spot in Temple Bar, full of tourists, the rugby crowd and plenty of young locals. The beer is great, and even committed fans of Guinness might come to think fondly of the range of Porterhouse stouts. It also does good bar food, including oysters.

Stag's Head I7
*1 Dame Court, **t** (01) 679 3701.* **Open** *Mon–Wed noon–11.30, Thurs–Sat noon–12.30am, Sun 12.30–11.*

One of the most authentic and unchanged Victorian pubs in the city, the Stag's Head is dark and wood-panelled, with snugs, stained glass and burnished mirrors. It's enormously popular with a varied crowd of tourists, shoppers, businessmen in suits, with a line of old regulars sitting at the bar. It also does limited bar snacks.

The Temple Bar I6
*47 Temple Bar, **t** (01) 672 5287.* **Open** *daily 11am–12.30am.*

The Temple Bar is one of the oldest pubs in the area, and has packaged its history in the form of T-shirts and baseball caps in the adjoining shop. It attracts a bewilderingly mixed crowd of young hipsters and tourists, and has a beer garden in summer.

Thomas Read's I7
1 Parliament St, t (01) 670 7220. **Open** *Mon–Wed 10.30am–11.30pm, Thurs 10.30am–12.30pm, Fri–Sat 10.30am–2.30am, Sun 12.30–11.*

A good spot for coffee and lunch as well as pint or two in the evenings, this airy modern café-cum-bar attracts Trinity students and literary types who linger over the newspapers. At weekends it gets very crowded, and there's a small dance floor.

Turk's Head J6
27–30 Parliament St, t (01) 679 9701. **Open** *Mon–Wed 10.30am–12.30am, Thurs–Sat 12.30pm–1.30am, Sun 12.30–midnight.*

Big, gaudy popular pub with two spaces in Temple Bar. It's usually packed with tourists out for a good time, so don't expect to find too many locals.

Northeast Dublin

Flowing Tide J6
9 Lower Abbey St, t (01) 874 0842. **Open** *Mon–Wed 10.30am–11.30pm, Thurs–Sat 10.30am–12.30am, Sun 12.30–11.*

Right opposite the Abbey Theatre, this is the classic pre-theatre drinking hole, lined with photographs of famous actors and celebrities. It's a great spot for a pint at any time of the day.

The Isaac Butt Bar K5
Store St, t (01) 855 5021, www.isaacs.ie. **Open** *daily: bar 11am–12.30am, restaurant noon–8pm.*

Attached to a hostel and hotel (see p.182), this bar is always lively and attracts a big backpacker contingent. Good live music.

Life I6
Irish Life Centre, Lower Abbey St, t (01) 878 1032. **Open** *daily 11pm–3am.*

This trendy, bright white bar has huge windows for people-watching, but is too far off the beaten track to get the crowds at night. It's best for a daytime pint or some very decent bar food, as it can feel a bit too empty at weekends.

Metropolitan J6
11 Eden Quay, t (01) 874 3535. **Open** *daily: bar 11am–12.30am, club until 3am.*

The Saturday night drum 'n' bass event run here by Bassbin is one of the best nights out in the city.

Morrison Bar/Lobo H6
Morrison Hotel, Upper Ormond Quay, t (01) 878 2999. **Open** *daily 8am–11.30pm (Fri and Sat until 12.30am).*

The Morrison's pared-down stylish minimalism draws Dublin's it-girls and celebs, and is the perfect spot for an elegant cocktail. The late-night bar, Lobo, is open until 3am at weekends. Dress the part or you won't get past the notoriously tough bouncers.

Nealon's I6
Capel St, t (01) 872 3247. **Open** *Mon–Wed 10.30am–11.30pm, Thurs–Sat 10.30am–12.30am, Sun 12.30–11.*

Nealon's has a fairly run-of-the mill bar on the ground floor, with lots of regulars and a good line in pub grub, and a smarter, stylish upstairs bar area for fashionable young locals.

The Oval I6
78 Middle Abbey St, t (01) 872 1259. **Open** *Mon–Wed 10.30am–11.30pm, Thurs–Sat 10.30am–12.30am, Sun 12.30–11.*

This traditional, slightly battered old bar is a popular meeting place for journalists. There's a pedestrian bar menu, but a very decent pint.

Patrick Conway I5
70 Parnell St, t (01) 873 2687. **Open** *Mon–Wed 10.30am–11.30pm, Thurs–Sat 10.30am–12.30am, Sun 12.30–11.*

Gorgeous Victorian decor and friendly bar staff, used to pulling pints for nervous fathers waiting for news from the Rotunda maternity hospital opposite,

Spi J6
3 Eden Quay, t (01) 874 6934. **Open** *daily 11am–12.30am.*

A hip bar which manages to be cool without trying too hard. Funky décor including a wacky wood and mirrored wall, a couple of sofas and great music downstairs in the cellar bar. Food is served in the restaurant upstairs.

The Vaults K6
Harbourmaster Place, IFSC, t (01) 605 4700, www.thevaults.ie. **Open** *daily 11am–12.30am, food until 8pm.*

Vast, fashionable bar in the cavernous vaults beneath Connolly train station, offering good food, DJs and the CineBar club on Monday nights with classic movie screenings.

Zanzibar I6
35 Lower Ormond Quay, t (01) 878 7212, www.capitalbars.com. **Open** *daily 4pm–2.30am.*

Another of the big superbars, this one has a slightly bewildering and overdone North African theme, but it's popular with fashionable young locals, and there's good live jazz on Sundays.

Northwest Dublin

The Cobblestones G5
77 North King St, t (01) 872 1799. **Open** *Mon–Wed 10.30am–11.30pm, Thurs–Sat 10.30am–12.30am, Sun 12.30–11.*

Battered, smoky (despite the new laws), labrythine pub with live performances (see p.118), and regular impromptu jams. Good range of beers from the nearby Dublin Brewing Company microbrewery, too. Highly recommended.

Dice Bar G6
Queen St, t (01) 872 8622. **Open** *Mon–Wed 10.30am–11.30pm, Thurs–Sat 10.30am–2.30am, Sun 12.30–11.*

This dark, black-painted, candle-lit bar is where Smithfield's young hipsters hang out, and has great DJs and friendly bouncers.

The Glimmer Man G5
*14–15 Stoneybatter, t (01) 677 9781. **Open** Mon–Wed 10.30am–11.30pm, Thurs–Sat 10.30am–12.30am, Sun 12.30–11.*

A good down-to-earth pub, well off the beaten track, but with a great beer garden in summer.

Hughes H6
*19 Chancery St, t (01) 872 6540. **Open** Mon–Wed 10.30am–11.30pm, Thurs–Sat 10.30am–12.30am, Sun 12.30–11.*

An excellent traditional bar tucked away down a back street behind the Four Courts. The impromptu Irish music sessions are excellent, and it's one of the city's best-kept secrets.

Pravda I6
*35 Lower Liffey St, t (01) 874 0076. **Open** Mon–Wed 10.30am–11.30pm, Thurs 10.30am–12.30pm, Fri–Sat 10.30am–2.30am, Sun 12.30–11.*

A big, smart, severely minimalist bar which has gone off the boil since first opening, but still draws a fashionable crowd. There's an incredible range of vodkas, if you've had enough black stuff.

Ryan's E6
*28 Parkgate St, t (01) 677 6097. **Open** Mon–Wed 10.30am–11.30pm, Thurs 10.30am–12.30pm, Fri–Sat 10.30am–2.30am, Sun 12.30–11.*

A traditional pub serving decent grub, which is handy for Phoenix Park, but is most famous for its pint of Guinness – the best in the city, say its fans.

Voodoo Lounge G6
*39 Arran Quay, t (01) 873 6013. **Open** Mon–Wed noon–12.30am, Thurs–Sat noon–2am, Sun noon–1am.*

A huge, eccentrically decorated bar, with strange murals, big candle-lit tables, guest DJs and a young, boho-chic crowd.

Outside the Centre: Dublin Suburbs

Brown's Barn OFF MAPS
*City West Bridge, Naas Rd, t (01) 464 0930, www.brownsbarn.ie. **Open** Mon–Wed 10.30am–12.30am, Thurs–Sat 12.30pm–1.30am, Sun 12.30–midnight.*

A handsomely restored 17th-century building houses this excellent bar and moderately priced restaurant. The bar is in a light-filled courtyard, and there's a beer garden in summer. Come during the week if you can, as it's always packed out at weekends.

Kavanagh's OFF MAPS
*1 Prospect Sq, Glasnevin Cemetery; no phone. **Open** Mon–Wed 10am–11.30pm, Thurs–Sat 10am–12.30am, Sun noon–11.*

Time has stood still in this wonderful ancient bar, which is better known as The Gravediggers and hasn't changed in centuries. Sit down on an old wooden bench and quietly mull the world over your pint.

Slattery's OFF MAPS
*217 Rathmines Rd, t (01) 497 2052. **Open** Mon–Wed 10am–11.30pm, Thurs–Sat 10am–12.30am, Sun noon–11.*

This is a great, old-fashioned bar full of 'hurleyheads' and a lively crowd of locals. It's well worth the trek out of town (take bus 14, 15, or 83). Great live music ranging from jazz to traditional in the upstairs room.

Rumm's OFF MAPS
*Shelbourne Rd, t (01) 667 6422. **Open** Mon–Wed 10am–11.30pm, Thurs–Sat 10am–12.30am, Sun noon–11.*

A laid-back traditional pub close to the RDS serving good food and offering occasional live traditional music.

Outside the Centre: Dublin Bay

Abbey Tavern OFF MAPS
*Howth, t (01) 839 0307, www.abbeytavern.ie. **Open** daily: bar 10.30am–12.30am, restaurant Mon–Sat 7pm–12.30am.*

A good old-fashioned pub, which often hosts live music and runs an equally old-fashioned restaurant (see p.200).

Duffy's OFF MAPS
*Main St, Malahide, t (01) 845 0735. **Open** Mon–Wed 10.30am–11.30pm, Thurs–Sat 10.30am–12.30am, Sun 12.30–11.*

A classic, old-fashioned seaside pub, complete with tacky mural depicting the harbour. Decent pub grub.

In OFF MAPS
*115–116 Coliemore Rd, Dalkey, t (01) 275 0007, www.indalkey.ie. **Open** Mon–Wed 11am–11.30pm, Thurs–Sat 11am–1.30am.*

A cool black-and-white minimalist bar with comfy sofas, good Asian-influenced food and an upmarket clientele.

The Queens OFF MAPS
*12 Castle St, Dalkey, t (01) 285 4569. **Open** daily noon–12.30am.*

A famous old pub, which contains a couple of good restaurants (see p.201).

Clubs
Southeast Dublin

Coyote Lounge J6
*21 D'Olier St, t (01) 671 2089, www.capitalbars.com. **Open** Wed–Sat 9pm–3am, Sun 9pm–late.*

Another big superbar, with the usual mix of modern, stylish surroundings and DJ nights.

D Two I8
*Harcourt Hotel, 60 Harcourt St, t (01) 478 3677. **Open** daily 9pm–3am.*

This cheerful, middle-of-the-road club offers a wide variety of dance music.

The Gaiety Theatre I7
*South King St, t (01) 679 5622, www.gaietytheatre.com. **Open** Fri–Sat 11.15pm–4.15am.*

This gorgeous old theatre is a great venue for weekend club nights, with live bands and DJs on the several different levels.

International Bar I7
*23 Wicklow Street, t (01) 677 9250. **Open** Mon–Thurs 10.30am–*

11.30pm, Fri–Sat 10.30am–12.30am, Sun noon–11.

An excellent, much-celebrated venue, with a traditional bar and separate areas for DJs, live music, comedy nights and other events.

Lillie's Bordello J7
Adam Court, off Grafton Street, t (01) 679 9204. Open Mon–Sat 11.30 till late.

The longest established of Dublin's currently fashionable clubs, ostentatiously frequented by models, visiting rock stars and other beautiful people. Wide-ranging in age. Be prepared to queue, and dress the part or you won't get past the sniffy doormen: this is, in fact, a private members' club and entry of non-members is entirely at the management's discretion. Jazz on Sunday nights.

Mono I8
26 Wexford St, t (01) 478 0766. Open daily 10.30pm–2.30am.

A huge, fashionable venue popular with students, with top DJs playing a wide range of music and plenty of big sofas for chilling.

Pod I8
35 Harcourt St, t (01) 478 0166, www.pod.ie. Open Wed–Sat 11pm–2.30am.

Serious dance music for late 20- and 30-something posers, tucked beside an old train station. They also run Red Box next door.

The Red Box I8
35 Harcourt Street, t (01) 478 0166. Open Wed–Sat 11pm–2.30am.

Huge dancefloor with house, techno and disco nights.

Renard's J7
Setanta Centre, 35 Frederick St South, t (01) 677 5876. Open daily 9pm–3am.

Once you get beyond the strict bouncers here, you might wonder what all the fuss was about, but the sweaty, crammed dance floor remains a favourite with media types and fashionistas. If the club nights don't appeal, it has live jazz and blues on Mondays to Wednesdays.

Ri Ra I7
Dame Court, t (01) 677 4835. Open Thurs–Sun 11.15pm–3am.

Funky, unpretentious and good for late-night drinking; two floors of music plus a quieter bar upstairs. Strictly Handbag on Mondays is a classic night out.

Spy/Wax Basement I7
Powerscourt Townhouse Centre, Clarendon St, t (01) 677 0067, www.spydublin.com. Open Mon–Sat 9pm–3am.

A big, ultra-cool space over three levels, with several bars and dance floors. The crowd dress to impress, but it's not too stuck-up to be fun.

The Sugar Club J8
8 Leeson St Lower, t (01) 678 7188, www.thesugarclub.com. Open Wed 7.30pm–2am, Thurs–Sun 8.30pm–2am; serving until 3am.

Another favourite with the fashion pack, the Sugar Club has a strict dress code and high admission prices. It's one of the most slickly designed clubs in the city, and presents everything from movie screenings to comedy.

Southwest Dublin and Temple Bar

Boomerang Nightclub I6
Downstairs from Bob's Bar, Temple Bar, t (01) 612 9200. Open Wed–Sat 11.30pm–late.

Chart music for party crowds.

Club M I6
Cope St, Temple Bar, t (01) 671 5622, www.clubm.ie. Open Mon–Thurs 11pm–2.30am, Fri–Sat 10pm–2.30am, Sun 10.30pm–1am.

Another run-of-the-mill club.

The Kitchen I6
East Essex St, Temple Bar, t (01) 677 6635, www.the-kitchen.com. Open daily 11.15pm–2.45am.

U2-owned club, hot, hip and friendly with an open-house music policy – which means anything from hardcore house and techno to drum 'n' bass.

Shelter/Vicar Street G7
58–59 Thomas St West, t (01) 454 6656, www.vicarstreet.com. Open Fri–Sat 11pm–3am.

Excellent club nights at the huge Vicar Street venue, which also offers live music and comedy.

Switch I6
Eustace St, Temple Bar, t (01) 668 2504. Open daily 11pm–3am.

For die-hard dance fans, tiny, sweaty Switch offers some of the best club nights in the city.

Temple Bar Music Centre I6
Curved St, Temple Bar, t (01) 670 9202, www.tbmc.ie. Open daily 9.30pm–2.30am.

This big venue has good club nights which follow live gigs. Check to see what's coming up but regular events include Lowe Phat on Tuesdays, the student night Blitz on Wednesdays, and Screamadelica on Thursdays.

Viperoom J6
5 Aston Quay, Temple Bar, t (01) 672 5566/7. Open daily 8pm–3.30am.

A cool bar with live jazz, salsa and R&B, and a big club serving up mainly chart and dance music.

Northeast Dublin

Spirit I6
44–47 The Lotts, t (01) 877 9999.

One of the newest of Dublin's hip clubs – with a VIP room and a VVIP room.

Temple Theatre I4
Temple St North, t (01) 874 5088, www.templetheatre.ie. Open Fri–Sat 10pm–3am.

A cool space in a converted church. Young, hip and energetic.

Outside the Centre: Dublin Suburbs

Whelans I8
25 Wexford St, t (01) 478 0766, www.whelanslive.com. Open Mon–Tues 11am–11.30pm, Wed 11am–1.30am, Thurs–Sat 11am–2.30am, Sun noon–1am.

Music almost every night: indie, rock, bluegrass, country and some styles that you never dreamed existed.

Entertainment

Music 211
Theatre 212
Dance 213
Comedy 213
Cinema 213

Dublin's dramatic tradition is legendary, and theatre is thriving. The Dublin Theatre Festival is one of the biggest and best-known in Europe, attracting huge crowds, and the Fringe Festival, which runs at the same time, displays some exciting emerging talents. Dublin is a fantastic city for live music – whether it's the latest European dance act, or a jam session with Irish musicians in a traditional pub. The listings guides (*InDublin* and *Hot Press*, available from most newsagents, or the freebie *The Event Guide*, available in most city centre bars and cafés) are the best sources of information.

Buying Tickets

The tourist information centre on Suffolk Street has a ticket-booking service, or you can contact box offices directly. The counter of Ticket Master (www.ticketmaster.ie) in the HMV music store on Grafton Street sells tickets for the big pop concerts, as well as for performances at most of the major theatres. Book well in advance for the big events.

Music

Pop, Rock and Jazz

There are always big-name pop and **rock** bands headlining at the annual Green Energy Festival in May, which takes place at Dublin Castle and other venues across the city. Whelan's is the classic venue for a whole range of acts, with Vicar Street and Shelter also offering a great selection of bands. Many bars offer **jazz**, particularly on Sundays.

Eamonn Doran's I6
3A Crown Alley, **t** *(01) 679 9114*,
www.eamonndorans.com.
Live traditional music nightly, plus rock and pop gigs downstairs.

International Bar I7
23 Wicklow St, **t** *(01) 677 9250*.
An old-fashioned bar with mainly jazz, blues and soul.

Irish Film Centre I7
6 Eustace St, **t** *(01) 679 3477*.
Mellow jazz and blues on Friday and Saturday nights.

McDaid's I7
3 Harry St, **t** *(01) 679 4395*.
Blues at this classic literary pub.

Mother Redcaps D7
Back Lane, **t** *(01) 453 8306*.
A relaxed pub with traditional music (Tues, Wed & Sun).

The Music Room J6
The Firestone, Abbey St Lower,
www.musicroomdublin.cjb.net.
Eclectic pub venue.

Olympia I7
72 Dame St, **t** *(01) 677 7744*.
A delightful former music hall.

The Point OFF MAPS
East Link Bridge, North Quay, **t** *(01) 836 6777*.
A huge arena on the outskirts.

J.J. Smyth's I8
12 Aungier St, **t** *(01) 475 2565*.
Relaxed pub for jazz and blues.

Temple Bar Music Centre I6
Curved St, Temple Bar, **t** *(01) 670 9202*, *www.tbmc.ie*.
Anything and everything.

Vicar Street/Shelter G7
58–59 Thomas St, **t** *(01) 454 6656*,
www.vicarstreet.com.
Two of the best venues for live gigs, offering everything from gipsy folk to rock bands and DJs.

The Village I8
25 Wexford St, **t** *(01) 478 0766*.
Another excellent live venue.

Whelan's I8
26 Wexford St, **t** *(01) 475 8555*,
www.whelanslive.com.
A Dublin musical institution.

Traditional Music

Baggot Inn K8
142 Lwr Baggot St, **t** *(01) 676 1430*.
Regular live sessions.

Brazen Head G7
20 Lower Bridge St, **t** *(01) 679 5186*,
www.brazenhead.com.
Live traditional music nightly in Dublin's oldest pub.

The Cobblestone G5
77 North King St, **t** *(01) 872 1799*.
Battered, smoky, labyrinthine pub with live performances.

Comhaltas Ceoltoiri Eireann
OFF MAPS
35 Belgrave Sq, Monkstown, **t** *(01) 280 0295*, *www.comhaltas.com*.
One of the best places to hear authentic Irish music; out of town but well worth the easy trip on the DART. This organization is dedicated to the promotion of Irish culture. The Friday night *ceili* gives visitors a chance to join in with the set-dances.

Fitzsimons of Temple Bar I6
Fitzsimon Hotel, East Essex St,
t *(01) 677 9315*, *www.fitzsimons hotel.com*.
Irish music packaged for tourists, but not a bad night out.

Harcourt Hotel I8
60 Harcourt St, **t** *(01) 478 3677*.
Sessions every night.

Hughes H6
19 Chancery St, **t** *(01) 872 6540*.
Regular jam sessions.

Mother Redcaps D7
Back Lane, beside Tailors' Guildhall, Christchurch, **t** *(01) 453 8306*.
Folk and traditional music.

O'Donoghue's K8
15 Merrion Row, **t** *(01) 660 1794*,
www.odonoghues.ie.
One of the city's original traditional music venues – the Dubliners started out here.

The Oliver St John Gogarty I6
Fleet St, Temple Bar, **t** *(01) 671 1822*,
www.gogartys.ie.
Live music in Temple Bar.

O'Shea's Merchants Bar G7
12 Lower Bridge St, **t** *(01) 679 3797*.
This big, classic pub offers traditional Irish and ballad music.

Rumm's M8
Shelbourne Rd, **t** *(01) 667 6422*.
Traditional music nightly.

Slattery's OFF MAPS
217 Rathmines Rd, **t** *(01) 497 2052*.
Regular gigs and sessions in an enjoyable and raucous pub.

The Temple Bar I6
47 Temple Bar, **t** *(01) 672 5287*.
Occasional traditional sessions.

Whelan's I8
26 Wexford St, **t** *(01) 475 8555*.
Excellent venue staging some of the best traditional Irish bands.

Classical and Opera

Handel's *Messiah* was famously first performed in Dublin, an event which is re-enacted annually on Fishamble Street. **Classical music** may not enjoy the prominence of other performing arts in Ireland, but there is always plenty going on. The National Concert Hall is the main venue, but you can also enjoy lunchtime concerts in the magnificent surroundings of the city's cathedrals. The Gaiety Theatre features **opera**, and Wexford stages an opera festival every October.

Bank of Ireland Arts Centre J6
Foster Place, t (01) 671 1488.
Regular classical music concerts.

Gaiety Theatre I7
South King Street, t (01) 677 1717, www.gaietytheatre.com.
Dublin's main opera venue.

Hugh Lane Gallery I4
Charlemont House, Parnell Sq North, t (01) 874 1903, www.hughlane.ie.
Regular lunchtime concerts.

The National Concert Hall J8
Earlsfort Terrace, t (01) 475 1666, www.nch.ie.
Home of the National Symphony Orchestra.

RDS Concert Hall OFF MAPS
RDS Society Showgrounds, Ballsbridge, t (01) 668 0866.
A large concert hall.

Churches Hosting Regular Concerts

Christchurch Cathedral
t (01) 677 8099, www.cccdub.ie.

St Mary's Pro-Cathedral
t (01) 874 5441, www.procathedral.ie.

St Patrick's Cathedral
t (01) 475 4817, www.stpatrickscathedral.ie.

St Stephen's Church
t (01) 288 0663.

Trinity College Chapel
t (01) 608 2320, www.tcd.ie.

Temple Bar Music Centre I6
Curved St, Temple Bar, t (01) 670 9202, www.tbmc.ie.
Home of the touring Opera Theatre Company.

Theatre

Ireland has produced some stellar **theatrical** talent, with a list of playwrights taking in Oscar Wilde, Sean O'Casey, J.M. Synge, Samuel Beckett, Brendan Behan and newer talents such as Conor McPherson and Martin McDonagh. Dublin's theatrical scene remains vibrant, with something to suit all tastes.

Abbey Theatre J6
Lower Abbey St, t (01) 878 7222, booking line t (01) 456 9569.
The famous theatre founded by Lady Gregory and W.B. Yeats. The old building burned down and has been replaced by an uncompromisingly modern version. The Abbey is best known for the Irish classics, but the Peacock Theatre, in the same premises, shows the work of contemporary playwrights. Make sure you book ahead.

Andrew's Lane Theatre I7
12 St Andrews Lane, t (01) 679 5720.
Mainstream fare, with more adventurous pieces in the studio.

Bank of Ireland Arts Centre J6
Foster Place, t (01) 671 1488.
A variety of performances, including a good programme of lunchtime events.

City Arts Centre K6
23 Moss St, t (01) 677 0643, www.cityartscentre.ie.
Cutting-edge fare.

Civic Theatre OFF MAPS
The Square, Tallaght, t (01) 462 7477, www.civictheatre.ie.
A wide-ranging programme of drama, comedy and musicals.

Crypt Arts Theatre I7
Chapel Royal, Dublin Castle, t (01) 671 3387, www.cryptartscentre.org.
Drama and multimedia events by new artists.

Focus Theatre K9
6 Pembroke Place, off Pembroke St, t (01) 676 3071.
Challenging productions of classic and contemporary theatre.

Gaiety Theatre I7
South King St, t (01) 677 1717, www.gaietytheatre.com.
A splendid, tiered Victorian theatre, showing traditional plays.

Gate Theatre I5
1 Cavendish Row, t (01) 874 4045.
International and classic drama.

Helix OFF MAPS
DCU, Collins Ave, Glasnevin, t (01) 700 0000, www.thehelix.ie.
A big, glassy theatre in Dublin College University.

Olympia Theatre I7
72 Dame St, t (01) 677 7744.
A delightfully old-fashioned theatre, with drama, ballet, and musicals as well as regular late night concerts.

Pavilion Theatre OFF MAPS
Dún Laoghaire, t (01) 231 2929, www.paviliontheatre.ie.
A community theatre with a varied line-up of theatre, dance, comedy and music. Schedules tally with the DART back to Dublin city centre.

The Point OFF MAPS
East Link Bridge, North Quay, t (01) 836 6777.
Stages big musicals and other crowd-pleasers.

Project Arts Theatre I6
39 East Essex St, Temple Bar, t (01) 679 6622, booking t 1800 260 027, www.project.ie.
Some of the most stimulating experimental theatre in Dublin, with art exhibitions alongside.

Samuel Beckett Centre J6
Trinity College, t (01) 608 2461, www.tcd.ie/drama.
This theatre is used for student performances, and is also often rented by independent theatre companies.

SFX City Theatre J3
23 Upper Sherrard St, t (01) 855 4673, www.sfx.ie.
Drama, comedy and dance.

Tivoli Theatre H7
Francis St, *t (01) 453 5998*.
Stages usually excellent musicals and plays.

Dance

Classical **ballet** performances take place in many of Dublin's theatres, including the Olympia, Gaiety, National Concert Hall and Helix. Unfortunately, Arts Council funding has been slashed for many of Ireland's ballet companies, and none has its own home. The **contemporary dance** scene is thriving, with two excellent dance theatres offering constantly challenging work.

Dance Theatre of Ireland
OFF MAPS
Bloomfields Centre, Lower George's St, Dún Laoghaire, t (01) 280 3455, www.dancetheatreireland.com.
This state-of-the-art centre for dance is home to one of Ireland's most exciting contemporary dance companies, and also runs an extensive programme of dance classes and courses for adults and young people.

Irish Modern Dance Theatre J3
23 Upper Sherrard St, t (01) 874 9616, www.irishmoderndancetheatre.com.
Another of Ireland's most innovative dance companies, the IMDT always offers cutting-edge theatre.

Dance Classes

A wide variety of dance classes are listed in the Noticeboard section of *InDublin* and in the Listings section of *The Event Guide*. The salsa nights at the Gaiety on Fridays (*see opposite*) are excellent.

B-Famous Studios
5 Wolfe Tone St, t (01) 878 9070. All kinds of dance classes, including salsa, flamenco and belly-dancing.

Morosini-Whelan School of Dancing
26 Parnell St, t (01) 830 3613. Salsa, Argentine tango and ballroom dancing.

Comedy

As well as these venues, see The Sugar Club (see p.xxx) and Spirit (see p.xxx) which both run regular **comedy** nights, and check listings for one-off events.

Comedy Cellar at International Bar I7
23 Wicklow St, t (01) 677 9250.
This is a Dublin institution, co-founded by Ardal O'Hanlon and still going strong. Every Wednesday night at 9pm.

Ha'penny Bridge Inn I6
42 Wellington Quay, t (01) 677 0616.
A popular comedy venue with a wide range of events nightly.

Irish Film Centre I7
6 Eustace St, t (01) 679 3477.
The Comic Strip – comedy from local and international acts – takes place every Saturday night.

Laughter Lounge J6
4–6 Eden Quay, t 1800 266 399, www.laughterlounge.com.
Dedicated comedy club, with shows Thurs–Sat at 9pm.

Cinema

Irish **cinema** has had a higher profile over the last few decades, with the success of directors such as Neil Jordan, and film stars such as Liam Neeson and Colin Farrell. The city regularly features in movies, from John Huston's *The Dead*, based on Joyce's short story, to *Michael Collins*, *The Commitments*, *In the Name of the Father* (filmed in Kilmainham Gaol) and *Nora* (which featured Ewan McGregor as James Joyce). By contrast, the domestic film industry is very small, but occasionally throws out some great films, such as Conor McPherson's *Saltwater* and the quirky, low-budget thriller *Dead Bodies*, a surprise box-office hit in 2003.

Going to the cinema is very popular in Dublin (the Irish attend the cinema more frequently than any other Europeans), but most of the cinemas are generic multiplexes in the city suburbs. A few delightfully old-fashioned stalwarts remain in the city centre, and the excellent Irish Film Centre, in Temple Bar, is a great place to find out what's going on in Irish cinema. Look out for the midweek cinema club at The Sugar Club (*see* p.209), one of the slickest nightclubs in Dublin, and CineBar nights at the Vaults bar (*see* p.207). Cinema listings are published daily in most newspapers, or you can get info from *Hot Press*, the (free) *Event Guide* and *The Dubliner*.

Classic Cinema G10
Harold's Cross Rd, t (01) 492 3699.
Long-running Friday-night screening of the *Rocky Horror Picture Show*, complete with crowd in fancy dress, plus theme nights once a month.

Irish Film Centre I7
6 Eustace St, Temple Bar, t (01) 679 3477.
Foreign and art-house releases, plus regular seasons featuring Irish directors. The IFC organizes the excellent International Film Festival in spring. Great café and bookshop, too.

Savoy Cinema I5
16–17 Upper O'Connell St, t (01) 874 6000.
A wonderful old-fashioned cinema with plenty of atmosphere and a huge screen. It shows the staple imports from Hollywood and elsewhere.

Screen Cinema J6
D'Olier St, t (01) 672 5500.
This battered little cinema shows some mainstream first-runs, along with a good selection of independent and less commercial films.

UGC Cinemas J5
Parnell St, t (01) 872 8444.
One of the most central of the big multiplexes, showing the usual Hollywood releases.

Shopping

Antiques 215
Auctioneers 215
Books 215
Children's Clothes and Toys 215
Commercial Art Galleries 216
Crafts 216
Department Stores 216
Fashion and Accessories 216
Food and Drink 217
Hair and Beauty 217
Markets 218
Music 218
Shopping Centres 218

Grafton Street is Dublin's most popular **shopping** street, home to the excellent department store Brown Thomas and several leading UK and Irish chains. There are more unusual shops on fashionable South William Street as well as the shopping mecca of the Powerscourt Townhouse, an elegant shopping centre in an 18th-century mansion. Dublin has become increasingly fashionable in the last decade or so, and you'll have no trouble finding all the usual international designer labels, plus some excellent and very imaginative Irish designers (check out the Design Centre in the Powerscourt Townhouse). North of the river, Henry Street has been pedestrianized and has a string of department stores and plenty more chain stores. Just off it is the earthy, atmospheric Moore Street market, which, even if you aren't interested in the slightly battered fruit and veg on offer, is worth a look for a taste of last-disappearing old Dublin. Another good place to get a sense of pre-boom Dublin without the gloss is the antique and junk shops that line Francis Street. Dublin's museum shops are excellent, and offer a wonderful range of books, gifts and prints: the shops at the National Gallery, IMMA, the Chester Beatty Library and the Dublin Writers Museum deserve a special mention.

Good buys have traditionally included tweeds and woollen sweaters as well as Waterford crystal, but you can also pick up some stylish, contemporary art, jewellery and other crafts at places like the excellent DESIGNyard in Temple Bar. Kitsch-lovers will be in heaven, as countless souvenir shops are stuffed with leprechaun snow-shakers, glow-in-the-dark shamrocks and neon-lit religious figures.

Most shops in Dublin are open Monday to Saturday 9am–5pm, although several have later opening hours on Thursday nights, and some others will also be open on Sunday afternoons. If you live outside the European Union, you qualify for a VAT refund on individual purchases over 990: fill out a VAT form when making your purchase and present it at Customs when you leave to claim the refund.

Antiques

The smartest and most expensive antiques shops are clustered around South Anne St, Molesworth St and Kildare St. Francis St in the Liberties is where to go to find bargains, with lots of individual antique shops and a battered antiques arcade.

Alexander Antiques J7
16 Molesworth St, t (01) 679 1548.
One of the most prestigious antique galleries on this elegant street. Come only if you have very deep pockets.

Delfi Antiques I7
Powerscourt Townhouse Centre, South William St, t (01) 679 0331.
This elegant shop specializes in fine 19th-century Irish, English and European porcelain, jewellery and silver.

Fleury Antiques H7
57 Francis St, t (01) 473 0878.
One of many good spots for a rummage along this street.

Auctioneers

De Vere's Art Auctions J7
35 Kildare St, t (01) 676 8300.
Auctions mostly Irish paintings.

Herman and Wilkinson I10
161 Lower Rathmines Rd, t (01) 497 2245.
Fortnightly auctions of silver, paintings and furniture.

Books

Cathach Books J7
10 Duke St, t (01) 671 8676.
A large independent bookseller which specializes in rare first editions and antique maps.

Dublin Writers Museum I4
18 Parnell Sq, t (01) 872 2077.
The museum shop has an excellent selection of books by and about Irish authors.

Eason & Son J6
Lower O'Connell Street, t (01) 873 3811.
The biggest Irish chain of booksellers, with several other branches in the city. This one also has a café, and is one of the biggest newsagents in Dublin, with a huge range of magazines and newspapers (including international titles).

Fred Hanna's J7
28–29 Nassau St, t (01) 677 1255, www.hannas.ie.
Independent bookseller.

Greene's Bookshop K7
16 Clare St, t (01) 676 2554, www.greenesbookshop.com.
One of the prettiest bookshops in the city, with an elegant wrought-iron canopy. It sells new and secondhand books, including a good selection of rare and out-of-print books.

Hodges Figgis J7
57 Dawson St, t (01) 677 4754.
Dublin's oldest bookstore, with an excellent coffee shop and an excellent range of titles, including a good selection of books relating to Dublin and Ireland.

Waterstone's J7
7 Dawson St, t (01) 679 1415.
The biggest branch of the well-known British chain.

Winding Stair Books I6
40 Lower Ormond Quay, t (01) 873 3292.
Has an excellent café and three floors of secondhand books, plus great river views.

Children's Clothes and Toys

Gymboree J7
75 Grafton St, t (01) 670 0331, www.gymboree.com.
An outpost of the smart childrenswear chain, with quality

mid-priced clothes in bright, fun fabrics.

Rainbow Crafts J7
5 Westbury Hotel Mall, Grafton St, t (01) 677 7632, www.teddybears-dolls.com.

A delightfully old-fashioned shop, with rocking horses, teddy-bears and wooden toys.

Commercial Art Galleries

ArtSelect I7
Meeting House Sq, Temple Bar, t (01) 635 1046, www.artselect.ie.

Offers an exciting and varied range of affordable art from Irish and international artists, including paintings, photography, sculpture, ceramics, prints and glass.

Hallward Gallery K8
65 Merrion Sq, t (01) 662 1482.

This gallery exhibits established and emerging Irish artists.

Kerlin Gallery J7
Anne's Lane, off South Anne St, t (01) 670 9093.

An elegant gallery showing established and new artists.

Oriel Gallery K7
17 Clare St, t (01) 676 3410, www.theoriel.com.

Mostly traditional and figurative early 20th-century works.

Crafts

Avoca J7
11–13 Suffolk St, t (01) 677 4215.

A beautiful range of contemporary Irish fashion, kidswear, beautiful blankets, shawls and throws, jewellery, ceramics, food and toys. There's a great café, too (see p.190).

Crafts Council of Ireland I6
12 Essex St, Temple Bar, t (01) 679 7368.

Contemporary Irish crafts from young designers.

DESIGNyard I6
12 East Essex St, Temple Bar, t (01) 677 8467.

This sleek modern gallery is set in a converted warehouse, and has a wide range of jewellery from artists from all over the world, plus an upper floor dedicated to contemporary Irish ceramics, glass, wood, textiles and furniture.

Irish Georgian Society K8
74 Merrion Sq, t (01) 676 7053, www.irishgeorgiansociety.org.

A good selection of gifts, including coffee-table books, placemats, lace, jewellery and knick knacks.

The Kilkenny Shop J7
5–6 Nassau St, t (01) 677 7066.

This is where to find sturdy Irish tweeds, thick sweaters, Waterford crystal and lots of Irish glass, ceramics, jewellery and much more. It's all classic stuff, so don't expect to find anything cutting-edge.

Tower Craft Design Centre L7
Pearse St, t (01) 677 5655.

Near the Waterways Visitor Centre, this has more than 35 separate crafts shops in a converted 19th-century factory. You'll find everything from glass, jewellery, woodcarving and hand-painted silks to textiles, prints and pottery.

Department Stores

Arnotts I5
12 Henry St, t (01) 872 1111.

A big, chaotic department store with everything from fashion and accessories to sports goods and things for the home. Prices are very reasonable.

Brown Thomas J7
88–95 Grafton St, t (01) 605 6666.

Dublin's best and most exclusive department store, selling a particularly good range of fashion and accessories from international and Irish names. It always carries Irish designer labels such as Paul Costelloe, Louise Kennedy, John Rocha and Michaelina Stacpoole.

Clery's J6
O'Connell St, t (01) 878 6000.

This famous, old-fashioned department store is good for classic fashion, things for the home and furniture, and has a useful gift section.

Dunnes Stores J8
St Stephens Green Shopping Centre, t (01) 478 0188.

A branch of the big Irish chain, with cheap groceries, household goods and fashion.

Marks & Spencer J7
15–20 Grafton St, t (01) 679 7855.

A big branch of the famous British department store, with good-quality fashion, accessories and household goods and an excellent grocery department. It also has a bureau de change, which offers good rates and doesn't charge commission.

Fashion and Accessories

Lots of the big UK fashion chains, including Karen Millen, Next, French Connection, Oasis, Principles and Marks & Spencer, can be found in the main shopping centres (*see* p.218) and along Grafton Street.

Avoca J7
11–13 Suffolk St, t (01) 677 4215.

Beautiful clothes and accessories from Irish designers, as well as gifts, food, ceramics. Great café, too.

Alias Tom J7
Duke Street, t (01) 671 5443.

Probably the most popular men's designer store, with cool designs at pretty high prices.

A-Wear J7
26 Grafton St, t (01) 671 7200, www.a-wear.ie. Branch at Henry St.

Young, funky, affordable fashion, with a diffusion range by Quin and Donnelly and bargain racks in the basement.

Acquiesce J7
31 South Anne St, t (01) 671 9433.

Elegant, sharply tailored women's clothing from Irish, British and European designers.

An Táin I6
13 Temple Bar, **t (01) 679 0523**.
Beautiful Irish fabrics in fashionable designs, including handmade sweaters and jackets.

BT2 J7
25 Grafton St, **t (01) 605 6666**.
An outpost of the Brown Thomas department store, this just sells fashion from the likes of Armani, DKNY and Miu Miu.

Boutique Homme J7
2 South Anne St, **t (01) 671 5122**.
Expensive men's designer clothing. Gorgeous but pricey.

The Blarney Woollen Mills J7
21–23 Nassau St, **t (01) 671 0068**.
Traditional Irish tweeds and woollen jumpers. Classic designs in good-quality fabrics.

Cleo J8
18 Kildare St, a little off Nassau St, **t (01) 676 1421**, www.cleo-ltd.com.
Gorgeous wools and tweeds in stylish designs.

Design Centre I7
Powerscourt Townhouse Centre, 59 South William St, **t (01) 679 4144**.
The best place to find Irish designer clothing, including fashion by Louise Kennedy and Sharon Hoey. It has men's and women's wear, along with a great selection of shoes. Prices are high, but there's always a bargain to be had during the sales.

Emma Stewart-Liberty I7
Powerscourt Townhouse Centre, 59 South William St, **t (01) 679 1603**.
Fabulous boutique selling original jewellery designs.

Hobo I7
13 Trinity St, **t (01) 679 1641**, www.hobocorp.com.
Hip, affordable streetwear from modern Irish designers.

Jenny Vander I7
50 Drury St, opposite the George's St Arcade, **t (01) 677 0406**.
One of the best for vintage clothing, with frocks, fabulous jewellery, beaded bags, evening shoes and silk lingerie.

Kennedy McSharry J7
39 Nassau St, **t (01) 677 8770**.
Beautifully tailored suits in Donegal tweed.

Louis Copeland J7
Wicklow St, **t (01) 872 1600**.
A very fancy tailors which makes some of the finest suits in Europe.

Platform I7
50 South William St, **t (01) 677 7380, platform@indigo.ie**.
Beautiful, floaty fashionable designs in a gorgeous shop. Highly recommended.

Se Si Progressive I6
11 Fownes St, Temple Bar. **t (01) 677 4779**.
Worth a visit for its inexpensive clubby gear, with new, young designer talent.

TK Maxx I8
St Stephens Green Shopping Centre, **t (01) 475 7080**.
Designer labels at sale price; rummage hard.

Zerep J7
57 Grafton St, **t (01) 677 8320**.
Wild and wacky fashionable footwear at affordable prices.

Food and Drink

Aya I7
Clarendon St, **t (01) 677 1544**.
Linked to a trendy noodle bar, Aya also has a great Asian deli.

Bretzel Kosher Bakery I9
1a Lennox St, **t (01) 475 2724**.
A famous kosher bakery which serves up tasty treats such as walnut loaves and challah – shiny twisted plaits of bread.

Butler's J7
51a Grafton St, **t (01) 671 0599**.
Delicious Irish chocolates.

Caviston's I6
Epicurean Food Hall, Liffey St Lower, **t (01) 878 2289**.
A fabulous deli selling oysters and other freshly caught fish, Irish cheeses and smoked salmon.

Down to Earth I7
73 South Great Georges St, **t (01) 671 9702**.
Reliable health food store.

Dublin Brewing Company G5
141–146 North King St, **t (01) 872 8622**, www.dublinbrewing.com.
An excellent microbrewery with on-site shop.

La Maison des Gourmets I7
15 Castle Market, **t (01) 672 7258**.
Delicious French pastries, tarts, croissants and other goodies.

Leonidas J7
Royal Hibernian Way, off Dawson St, **t (01) 679 5915**.
Superb Belgian chocolates.

Magill's I7
14 Clarendon St, **t (01) 671 3830**.
A wonderful old-fashioned deli for bread, cheese and charcuterie.

Mitchell & Son J8
21 Kildare St, **t (01) 676 0766**.
One of best wine merchants in the city, also with a great range of Irish whiskeys.

Panem I6
Ha'penny Bridge House, 21 Ormond Quay Lower, **t (01) 872 8510**.
Among the tastiest breads, muffins, croissants and other baked goodies in the city. It also has a tiny café (see p.198).

Sheridan's Cheesemongers J7
South Anne St, **t (01) 679 3143**.
Perhaps the finest cheese selection in the city, with a huge array from Ireland and Europe. Sheridan's supplies most of the smartest restaurants, and also sells a fabulous array of chutneys and jams which make great presents.

Hair and Beauty

Thérapie J7
8–9 Molesworth St, **t (01) 472 1222**.
A chic, minimalist and exclusive spa, offering holistic health and beauty treatments including massages and facials. It uses products by Eve Lom, Elemis and Anne Sémonin, among others.

Toni and Guy I7
53 Dame St, **t (01) 670 8745**.
A branch of the popular hairdressing chain; stylish haircuts at reasonable prices.

Shopping

Markets

Art Market K7
Merrion Sq.
Local painters display their works every weekend across the street from the National Gallery. The quality varies wildly, with some horrible sentimental scenes rubbing shoulders with some exceptional and interesting work.

Camden Street Food Market I9
Camden St.
A daily market for cheap fruit, vegetables and flowers.

Cow's Lane Natural Food Market I6
Temple Bar.
Every Saturday, a range of food stalls sell certified organic fruit, freshly caught fish, cheeses, breads and preserves.

Georges Arcade I7
South Great Georges St.
A pretty, wrought-iron-covered market, with a great range of stalls selling everything from olives (which are generally considered the best in the city) to fashion, incense, crafts, fresh bread and much more.

Moore Street Market I5
Moore St.
This is the place for fruit and vegetables, although some of the produce is rather suspect, so watch out for the rotten ones. It is also a good place to observe Dublin life. Here the warmly wrapped pram people wait with their wares: in place of a gurgling infant, veteran market-traders, usually women, use prams to carry jewellery, fish, turf, concrete blocks, flowers and evening newspapers. You can buy their vegetables, fruit and the most gaudy of Taiwanese toys. The 'perambulators' are not strictly allowed, as they do not pay rent, unlike the properly established stands; so if the boys in blue appear, they melt away into the crowds. Some of the prams are as old as 70 years and still going strong.

Mother Redcap's Market H7
Back Lane near Christchurch.
Pottery, books and bric-a-brac. Check out The Gallic Kitchen, for delicious pies and cakes (see p.195).

Temple Bar Book Market I6
Temple Bar Sq.
A popular book market, open Saturday and Sunday 10am–6pm.

Temple Bar Food Market I6
Meeting House Sq, Temple Bar.
A fantastic Saturday food market: there's a wonderful range of Irish cheeses, French cakes, great breads, lots of organic produce (including meat, vegetables and fish), and all the ingredients for a very fancy picnic.

Music

Celtic Note J7
12 Nassau St, t (01) 670 4157.
They have a decent range on offer with the emphasis on Irish music.

Claddagh Records I6
2 Cecilia St, t (01) 677 0262, www.claddaghrecords.com.
Specialists in traditional Irish music.

Freakout Aural Stimulation I7
22 South William St, t (01) 677 4667.
Every kind of dance music imaginable.

HMV J7
66 Grafton St, t (01) 679 5334.
A branch of the big music store chain, with lots of mainstream CDs, tapes, videos, records. It also has a branch of Ticket Master for concert tickets.

Waltons I7
69–70 South Great Georges St, t (01) 475 0661.
Irish and world music and musical instruments.

Shopping Centres

Irish Life Mall J5
Talbot St, t (01) 704 1452.
The usual array of department stores and chain stores, and a smattering of fast-food restaurants and cafés.

Ilac Centre I5
Henry St, t (01) 704 1460.
This was Dublin's first big shopping centre, and has a couple of department stores, lots of chain shops and several restaurants.

Jervis Shopping Centre I6
125 Upper Abbey St, t (01) 878 1323.
Another of the big shopping centres on the northside, this has the usual array of department stores and chain stores, but it's slightly more upmarket than its competitors.

Powerscourt Townhouse Centre I7
Design Centre, 59 South William St, t (01) 679 5718.
If you only shop in one place in Dublin, make it here. The elegant 18th-century Georgian home of Lord Powerscourt has been magnificently converted into the city's most prestigious shopping centre, set around a glassed-over courtyard. There are antique shops, jewellers, lots of fashion, plenty of craft shops and several great bars and restaurants.

Royal Hibernian Way Shopping Centre J7
Dawson St, t (01) 679 5919.
A small, rather chi-chi shopping centre with a couple of dozen elegant boutiques, where you can pick up anything from beautiful lingerie to jewellery and Belgian chocolates.

St Stephens Green Shopping Centre I8
St Stephens Green, t (01) 478 0888.
A big glassy mall with a couple of department stores, knock-down designer fashion at TK Maxx, and plenty more.

The Westbury Centre I7
Near the Powerscourt Centre, off Grafton St, t (01) 679 1964.
Has an Aladdin's cave of a lingerie shop, a leather studio, a good Costa Coffee shop and Angles, a shop with the best of contemporary Irish jewellery.

Sports

Spectator Sports 220
Participation Sports 220

Dublin has a busy **sports** calendar, which features everything from showjumping to hurling and Gaelic football. The Six Nations rugby championship in February and March is always a huge event, or, for something altogether more relaxed, you can spend a lazy day in Phoenix Park watching the polo. Dubliners like a flutter, and the horseracing and greyhound racing tracks always do very good business. The coastline offers plenty in the way of watersports, from sailing and wind-surfing to diving and snorkelling, and companies offering lessons and trips. The city has lots of public amenities for keeping fit, including leisure centres, gyms, tennis courts, and swimming pools.

Dublin must rate as one of the greenest cities in Europe, with a swathe of beautiful public parks to relax in when the grit and clamour of the city streets get too much. Garden-lovers will delight in the spectacular formal gardens which circle the city, described in more detail in the Day Trips chapter, starting on p.153.

Spectator Sports

Basketball

Basketball has become increasingly popular in Ireland in the last few years. All the big events take place in Dublin's national stadium.

National Basketball Stadium OFF MAPS
*Tymon Park, Tallaght, **t** (01) 459 0211, www.iba.ie.*

Boxing

Ireland has produced several boxing champions, and Dublin has the world's only purpose-built boxing stadium.

Irish Amateur Boxing Association G10
*145 South Circular Rd, **t** (01) 453 3371, www.iaba.ie.*
The IABA can provide information on boxing matches.

National Stadium of Ireland G10
145 South Circular Rd, Kilmainham.
Information from the IABA.

Greyhound Racing

Dubliners like nothing more than a flutter, and Dublin's two big dog-tracks are always packed.

Shelbourne Park OFF MAPS
*Lotts Rd, Ringend, **t** (01) 668 3502, www.shelbournepark.com.*

Harold's Cross Stadium OFF MAPS
*151 Harolds Cross Rd, **t** (01) 497 1081.*

Hurling and Gaelic Football

The excellent GAA museum (*see* p.131) gives a fascinating insight into Gaelic games, but nothing beats attending a match. The tourist office has details of minor games around the city, as well as the main events at the huge Croke Park stadium.

Croke Park K3
*Jones Road, Drumcondra, **t** (01) 836 3222, www.gaa.ie.*

Horse-racing

Kildare (*see* p.166) is still the home of Irish horse-racing, but Dublin has its own racecourse to offer plenty of excitement.

Leopardstown Racecourse OFF MAPS
*Leopardstown, **t** (01) 289 3607, www.leopardstown.com.*
Several prestigious horseracing events are held here, including the 4-day Christmas National Hunt Festival and the Irish Champion Stakes, part of the World Series Championship.

Polo

The All-Ireland Polo Club plays in the beautiful surroundings of Phoenix Park (*see* p.121), and spectators are welcome at matches, held in summer.

All-Ireland Polo Club C4
*Phoenix Park, **t** (01) 677 6248, www.allirelandpoloclub.com.*

Rugby

Catch a game at Lansdowne Road, one mile south of the city centre, where in Feb or March you can catch the mighty Six Nations rugby tournament, held every year between Ireland, Wales, England, Scotland, France and Italy.

Lansdowne Road Stadium OFF MAPS
*4 Lansdowne Rd, Ballsbridge, **t** (01) 668 4601, www.irishrugby.ie.*
Ireland's national stadium.

Showjumping

The Kerrygold Horse Show is one of Dublin's most prominent social events. The bigger the hat, the better you'll fit in.

Royal Dublin Society (RDS) OFF MAPS
*Ballsbridge, **t** (01) 660 1700, www.rds.ie.*

Participation Sports

Diving

Irish Underwater Council OFF MAPS
*78a Patrick's St, Dún Laoghaire, **t** (096) 31215, www.scubaireland.com.*
Has details of companies offering diving trips and courses. They also publish a guide to Irish dive sites.

Discover Scuba OFF MAPS
*20 Terenure Park, **t** (01) 492 7392, www.discoverscuba.net.*
Diving trips in Dublin Bay for certified divers, plus courses for beginners and advanced.

Golf

It's strange that a sport so dependent on the weather should be so popular in Ireland, but the country has become one of the most golfing destinations in

Europe. It hosts several major golfing events throughout the year, and the prestigious Ryder Cup will be held in 2006 at the exclusive K Club in Straffan, County Kildare (www.kclub.ie).

The Golfing Union of Ireland OFF MAPS
Glencar House, 81 Eglinton Rd, Donnybrook, t (01) 269 4111, www.gui.ie.

There are more than fifty golf courses within an hour of Dublin; the following is a list of some of the nearest. All accept visitors, although you should call in advance to check fees and restrictions. Most also offer tuition, although this may need to be arranged in advance. Book your tee time well in advance.

Edmondstown Club OFF MAPS
Rathfarnham, t (01) 493 1032, www.edmondstowngolfclub.ie.

An 18-hole championship course, which has recently emerged from a major makeover.

The Island Golf Club OFF MAPS
Corballis, Donabate, Co. Dublin, t (01) 843 6205, www.theislandgolfclub.ie.

This coastal 18-hole course has recently hosted the Irish PGA, the Irish Men's Close and the Irish Women's Close.

Deer Park Hotel and Golf Courses OFF MAPS
Howth, t (01) 832 2624.

Smart, modern hotel (see also p.184) in a beautiful rural location in Howth, with Ireland's largest golf complex right on the doorstep. An 18-hole course and two 9-hole courses.

Portmarnock Hotel OFF MAPS
Portmarnock, Co. Dublin, t (01) 846 0611, www.portmarnock.com.

An elegant golf hotel set in an 18th-century mansion, with an 18-hole links course.

St Margaret's Golf and Country Club OFF MAPS
Co. Dublin, t (01) 864 0400, www.stmargaretsgolf.com.

An 18-hole championship course.

Gyms

Many of the smart hotels have gyms, or have special arrangements with local gyms. Most require membership, but the following are open to non-members. The gym at the Markievicz Leisure Centre (see Swimming, below) is also open to non-members.

Buzz Fitness OFF MAPS
75a Orwell Rd, Rathgar, t (01) 492 3146, www.buzzfitness.com.

Three gyms in one.

Crunch Fitness OFF MAPS
Bellfield Campus, UCD, t (01) 260 3155.

One of Ireland's biggest gyms, located in the campus of University College Dublin.

Pulse Fitness Centre I6
1 Temple Bar, t (01) 679 9620.

Gym in the heart of Temple Bar.

Horse-riding

There are dozens of riding stables around Dublin. Most will provide riding hats, but you should check in advance.

Ashtown Equestrian Centre OFF MAPS
Castleknock, t (01) 869 0500.

Trail rides and treks in Phoenix Park, suitable for beginners.

Carrickmines Equestrian Centre OFF MAPS
Glenamuck Rd, Foxrock, t (01) 295 5990.

Beginners a speciality.

Paddocks Riding Centre OFF MAPS
Woodside Rd, Sandyford, t (01) 295 4278.

Organizes treks in the Dublin mountains and runs pony camps for children.

Sailing and Watersports

Irish National Sailing School OFF MAPS
West Pier, Dún Laoghaire, t (01) 284 4195.

All kinds of sailing courses, plus windsurfing, canoeing and orienteering.

Wind and Wave OFF MAPS
16a The Crescent, Monkstown, t (01) 284 4177, www.windandwave.ie.

Windsurfing and canoeing courses, plus a shop selling equipment.

Swimming

The classic place to go for a swim is the Forty Foot Pool in Sandycove, by the James Joyce Museum (see p.136). Hardy chaps can be found there all year round (women are allowed, but few seem to use it). There are gorgeous beaches along the coast: Brittas Bay is the loveliest, but you'll need a car to get there. Other good sandy beaches include Bull Island, Sutton and Portmarnock, Malahide and Donabate. Some have lifeguards in summer (these beaches have a flag code in operation).

Many of the big hotels have swimming pools, or arrangements with local leisure centres. There is a list of municipal swimming pools on the Dublin Corporation website (www.dublincorp.ie), or you could try one of the following:

Markievicz Leisure Centre K6
Townsend St, t (01) 672 9121.

The best and newest leisure centre.

Mespil Pool K9
Mespil Estate, Sussex Rd, t (01) 668 4626.

Tennis

Most tennis clubs in Dublin are private, but many parks have public courts which are available for hire (full listings at www.dublincity.ie/parks). These are usually open from 10am to 9.30pm, with the last evening booking at 8.30pm.

UCD and Trinity College also rent out their courts to the public.

Children's and Teenagers' Dublin

Babysitting 223
Eating Out 223
Museums and Attractions 223
Activity Centres 223
Theatres 224
Parks and Beaches 224
Attractions outside Dublin 224
Teenagers 224

Much of Dublin's life centres around the pubs, which means the city is not an obvious destination for kids. And yet, Dublin offers plenty to keep kids interested.

The big museums have made great efforts in recent years to make their collections more accessible to children, and in the excellent Museum of Modern Art there are even special rooms full of paper and paints for kids to create their own response to what they've seen. There are lots of child-friendly exhibitions, such as the multimedia Dublinia, for kids to learn about the city without it being too much like a dull history lesson. Children get discounted admission at most museums and attractions, and on buses and trains; in addition family tickets, offering discounts for two adults and two (or more) children, are usually available.

Babysitting

Most of the big hotels offer babysitting services, and smaller ones can usually arrange babysitters with some notice. Most shopping centres and leisure centres offer crèche facilities.

Eating Out

Children are generally made very welcome in Dublin restaurants, although it's unusual to see children in any restaurants after about 8pm. Child menus are rare, but most places will happily prepare smaller portions.

Bad Ass Café I6
9–11 Crown Alley, Temple Bar, t (01) 671 2596, www.badasscafe.com. Open daily noon–11.30.

Diner-style spot for pizza, chops and burgers, famous because the singer Sinead O'Connor used to waitress here. It's a good place to take the kids, who will also enjoy the pulley system that whips orders into the kitchen. Good set menu for less than €15.

Chompys Deli I7
J22 Powerscourt Townhouse Centre, Clarendon St, t (01) 679 4552. Open Mon–Sat 8–6.

An institution for its American-style breakfasts – great pancakes, bagels and eggs benedict.

Elephant & Castle I6
18 Temple Bar, t (01) 679 3121. Open Mon–Fri 8am–11.30pm, Sat 10.30am–11.30pm, Sun noon–11.30.

Popular, relaxed place serving up good burgers, omelettes and spicy chicken wings. Always busy, and good for brunch on Sundays.

Gallagher's Boxty House I6
20–21 Temple Bar, t (01) 677 2762. Open daily noon–11.30.

Yes, it's touristy, but the food is authentically Irish and reliably good. A boxty is an Irish potato cake, and these are among the best you'll taste.

Ocean M7
Charlotte Quay Dock, t (01) 668 8862. Open daily for food 12.30–10.

Huge contemporary bar and restaurant with great views of the canal and a big terrace in summer. The food is simple bistro fare, but made with quality ingredients.

The Vaults K6
Harbourmaster Place, IFSC, t (01) 605 4700, www.thevaults.ie. Open for food daily noon–8.

This vast bar-brasserie in the vaults under Connolly train station has a special Kid's Club on Saturdays and Sundays (1–6pm), with treasure hunts, kid's movies, face-paintings and balloon-making.

Museums and Attractions

Most of the big museums, including the National Museum of Ireland and the National Museum of Modern Art, have a regular programme of family events and offer special activity packs for kids.

Dublin Bus Tours
See p.45.

A good way to see the city without tramping around on foot.

Dublinia
See p.90.

This is a very child-friendly exhibition on Dublin in the Middle Ages, with lots of interactive stuff.

GAA Museum
See p.131.

An excellent hands-on sport museum, where kids can try their hand at Gaelic sports in specially constructed booths.

Natural History Museum
See p.78.

Some kids might enjoy this old-fashioned museum, with its cabinets full of stuffed wildlife.

Smithfield Chimney
See p.119.

Ride up in a glass lift for panoramic views of the city.

St Michan's Church
See p.117.

Older children will enjoy the crypt, where you can shake hands with the mummified 'Crusader'.

Viking Splash Tours
t (01) 855 3000, www.vikingsplashtours.com.

A First World War amphibious vehicle trundles through the city streets before taking to the water in the Grand Canal Docks. Book through the tourist information centre on Suffolk Street.

Wax Museum
See p.110.

Every big city has one.

Zoo
See p.123.

One of the oldest zoos in Europe includes a petting zoo for littlies.

Activity Centres

Kids who love sports will enjoy a hurling or Gaelic football match at Croke Park (see p.131).

Fort Lucan
Off Strawberry Beds Rd, Westmanstown, Lucan, t (01) 628 0166.

An excellent adventure centre with climbing, sliding, suspension bridges and a special area for toddlers. Open in summer in good weather – call for opening times.

Leisureplex
Stillorgan Bowl, Stillorgan, t (01) 288 1656.

This contains a fun softplay

centre for toddlers to 8-year-olds, plus bowling alleys and Quasar for older kids. The complex also has a ceramic-painting studio, Pompeii Paints. There are three branches: in Blanchardstown Centre, **t** *(01) 822 3030*; Malahide Rd, Coolock, **t** *(01) 848 5722*; and Village Green Centre, Tallaght, **t** *(01) 459 9411*.

Premier Indoor Kart Racing
Unit 1a, Kylemore Industrial Estate, Killeen Rd, **t** *(01) 626 1444*.

Indoor karting track where kids can race against the clock. It's expensive – €21 for 20 minutes – but guaranteed to be popular. For children aged 9 and up, and at least 4 feet 6 inches tall.

Theatres

Many of Dublin's theatres offer events geared specifically towards children; some, such as The Pavilion in Dún Laoghaire and the Civic Theatre in Tallaght, have a regular programme of storytelling and other children's activities. The Gaiety often has a pantomime around Christmas.

The Ark
11a Eustace St, Temple Bar, **t** *(01) 670 7788, www.theark.ie*.

This is Europe's only custom-designed and dedicated cultural centre for children aged 4–14, with all kinds of events from theatre to music and new media.

Lambert Puppet Theatre
5 Clifton Lane, Monkstown, **t** *(01) 280 0974*.

Open year-round, this delightful puppet theatre retells classic fairy tales for children.

Parks and Beaches

Dublin's city parks are a delight for kids. Few have special play areas, but there is lots of room to run around and picnic and, in St Stephen's Green at least, they can feed the ducks. Phoenix Park offers everything from live polo to horse-riding, the zoo and even a miniature castle.

The best sandy beaches are generally north of the city, with the pebbly coves at Dalkey and further south also popular. The seafront at Bray, with its amusement arcades and Sea Life Centre, is also great for kids. The beautiful wild expanse of Brittas Bay is fabulous, but is not accessible by public transport.

There are some excellent cliff walks at Howth and Bray for older children.

Attractions Outside Dublin

Brú na Bóinne
See p.160.

The spectacular passage tombs at Newgrange will impress all children – even those who are bored stiff by history. The visitor centre brings the past to life with lots of child-friendly videos and activities.

Dalkey Castle
See p.137.

This small seaside castle has a 'murder hole' and great views from the battlements.

Malahide Castle
See p.133.

A grand castle with a resident ghost and huge gardens.

Model Railway Museum, Malahide
See p.134.

A great spot for all fans of model railways, where you can see the enormous track in action. Unfortunately, this is not a very hands-on museum: you get the impression that it is run by passionate collectors (mainly elderly gents) who don't want dirty fingerprints on their beautiful shiny trains.

Newgrange Farm
See p.160.

This delightful, family-run farm and tearoom close to the Brú na Bóinne visitors centre will keep kids happy with its puppies, kittens, chickens and ducks.

National Sea Life Centre, Bray
See p.138.

A seaside aquarium, with special areas for kids to pick up sea creatures such as crabs and starfish, and a new exhibit with seahorses.

National Stud Farm, Kildare
See p.167.

Horse fans might appreciate a visit to this impressive stud farm, with an excellent museum attached.

Newbridge Demesne Traditional Farm
See p.155.

This 18th-century-style traditional farm is always popular with children, with lots of animals, including cows, sheep and ponies.

Skerries Watermill and Heritage Centre
See p.156.

Try your hand at grinding at these restored watermills, a long-standing family attraction and well set up for kids.

Tara's Palace and Museum of Childhood, Malahide
See p.133.

Some children may enjoy these antique toys and rocking horses, and the enormous and unfinished dolls' house upstairs.

Teenagers

There is plenty to keep teenagers happily occupied in Dublin. Sports fans will enjoy the GAA museum (see p.131) and arty teenagers will get at least something out of the slick, fashionable Museum of Modern Art in Kilmainham. Temple Bar is full of shops geared towards teenagers, with funky clothes, jewellery and kitsch souvenirs, and there are plenty of hip boutiques across the city selling clubbing gear to keep fashion victims happy; for more, see p.216.

Gay and Lesbian Dublin

Dublin's gay community is still small, but has gained in confidence over the last decade or so. Homosexual behaviour was illegal until 1993, but the 1990s saw long-overdue liberalizing legislation. There are few dedicated gay venues, but plenty of gay-friendly ones. The free monthly *Gay Community News* (available from bookshops, cafés, bars – and at www.gcn.ie) has plenty of listings.

Information

OUThouse
105 Capel St, t (01) 873 4932, www.outhouse.ie.
An excellent resource centre which represents all sections of the gay, lesbian, bisexual and transgender communities.

Gay Men's Health Project
19 Haddington Rd, t (01) 660 2189.
Support and information.

Phone lines

Gay Switchboard Dublin
t (01) 872 1055. Sun–Fri 8pm–10pm.

Lesbian Line
t (01) 872 9911. Thurs 7pm–9pm.

Bookshops

There are no gay bookshops in Dublin, but the following have good gay and lesbian sections.

The Winding Stair
40 Ormond Quay, t (01) 873 3292.
A delightful, rickety bookshop with a wonderful café.

Books Upstairs
36 College Green, t (01) 679 6687.
Probably the best gay selection.

Waterstone's
7 Dawson St, t (01) 679 1415.
Well-known chain.

Hotels

There are few gay hotels, but some are more open-minded than others. These include Abrae Court, Albany House, Longfield's Hotel and Waterloo House (all listed from p.172). In addition, there are the following options, all priced at around €75–85 for a double.

Frankie's Guesthouse
8 Camden Place, t (01) 478 3087, www.frankiesguesthouse.com.

Inn on the Liffey
21 Upr Ormond Quay, t (01) 677 0828.

Alternative Guesthouse
61 Amiens St, t (01) 855 3671.

Horse and Carriage Hotel
15 Aungier St, t (01) 478 3537.

Cafes and Restaurants

Aside from the Rainbow Café within the OUThouse, many places are gay-friendly.

Cornucopia
19 Wicklow St. See p.191.

Gruel
68a Dame St. See p.194.

Irish Film Centre (IFC)
6 Eustace St, Temple Bar. See p.213.

Juice
73–83 S Gt George's St. See p.191.

Rainbow Café Coffee Bar
In OUThouse, 105 Capel St, t (01) 873 4932. Open to all Mon–Fri 12.30–2.30pm, Sat 1–5pm. In addition, Wed is mixed night, Thurs is women's night, Fri is men's night (all 7–10pm).

Stonewall Café
18 Exchequer St. See p.191.

Bars and Clubs

The George
89 South Great Georges St, t (01) 478 2983, www.capitalbars.com. Open bar: Mon–Tues 12.30–11.30; club: Wed–Sun until 2.30am.
The matriarch of Dublin's gay bars, for mostly gay men and transvestites. Sunday's Bingo! session features cabaret and DJs.

GUBU
7–8 Capel St, t (01) 874 0710.
A trendy gay (straight-friendly) bar: Wednesday's G-Spot is a classic night out, with drag artists and comedy.

The Front Lounge
33 Parliament St, t (01) 670 4112.
A swish bar, not strictly gay – but it feels like it. Tuesday's Casting Couch is popular, with a karaoke competition from 10pm.

Out on the Liffey
27 Upr Ormond Quay, t (01) 872 2480.
A comparatively quiet bar, which has the reputation for being a bit rough

Gay nights at mainstream clubs

Pink at SPI
3 Eden Quay, t (01) 874 6934.
Great gay-friendly night (Wed).

HAM at PoD
Old Harcourt St Railway Station, t (01) 475 8581.
HAM (Homo Action Movies) every Fri from 11pm. A massive gay night out, with excellent music.

Club Soho at the Earl of Kildare Hotel
Kildare Street, t (01) 679 4388.
Gay nights at this young, poppy club are Sat, Sun, Tues and Thurs, plus monthly. Queer & Alternative

Diversion at Traffic
54 Middle Abbey St, t (01) 873 4800.
Stylish gay night (Thurs).

Freedom at Spi Bar
3 Eden Quay, t (01) 874 6934.
Monday nights from 11pm.

Fruit at PoD
Old Harcourt St Railway Station, t (01) 475 8581.
A very popular Saturday night.

Libida at Chief O'Neill's Hotel
Smithfield Village, t (01) 817 3860.
Gay club (last Sat in month); also a night for women (men also welcome) on the third Friday.

Queen at Tomato
60–61 Harcourt St, t (01) 476 4900.
Thursday is gay student night.

Sharpshoote at Eamonn Dorans
3a Crown Alley, Temple Bar, t (01) 679 9114.
A gay indie night on Tuesdays.

Slam at Spy/Wax
Powerscourt Centre, South William St, t (01) 677 0067.
One of the biggest and best gay club nights. Mon from 11pm.

Tease at Temple Bar Music Centre
Curved St, Temple Bar, t (01) 670 9202, www.tbmc.ie.
Monthly gay night.

The Tivoli
Francis St, t (01) 453 5998.
Fridge Lite (Tues), and The Big Fridge Lite (last Sun of month), with male strip acts.

Festivals and Events

Dublin has a packed calendar of events, ranging from the giddy week-long party celebrating St Patrick's Day to a massive outdoor music festival in May.

February

Six Nations rugby
February and March (dates vary); Lansdowne Rd Stadium t (01) 647 3800, www.irishrugby.ie.

Tickets quickly sell out for this hugely popular championship, staged annually between Ireland, Wales, Scotland, England, France and Italy.

March

St Patrick's Day
17 March; t (01) 676 3205, www.stpatricksday.ie.

'Paddy's Day' is celebrated with a week-long party (check the website for exact dates, which vary). On the day itself, a parade with floats and marching bands wends its way through huge crowds from St Patrick's Cathedral to O'Connell Street. There are dozens of events, including fireworks, street theatre and a free concert on Merrion Square.

April

Easter Rising Commemoration
Easter Sunday.

A Republican march begins at the GPO on O'Connell Street and continues to Glasnevin Cemetery, where many of the major figures in the uprising are buried.

International Film Festival
March–April; www.dubliniff.com.

A celebration of the best Irish and international cinema.

Pan Celtic Festival, Kilkenny
Mid-April; www.panceltic.com.

A week-long festival of traditional music, dance and sporting events from the Celtic territories of Ireland, Scotland, Brittany, the Isle of Man, Cornwall and Wales.

May

Green Energy Music Festival
First week of May; t (01) 456 9569, www.mcd.ie.

A popular week-long event, held at Dublin Castle and elsewhere.

Wicklow Gardens Festival
May–July; t (0404) 20070, www.wicklow.ie.

Open days at private gardens throughout County Wicklow.

June

Bloomsday
16 June; t (01) 878 8547, www.jamesjoyce.ie.

The events of James Joyce's *Ulysses* took place on 16 June 1904, and the anniversary is marked annually with a series of events: at Davy Byrne's pub, you'll be served Leopold Bloom's lunch of a glass of Bordeaux and a gorgonzola sandwich. People wear Edwardian costume, make recitations or just tag along for the pub crawl.

Music in Great Irish Houses.
Throughout June; t (01) 278 1528.

A festival of chamber music, with many evening concerts held in great houses in the Dublin area.

Diversions
June–Aug; t (01) 677 2255, www.templebar.ie.

Outdoor performances of all kinds in Temple Bar.

July

Dublin Jazz Festival
First week of July; t (01) 670 3885.
A five-day citywide jamboree.

Anna Livia Opera Festival
Second week of July; t (01) 661 7544, www.operannalivia.com.

A cycle of opera at the Gaiety Theatre and the National Concert Hall, with supporting events.

August

Kerrygold Horse Show
First week of Aug; t (01) 668 0866, www.rds.ie.

One of the world's top equestrian events, attracting top national and international showjumpers, held at the Royal Dublin Society in Ballsbridge.

Dún Laoghaire and Rathdown Festival of World Cultures
Early Aug; t (01) 286 0213, www.dlrcool.ie.

A lively three-day festival featuring music, dance, theatre, circus and club nights.

Kilkenny Arts Festival
Second week of Aug; t (056) 776 3663, www.kilkennyarts.ie.
Performing arts festival.

Liffey Swim
Late Aug/early Sept; t (01) 833 2434

It's hard to see why anyone would want to throw themselves into the filthy Liffey, but this has been a tradition since 1920.

September

All-Ireland Finals
Second and fourth Sundays; t (01) 836 3222, www.rds.ie.

First the hurling finals at Croke Park, then the football finals.

Dublin Theatre Festival
End-Sept–mid-Oct; t (01) 677 8439, www.dublintheatrefestival.com.

Prestigious event founded in 1957. More than 140 performances citywide, plus associated events.

Dublin Fringe Theatre Festival
End-Sept–mid-Oct; t (01) 872 9433, www.fringefest.com.

Original drama, comedy and dance, in venues across the city.

October

Wexford Opera Festival
Late Oct; t (053) 22400, www.wexfordopera.com.

Major opera productions staged in Wexford Town.

Dublin City Marathon
Last Mon in Oct; t (01) 626 3726, www.dublincitymarathon.ie.

Long-standing race that starts and finishes on O'Connell Street.

Samhain Festival (Halloween)
31 Oct; t (01) 855 7154.

The ancient Celtic festival of Samhain forms the basis for Dublin's Halloween events. The kids still go out 'trick-or-treating' but there's also a big parade.

December

Dublin Grand Opera
Gaiety Theatre, S. King St, t (01) 677 1717, www.gaietytheatre.com.
Dublin's winter season of opera.

Leopardstown Winter Festival
26–28 Dec; t (01)239 3607, www.leopardstown.com.

Hugely popular horse-racing meet at Leopardstown racecourse.

Language

Ireland's official first language is **Gaelic** (Gaedhilge in Gaelic). All official documents are published in both English and Gaelic, and road signposts are usually written in both languages. Everyone speaks English, so you won't need to speak Gaelic when you are visiting, but efforts to say even a few simple words are always very much appreciated.

The recent resurgence of the Gaelic language is inextricably linked to the struggle for Irish independence. Its earliest form was Goidelic, the name derived from the earliest Celts who spoke it. Early evidence of Gaelic dates from the 4th and 5th centuries AD, and is found on sepulchral inscriptions in the Ogham alphabet involving a system of strokes and notches (which you can see at the Book of Kells exhibition in Trinity College). The language gradually fell into disuse after the arrival of the Anglo-Normans in the Middle Ages. Nonetheless, it is estimated that at the beginning of the 19th century more than half the population spoke Gaelic. This proportion declined dramatically through death and emigration during the Great Famine of the 1840s, which particularly affected the western areas of Ireland where Irish was most spoken.

At the end of the 19th century, there was a remarkable Irish Gaelic revival, associated with the nationalist struggle and independence, with a resurgence of traditional Irish culture and an Irish literary renaissance including the growth of an active Irish Gaelic literature based on long oral traditions. All led to a considerable increase in the numbers of Irish speakers.

By its constitution, the Republic of Ireland designated Irish as its first official language, thus making it a symbol of independence. It has been compulsorily taught in schools since 1922, and a standard grammar and simplified spelling system has replaced diverse dialects. In the 2002 census, it was discovered that 47% of the population had knowledge of Irish, although the numbers of vernacular speakers are steadily shrinking. The western districts, including all the western peninsulas, and parts of Donegal, Connacht and Munster, are the traditional areas of Irish speaking, known as the Gaeltacht.

In Dublin there are lots of places to try your language skills, including the Irish-speaking Caife Tri-D on Dawson Street (see p.192).

Pronunciation

Pronunciation is not easy to grasp: there are few points of contact with English, and the unfamiliar consonant clusters – which also vary in sound depending on the letters around them – make for a linguistic minefield. We've given just a few basic guidelines.

Vowels take an accent to lengthen the sound.
- **a** is short, as in cat
- **á** is long, as in law
- **e** as in bet
- **é** as in say
- **i** as in bit
- **í** as in been
- **o** as in cot
- **ó** as in cone
- **u** as in put
- **ú** as in pool

Consonants are deemed to be "broad" if they stand before *a*, *o* or *u* – or "slender" if they stand before *e* or *i*.
- broad **bh** is a *w* or *v* sound
- slender **bh** is a *v* sound
- **c** is always hard, as in cat
- **ch** is guttural, as in loch
- broad **d** is a voiced *th* sound, as in that
- slender **d** is almost a *t* sound
- broad **dh** is a gargle, like a voiced *ch*
- slender **dh** is as in yes
- **fh** is silent
- **g** is always hard, as in get
- broad **gh** is a gargle, like a voiced *ch*
- slender **gh** is as in yes
- broad **mh** is a *w* or *v* sound
- slender **mh** is a *v* sound
- **ph** is an *f* sound, as in phone
- broad **s** is as in sign
- slender **s** is as in shine
- **sh** is an *h* sound, as in hat
- broad **t** is aspirated
- **th** is an *h* sound, as in hat

Simple Phrases and Greetings

yes *sea, tá*
no *ní hea, nil*
thank you *go raibh maith agat*
you're welcome *tá fáilte romhat*
please *más é do thoil é, le do thoil*
excuse me *gaibh mo phardún*
hello *dia dhuit*
goodbye *slán agat/slán leat*
What is your name? *Cad is ainm duit?*
Nice to meet you. *Tá áthas orm bualadh leat*
How are you? *Conas tá tú?*
good/bad *maith/olc*

Numbers

one *aon*
two *dó*
three *trí*
four *ceathair*
five *cúig*
six *sé*
seven *seacht*
eight *ocht*
nine *naoi*
ten *deich*

Shopping/Eating Out

How much does this cost? *an mór atá air?*
I would like to buy... *ba mhaith liom ... a cheannach*
Do you have... *an bfhuil ... agat*
open *oscailte*
closed *dúnta*
breakfast *bricfeasta*
lunch *lón*
dinner *dinnéar*
cheers! *sláinte*
bread *arán*
coffee *caife*
tea *té*
water *uisce*
beer *beoir*
wine *fíon*
meat *feoil*
beef *mairteoil*
pork *muiceoil*
fish *iasc*
potato *práta*
salad *sailéad*
dessert *milseog*

Directions/Place Words

left *ar chlé*
right *ar dheis*
straight *díreach*
up *suas*
down *síos*
far *fada*
near *gearr*
long *fada*
short *gearra*
tourist information *oifig eolais*
post office *oifig an phoist*
museum *músaem*
bank *banc*
police station *staisún na ngardaí*
hospital *óispidéal*
pharmacy *cógaslann*
school *scoil*
church *séipéal*
restrooms *seomra folctha*
street *sráid*
square *cearnóg*
mountain *sliabh*
hill *cnoc*
valley *gleann*
lake *loch*
river *abhainn*
tower *túr*
bridge *droichead*

Places

Where is...? *Cá bfhuil...?*
How much is the fare? *Cad é an táille?*
ticket *ticéad*
A ticket to ... please *Ticéad amháin ... le do thoil*
Where are you going? *Cá bfhuil tú ag imeacht?*
Where do you live? *Cá maireann tú?*
train *traen*
bus *bus*
airport *aerphort*
train station *staisún an traen*
bus station *staisún an bhus*
parking *páirceáil*
hotel *ostán*
room *seomra*
reservation *áirithint*
Are there any vacancies for tonight?
 An bfhuil aon seomraí ar fáil anocht?

Index

Numbers in **bold** indicate main references. Numbers in *italic* indicate maps.

Abbey Street 142
Abbey Theatre 36, **103–4**, 142
abbeys *see* churches
abortion 30
accommodation *see* where to stay
Act of Union 25
activity centres 223–4
Ahern, Bertie 30
airlines 38–9
airport 42
Anna Livia fountain 102
antiques shops 215
Áras an Uachtaráin 123
Arbour Hill cemetery 121
Ardagh Hoard 69
Ardgillan Castle 157
art and architecture **32–6**
art galleries (commercial) 216
Arts Centre (Bank of Ireland) 65
Arts and Crafts Movement 35
Ashtown Castle 123
Áth Cliath 20
auctioneers 215

babysitting services 223
Bacon, Francis 36, 106–7
Ballsbridge 151, 172
bank holidays 53
Bank of Ireland 33, **64–5**
Banking Museum 65
banks 52–3
Barry, Kevin 129
bars *see* pubs and bars
basketball 220
beaches 224
Beaker People, The 20
Beatty, Chester 87
beauty salons 217
Behan, Brendan 67, 107, 110, 130
Belvedere College **108**, 141
Beresford, Lady Elizabeth 155
Berkeley, George 63

Bewley's Oriental Café 35, **66**, 142
bicycles 44–5
Black Church 35, **111**
Black Death 22
Black and Tans 28
Black Tom (Thomas Wentworth) 23
Bleeding Heart pub 95
Blessington Lakes 171
Bloody Sunday (1971) 29
Bloody Sunday Massacre (1920) 28, 131
bodysnatchers 130
Book of Kells 20, 32, **61–2**, 164
bookshops 215, 226
Ború, Brian 21, 110, 155
Botanic Gardens 130
Botany Bay 61
boxing 220
Boyd, John McNeill 92
Boyle Monument 92
Boyne, Battle of 23, **158**
Boyne Valley 32, 157–65
Bray 138
breweries and distilleries
    Dublin Brewing Company 120
    Jameson Distillery 119–20
    St James's Gate Brewery 95–6
Bride Street 146
Bridge Street 146
Brigid, Saint 166–7
Britain Quay 150–1
Brown Thomas department store 66
Brú na Boinne 160–2
Bull Island Nature Reserve 132
Burgo, William de 21
Burke, Thomas 122
Busáras 36
buses and coaches 39–40, 42, 43, 45–6
Butt Bridge 142, 149
Butterstream Gardens (Trim) 164

cafés
    Around Dublin Bay 201
    gay and lesbian 226
    northeast Dublin 198
    southeast Dublin 192–3
    southwest Dublin 195
    suburbs 200
    Temple Bar 195
    see also food and drink; pubs and bars
Campanile 61
Campshires 150
Carmelite order 67–8
cars 40, 45
Casino at Marino 34, **131–2**
castles
    Ardgillan 157
    Ashtown 123
    Dalkey 137–8
    Drimnagh 128–9
    Dublin 21, **85–7**, 145
    Goat 137
    Howth 135
    Malahide 133
    Rathfarnham 128
    Slane 159–60
    Trim 163–4
Castletown House 165–6
Catholic Emancipation Act 25
Cavendish, Lord 122
Celbridge 165–6
Celbridge Abbey 165, **166**
Celts 20
cemeteries 121, 129–30
Chambers, Sir William 34
Charlemont House 106
Charles I 23
Chester Beatty Library **87–8**, 145
Chesterfield Avenue 122
Childhood Museum 133–4
children's Dublin **223–4**
    shops 215–16
Chimney Viewing Tower 119
Christ the King 135

Index: CHR–FAS

Christchurch cathedral 33, 35, **89–90**, 147
Christchurch Place 147
Christianity 20, 32
churches and abbeys
  Black Church 35, 111
  Celbridge Abbey 165, **166**
  Christchurch cathedral 33, 35, **89–90**, 147
  Glendalough 21, 32, 167–9
  Mellifont Abbey 158–9
  Newman University Church 73–4
  Peppercanister 151
  religious services 54
  Rotunda Chapel 105
  St Anne's 72
  St Audoen's **90–1**, 146
  St Augustine and St John 95
  St Brigid's cathedral (Kildare) 166–7
  St Catherine's 95
  St Francis of Assisi 147
  St Francis Xavier 35, **110**
  St Kevin's (Glendalough) 169
  St Mary's Abbey 116–17
  St Mary's Abbey (Trim) 163
  St Mary's Chapel of Ease 111
  St Mary's Pro-Cathedral 35, **104**
  St Michan's 117
  St Nicholas of Myra 95
  St Patrick's cathedral 33, 35, 91–3, 146
  St Stephen's 35, 80
  St Teresa's Carmelite Church and Friary 67–8
  St Werburgh's 91
cinema 213
City Hall 34, **88–9**, 144
City Quay 150
city walls 33
Civic Museum 67
Civil War in England 23
Civil War in Ireland 28–9
Clanwilliam House 34, **73**
classical music 212
Clery department store 102, 103
climate 48
Clondalkin 32
Clonmacnoise crozier 69

clothes shops 215–16
clubs 208–9
  gay and lesbian 226
coaches and buses 39–40, 42, 43, 45–6
coast *154*, 155–7
  see also Dublin Bay
College Green **64–5**, 142, 144
Collins Barracks 34, 36, **120–1**
Collins, Michael 28
Colum Cille, Saint 62
comedy clubs 213
Concert Hall 74
consulates 50
contemporary Dublin 30
Cook Street 146
The Coombe 94–5
Cornmarket 146
Corporation Buildings 36, **89**
craft shops 216
crannógs 20
credit cards 53
crime 48–9
Croke Park 131
Cromwell, Thomas 23
Croppies 24
Croppies Acre 121
Cross of Cong 69
curraghs 20
Curran, John Philpott 130
Custom House 34, **111–12**, 149
Custom House Quay 149–50
customs formalities 41

Dáil Éireann 71
Dalkey 136–8
Dalkey Castle 137–8
Dalkey Island 20, 32, 137
Dame Street 144
dancing 213
DART services 43–4
Davitt, Michael 96
Davy Byrne's 66
De Valera, Eamon 28, 29
department stores 216
DESIGNyard 36
Dillon garden 129
disabled travellers 49
distilleries *see* breweries and distilleries
diving 220
divorce 30
dockers statue 150

Docks and the Grand Canal walk *148–9*, 149–52
Dollymount Beach 132
dolmens 20
Donabate 155–6
Donore 158
Douglas Hyde Gallery 63
Dowth 32, 160, **162**
Drimnagh Castle 128–9
Drogheda 23, **157–8**
Dubh Linn 20, **145**
Dublin Bay *126*, 132–8
  accommodation 173, **184**
  cafés 201
  food and drink 200–1
  pubs and clubs 208
Dublin Brewing Company 120
Dublin Castle 21, **85–7**, 145
Dublin Civic Museum 67
Dublin Experience 63
Dublin Port *see* Quays
Dublin Writers Museum **107–8**, 141
Dublinia 33, **90**, 147
Duke Street 142
Dún Laoghaire 42, **135–6**
duty-free shopping 41
Dwyer McAlister Cottage 171

E111 forms 51
Easter Rising 27–8, 96, 103, 127
  monument 151
economy 30
Eden Quay 142
Edward the Bruce 21–2
electricity 49
Elizabeth I 22
embassies 50
emigration 25
Emmet, Addis 96
Emmet, Robert 95, 96, 97, 117, 127, 142
entertainment *see* nightlife and entertainment
Essex Street West 147
etiquette 50
euro 52
Examination Hall 61

Famine 25–6
  memorial 150
fashion shops 216–17

Father Mathew Bridge 146
Fenian Brotherhood 26
ferries 40
festivals 228
Ffoliot's Revenge 132
Fianna Fáil 29
Finglas 32
First World War 27
Fishamble Street 147
Fitzgerald, Sir Edward 95
Fitzwilliam Square 79, 143
Fitzwilliam Street 36, 79
Flight of the Earls 22
food and drink 186
  Bewley's 35, **67**, 142
  Boyne Valley 157–65
  Celbridge 165
  for children 223
  Donabate 155
  Dublin Bay 200–1
  fruit and vegetable market 117–18
  Guinness 95–6
  Kildare 166
  northeast Dublin 101, 195–8, *196–7*
  northwest Dublin 115, 199
  shopping 217
  Skerries 156
  southeast Dublin 58, 186–93, *188–9*
  southwest Dublin 83, 193–5, *194*
  suburbs 199–200
  Swords 155
  Temple Bar 193–5, *194*
  whiskey 119–20
  Wicklow Mountains 167–71
  see also pubs and bars
Fort Lucan 223
Forty Foot Pool 136
fountains 102
Four Courts 34, **116**
Francis Street 95, 146
Free State 28
Freemason's Hall 71
fruit and vegetable market 117–18
Fry Model Railway Museum 134

GAA (Gaelic Athletics Assoc.) museum 131
Gaelic phrases 230–1

Gaelic sports **131**, 220
Gaels 20
Gandon, James 116, 118
gardens *see* parks and gardens
Gardiner Place 141
Gate Theatre 105
gay and lesbian Dublin 226
genealogy 50–1
General Post Office 34, 102, **103**, 142
General Register Office 50
George IV statue 135
George's Quay 149
Georgian Dublin 23–5, 33–4, 59–60
Geraldines 22, 146
Gladstone, William 26
Glasnevin cemetery 129–30
Glen Pond 123
Glendalough 21, 32, **167–9**
Gleninsheen Collar 20, **69**
Goat castle 137
gold rush 137
golf 220–1
Graduates' Memorial Building 61
Grafton Street **65**, 142
Grand Canal Quay 151
Grand Canal Square 150
Grand Canal walk *148–9*, 149–52
Grattan Bridge 112
Grattan, Henry 24, 166
  statue 65
Great Denmark Street 141
Great Famine *see* Famine
Gresham Hotel 102
greyhound racing 220
Griffith, Arthur 27
Guerin, Veronica 30
guided tours 45–6, 60
Guinness 95–6
gyms 221

hair and beauty salons 217
Hanover Lane 146
Ha'penny Bridge 112
Haughey, Charles 30
Hawkins Street 142
Head of Howth 32
health 51
Henrietta Street 34, **118**
Henry II 21

Henry VII 22
Henry VIII 22
Henry Street 103
Heraldic Museum 71
Herbert Place 151
high crosses 32
High Street 146, 147
Hill of Slane 159
Hill of Tara 32, 159, **162–3**
hiring cars 45
history **20–30**
  contemporary Dublin 30
  early Christianity 20, 32
  Famine 25–6
  Georgian 23–5, 33–4, 59–60
  Home Rule struggles 24–6
  Independence 26–9
  Medieval Dublin 21–2, 33, 70, 143–7
  prehistoric Ireland 20, 32, 68–9, 160–2
  Troubles 29–30
  Vikings 20–1, 32–3, 69–70, 143–7
Home Rule struggles 24–6
Hopkins, Gerald Manley 130
horse market (Smithfield) 119
horse-racing 220
horse-riding 221
hospitals 51
Hot Press Irish Music Hall of Fame 104
hotels *see* where to stay
House of Lords 65
Howth 134–5
Huband Bridge 151
Hugh Lane Gallery 34, 35–6, **106–7**
hurling 131, 220
Hyde, Douglas 142

IFSC (International Financial Services Centre) **111**, 150
Independence 26–9
Internet access 51
Invincibles 122
IRA (Irish Republican Army) 28, 29
Ireland's Eye 32, 134
Irish Civil War 28–9
Irish Free State 28
Irish Jewish Museum 74–5

Index: IRI–MUS

Irish Museum of Modern Art (IMMA) 36, **97**
Irish Parliament 33, **64**
Irish Republican Brotherhood (IRB) 26, 127
Irish Volunteers 27
Irish Writers Centre 107–8
Ivar the Boneless 21
Iveagh Baths 93, 146
Iveagh Buildings 93
Iveagh Gardens 74
Iveagh Market 95
Iveagh Trust 35

James I 23
James II 23
James Joyce bridge 121
James Joyce Centre 108–9
James Joyce museum (Sandycove) 136
Jameson Distillery 119–20
Japanese Gardens (Kildare) 167
jazz music 211
Jewish Museum 74–5
Joyce, James **109**, 138
  James Joyce Centre 108–9
  museum (Sandycove) 136
  statues 73, 102, 141
Joyce, John Stanislaus 130

karting 224
Kavanagh, Patrick 151
Kells 164–5
  Book of Kells 20, 32, **61–2**
Kevin, Saint 167–8, 169
Kildare Street 68–72, 143
Kildare Town 166–7
Killiney Bay 137
Killruddery House 138
Kilmainham Gaol 96–7
Kilmainham Royal Hospital 33
King's Inn 118
Knowth 32, 160, **162**

Lambey Island 134
Land Acts 26
Lane, Sir Hugh 106
language 26–7, 230–1
Larkin, Jim 102
Lawrence O'Toole, St 158
Leeson Street 143
Leinster House 34, **71**

Lemass, Séan 29
Lennox Street 152
Leopardstown racecourse 220
lesbian Dublin 226
Lia Fáil 163
The Liberties **95–6**, 146
Liberty Hall 36
libraries
  Chester Beatty **87–8**, 145
  Marsh's 94
  National Library 35, **70–1**
  New Berkeley 63
  Old Library (Trinity College) 61–3
Library Square 61
Lincoln Place 143
literary walk 140, 141–3
long stays 56
Lord Edward Street 147
lost property 52
Lower Abbey Street 142
Lower Baggot Street 143
Lower Rathmines Road 152

McAlister, Sam 171
McBride, Maud Gonne 130
McDaid's 66–7
MacMahon Bridge 151
MacMurragh, Dermot 21
McQuaid, Archbishop 29
magazines 52
Malahide 132–4
  Botanic Gardens 133
  Castle 133
Malone, Molly 65–6
Mansion House 72
Marino crescent 132
Maritime Museum 135
Markievicz, Countess 74, 96–7
  grave 130
  statue 73
Marsh's Library 94
Mary, Queen 22
Matt Talbot Memorial Bridge 150

Meath Street market 94
media 52
Medieval Dublin 21–2, 33, 70
  walk 143–7, 144–5
Mellifont Abbey 158–9
Merrion Square **76**, 143
Merrion Street 143
Millennium Bridge 112
millennium celebrations 30
Millennium Spire 102
Millmount Museum (Drogheda) 158
mobile phones 53–4
Model Railway Museum 134
Modern Art Museum (IMMA) 36, **97**
Modernism 36
Monasterboice 158, **159**
money 52–3
monuments see statues and monuments
Mooghaun Hoard 69
Moore Street market 103
Moore, Thomas 65, 107, 142
Mountjoy Square 110, 141
Mulligan's 95
multiculturalism 30
mummified bodies 117
museums
  Arts Centre (Bank of Ireland) 65
  Banking 65
  Chester Beatty Library 87–8
  Childhood 133–4
  for children 223
  Civic 67
  Douglas Hyde Gallery 63
  Freemason's Hall 71
  Fry Model Railway 134
  GAA (Gaelic Athletics Association) 131
  Heraldic 71
  Hugh Lane Gallery 34, 35–6, **106–7**
  James Joyce Centre 108–9
  James Joyce (Sandycove) 136
  Jewish 74–5
  Maritime 135
  Millmount (Drogheda) 158
  Modern Art (IMMA) **97**
  National Gallery of Ireland 34, 35 **76–8**

National Museum of
  Ireland 32, 34, 35, 36,
  68–70, 120–1
Natural History 78–9
Old Museum (Trinity
  College) 63
opening hours 53
Pearse 126–7
Print 80
Temple Bar Gallery 85
Transport 135
Wax 110–11
Writers **107–8**, 141
Yeats 77
music 211–12
  Hot Press Irish Music Hall
    of Fame 104
  shops 218

National Archives 51
National Botanic Gardens
  130
National Concert Hall 74
National Gallery of Ireland
  34, 35 **76–8**
national holidays 53
National Library 35, **70–1**
National Maritime Museum
  135
National Museum of Ireland
  32, 34, 35, 36, **68–70**,
  120–1
National Photographic
  Archive 85
National Print Museum 80
National Sea Life Centre 138
National Stud 167
National Transport Museum
  135
National Wax Museum
  110–11
Natural History Museum
  78–9
Nelson, Horatio, statue 102
Neoclassical architecture
  33–4
New Berkeley Library 63
Newbridge House 155–6
Newgrange 32, 160, **161–2**
Newman House 34, **73**, 143
Newman University Church
  73–4
newspapers 52

nightlife and entertainment
  202–13
  cinema 213
  comedy clubs 213
  dancing 213
  Dublin Bay 208
  music 211–12
  northeast Dublin 207, 209
  northwest Dublin 207–8
  opera 212
  southeast Dublin 203–4,
    208–9
  southwest Dublin 205–7,
    209
  suburbs 208, 209
  Temple Bar 205–7, 209
  theatres 212–13
  ticket booking service 211
Nine Years' War 22
Normans 21
North Great Georges Street
  141
northeast Dublin **100–12**,
  100–1
  accommodation 179–82,
    180–1
  food and drink 101, 195–8,
    196–7
  pubs and clubs 207, 209
Northumberland Road 151
northwest Dublin **114–24**,
  114–15
  accommodation 182
  food and drink 115, 199
  pubs and clubs 207–8
Number Twenty-Nine
  (Fitzwilliam Street) 79

O'Brae, Patrick Cotter 67
O'Casey, Séan 141
O'Connell Bridge 103
O'Connell, Daniel 25, 76
  monument 129
  statue 103
O'Connell Street **100–2**, 141–2
  statues and monuments
    102
O'Connor, Rory 21
O'Donnell, Hugh 22
Old Jameson Distillery
  119–20
Old Library (Trinity College)
  61–3

Old Museum (Trinity
  College) 63
Oldtown Wood 122
Oliver Plunkett, Saint 158
O'Malley, Grace 135
O'Neill, Hugh 22
opening hours 53, 215
opera 212
Ormonds 146
O'Toole, Lawrence, St 158

packing 53
The Pale 21
Papal Cross 122
parks and gardens 224
  Ardgillan Castle 157
  Botanic Gardens 130
  Butterstream Gardens
    (Trim) 164
  Dillon Gardens 129
  Drimnagh Castle 128–9
  Dubh Linn Gardens 145
  Iveagh Gardens 74
  Japanese Gardens (Kildare)
    167
  Killruddery House 138
  Malahide Botanic Gardens
    133
  People's Park 122
  Phoenix Park 121–3
  Powerscourt Estate
    (Wicklow) 169–70
  Rathfarnham Castle 128
  Remembrance Gardens
    105
  Russborough House
    (Wicklow) 171
  St Patrick's Park **93**, 146
  St Stephen's Green **72**, 142
  War Memorial Gardens
    97–8
Parliament 33, **64**
Parliament House 33
Parliament Square 61
Parliament Street 144, 147
Parnell, Charles Stewart 26,
  96, 97, 122
  grave 129–30
Parnell Square 34, **105**, 141
passports 41
Pearse, Patrick Henry 27, 127
  museum 126–7
Penal Laws 23–4
People's Park 122

Peppercanister Church 151
Phoenix Park 32, **121–3**
  statues and monuments 122
Photographic Archive 85
Physics Theatre 73
pilgrimage path 169
plantations 23
Plunkett, Oliver, Saint 158
police 48–9
polo 220
Poolbeg Street 142
pop music 211
Portobello **74–6**, 151
Portobello Bridge 151
Portobello Harbour 151
Portobello House 151
Portobello Road 151
post offices 54
  General Post Office 34, 102, **103**, 142
Powerscourt Estate 169–70
Powerscourt Townhouse 67
practical A–Z **48–56**
prehistoric Ireland 20, 32, 68–9, 160–2
President's House 123
Print Museum 80
Printing House 64
Prospect cemetery 129–30
Provost's House 63
public holidays 53
pubs and bars 53
  Bleeding Heart 95
  Davy Byrne's 66
  Dublin Bay 208
  gay and lesbian 226
  McDaid's 66–7
  Mulligan's 95
  northeast Dublin 207
  northwest Dublin 207–8
  Sky Bar 95, 96
  southeast Dublin 203–4
  southwest Dublin 205–7
  suburbs 208
  Temple Bar 205–7
  see also cafés; food and drink

Quays 42, **111–12**
  walk 148–9, 149–52

radio 52
Railway Street 141

railways 39, 42, 43–4, 46
Ráth na Ríoch 163
Rathfarnham Castle 128
Registry of Deeds 51
religious services 54
Remembrance Gardens 105
resident cards 56
restaurants see food and drink
Robert the Bruce 21–2
Robinson, Mary 30
rock music 211
Rotunda Hospital and Chapel 105
round towers 32
Royal College of Surgeons 74
Royal Hospital Kilmainham 33
Royal Plate 90
Rubrics 61
rugby 220
Russborough House (Wicklow) 171
Russell Street 141
sailing 221
St Anne's Church 72
St Audoen's Church **90–1**, 146
St Audoen's Gate 146
St Augustine and St John Church 95
St Brigid's cathedral (Kildare) 166–7
St Catherine's Church 95
St Columba's House 164
St Francis of Assisi Church 147
St Francis Xavier Church 35, **110**
St James's Gate Brewery 95–6
St Kevin's Church (Glendalough) 169
St Mary's Abbey 116–17
St Mary's Abbey (Trim) 163
St Mary's Chapel of Ease 111
St Mary's Pro-Cathedral 35, **104**
St Michan's Church 117
St Nicholas of Myra Church 95
St Patrick's cathedral 33, 35, **91–3**, 146
St Patrick's Hospital 95

St Patrick's park **93**, 146
St Stephen's Church 35, **80**
St Stephen's Green **72**, 142
  statues and monuments 73
St Stephen's Green Centre 74
St Teresa's Carmelite Church and Friary 67–8
St Werburgh's Church 91
Samuel Beckett theatre 63–4
Sandycove 36, **135–6**
Scott, Etty 137
Scottish invasion 21–2
Sea Life Centre 138
Seaman's Memorial 150
Seanad Éireann 71
Second World War 29
self-catering accommodation 173
Shaw, George Bernard **75–6**, 77
Sherbourne Hotel 143
Ship Street 145
shopping **215–18**
  Brown Thomas department store 66
  Clery department store 102, 103
  duty-free 41
  fruit and vegetable market 117–18
  Gaelic phrases 231
  horse market (Smithfield) 119
  Iveagh Market 95
  Meath Street market 94
  Moore Street market 103
  opening hours 53, 215
  Powerscourt Townhouse 67
  St Stephen's Green Centre 74
  tax refunds 52
  weights and measures 49, 50
showjumping 220
Shrine of St Patrick's Bell 69
Silken Thomas 22
Sinn Féin 27, 28
Sitric (Silkbeard), king 21
Skerries 156–7
Skerries cliff walk 156
Sky Bar 95, 96
Slane 159–60

Smithfield 36, **118–19**
smoking 54
Soup Kitchen Act 25–6
South King Street 142
South Richmond Street 152
southeast Dublin 58–9, *59–80*, *64*
  accommodation 173–8, *174–5*
  food and drink 58, 186–93, *188–9*
  pubs and clubs 203–4, 208–9
southwest Dublin **82–98**, *82–3*, *85*
  accommodation 178–9
  food and drink 83, 193–5, *194*
  pubs and clubs 205–7, 209
sports **220–1**
  Gaelic sports **131**, 220
state apartments (Dublin Castle) 86
statues and monuments
  Boyle Monument 92
  Christ the King 135
  dockers statue 150
  Easter Rising monument 151
  Famine memorial 150
  George IV 135
  O'Connell monument 129
  O'Connell Street 102
  Oscar Wilde 143
  Phoenix Park 122
  St Stephen's Green 73
  Seaman's Memorial 150
  Trinity College 65–6
Stella (Esther Johnson) **93**, 94
Steyne Monument 65
Stone of Destiny (Lia Fáil) 163
Stoneybatter 120
Strongbow (Richard de Clare) 21, 89
students 54–5
  travel discounts 38, 55
Suburban Rail services 44
suburbs
  accommodation 182–4
  food and drink 199–200
  north *126*, 129–32
  pubs and clubs 208, 209
  south *126*, 126–9

Swift, Jonathan 91, **93**, 94, 166
  grave 146
swimming 221
Swords 155
Synod Hall 90

Talbot, Matt 102, 110, 150
Talbot Street 141
Tallaght 32
Tara Brooch 69
Tara's Palace 133–4
tax refunds 52
taxis 42, 44
teaching English as a foreign language 56
teenagers 224
telephones 53–4
television 52
temperature chart 48
Temple Bar 36, **84–5**, *85*
  accommodation 173, **178–9**
  food and drink 193–5, *194*
  pubs and clubs 205–7, 209
Temple Bar Gallery 85
tennis 221
theatres 212–13
  Abbey 36, **103–4**, 142
  The Ark 36
  for children 224
  Gate 105
  National Concert Hall 74
  Physics 73
  Samuel Beckett 63–4
Thomas Street 95
ticket booking service 211
time 55
tipping 55
toilets 55
Tone, Wolfe 24
  statue 73
tour operators 40–1
tourist information offices 53, 55–6
tower houses 33
toy shops 215–16
trains 39, 42, 43–4, 46
trams 44
Transport Museum 135
travel **38–46**
  airlines 38–9
  airport 42
  bicycles 44–5
  cars 40

  hiring 45
  coaches and buses 39–40, 42, 43, 45–6
  customs formalities 41
  disabled travellers 49
  ferries 40
  Gaelic phrases 231
  guided tours 45–6
  lost property 52
  packing 53
  passports 41
  student discounts 38, 55
  taxis 42, 44
  tour operators 40–1
  trains 39, 42, 43–4, 46
  trams 44
  visas 41
  when to go 48
  women travellers 56
Trim 163–4
Trinity College 35, **60–5**, *64*, 142, 144
  statues and monuments 65–6
Troubles 29–30
Tullylough Cross 69

Ulster Volunteer Force 27
United Irishmen 24
university dorms 177

VAT refunds 52
Victoria, Queen 26
Viking Splash Tours 223
Vikings 20–1, 32–3, 69–70
  walk 143–7, *144–5*
visas 41

walks
  Docks and the Grand Canal *148–9*, 149–52
  guided tours 46, 60
  Howth cliff walk 134–5
  Literary walk *140*, 141–3
  pilgrimage path 169
  Skerries cliff walk 156
  Viking and Medieval Dublin 143–7, *144–5*
  Wicklow Way 168
Walworth Street 151–2
War Memorial Gardens 97–8
watersports 221
Waterways Visitor Centre 36, **80**, 151

Wax Museum 110–11
weather 48
websites 51
weights and measures 49, 50
Wellington monument 122
Wentworth, Thomas (Black Tom) 23
Werburgh Street 145–6
Westland Row 143
when to go 48
where to stay **173–84**
 Dublin Bay 173, **184**
 gay and lesbian hotels 226
 Gresham Hotel 102
 northeast Dublin 179–82, *180–1*

northwest Dublin 182
self-catering 173
Sherbourne Hotel 143
southeast Dublin 173–8, *174–5*
southwest Dublin 178–9
suburbs 182–4
Temple Bar 173, **178–9**
university dorms 177
whiskey 119–20
Wicklow Mountains 167–71
Wicklow Way 168
Wide Streets Act 24
Wilde, Oscar 76, **79**, 143
 statue 143
William of Orange 23

Windmills Industrial Heritage Centre 156–7
Winetavern Street 146–7
women travellers 56
Wood Quay 33, **89**, 147
work permits 56
working in Dublin 56
Writers Museum **107–8**, 141

Yeats, Jack B. 35
Yeats, W.B. 76, 142
 museum 77
 statue 73

Zoo 123–4

Also available from Cadogan Guides in our European series...

France

France
Brittany
Côte d'Azur
Corsica
Dordogne & the Lot
Gascony & the Pyrenees
Loire
Normandy
Provence
Rhône-Alpes
Short Breaks in Northern France
South of France

Italy

Italy
The Bay of Naples and Southern Italy
Bologna and Emilia Romagna
Central Italy
Italian Riviera and Piemonte
Lombardy and the Italian Lakes
Northeast Italy
Rome Venice Florence
Sardinia
Sicily
Tuscany
Tuscany, Umbria and the Marches
Umbria

Spain

Spain
Andalucía
Bilbao and the Basque Lands
Granada Seville Córdoba
Northern Spain

Greece

Greece
Athens and Southern Greece
Crete
Greek Islands

The UK and Ireland

England
London–Paris
London Markets

Scotland
Scotland's Highlands and Islands

Ireland
Ireland: Southwest Ireland

Other Europe

Portugal
Madeira & Porto Santo
Malta, Gozo & Comino

The City Guide Series

Amsterdam
Barcelona
Bruges
Brussels
Edinburgh
Florence
London
Madrid
Milan
Paris
Prague
Rome
Venice

Flying Visits

Flying Visits France
Flying Visits Germany
Flying Visits Ireland
Flying Visits Italy
Flying Visits Scandinavia
Flying Visits Spain
Flying Visits Switzerland

Cadogan Guides are available from good bookshops, or via **Littlehampton Book Services,** Faraday Close, Durrington, Worthing, West Sussex BN13 3RB, **t** (01903) 828800, **f** (01903) 828802; and **The Globe Pequot Press**, 246 Goose Lane, PO Box 480, Guilford, Connecticut 06437–0480, **t** (800) 458 4500/**t** (203) 458 4500, **t** (203) 458 4603.

Dublin Street Maps

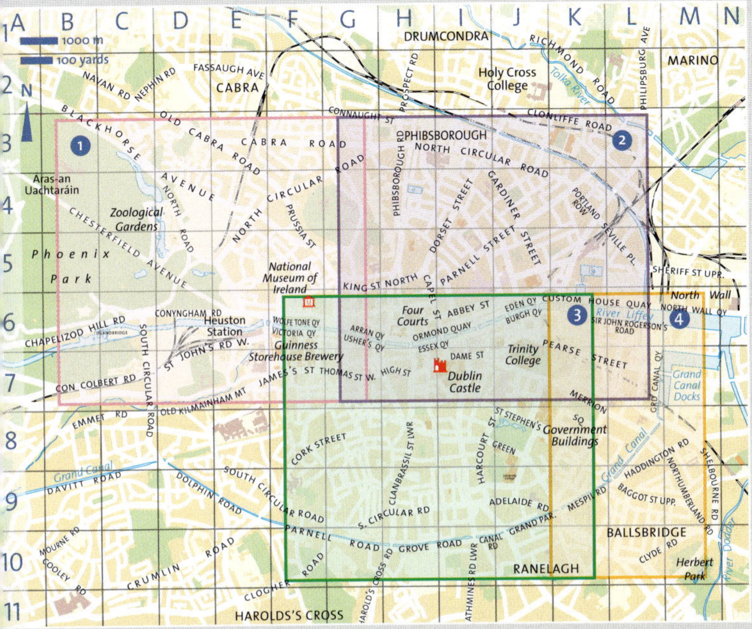

Key

i	Information	✉	Post Office
M	Museum	POL	Police Station
A	Art Gallery		Pedestrianized Road
	Theatre		Park
	Cinema		River/Canal
	Market		Place of Interest
	Library		Public Building
N		✝✝	Cemetery

250 m
250 yds

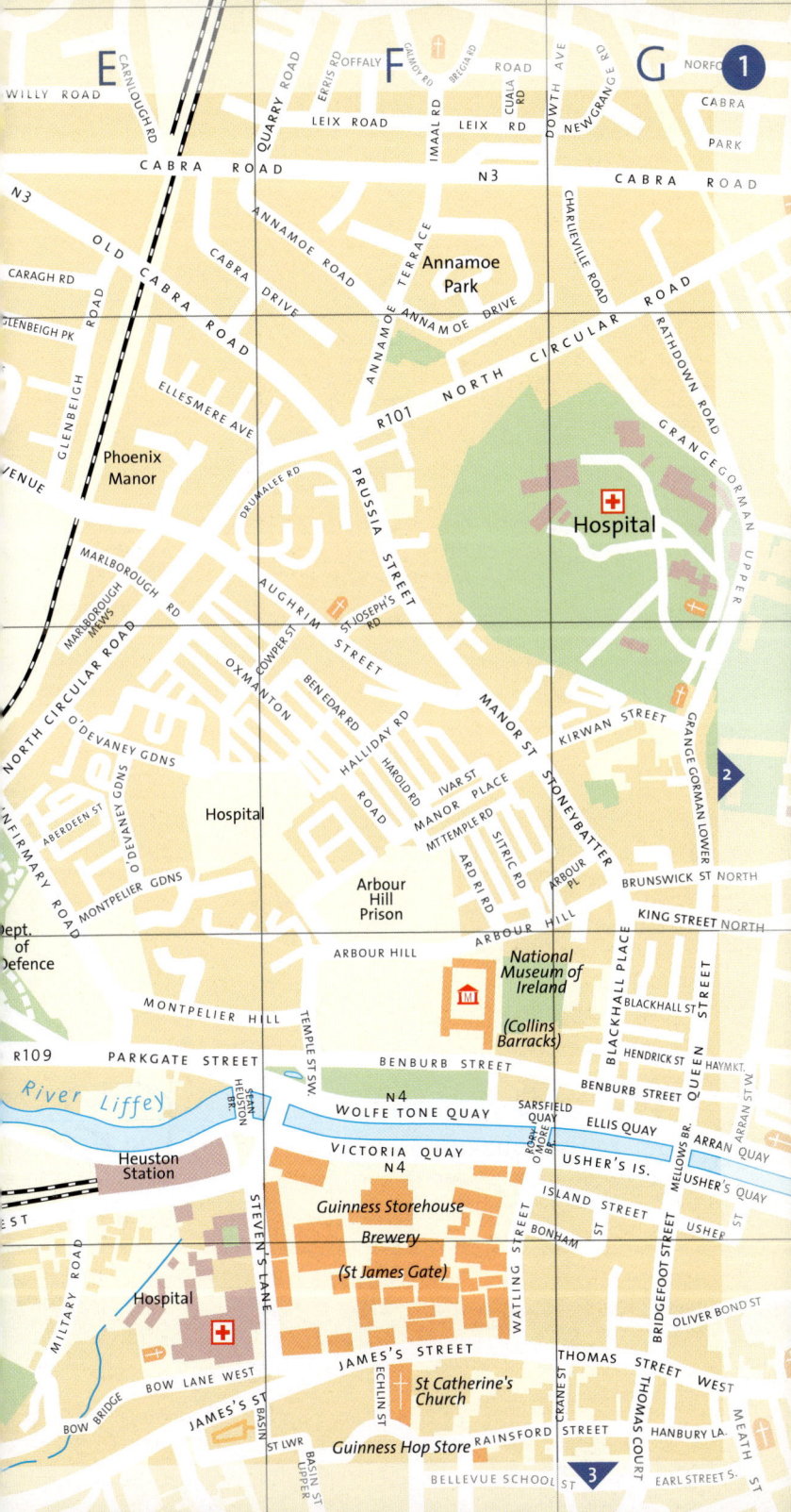

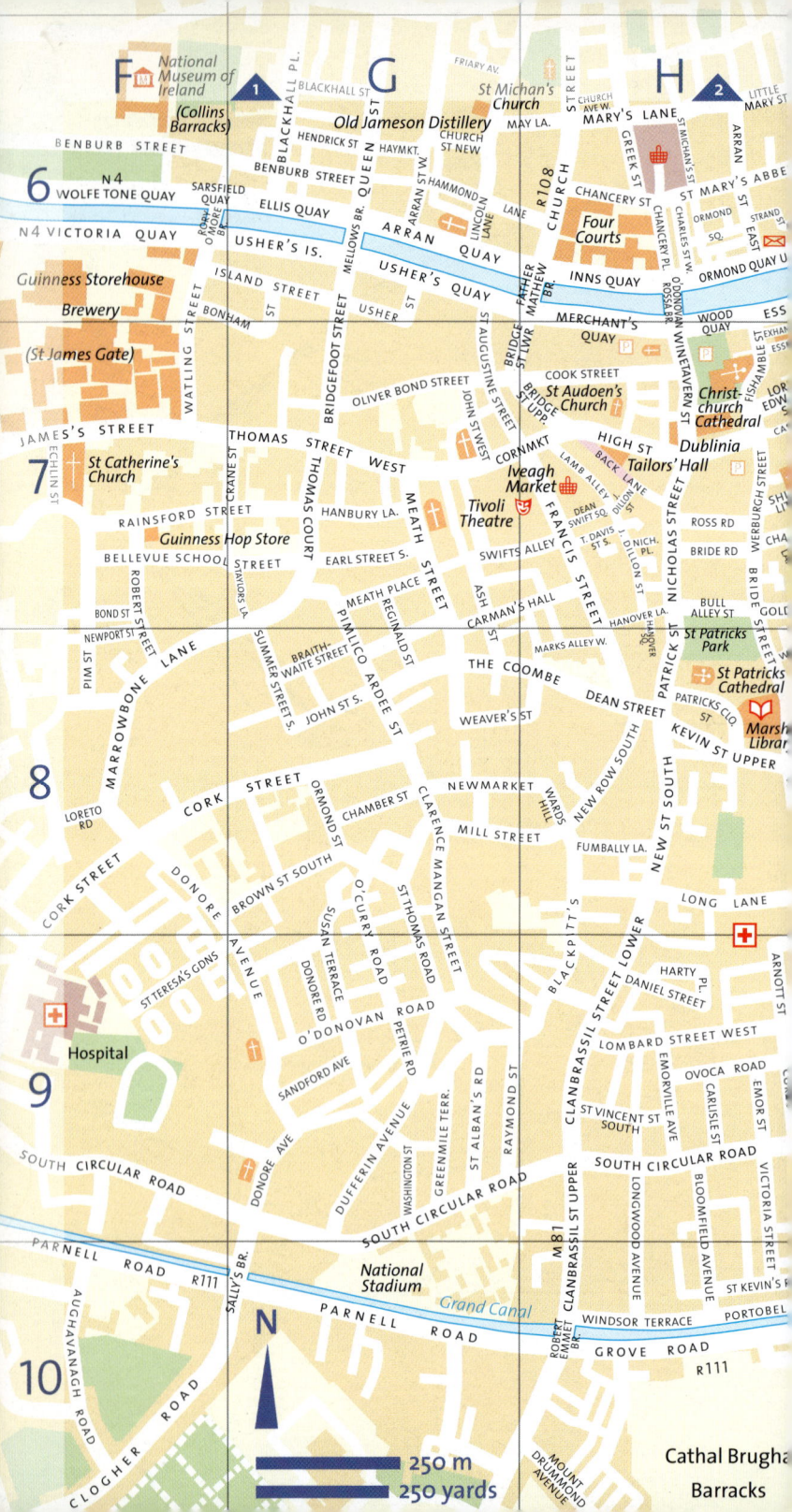